LOUIS ZUKOFSKY

MAN AND POET

TO CELIA

LOUIS ZUKOFSKY

NATIONAL
POETRY
FOUNDATION, INC.

Man and Poet

Edited
with an introduction by
Carroll F. Terrell

Published by

The National Poetry Foundation
University of Maine at Orono
Orono, Maine 04469

Printed by

The University of Maine at Orono
Printing Office

The National Poetry Foundation
University of Maine at Orono
Orono, Maine 04469

Library of Congress No. 79-89637
ISBN 0-915032-50-3

PREFACE

The unexpected death of Louis Zukofsky, May 12, 1978, prompted acknowledgment from the community of poets in America and England of the debt they in particular and the literate public at large owed to this most talented, dedicated, and retiring of men. Quickly came the sense of sorrow that that debt had not been acknowledged appropriately in his own lifetime and a sadness that he had not lived a few months longer to see the complete one-volume edition of his masterpiece *"A"* in 826 pages through the University of California Press. Hugh Kenner in a *New York Times Book Review* obit expressed the feeling of us all. By phone, I expressed my thanks to him for the note. His response then was even more to the point: "Yes, but how sad that he had to die to get the attention." Because of the personal friendship of 45 years (1927-1972) between Ezra Pound and Louis Zukofsky and their respect for each other as poets, that phone call resulted in a decision to dedicate the Winter issue, 1978, of *Paideuma: A journal devoted to Ezra Pound Scholarship* to the memory of Louis Zukofsky. My experience with that project led to the decision made in December, 1978, to publish this much needed book as quickly as possible.

To produce such a book from inception of idea to funding to actual publication in less than a year was no easy task. It could not have been done without the help of many people. First of all, I must acknowledge the subsidy given by the Faculty Research Funds Committee of the University of Maine at Orono. Without the assistance they provided with astonishing speed (faculty committees usually move at a rate best described as glacial), the book could not have been done at all, let alone so quickly.

But I am even more indebted to dozens of other people who helped make it a reality with such speed. Celia Zukofsky and Hugh Kenner in particular have been ready with information, assistance and advice. The work of the writers speaks for itself but does not show the deadlines many of them met which cannot be described as leisurely. It was the urgent need for the book, recognized by all, which acted as a more powerful stimulant to a speedy performance than did persuasion or other blandishments from me. To several of my colleagues in the English department here, especially Burton Hatlen, I owe thanks for help in the chores of indexing and proofreading. I am most grateful to many of the library staff: James MacCampbell, Director; Lorraine LeBlanc, Purchasing; Margaret Menchen, Interlibrary Loans; and Thomas Patterson, Reference Department, all have helped quickly when called upon. My immediate assistants are to be congratulated as heroes for doing this job on top of their regular duties with only passing thoughts of revolution: Sharon Stover, IBM Selectric Composer operator; Nancy Nolde, Research Assistant; Winifred Hayek and Roland Nord, graduate students in English, were aides and workers in the vineyard for many months: I owe them a great debt for their patience and dedication.

Several of the pieces in the book appeared first in the memorial issue of *Paideuma*, Vol. 7, No. 3 (Winter, 1978), either completely or substantially in their present forms: the biographical studies by Robert Creeley, Charles Tomlinson, Hugh Seidman, Fielding Dawson and Barry Ahearn as well as the pieces in THE POET section done by Don Byrd, Harold Schimmel, and John Taggart. Permission to reprint three pieces from *MAPS*, No. 5, 1973, edited by John Taggart, has been granted by John Taggart and the authors: Hugh Kenner for his "Too Full for Talk: *"A"* -11"; Jonathan Greene, "Zukofsky's Ferdinand"; and Guy Davenport's "Zukofsky's English Catullus." We are grateful to L.S. Dembo for permission to reprint the Zukofsky segment of his "Four Interviews" which appeared in *Contemporary Literature*, 10 (Spring, 1969), pp. 203-19; to Professor Dembo and the editors of *American Literature* for permission to reprint his "Louis Zukofsky: Objectivist Poetics and the Quest for Form" which appeared in Vol. 44, No. 1 (March, 1972). And to *Poetry* for permission to reprint Hugh Kenner's piece "Of Notes and Horses." For the Neil Baldwin essay, "Zukofsky, Williams, and *The Wedge*," special acknowledgment must be made to New Directions Publishing Corporation for permission to publish excerpts from several works of William Carlos Williams: *Selected Essays*, Copyright 1931, 1936, 1938, 1939, 1940, 1942, 1944, 1946, 1948, 1949, 1951, 1954 by William Carlos Williams; *The Autobiography of William Carlos Williams*, Copyright 1948, 1949, 1951 by William Carlos Williams; *The Collected Later Poems*, Copyright 1944, 1948, 1950 by William Carlos Williams; *The Collected Earlier Poems*, Copyright 1938, 1951 by William Carlos Williams;

C.F.T.
Orono, Maine
August, 1979

TABLE OF CONTENTS

LOUIS ZUKOFSKY

MAN AND POET

L.Z., Nov. 7, 1941 (Photo by Dushan Hill)

INTRODUCTION

I

Louis Zukofsky was a total poet: during a long life he practiced the craft of poetry with a single-minded passion. In his first maturity, he took the ideas of Pound about phanopoeia, melopoeia, and logopoeia as a point of departure for his own art. He also took Pound's ideas of composing in the musical phrase and the rhythms of great bass and such larger musical structures as the fugue. But Zukofsky extended Pound's range to include other musical patterns such as the sonata, the quartet, and the ballade and developed them in practice for over fifty years until he became not only the inventor but also the master of a new tradition.

He was and is a poet's poet. Although his work circulated in mimeographed sheets and little magazines, it was published in book form so rarely and in such limited editions that the public at large as well as academia could not hear of it through traditional channels. But practicing poets knew about it and found both Zukofsky and his work. Many of his followers and devotees, more widely known and anthologized than he, owe much of their music and polish to hard study of his premises and practices.

Thus as with the work of Pound and many innovators before him, we have with Zukofsky a tragic rehearsal of an old story: their inventions put them beyond the reach of most critics and readers who are trained to respond only to more traditional forms. With the mature work of Pound, almost all critics now find what they call "lyric passages" to praise, but the music and harmonies of much of *The Cantos* still remain much too subtle to reach the ears of many. Since Zukofsky went far beyond Pound in refining his lines until often only the harmonies are left, an even greater barrier exists which will take even more time for the poetry-reading public to cross. But since we have in Zukofsky the work of the greatest poet born in this century, cross it they will in time. Like Dante, Pushkin, Whitman and many another inventor/ master before him, Zukofsky will inevitably have his day.

But the sad past is still a condition to contend with. Getting Zukofsky's work out and known to those who would be glad to know of it is a task of no mean proportions. As Guy Davenport put it over five years ago [*Parnassus*, Spring-Summer, 1974] :

> Zukofsky's work has been published for forty years and the reviewers and scholars, except for a few, have been silent and indifferent. Only recently has the poet begun to appear in reference works of American poets, and in an occasional anthology. He has had the pleasure of riding along a London street under a banner tied from lamp post to lamp post on which he could read WEL−COME TO CAMBERWELL LOUIS ZUKOFSKY. He has with incredible and disgusting difficulty seen his *Bottom: On Shakespeare* and his *Catullus* into print, agonies comparable to Joyce's, the details of which constitute a formal indictment of the American publishing industry on charges of critical dullness, terminal stupidity, and general mopery.

In this same essay, Davenport discriminates some of the problems which make the poetry seem foreign. In spite of a long history in the English tradition of mixing the sacred and profane, we don't even in these parlous times identify abrupt changes in mood. In the *Secunda Pastorum*, we can accept the tomfoolery of having Mak tossed in a blanket just before the scene switches center stage for the birth of Christ. The reader can cite his own numerous examples from Shakespeare where at the most serious moments Bottom can reign supreme, but accepting Pound's "hilaritas" or Zukofsky's sense of fun is not so easy. Davenport says:

> Zukofsky's poetry is out of time in another sense. For all his kinship to the harmonies of Pound and the perpetual motion of Bach, its native enterprise is to *play*, if we can grasp all the punning senses of that dangerous word. The immediate sense must be that of *ludens*−the play of thought over a subject. [Pound put it, "the dance of the intellect among words."] This sense must not be detached from that of *playing* music. Neither discursive, incantatory, nor molendinary [the unabridged says, "Of or pertaining to a mill or miller"], Zukofsky's poetry is a playing of the intellect over a choice inventory of observations and predilections.

This sad history has taken place even though many of the greatest poets and critics of the 20th century early recognized Zukofsky's talents. Fifty years ago, when they were editors, Pound [*Exile*], Eliot [*The Criterion*], and Marianne Moore [*The Dial*] identified his real poetic passion and published his work.* In 1937

---

*But as usual Pound was the first to publish him and put pressure on the others to do so. He published "Poem beginning "The" " in *Exile*. Later Marianne Moore asked Zuk why he hadn't sent it to her. Since he had sent it to her first, he said: "I did but you sent it back." [C.Z. When the source of unpublished information is Celia Zukofsky, it will be followed by her initials in brackets.]

Pound, who was not given to dedicating his work to other poets, dedicated *Guide to Kulchur* to "Louis Zukofsky and Basil Bunting, strugglers in the desert." In the years following, William Carlos Williams said of his work: "I hear a new music of verse stretching out in the future." Kenneth Rexroth, one of the greatest of the next generation of poets, said of *All*: "These poems are absolute clarification, crystal cabinets full of air and angels."

The weight of an authority which includes all the major poets of the 20th century early and late as well as distinguished critics such as Kenner and Davenport is massive: it must not longer be ignored. Time and events press upon us: Zukofsky's recent death (May 12, 1978) has provided an impetus as well as an opportunity: hence this book, which is specifically designed as a stopgap measure to meet an urgent need. It is not designed for the poets, critics, and professors of literature who already know Zukofsky's work; it is designed for that small segment of the public which keeps the humanist tradition alive, whose members until recently have seldom heard of Zukofsky but who would now like to be introduced. It is designed as a first book of many which will eventually appear. Zukofsky's work, like all great art, is intricate and complex. As Kenner put it, "Scholars will still be elucidating parts of *"A"* and *All* in the 22nd century." Thus, the book is designed to answer the reader's first questions rather than his last, but an apparatus has been provided which will direct those who desire more information where to go to get it.

II

The division of the book into sections is a contrivance and no more. Neither a poet nor his work can be neatly divided into such aspects as The Man, The Poet, The Thinker, and so forth. Essays under the heading, "The Man," are more biographical than anything else, but essays under the heading "The Poet" cannot avoid being also about the man. The best that can be said about such an organization is that it is likely better than none, or if the work were alphabetized by title or author. The first piece, "Louis Zukofsky an Eccentric Profile," and the final piece, "An Annotated Checklist with Occasional Extended Commentary," were written last and after the editorial work on all the rest of the book was done. The first piece is called "Eccentric Profile" because it was not written to be read alone: it was deliberately written to emphasize materials not found elsewhere in the book and to leave out materials which are. It is therefore supplementary. The same thing is true of the Annotated Checklist at the end of the book. It has a sub-title of "Occasional Extended Commentary" because articles containing valuable information and stimulating opinions not found elsewhere in the book are summarized at greater length than are some others. The other pieces in the section entitled "The Man" give a variety of pictures from a variety of poets and friends who saw Zukofsky from different angles and with different "eyes" and "I's."

Robert Creeley's heart-warming memory could almost be excerpted from Henri Murger's *Scènes de la Vie de Bohème*: a series of unfortuitous events brought him first to Louie's door literally penniless and rain-soaked. One can use such phrases as "these extraordinarily dear and tender people" but actions have a compelling force words do not: as Creeley recalls his first meetings with Zuk and Celia all his feelings at that moment come crowding back, and he evokes them so well that the reader feels with him.

The piece by Charles Tomlinson is quite the opposite. His memoir traces the first encounter of a Britisher with Zukofsky's work, the growing interest, and subsequent meetings with Zukofsky and Oppen and the long productive associations of as significant a poet as Tomlinson himself with the poets associated with Zukofsky and Oppen, such as Creeley, William Carlos Williams, Jonathan Williams, and Charles Reznikoff. Tomlinson has an extraordinary ear for the nuances of sound in verse but also a candid-camera eye. Of Louie, after "recent illness," he writes, "Zukofsky had a curious dancing lightness in his build [Jonathan Williams cast him as Fred Astaire in a mythical movie], movement and talk ... a touch of elegance given sartorial precision...." Those words are a descriptive judgment, but the following lines are camera oriented: "What did not fit Jonathan Williams' casting was the densely black thick line of the eyebrows, the continuously re-lit cigarette, the nervous puckering of the forehead as the face flickered from anxiety to humour, the voluble, mercurial, ceaselessly inventive talk." The article ends with an objective account of the sad rift that developed between Louis and Oppen. No one was at fault, but a condition of human frustration with things as they are in the world of publishing poets exacerbated misunderstandings. Tomlinson's account leads to a happy conclusion: all involved should be understood and then forgiven.

Hugh Seidman, a student of Zuk's at Brooklyn Polytech, gives us a picture of Zukofsky as teacher in action: here, too, we have a poet reminiscing, and recalling a whole range of events from the ironic, to the hilarious, and even to the sad. But a poet of such sensitivity as Louis at any Polytechnic institute with no liberal arts commitment at all would make a situation fraught with potential ironies. Hugh Seidman cites many, but his account always returns to base: "I must simply say that I loved him. He was my poetic father who initiated me into the vision of the poem as a sacred and all pervading act. My debt to him is unpayable, and I have never forgotten the lesson of his commitment."

Hugh Seidman was born in Brooklyn in 1940, and thus knew the milieu and scene of Polytech. It is not too much to say that his experience with Zuk launched him from mathematics into the sea of poetry with such effect that he won the Yale Younger Poets Award for his volume, entitled *Collecting Evidence*, in 1970. But the next writer is from a quite different scene: Fielding ("Fee") Dawson (né 1939) is described in *Black Mountain* in the summer of 1950 as "just over the edge of being a boy" with "a touseled-haired innocence, a Missouri drawl and a noisy enthusiasm." These traits were all present 30 years later when he wrote of his memories and relationships with Zuk. His account is quite different from that of Seidman or the others who have written about Zuk, but the man portrayed is the same. Of a subtle and indirect praise Louis once gave him, "Fee" wrote: "*I couldn't believe it*! Talk about dancing on the ceiling, I danced down the walls, across the floor and out the door and around town for a few days, dazed and happy out of my mind. *Only* Louie would say that. . . ." His piece gives numerous examples of how Louie's just "being in the world" was a catalyst to those who came within his verge.

The final two pieces in "The Man" section were done by young post-doctoral scholars and see Zukofsky with the "Eyes" and "I's" of a new generation. Barry Ahearn takes note of the many ways in which Henry Adams, the man, and Zukofsky, the man, show affinities for similar ideas and feelings and how alike they are when observing the social scene. Henry Adams did not influence the poet so much as the poet recognized a lot of himself—including a wry sense of humor—in Henry Adams. Similarly, Neil Baldwin traces the affinities W.C. Williams and Zukofsky had for each other. But we have here a fascinating twist: the young Baldwin seeing the old Zukofsky as a young man looking at the older Williams.

III

The decision to publish the verse which Zuk himself discarded

was not made easily. In the end Celia, Hugh Kenner, and I decided
to do so only after searching conversations. We did so finally not
to add new items to the official canon, but to make the few works
kept in ms. available to scholars for comparison purposes. Zukofsky himself destroyed hundreds (?) of verses he wrote while
quite young. The ones published here are among those left which
Celia persuaded him not to destroy, but to include in the archive
as done by a person known as Dunn Wyth. Always the punster,
Louis agreed that since he was done with them, why not! The
several included here have been useful to me as a test: the more
familiar I become with Louis's work, the clearer it becomes why
these were finally discarded from the canon.

Don Byrd's piece, "The Shape of Zukofsky's Canon," is not
only the best, it is the only attempt made to date by a serious
student of Zukofsky to step back, as it were, and view all of the
work, prose and poetry, as a single body. Somewhere, early on,
Eliot said about Pound that it was necessary to read the prose to
understand the poetry and necessary to read the poetry to understand the prose. Byrd makes a similar point about Louis: "The
Zukofsky canon is a single work, no part of which can be fully
understood without reference to the whole." Thus in the course
of an intelligent and provocative account he glances briefly at all
items in the canon starting with *All: The Collected Shorter Poems,
1923-1964*. This volume, which originally appeared in two hard-
cover volumes (first *1923-1958* in 1965; second *1956-1964*
in 1966), was the first of Zukofsky's work to appear under the
imprint of a commercial press. Thus, the astute George Brockway,
President of W.W. Norton, who broke the ice, can be excused
from Guy Davenport's minatory judgment of the publishing
world at large which, as noted earlier, he says is guilty of "terminal stupidity and general mopery." Mr. Brockway followed
the original volumes by a combined, paperback edition of both in
1971.

As for the rest of the canon, Byrd says: " *"A," Bottom: On
Shakespeare*, and *Catullus* (the translations of Catullus which Zuk
referred to as his *Cats*) are the ABC of another order which arises
from the fragmented whole. These three works . . . are a critique
of and are critiqued by *All. All* is an inquiry into the dialectical
nature of objectivity; *"A," Bottom*, and *Catullus* are inquiries
into the dialectics of intersubjectivity." My first reaction to this
sentence was "Hear! Hear!" But after calming down and listening
to what he says in defense of this thesis I eventually recalled what
Melville says about Narcissus, who not being able to grasp the

"image he saw in the fountain plunged into it and was drowned."
That image became for Melville and Ishmael "the ungraspable
phantom of life; and this is the key to it all." Byrd's "tentative"
exploration of this thesis we might accurately say is *a* or *one*
rather than *the* key to it all. "Tentatively," he says, "and to avoid
temporarily matters which could become very complex, I will
suggest these three books are related to one another after the
order of three principles. . . ." He then has recourse to one of Zukofsky's favorite thinkers, Charles Sanders Peirce, to develop the
principles. Finally, we can only say of Byrd's piece, the more we
re-read and linger over it the more we find in Zukofsky, and the
more we read Zukofsky the more apt and full of insight do we
find Byrd.

Where Byrd's view is panoramic, Kenner zeros in with a mic-
roscope. His two pieces were written on different occasions to
satisfy different requests. The first, entitled "Of Notes and Horses,"
is mostly an ingenious reading of a very ingenious movement: *"A"*
-7 which Kenner expertly locates in the context of the larger poem
as then (1967) available. He has permitted us to re-use the second,
on *"A"*-11, as an example of what a person can do with Zukofsky's
text without bringing external information to it. The piece is
dated (1973), but since that time he has gathered a considerable
amount of information which shows that his interpretations were
in some instances inaccurate. But as he is presently writing an account to be published elsewhere which will correct the record, it
seemed best to leave the early piece as it appeared. What the
earlier piece did for *"A"*-7, the second entitled "Too Full for
Talk: *"A"*-11," written for *MAPS* six years later, does for *"A"*
-11. In this piece, Kenner shows his own most extraordinary ear
for the nuances of sound—the kind of ear required to register
fully Zukofsky's intricate patterns: "Reading in the normal sense—
collecting a sequential meaning—is all but out of the question, so
impacted are the formalities and the syntax. The first impulse is
simply to listen, as to violin music, while intricate recurrencies
sound and tease. It's as if the poem *approximated* human speech,
the way a fiddle does when the fiddler 'makes it talk.'" Listen,
Kenner does, and reports on a few of the remarkably intricate
sound patterns Zuk has woven into the fabric of *"A"*-11.

Of *"A"*'s 24 movements, *"A"*-9 is the only one, parts of
which were written at widely different times: the first half was
written from 1938-1940; the second half, 1948-1950. Each half
contains 5 sonnets followed by a 5 line coda, and is, as Robert
Creeley says, "an extraordinary reading of Guido Cavalcanti's

Donna mi prega." Peter Quartermain's essay, a reading in depth of
the first half of *"A"-9*, is entitled "Not at All Surprised by Science." The reader has an excuse for being quite surprised at what
Zukofsky, glancing at the various translations Pound had made of
this canzone, particularly for Canto XXXVI, makes of Cavalcanti's
insights into the nature of love—or rather "Love." All the phrases
in the 1st half of *"A"-9* are taken from the *Capital* of Marx. The
last half of the movement is a response to the first half—an answer
as it were. But these fairly simple considerations are enriched by
an unbelievable complication, echoing the use of "r" and "n"
sounds systematically through the poem, all this intending to be
"the poetic analog of a conic section—i.e. the ratio of the acceleration of two sounds." Quartermain deals with these and other formulaic elements in some detail. But he also places *"A"-9* in the
larger context of *"A" 1-12*.

M.L. Rosenthal looks briefly at a few of the poems in *All* and
finds some of them musical and others not. He finds a Zukofsky
of two sides: one a sad example, the other "the true poet"; or, "a
beautiful Z." and "a tiresome Z." Rosenthal, a poet who was also nourished by the power of Yeats, Pound and Eliot, is hard put
to it to accept the often subtler tones and nuances of Zukofsky.
As is usual with those literary critics who record their personal responses to a work of art, Rosenthal reveals as much of himself as he
does of Zukofsky in showing the why of his reactions; thus in the
end we are brought closer to the critic than we are to the poetry.

Quite different is Harold Schimmel's brilliant piece which we
finish reading knowing more than we did when we started. Schimmel places the early work, especially "Poem beginning "The,""
firmly in the Yiddish literary traditions of the Lower East Side
where everything, including Shakespeare, was advertised as "translated and made better by." Yehoash (the pen name of S. Bloomgarden) was such a favorite with Zuk that he adapted 60 of the
330 lines of ". . ."The"" from Yehoash's *In the Web*. Schimmel
speculates, reasonably enough, that Louis's father, Reb Pinchos,
was a reader of Yiddish verse and thus knew Yehoash. But Reb
could neither read nor write Yiddish or English at all. Only a perceptive reader such as Schimmel who is himself immersed in Jewish culture could have shown how much and in what ways Zukofsky was immersed in it himself and reacted to and with it.

The Poet section closes with a detailed look at "Mantis" by
John Taggart. Mr. Taggart, a poet in his own right (his most recent book is *The Pyramid is a Pure Crystal*), edited the best collection of Zukofsky criticism and exegesis available in 1973 in

MAPS, No. 5, now out of print. The "Mantis" piece is based on a chapter of a doctoral dissertation, entitled *Intending A Solid Object: A Study of Objectivist Poetics*, submitted to Syracuse University in 1974. "Mantis" and another poem *"Mantis," An Interpretation* were written in 1934. They first appeared in *New Directions in Prose and Poetry* for 1936, edited by James Laughlin; later they became part of the collection entitled *55 Poems,* published by The Press of James A. Decker in 1941; and thereafter are all included in all the Norton collections of *All*. From the beginning, the companion poems have been a problem and a challenge to all who would seek to get at the heart of Zukofsky's work. The form of the poem, the sestina, is part of Zukofsky's problem, but *our* problem became Zukofsky's solution to his problem: how to bring together the coincidence of a praying mantis encountered in, of all places, a New York subway station and the ragged poor in the depths of the depression. The solution, which would reflect the "Actual twisting" of many diverse thoughts in consequence, became in part the sestina. John Taggart makes everybody's problem his problem and works out some very ingenious patterns in the way the poet's mind works to create a poetry with polish and edge.

IV

During a conversation with Celia, we worked out a sequence of famous thinkers who meant most to Zuk. Both he and Pound were partial to the magnificent perceptions about music and number attributed to Pythagoras. Numbers and dates had a mysterious meaning: e.g. that Emperor Yong Cheng, son of K'ang Hsi of the Manchu Dynasty in China should have died in October 1735 and John Adams (whose ethical perceptions were mightily influenced by Neo-Confucianism) should have been born in October 1735 is not without significance. And that Pound was born in October 1885 (exactly 150 years later) is not without significance. Exactly what significance such coincidence might have, one would be hard put to it to state. Again, Zuk knew Pound first in 1927. Their friendship continued strong until Pound's death in 1972. The fact that the 27 is reverse of 72 in these dates is not without significance. The fact that the complete *"A"* turned out to be 803 pages in length which is exactly the length of *The Cantos* was certainly not arranged deliberately by Zukofsky since it was done at the California Press without consultation. It just came out that way. But, somehow, the fact that the numbers are the same is not without significance. Dozens of other examples could be adduced here.

Let us just say that both men were so extraordinarily attuned to nuances of design in the universe at large and the air around them that everything had significance. Thus the "tetraktys" of Pythagoras is a revelation of universal design somehow tied up with the music of the celestial spheres. It would take the antennae of the poet to pick up such vibrations and the greatest of all thinkers to rationalize them. With Zukofsky, the major minds of the western world to whom he gave major attention were (after Pythagoras) Aristotle, Aquinas, Shakespeare, Spinoza, Pierce, and Wittgenstein. But to Wittgenstein he came quite late—Celia says around 1960—and it was Wittgenstein the Second rather than the First that he was most taken with. But after discovering his *Philosophical Investigations*, he returned to the *Tractatus Logico-Philosophicus* of 1921 and worried this dense text with much thought and marginalia. An overlap of the philosopher's ideas of objects in the world as the relationships of fact/events [Tatsachen] and not objects/things [nicht der Dinge] and what Zukofsky was feeling about objectivists [not objectivism] in 1931 can be demonstrated. It is not without significance that Spinoza's numbered "Propositions" are looked at finally with the insight of Wittgenstein's "Propositions" which in turn have something to do with Zukofsky's title for his book of critical essays, *Prepositions*. The title here has at least a dual significance and implies the "positions" the poet took "before" he came to write as well as the relationships of objects as fact/events rather than "things" in the world. Wittgenstein's first two propositions are: "1.I Die Welt is Alles was der Fall ist." [The world is everything that is the case.] And "1.2 Die Welt ist die Gesamtheit der Tatsachen, nicht die Dinge." [The world is the totality of facts not of things].

Finally, there is a connection between Wittgenstein's act of rejecting philosophy at the end of his first period when he said that those who understood him would see that everything he had done showed philosophy to be pointless and Zukofsky's response in the Dembo interview: "Well, I don't want to get involved in philosophy; I might as well say that *Bottom: On Shakespeare* was written to do away with philosophy."

But some branches of philosophy such as Ethics continued to engage the poet's mind with attendant frustration. Zukofsky knew as did Aristotle, Spinoza, and Wittgenstein that the factitious world can be enormously complicated for ethical action while action itself can be nothing except simple in time and space. One can, as people did, gather volumes of complicated analyses about the situation at the end of WW II to justify the decision to drop the atom bomb. A human impulse seems to be to contrive an action that would be equally complicated. But that cannot be done. In the end any president could only say either, "Drop it" or "Do not drop it." Then the order could be carried out only in a simple fashion at one moment in time at one location of space. In the first piece in the section entitled The Thinker, Zukofsky says to Dembo: "All you have to do is say 'yes' or 'no.' That's about all we have ever done as far as action is concerned. The trouble is most people just won't be that definite." And this perception leads to a notion of design: "the scheme that seems to be running everything, God, whatever you want to call it."

The age old conflict between free will and determinism has been a mind-breaker for many a thinker in the western world, but Zukofsky experienced it more intensely than most. For him a fervent belief in universal rhythm and design as well as what he called the *"Aleatorical indeterminate"* [a fancy phrase for "accident of fate"] became a double-bind. Such complications in situations should somehow be reflected in the complication of poetic design. Hence his use of old and difficult Italian forms such as the sestina, an old bottle that he warped into a new bottle in which to pour something old: "Musicians have done that with fugues; there are some today who try to do counterpoint or traditional harmony, but most won't even talk in that terminology."

Still, harmony with whatever gods there be or whatever design one perceives in nature is a *sine qua non* of Zukofsky's epistemology and ethics. But his way of saying "It's not nice to fool mother nature " is to glance at Spinoza via Santayana:

> "Where they sin against nature," says Santayana in his preface, "Nature will take her revenge." Many years ago nature casually turned him over to Spinoza who said: "the superstitious, who know better how to reprobate vice than to teach virtue, have no other intention than to make the rest as miserable as themselves." [*Prepositions* 50]

So we have the difference between the righteous or the self-righteous (surface matters) and the man who thinks about ethical actions in the world of things that are real. For things do exist as even the Hindu knew, and one could worry the problem and the efforts to discriminate until one were thoroughly sick of even thinking about it: "You can get lost, really lost. . . . So much for epistemology. When I'm sick of it, thoroughly sick of it, I handle it this way [have done with it]. It was *enough* that I wrote five hundred pages of *Bottom*."

The Dembo interview ends with speculations about form in long poems and the structure in *"A"*: "I don't care how you

consider it, whether as a suite of musical movements, or as something by a man who said I want to write *this* as I thought I saw the
'curve' of it in twenty-four movements, and lived long enough to
do so." Or again: "Written in one's time or place and referring to
other times and places, as one grows, whatever way one grows,
takes in, and hopes to survive them, say like Bach's music." Then
with some references to the long poems of Pound and Williams, he
says: "A long poem is merely more of a good thing, shall I put it
that way?" And finally quoting from the *Cantos*:

> Imperial power is? and to us what is it?
> The fourth; the dimension of stillness.

> [49/245]

That's the great Pound. Or in a very late canto:

> When one's friends hate each other
>   how can there be peace in the world

> [115/794]

And with that I leave you.

    Dembo's interview with Zukofsky is followed by his classic
piece, entitled "Louis Zukofsky: Objectivist Poetics and the Quest
for Form," which appeared in *American Literature* in Spring of
1972. The two pieces together mark a new epoch in Zukofsky
studies not only because they précis the most important elements
of Zukofsky's practices and precepts as perceived at that time, but
because the combined circulations of *Contemporary Literature*
and *American Literature* introduced the poet to a much wider
audience. Heretofore known mostly to poets, his name became
with these articles known also in academe. Dembo reviews the original ideas in action of the objectivists and follows these ideas as
they ramify and transpire in work and criticism during the next
forty years.

    Cid Corman, as a poet, can be said to revel in the laconic na-
ture of much of L.Z.'s poetry and uses a similar concision in his
own work with an enthusiasm that verges upon love. Since Corman himself set the type and printed *"A" 1-12* in Japan, he has
had as complete a sense of Zukofsky's ideas of sound, noise, vibration, or music as anyone ever had. A devotee also of Pound's
work and critical premises, he believes the best kind of criticism
is that which allows the artist or poet to be seen best. Hang the
painting in a good gallery with good light, without a distracting
environment and let the work speak for itself. After that the critic should do little except say, "do you notice in the lower
left. . . ?" etc. Thus, if one wants to get a sense of Zukofsky as
"thinker," one should set forth his thought in his own words and

let it speak for itself. He does exactly this in his piece, "In the Event of Words." He gives up a brief introduction and then lines up brief excerpts from Zuk's work which in effect summarize the story of his thought. His piece might well have been sub-titled: "The heart of the matter."

Jonathan Greene's brief piece on *Ferdinand* is used to close the thinker section in order to include some references to Zukofsky's fiction which can be described (except for the novel, *Little*) as "short" or "shorter." The author is disinclined to waste words in fiction anymore than he is in poetry or criticism. But Zukofsky's fiction, short or not, is fiction with a difference. Ferdinand is so much a metaphor (L.Z. did not like the word, symbol) for so many aspects of the machine-age with all its dehumanizing attributes that he becomes a non-person: in fact, that is his problem. Quite reasonably, Greene is reminded of another such hero-non-hero: "Without the self-awareness and self-humour of Musil's 'hero' in *The Man Without Qualities*, both Ulrich and Ferdinand share similar reclusive natures through which they perceive the world as too absurd to be intimate with or accept." With as much justification, Greene might have been reminded of Musil's *Young Torless* about whom John Simon said: "There are two worlds within him corresponding to two worlds without him: a quotidian existence of rational, routine activity . . . and also a dark, exciting realm of violent, often destructive . . . impulses and adventures." In a critical sense, Greene finds realism stretched by "Zukofsky's penchant for literary quotes and allusions." But he adds, "Perhaps these can be excused since Ferdinand's background is cultured. . . ." They can indeed. Ferdinand is a Jew. He is not pictured as deriving from a very particular geographic area, but we must not forget that Zukofsky as well as most Jewish youth attended much theater at the turn of the century in the Lower East Side. Greene says: "The later allusions to Villon and Antigone seem . . . precious and forced." In almost any other context they would indeed. But we must remember that the Yiddish there included many productions of Shakespeare plays and Greek drama, "Translated and made better by" any number of Jewish writers.

V

The title, The Translator, for section V of the book gives Burton Hatlen an opportunity to consider together the *Catullus* translations as well as the translation of *Rudens*, the main content of *"A"*-21, which L.Z. dedicated to "the memory of John

Gassner and my brother Morris Ephraim." And since *Rudens* is a drama, Hatlen takes the opportunity to glance at LZ's own drama, written in 1930-1931, *Arise, Arise*. Together Guy Davenport, David Gordon, and Hatlen manage to review *The Cats* (as L.Z. called his *Catullus*) from a number of different angles and take both long and short views of the criticism about them since they first appeared and pleased (in some cases) or alarmed (in a lot more cases) a public quite unprepared for them in 1969.

The final section, entitled The Testament, was required to fulfill the last part of the original idea of the book: direct the reader to additional sources of information. It starts off with Celia's "Year by Year Bibliography of Louis Zukofsky" which lists with brief annotations all his published work from the first in 1922 to post-mortem publications in 1978. This is followed by a brief description by Marcella Booth of the Zukofsky papers at the Humanities Research Center, University of Texas at Austin, where by far the largest collections of Zukofsky materials is housed. The last item in the book, "A Bibliography of Works about Louis Zukofsky with Extended Criticism," gives fairly detailed summaries of all the significant critical articles about Zukofsky's work which have appeared since WW II. Again, I wrote the summary after the rest of the book, except for the introduction, was completed and gave most of the space to materials not covered elsewhere. The 70 items are indexed first, alphabetically, but they are numbered and considered in the order and time they appeared. With this organization, the flow of thought and change of attitude about Zukofsky and thus a fuller realization of his significance may be evoked in the reader's mind. If that is not the case, as some fella said, it ought to be.

THE MAN

L.Z., Flushing, N.Y., Nov. 25, 1945

CARROLL F. TERRELL

LOUIS ZUKOFSKY: AN ECCENTRIC PROFILE

Artists who are said to be possessed by the divine afflatus are probably no different from other people except in the intensity of their response to experience. Love is a fine example. When some people fall in love they experience a slight quiver; but, as a person who knew Hemingway said, "When Papa falls in love it's like a great tree crashing in the forest." The experience for all is the same in kind and derives from the same psychosomatic and perhaps spiritual sources. The only difference is in the degree of intensity. So with poets: not only is their experience variously intense but they are also impelled to record it. And to the degree that they are born to greatness, they will be satisfied only with perfection of form and its articulation with content as they struggle to get the experience into words.

Talent is cheap in the world and can be found everywhere; but strength of character and the discipline necessary to nurse the talent to a full maturity is rare. Many a potentially great artist loses the battle to express that potential and succumbs to drink, drugs, or other mechanisms of escape from the anguish of an intense emotional life. But happily a few summon up the resources of character necessary and dedicate themselves with single-minded passion to their art. Such a man was Louis Zukofsky. The train of thought adduced here is not recorded lightly, for therein is the germ of the man and the key to his work: love, intensity, discipline, simplicity, music, and poetry. These ingredients of a life in action cannot be separated. Love comes first but quickly ramifies through all else: the power given and developed to love wife and son becomes in Zukofsky and his work the power to love family, friends, and humanity at large. But different from many others, with Zukofsky these attributes of the poet and man are a single unwavering entity: the public and private images are the same. But with such poets as Pound and Eliot the private person appears to differ from the public image. And Eliot, at least, cultivated a particular image of poet-critic in action which was quite different from the person to whom people wrote letters beginning, "Dear Tommy." But not Zukofsky. The Zukofsky profile as man and poet is starkly and simply, early and late, the same.

While a young poet seeking to perfect his craft, Zukofsky hunted out the work of the great poets of the past as well as those of his own time. He read everything he could lay hands on in order to learn as Dylan Thomas put it "the tricks" of the poet's "trade." But he knew well that a composer, although he might have the technical competence, could not in the 20th century write a symphony in the manner of Beethoven. Thus, it was logical that Ezra Pound, the greatest poetic innovator of his time, should become his master. It was also logical that in time Zukofsky should become a master and be sought out as a model by the generation of young poets who came after him. Although the poetry reading public at large seldom or never heard of Zukofsky, young practicing poets heard about him all the time. By a sort of underground grapevine the word spread. They obtained his work from obscure sources; they read his few and sparse critical statements avidly; they studied his musical effects and forms enthusiastically; and they came away from his work changed in themselves. It can now be flatly stated: no serious poet of any consequence exists in the USA or England who has not been influenced by the work of Louis Zukofsky. Like the work of Pound, Epstein, and Stravinsky, it is pandemic and pervasive.

Thus the state of affairs at the moment is extraordinary: Here we have one of the most important and influential literary figures of the 20th century, but we know next to nothing about his background, heritage, milieu, or working life. One of the difficulties has been Zukofsky himself who has had no enthusiasm for talking or writing about his private life. But with the help of his widow, Celia Zukofsky, this unhappy situation can now be ameliorated: this profile is a gesture in that direction.

I

Like T.S. Eliot, Basil Bunting, and many another public figure, Louis Zukofsky had little patience with gossip mongers, tale-bearers, or biographers. But different from Bunting and Zukofsky, Eliot was passionately concerned to protect his private life.* Zukofsky's concern for privacy is not like Eliot's. His is rather an impatience, or frustration, even at times an irritation, that one should waste time on such concerns rather than read the poetry. If anything matters, the poetry matters. The rest is dross. Besides that, he thought that the facts of his personal life could not help but be boring to someone outside his circle of family and friends. It's true that he never spent any time at the forefront of battle, did not attempt to scale the Matterhorn, did not serve before the mast, did not even hitchhike so far as Staten Island let alone across the USA. But what went on in his mind as he poked along in Brooklyn or sat alone before his desk is far more dramatic and exciting than any number of barroom brawls, shoot-ups of any kind of drugs, or shoot-outs at the Kay-o, O-kay, or whatever corral. If this is true, his poetry and other writings would surely show it, while chatter about other things would not.

His attitude is quite well expressed in a small book he wrote with Celia in 1970 entitled *Autobiography*. This 63-page work contains all he considered of note about his life, love, and pursuit of the impossible dream. In fact it contains many an instructive cue. Most of it is made up of eighteen short poems by Zukofsky written between 1937 and 1952 set to the musical scores of Celia done between 1940 and 1952. The 18 different songs are introduced and interrupted occasionally by a brief prose statement. The first, taken from *Little*, says: "I too have been charged with obscurity, tho it's a case of listeners wanting to know too much about me, more than the words say." This statement is followed by another: "As a poet I have always felt that the work says all there needs to be said of one's life."

But Zukofsky is wrong: once a reader becomes convinced that Mr./Ms. X is a great poet, artist, singer or a genius of any kind, that reader or devotee begins to develop a nagging thirst to know as much about the person as possible—as if he were impelled to discover how such a genius came to be. Although the quester for information is hardly to be satisfied (a lot of information only seems to spark the desire for a lot more) and sometimes seems to become highly personal, his quest is not really personal

---

*In 1957, at the end of a two hour conversation, Eliot asked me what my plans were. I told him that for years I'd been collecting materials for an Eliot biography, a book which was badly needed because at that time there was none in fact or in the offing; and further that one of the reasons I'd come to see him was to ask his help with the project. But before I could go on to say that my plans were for an intellectual and religious history rather than details about his personal life, he interrupted me with such vigor that I never got a chance to say it. He was not just upset; he was visibly disturbed. I no longer remember exactly what he said, but I remember quite well the emotional concern. When I finally had a chance to say something, I promised to give the project up and do nothing more about it.

at all. If we have a great poet to deal with, it hardly matters who the poet is personally. It's the *poet* not the *person* that matters.

Although the *Autobiography* was not published until 1970, L.Z. wrote a preface for it dated February 17, 1962:

C. Z.
music for poems by
Louis Zukofsky

> *the poem . . . the completed action of one writing words to be set to music.* For all the good sense one must owe to Dante, these twenty-two settings to eighteen poems ["Song 8" from *55* has two versions, "Song 29" from *Anew* three, and "que j'ay dit devant" again two] have always acted to complete the words for me. I find some notes intended for comment at a reading, going back some twenty years, which point to the final intention of the words: "madrigal," "plain chant," "organum," "Adoration" (no doubt in the medieval sense), "for one voice," "for several" and so on. The composer set the words to the "forms" I asked for—to which I had perhaps no right, unable to compose them myself; but in following my wish or whim she also did something else— showing me that apart from my impositions on my words and her, the words had potentially their own tunes which she followed even more carefully to complete for me.

The first song is "Motet" from *Anew* [*All, The Collected Shorter Poems 1923-1964*, p. 212]:

> General Martinet Gem
> Coughed Ahem, and Ahem, and Ahem
> Deploying the nerves of his men
> Right, and about face, to his phlegm
>
> Their whangs marched up to the sky,
> His 'eyes telescoped' in his head
> A pillow that as pillar of Europe
> He flung to his rupture Ahead.

Obviously for one who has so strong a sense of design as Zukofsky, placing this song first in his *Autobiography* is significant. It must imply one of the most important elements in his life. And it does: both Louis and Celia abhorred war, violence, and discord of any kind. And they had that sense of despair so common in the 30's about the "military mind," either in the generals who postured around in uniform and braid or the men who blindly followed them. The verses also imply a lifelong dislike of sham, hatred, and hypocrisy, or put another way, the obverse of the things he celebrated in his poetry: Truth, Love, and Life.*

---

*Since these reflections are so theoretical, I sent them to Celia with a request which said: "Celia, would you react to these ideas and correct them where wrong." She wrote,

The motet is followed by another brief note called bare facts:

> But the bare facts are: I was born in Manhattan, January 23,
> 1904, the year Henry James returned to the American scene to
> look at the Lower East Side. The contingency appeals to me as a
> forecast of the first-generation American infusion into twentieth-
> century literature. At one time or another I have lived in all of
> the boroughs of New York City—for over thirty years in Brook-
> lyn Heights not far from the house on Cranberry Street where
> Whitman's *Leaves of Grass* was first printed.

Bare indeed. And quite characteristic to find such appeal in a date as a symbol of the melding of the generations. As for Zukofsky's own heritage and parentage facts are hard to come by. His parents were from obscure backgrounds in Russia and as was traditional among immigrants they did not talk about it. If they'd been weal- thy landowners, Collegiate Councilors, or something to brag about —everybody would have heard about it. As Celia put it, "You didn't talk about coming to the new world by steerage. Now if you came by first class it would have been something to talk about."*

Louis' father, Pinchos Zukofsky, was born about 1860 in the outlying districts of a town called Most (Must) in Kovna Province, an area which for a short time became Lithuania. His father's name was Maishe Afroim Zukofsky. Both Pinchos and Maishe were probably farmhands without land and without hope for the future. Louie's mother, Chana Pruss, was born in Most about 1862. His parents met because they were distantly related and lived in the same village. In the tradition she would have had no education nor interests other than being a housewife and mother. They were married, probably in 1887, and had five children before Pinchos came to the United States in 1898. Two of the children died in infancy but three survived: a daughter born in 1888, a daughter born in 1890, and a son born in 1892.

Pinchos was obviously a man of character and determination. All we can do now is imagine the kinds of conferences in a highly orthodox Jewish family, both sides being very religious, which could lead the father to leave his wife and three children to come

---

"Your ideas and statements are correct concerning Louis' reaction to questions about his personal life," as well as "you are correct in your set-up of the poem 'General Martinet Gem.'" Other excerpts from her letter will be given in context later.

*The factual data in this account come from several sources: (1) information already a matter of record; (2) a series of interviews with Celia Zukofsky taped in September, 1978 or in August, 1979; (3) correspondence with Celia between June, 1978 and August, 1979. Occasionally, segments from the tapes will be introduced to develop significant relationships. The material recorded on the tapes has been edited for brevity but the sense of what was said and the order in which it was said have not been changed.

to the USA with the object of saving enough money to bring them
to America too. But like a great many hardy immigrants at the
turn of the century, he did it. Although it took 5 years, working
night and day at odd jobs, as a night watchman and as a pants
presser in a men's clothing factory, in 1903, he was able to send
enough money to bring them, steerage, to this country. Pinchos
had no education of any kind, but he had ideas. To the question,
"Which would you call him: Rigid? Easy going? or Domineering?"
Celia picked "domineering." To the question "What are the most
significant effects he had on Louie?" she wrote: "His persistence
and hardwork; also his uncompromising attitude when he thought
he was right." But Pinchos' life-long dedication to work, night and
day, during the week and religion during the Sabbath resulted in
Louis seldom seeing his father: he was off before Louis was up in
the morning and arrived home after he had gone to bed.

Chana, his mother, had much stronger influences on him.
But they were influences less of ideas or persuasion than the consequences of constant presence. To the question "What did she
look like? Tall? Fat?" Celia wrote: "Louis resembled his mother
very closely; she was very thin, even emaciated looking." And to
the question, "What about her influenced Louis most?" she
wrote: "Her quiet resignation and acceptance of a very hard life."

As Louis was the only child born in the United States, his
two sisters and one brother born in Russia much earlier, all seemed
to him from another generation: when he was 5, Morris was 17,
and his sisters were 19 and 21. Since the family spoke only Yiddish at home that was the only language Louis knew until he
started school on the Lower East Side of Manhattan, a district
referred to until recently as "Hell's Kitchen."

The following excerpts from tapes made September 1, 1978
contain additional detail of his early years:

T. Did Louie remember specific things about growing up that he
    used to talk about?

C. There was one incident about chasing a kitten down a flight of
    stairs and down an iron stoop and then falling on his head.

T. What about that? How old was he?

C. Five or six. He probably got a lot of bumps and lumps on his
    head. So, of course, we made a jest: decided that's what made
    him the genius.

T. He was trying to save the kitten?*

C. Yes.

T. Did he ever talk about growing up?

C. No, not really. He never participated in games like baseball—all the games the other youngsters played in; obviously he just wasn't sufficiently coordinated to know what to do with a ball or a bat so he was always put on the outside as observer or whatever.

T. Who put him there?

C. Youngsters in the group. Oh, they liked him! In fact a number of them kept up a friendship with him for many many years. They respected his judgment, his impartiality, but he was always on the sidelines but never a participant and as I said he was just never sufficiently coordinated.

T. Maybe he became a referee or umpire?

C. Could have been that eventually. He could follow the games. Even in his later years he knew all the rules of baseball and enjoyed baseball games on the television and knew who was doing what and so on.

T. He went to a public school near Christie Street?

C. The public elementary schools and then he went to Stuyvesant, which at that time was a specialized high school; it was primarily for students who would be interested in engineering; technical, rather than a general or liberal arts high school. As a

---

*Some of the tape sequences are included because they are a comment on the poetry. The kitten incident and the fall are noticed at *"A"*-14, p. 355 [All page references to *"A"* are to the University of California edition of 1978]:

> an escaped cat
> ran down three
> flights of stairs,
>
> a little boy
> after, he caught
> it and climbed
>
> back up the
> three flights and
> before closing the
>
> door on it,
> stroked it, 'you
> pussy stay upstairs,
>
> now I'll go
> downstairs.' It became
> the family joke —

matter of fact he had hoped at one time to go into engineering. It was at Stuyvesant High School that he first took English literature. It was a part of the curriculum and he found himself becoming far more interested in that than the other. He had to take a course in mechanical something or other, and by the end of the term he had to build something: he made just one little bit of a shelf, sort of two little bookends. Kind of a miniature book shelf.

T.   What they called shop?

C.   Shop. Yes.

T.   Let us talk about his parents. When did his mother die?

C.   In 1927.

T.   They were both orthodox?

C.   Oh, yes, very. His mother wore a wig so that he never knew what the color of her own hair was. Orthodox women wore wigs. My mother never did, but apparently Lou's mother did.

T.   They spoke only Yiddish at home?

C.   Well, that was his sister. I never met his mother. When I met Louie his mother had been dead for several years and the eldest sister had been dead by that time so the only ones I really knew of his family were his sister Fanny and his brother, Morris.

T.   Did Louis mention his mother much?

C.   No, only incidentally in his work. *Arise, Arise* was built around his mother's illness. She'd had a pulmonary infection and she was hospitalized and then they brought her home. It's almost autobiographical. This business of the aunt in the play *Arise, Arise* is not really an aunt: it's a distant relation that had some sort of a factory and Louie's brother made an attempt to work there for awhile, and his two sisters, but other than that, he didn't mention her. They did bring his mother home and in a month she was gone. It was not tuberculosis nor was it pneumonia. I suppose the doctors were either remiss or weren't quite aware and didn't diagnose it correctly.

T.   They lived in the same place in NY all their lives?

C.   First they lived on Christie Street until Louie was 10 or 11; then they moved to East Harlem, East 111 Street. And it was from there that he entered Columbia College and could walk from East 111th Street up to the Columbia campus.

T. It was quite a walk.

C. Not too bad because if you wanted to you could walk down one block to 110th Street, down to what was Cathedral Parkway, and then walk up to Broadway.

T. Let's go back down town. What synagogue did they go to?

C. The synagogue his father attended was called Tifereth Jerusalem. It was not the largest synagogue but one of the larger ones. It was on East Broadway, Manhattan.

T. How far north of say Wall Street was it?

C. About two miles.

T. How far south of Houston Street?

C. Oh, about one-fourth of a mile. No more than five blocks.

T. When did Louie become unorthodox?

C. Probably the moment he was aware; he always refused to wear the phylactaries. They did have a rabbi or a biblical student (I don't know what he was) come and make an attempt to teach him to say his prayers in Hebrew and to read the Hebrew prayer book, but that didn't last very long either. He refused to do that.

T. Did he behave in this way until his Bar Mitzvah?

C. As a matter of fact he probably just went through a very perfunctory Bar Mitzvah where you go to the synagogue on a particular Saturday morning. I'm not certain but they probably pronounce your name and say you are the son of so and so and the grandson of so and so and that you are now arrived at manhood at 13 and that was it. As far as I know there was no celebration and there was no special attention paid to it. Louis always said that he barely knew his father because his father worked very late hours at this men's clothing factory where he was the presser and wouldn't come home till close to midnight and then be up first thing in the morning. I know my father did, too. My father would wake at four. He would go to the synagogue for morning prayer, then one at sunset, and then one in the evening. And every orthodox Jew, if he is not near a synagogue will at least recite the prayer. It is preferable that you attend the synagogue because if they are saying prayers for the dead you might be needed; they must have a group of at least ten men present. So most orthodox Jews always felt an obligation to arrive at a synagogue just in case they were needed. My father always went to the synagogue for his morning prayers and so did Louie's father. And also the evening prayer. The late afternoon or early evening prayer was different except on Friday. Of course on Friday they would leave work early to be home before the sunset.

T. Was it much cause of concern to his father that Louie became perfunctory?

C. Yes it was: he was always irritated by it, but then there was already a precedent. Louie's older brother, Morris, had already shaken off all of that as well, so the elder Zukofsky just accepted it. There was no use. I mean you could argue just so much and that was it.

T. If Louie ever (after you were married) talked about his early days, what kind of things would he say about them?

C. Never really. As I said he felt that whatever he could say about it he put into his work and *Arise, Arise* is built around his mother's illness and death. "Poem beginning "The"" has a great many hints of his mother. The novel, *Little*, bears heavily on a kind of description of his surviving sister and her husband, and Louie.

T. Do you remember the character's name in *Little*?

C. Yes, she is the Contessa Murda-Wonda.

T. Really! That's Louie's sister?

C. Yes, and the count was his brother-in-law, his sister's husband. He apparently came from the same village that the Zukofskys came from in Russia. That was how they knew one another. His name was Al: Count Murda-Wonda. Al was a very charming creature but Louie's sister could be very depressing always moaning and bewailing her fate because she couldn't have the latest furniture, the latest clothes, and the latest this and that. Al was always charming and gay; not very good at holding down any kind of job, but he was a fine dancer, a great baseball fan and all in all, though he was poor, he was a very cheerful man indeed. They have the one son who in the novel is called "the young count": he is Louie's nephew. Louie's father lived with that family group until his death.

As Celia suggested on the tapes, Louie's mother is present everywhere in "Poem beginning "The"." At the beginning:

    4   A boy's best friend is his mother,
    5   It's your mother all the time.
    6   Residue of Oedipus-faced wrecks
    7   Creating out of the dead,—

In the middle:

        186   Speaking about epics, mother,
        187   How long ago is it since you gathered mushrooms,

        . . .
        203   Is it your Russia that is free mother.
        204   Tell me, mother.

        . . .
        238   If horses could but sing Bach, mother, —
        239   Remember how I wished it once —
        240   Now I kiss you who could never sing Bach, never read Shakespeare.

Elsewhere at lines 241, 243, 248, 249, 250, 270, 271, 273, 276, 277, 278 as well as near the end:

        313   O my Sun, my son, my son Sun!
                    would God
        314   I had died for thee, O Sun, my son,
                    my son!

Further, after plays on the word son, we have the line:

        315   I have not forgotten you, mother, —

Sometimes, in fact, he addresses his mother with the tone of voice and chuckle of a comic-strip fiend:

        251   Assimilation is not hard,
        252   And once the Faith's askew
        253   I might as well look Shagetz just as much as Jew.
        254   I'll read their Donne as mine,
        255   And leopard in their spots
        256   I'll do what says their Coleridge,
        257   Twist red hot pokers into knots.
        258   The villainy they teach me I will execute
        259   And it shall go hard with them,
        260   For I'll better the instruction,
        261   Having learned, so to speak, in their colleges.

The poem was written more than four years before his mother's death and the drama *Arise, Arise* started forming in his mind probably within a year after her death. A fascinating play, it shows that Zukofsky was familiar with the new modes of German Expressionist drama which derived in part from Strindberg and led to the Surrealist theatre of Apollinaire [e.g. *The Breasts of Tiresias*, 1917] and Cocteau [e.g. *The Wedding on the Eiffel Tower*, 1921]. Such German dramatists as Oskar Kokoschka, Georg Kaiser, and Reinhard Sorge are quite likely behind the form and feeling of *Arise, Arise* as well as the drama of Apollinaire. Zukofsky was a thorough researcher: it is quite unlikely that he would have written a book about Apollinaire's style without looking into the European genesis of that style. It is probable that early work on *Arise, Arise* led to the work which Zukofsky entitled *The Writings of Guillaume Apollinaire.**

A preliminary note to the drama says: "The play requires two curtains: the familiar one of the theatre, and the dream curtain of dark, heavy indefinite voile back of the theatre curtain. The actors should be dancers. The costumes, not confined to a realistic locale, are essentially theatrical and as such never give the feeling of being anachronous." This note evokes a number of associations reaching from Strindberg's *Ghost Sonata* to Bertold Brecht's "Verfremdungseffekt" theatre of post WW II, a concept variously translated (always inadequately) as "Alienation effect" or "effect of estrangement" and before *Arise, Arise* is finished we have a sense of the "theatre of the absurd" stirring.

The main curtain rises on Act I, scene 1, with the sound of a train whistle coming out of the distance: the voices of a mother and son are heard behind the second curtain. The son is reading the opening lines of Donne's Holy Sonnet VII from which the title of the play is taken:

> At the round earth's imagined corners, blow
> Your trumpets, angels, and arise, arise
> From death, you numberless infinities
> Of souls, and to your scattered bodies go.

Donne's poem concerns an idea in 17th-century eschatology which assumes the resurrection in the flesh of all Christians called to life to enter the New Jerusalem. In part Zukofsky is adapting this tradition into the poetic feelings appropriate to a Jewish Kaddish for his mother. But the hard sweat-shop life of both his mother and father lead to another source for the title: "Arise ye workers of the world, you have nothing to lose but your chains." Thus the despair of death is tempered by hope. The play closes with two characters (attendants R. and D.) who represent the unnamed and unsung proletariat anticipating a revolution. R. says to D. "I vaticinate a revolution." Since both R. and D. are black, menial laborers about a hospital and its grounds, we may assume that the revolution now anticipated, which will result in radical changes in a sick society, is not a violent or bloody one, but a drastic change in social thinking. The Civil Rights Bill and all that followed it to the chorus of "We shall overcome" accord with such a theory and the Marx-Engels refrain is seen in a new perspective.

Returning to the scene behind the dream curtain, we note

---

*Zukofsky's own English work was never published. But the translation by his good friend René Taupin was published in France in 1934 as *Le Style Apollinaire.*

that the mother seems not to hear the son reading. She recalls dramatic moments in the mind of an immigrant arriving in this country from Russia, but even more, she is concerned with the death of her daughter: "My life was cut short when your sister was put in the grave. You place something on an upper shelf and cannot find it again." But the son, concerned with the idea of arising from death, accuses her of not listening. But she has heard and proves it by citing phrases from the same Holy Sonnet: "let them sleep . . . . mourn a space. . . ." The interchange suggests the difference between the generations: the mother's "let the dead past sleep" and the son's "let the sleeping giant rise from its chains and enter the world which awaits them."

Finally, the dream curtain rustles and lifts, and the mother and son are seen in partial darkness walking along some country road. The dialog continues with more reflections on death and its implications for the living. But it soon appears that the mother has been long dead and the dialog is part of a dream. At the end of the scene, the mother and son listen to the voice of the father said to come from the grave. The voice says:

> they do not return child. There is a legend that they would speak from their graves outside a village before morning. Someone came to listen, stretched out, put his ear to the ground, and they whispered: "Sisters, brothers, we are being overheard, we must not speak." My son dreams often about your grandma, he tells me that he knows she is dead in the dream and she knows but does not mention it. They say nothing about it for love of each other, so that there will be no difference between them or a fear that he will wake.

That is it: *for love of each other*. Love, familial love, is a major theme in *Arise, Arise* as indeed in all of Zukofsky's work. And this love is most significant: for it is the power of love within the particular family that can be—nay *must be*—enlarged to encompass the family of man. It is the psychological or emotional basis on which any New Jerusalem may—indeed *must*—be built. No new kingdom will come and survive if it is engendered, nurtured, and perpetrated by spilling blood.

Upon hearing the father's voice the mother says "One moment." She turns a knob, which is all that is seen of a door on this dream-like set, and hurries in. That's all the stage direction says: "She hurries in." The scene ends with the son calling after her: "Mother, the door—leave the keys with me!" He tries the door, "nervously." It rattles. The Dream Curtain lowers. The audience is left with a question. "What keys?" or "keys to what?" Since Zukofsky was an avid, life-long student of the Bible, both Old and

New Testaments, we may have a metaphor of one generation asking another for "the keys to the kingdom." The thought sets up ripples in many directions. Before the final curtain at the end of two acts and nine scenes, we find that the play's purpose, operating on several levels at once, is to pose many kinds of questions and leave hope if there is any to future generations. Zukofsky sees and dramatizes an age old dilemma: a vision of a new and more decent world is not difficult to state or aspire to, but such a world if it is to transpire can transpire only with the help of new and more decent people—a condition not likely to be met in any near century.

II

Returning to the *Autobiography*, we find that it continues, after the brief prose statement concerning "the bare facts," with five poems set to sixteen pages of music, all except the first to be found in *All*: "Song 11," "Song 8," "No. 5," "Song 22," and "Light: No. 10."

The verses as well as the lilting music celebrate the changing seasons, especially spring:

When is winter spring?
When, tho ice is not breaking,
One has what one does not expect to be taking

It is against the winds
It is against firm ice
But with the sun, that falling asleep
    winter is spring
    one-sixth of the earth.

["Song 11"]

The next piece continues for five pages in a tone of delight:

Happier, happier, now
For whom in snowsleet barberries see;
If not that, if not that, how
Are red berries for their windsleights free?

["Song 8," *All*, 50]

So does the next which is done in just one page:

Ah spring, when with a thaw of blue
Sun in the street will she be as today?
Seaplane up to sky over sky
Avenues without empire on earth of May

["No. 5," *All*, 25]

The next one has a telling change in content and tempo. It has 15 1/2 stanzas of which the first two are:

> To my washstand
> in which I wash
>   my left hand
> and my right hand
>
> To my washstand
> whose base is Greek
>   whose shaft is marble
> and is fluted

["Song 22," *All*, 59]

We infer from this song that after celebrating the happiness of each new season, the poet is now celebrating the happiness of each new day. And by implication all activities of life both small and smallest, even the sensuous pleasure of washing one's hands if one consciously maintains continuous contact with the universe at that place where it really counts: as it impinges upon the skin. This is clearly a Zen insight which says by further implication, "Life is a reality to be experienced [one can feel at the skin/nerve level, the Zen Master's stick] not a problem to be solved." But with Zukofsky we may have it both ways: "Yes, life is a reality to be experienced but also a problem, at the epistemological and ontological levels, to be engaged if not solved."

In any hierarchy of Zukofsky values we could anticipate the next important thing in life would be words: words, words, words. All words! The *Autobiography* does not disappoint us. In the next brief prose statement after the songs, he says so:

> My first exposure to letters at the age of four was thru the Yiddish theaters, most memorably the Thalia on the Bowery. By the age of nine I had seen a good deal of Shakespeare, Ibsen, Strindberg and Tolstoy performed—all in Yiddish. Even Longfellow's *Hiawatha* was to begin with read by me in Yiddish, as was Aeschylus' *Prometheus Bound*. My first exposure to English was, to be exact, P.S. 7 on Chrystie and Hester Streets. By eleven I was writing poetry in English, as yet not "American English," tho I found Keats rather difficult as compared with Shelley's "Men of England" and Burns' "Scots, wha hae."

This brief statement is followed by 7 more pages of music. "Song 21":

> Snows' night's winds on the window rattling
> Would seem to leap out of the bedspring
>
> What prevents a feat like that occurring
> Reason—but the more actual bedding

Springs of steel mercurial spirallings
Making a body's night a changeable singing

The winged boots of the frozen seek of it sheltering
Safety from the window's pommelling

[*All*, 58]

These verses are orchestrated for three voices in the music. Love, sex, procreation, and the strength of a close family relationship as a defense against the cold impersonal world seem implied.

The next song (16) is more enigmatic. Spread horizontally along three lines of music on one page it seems one thing. But as it's given vertically in *All* (p. 55) it seems another:

Crickets'
thickets

light,
delight:

sleeper's eyes,
keeper's;

            Plies!
lightning

frightening
whom. . . ?

doom
nowhere. . .

where eyes. . .
air,

are crickets'
air.

Since the poem and music in 2/4 time are squarely there in the center of the book it must have great biographical significance. Since I was left without a cue I queried Celia. Her response to these interpretations contained additional insights and information especially about the crickets' / thickets:

Your "Zen" insight into "Song 22 (To my washstand)" is exactly what Louis intended. "Song 22" was one of his favorite poems. The melodic line is his. I simply recorded it as he "chanted" the words. I added the harmonic bass because he liked to hear instrumental timbre as he read (chanted) the poem.

Your interpretation of "Song 21" is right too. An added note is that in the Pythagorean Theory of Numbers, 3 is the number of mediation.

Re "Song 16 (Crickets')"—We spent the summer and early fall of 1942 in Diamond Point, Lake George, N.Y. where we were constantly entertained (?) by crickets. Louis said he had prophesied the summer of 1942 ten years earlier, in 1932, and wanted to use the poem as his Xmas greeting to friends in 1942.

Some excerpts from the tapes bear on the issues of early work, education, and the call to be a poet:

T. When did he start writing poetry? Did he ever tell you?

C. Well, he said he'd written and discarded 500 poems. A manuscript at Texas under the name of Dunn Wyth is Louie's work. He called the poems "juvenelia" and he wanted never to be reminded of it. He wanted to throw it out. But I said that would be foolish and he ought to send it on to Texas since another name was on it. Nobody would find out who Dunn Wyth was. It would make a nice little problem for scholars. Anything he wrote before he was 22 is discarded, although he started writing very early.

T. He said he started at age 11. When did he start seriously?

C. In his last year at high school he probably wrote something; at Columbia he wrote a great deal.

T. He was writing poetry seriously as early as 15 or 16?

C. Yes. The Columbia college magazines like *Varsity* have a number of early poems which Louie never had reprinted. He refused to have them in *All*. Oh, there they are in *Varsity* and *The Columbian*. He never kept any of these, but he wrote them as early as 1920. Those two were done with. He did not want them as part of [his mature work].

T. Did he ever tell you who his favorite poets were when he was young?

C. Well, he read Longfellow in Yiddish. That was *Hiawatha*.

T. A Yiddish *Hiawatha* staggers the imagination.

C. Apparently, in high school he had excelled in something and the first prize he had hoped to get was to have been a collection of Shakespeare's plays. But he was given some book on Engineering and of course he was very distressed by that. His interest probably started when he was attending the Yiddish

theatre and they did Yiddish translations of Aeschylus and
Shakespeare. It is a fact that until he attended school he knew
no English at all. But once he knew Longfellow in Yiddish
there was no problem when he could read English, to go and
find Longfellow at the library and read it or to start reading
Shakespeare.

It is clear from the tapes and the record everywhere else that
great literature in all its forms became a passion for Zukofsky. As
he matured, the idea grew that not only could he become an expert in the interpretation of literature, he could also produce it.
But he approached the vocation of poet with trepidation, deadly-
seriousness, and the conviction that he would have to serve a long
and painstaking apprenticeship. It was by such means that his
practice approached the perfect.

Among his English teachers at Columbia were John Erskine
and Mark Van Doren. With Mark and his wife he formed a life-
long friendship. The prose squib in the *Autobiography* summarizes:

> My poems first appeared in print in 1920 and continued to ap-
> pear in more than one hundred "little" magazines, national and
> international. The appearances led to friendship with Ezra Pound
> and William Carlos Williams beginning in 1927. I wrote the first
> extended essay on Pound's *Cantos 1-27*, which appeared in
> French in *Echanges* (Paris) 1930. It was thru Pound's efforts that
> Harriet Monroe invited me to edit the February 1931 issue of
> *Poetry* (Chicago). But it was not until 1965 that an easily acces-
> sible volume of my poetry appeared on the American scene. My
> thanks for this fact are due to W.W. Norton & Company.

During these years he also went to teach at the University of Wisconsin [1930-31] where he was a colleague of Kenneth Rexroth.
An excerpt from the tapes takes up on this point:

T.   After he returned from Wisconsin, he took Pound up on his
     invitation and went to visit him at Rapallo?

C.   Yes.

T.   Was J. Laughlin there at the same time that Louie was?

C.   Louie met Laughlin at Rapallo, yes.

T.   Did he talk about being at Rapallo to you?

C.   Well, Louie never forgot Homer Pound, that's Ezra's father.

T.   He was there?

C.   Yes, because Louie was put up in the father's apartment.

Homer Pound would ask Louie to come out on the beach, and he'd say, "See that over there floating? That's my boy!" pointing to Ezra. Homer Pound was very proud of Ezra.

T. Floating? You mean swimming?

C. No, just floating, just lying there floating like a [log].

T. Way out there?

C. Way out there.

T. Half a mile at sea?

C. Half a mile at sea out on the Mediterranean. And Louie's first impressions of James Laughlin were probably very true: he said he just looked like a young god. He was very tall, very handsome, strikingly handsome.

T. I understand he was a rebel when he was there as a young man.

C. I don't know that. Louie never thought of Laughlin as a rebel.

T. Never talked about what he was doing there?

C. No. But, Laughlin is probably 10 years younger than Louie was and whether Louie thought he was very young, 10 years younger, a very young boy, I don't know. But he was struck by his physical appearance.

T. Then Laughlin would have been 17?

C. Laughlin would probably have been 17 or 18. Well, no, if this was 1933 and Louie was about 29, then Laughlin would have been 19 or 20. If I'm correct, if there is a ten year difference, I don't know Laughlin's age, but I think they are approximately 10 years apart. [J. Laughlin was born Oct. 30, 1914.]

T. Let's go back and pick up his Columbia days. When did he enter?

C. He was probably not quite 16 when he entered. He graduated from Columbia in 3 1/2 years when he was approaching his 20th birthday. He stayed on to get his MA, and graduated in the class of 1923. He was not quite 20: he was just a little past 19 approaching his 20th birthday.

T. What then?

C. Then he had odd jobs. He worked for awhile for the National Industrial Conference Board. That was the job he got through a close friend at Columbia known as Kappy. His real name was Kaplan, Irving Kaplan. Everybody called him Kappy. He was a statistician on Wall Street. Louie continued to see him for quite a number of years until they moved to Washington when Kappy got a job working for somebody important in the Roosevelt administration. Another friend he met at Columbia with whom he maintained a great friendship was Ted Hecht.

T. Ted who?

C. Hecht. Samuel Theodore Hecht. One of the poems in *All* was dedicated to him. Louie used the initials: "My friend STH."

T. Were there others who became well known?

C. His closest friend at Columbia was Whittaker Chambers. Witt at that time was interested in poetry—in writing it. He would always show Louie what he was doing. But he went on a tangent which was political and then came the split though it was purely for political reasons because they did like each other. This was in the 30's. Many years later during the Chambers [-Hiss] trial the FBI came to ask about their friendship. Witt had given Louie's name as a character reference. Back there, he had gone wild: first he had been a Calvin Coolidge admirer and then suddenly had gone to the other end of the pendulum and joined the communist party.

T. Was he a card carrying member?

C. Witt? Yes. In fact Witt took Louie to one of the party meetings. That was on the west side and apparently the people there felt that Louie was too well dressed and too neat and too natty. All in all he didn't strike them as being the proper kind of member and so they suggested that he join someplace on the east side. Louie thought, "What a thing to be going to! East side or west side!" But to his dying day he never knew if they had made out a card for him. And Witt, of course: even that Louie was never certain of. Witt would jest and say that his name in the party was so and such and he had several names and when Witt would say things about espionage, etc. Louie always thought that Witt was jesting. He didn't think that anything like that was possible. He didn't see how Witt could get to the upper echelon of the communist party. It just seemed incredible to him. Well, to go back to this business of a character reference, two FBI agents arrived one day when we were still living at Willow Street in Brooklyn to question Louie about his friendship with Witt and where Louie had been in 1930-1931. Louie was never a member and he couldn't even remember when he had been in Wisconsin and of course Louie was so mixed up that the FBI was correcting him and saying "Oh no, excuse me, you were in Wisconsin in 1930, you're getting your dates mixed up." And finally they said, "We're sorry but we really couldn't use you as a character reference because you haven't seen him in so many years." That was it. In his book Whittaker Chambers never mentions Louie by name. I think the name of the book was *Witness.* But there is a reference where he talks to this young man with tortoise shell glasses who approached him one day, and I forgot how he put it, "Well what are you going to do now? Are you going to . . ." something about using a gun or something? But Louie always thought that Witt was jesting—that all these stories of espionage and Kerensky and all this name dropping was just Witt's wild imagination and thought it was probably Witt preparing some novel or some story because he was interested in writing then. I don't know what he did with the material he wrote.

T. He took that direction after the crash of 1929?

C. Yes, he went completely to the other end of the pendulum. Louie knew Witt's mother and his father. And of course he knew his younger brother, Richard, who was known as Dickie. Some of the poems in *All,* even "Poem beginning "The,""" have references to Witt's younger brother.*

T. His own family background was generally democratic, New Deal and that sort of thing?

C. You mean Louie's family?

T. Yes.

C. Yes. They always veered away from the conservative elements. Of course, with his sister, the background would be nil, just bland. She never became a citizen. Even though she arrived here as a young girl of 16 and lived till the age of 85, she never became a citizen of the U.S. Couldn't speak more than two words of English; I think the two words were "hello" and "goodbye." Even her husband Al never became an American citizen.

T. You had to learn English to do that?

C. Yes, but also you had to know who was the president of the U.S. and I suppose you had to know who was the mayor of

---

*Richard Chambers, called Ricky in *"A,"* is recalled often in the early movements. His suicide is central to *"A"*-3. Celia is referring to lines 76-129, which is known as the "Ricky section" of . . . "The."

New York City: these were insurmountable [obstacles]! I
mean how could you learn things like that!

T. Now, let's check back. Louie had some odd jobs after Columbia College in 23 and 24?

C. Yes. The job Kappy got for him with the National Industrial
Board. It probably had to do with editing reports some of the
writers were getting out. He did have a part-time job for awhile
at Nedicks, as a soda jerk and a part-time job at a local post
office that didn't last too long. Louis could be contrary even
though he was not a practicing Jew. He was fired from the
post office job because he refused to come to work on Yom
Kippur. He wasn't going to any synagogue, but he wasn't
going to work on Yom Kippur either.

III

To return to the *Autobiography*, the prose passage cited
above is followed by the words and music of several brief songs:
(1) "A song for the year's End: No. I"; (2) "No. 29"; (3) "que j'ay
dit devant: No. I"; and (4) "So that even a lover: No. I." The first,
arranged for four voices (sopr., alto, tenor, bass), reads

> Daughter of music
> and her sweet son
> so that none rule
> the dew to his own hurt
> With the year's last sigh
> Awake
> the starry sky and bird.
>
> [*All*, p. 119]

Song 29 of *Anew* goes:

> Glad they were there
> Falling away
> Flying not to
> Lose sight of it
> Not going far
> In angles out
> Of ovals of
> Dances filled up
> The field the green
> With light above
> With the one hand
> In the other.
>
> [*All*, p. 102]

The third, from "Some Time," goes:

Day that passes,
Day that stays,
Day that passes
Other days'

Crow's-foot, sieges,
Tears, bare way,
A god's egis,
Catspaw spray.

[*All*, p. 121]

The last, also from "Some Time," reads:

Little wrists,
Is your content
My sight or hold,
Or your small air
That lights and trysts?

Red alder berry
Will singly break;
But you—how slight—do:
So that even
A lover exists.

[*All*, p. 122]

These songs are followed in the *Autobiography* by a single prose sentence alone on a page:

As for subsistence I can only quote with
affection e.e. cummings: "no thanks."

Two additional songs with music are given ["Xenophanes," *All*, p. 130 and "As to how much," *All*, p. 137], after which we have a final prose statement which brings us to the heart of L.Z.'s matter:

My wife Celia and son Paul have been the only reason for the poet's persistence. She has collaborated with me in my work on Shakespeare and Catullus. Paul is a violinist and composer. I trust, considering his gifts, that his art will be welcomed sooner than mine.

The *Autobiography* ends with two brief songs:

To My Valentines

From one to two
is one step up
and one and two
spell three
and we agree
three is the sum
        a run
of two and one.

[*All*, p. 140]

And

Old

"More do I love cold
than do I hate warm."
If what the child hear
sound old, neither does
cold hate warm.
The more if less love
may do hate out
of its charm.

[*All*, p. 142]

Clearly implied and underlined by repetition in the *Autobiogra-phy* is L.Z.'s message that music, song, and poetry are at the center of his life but Celia and Paul (Daughter of music/and her sweet son) become with the years the center of the poetry and song.

Celia's first meetings with Zuk were hardly promising, still less dramatic, as this segment from the tapes shows.

T. When did you first meet Louis?

C. In the fall of 1933. He was a supervisor on a WPA project which had just been started. I went to work there.

T. Love at first sight?

C. Oh, no.

T. When you first saw him, didn't you take a look and sort of say: "That's for me!"

C. Certainly not. I didn't even notice him—much. My mind was on other things—the new job.

T. What about him? Did his face light up when he first saw you?

C. Not at all. He didn't notice me either.

T. What kind of contacts did you have with him?

C. Just the same as the others. There were five or six people in the room writing different things—jobs given us to do. When they were finished we'd hand them to him. That's all.

T. When you took your pieces up didn't he make a special sign different from the others . . . maybe say thank you a little different?

C. He didn't say thank you to me or anyone. He didn't look up or do anything. He just sat there.

T. Okay. But a day must have come when he became aware that you were special. What happened?

C. [long pause]. Well he noticed a book on the corner of my desk one day and asked if he could look at it. It was *In the American Grain* by Carlos Williams. I'd bought it in some sale to read on the long subway ride. It was just lying on the corner of the desk while I was working, and he saw it.

T. So! You thought Williams! That'll get his attention!

C. No! I'd never heard of Williams at the time. And I certainly didn't know Louie had.

T. What happened next?

C. He kept the book for a couple of hours and then brought it back. He said thank you. Then at the end of the day he asked if he could borrow it over night. I told him he could, but to take care of it because I didn't have too much money to spend for books. He gave it back the next morning and then gave me some other pages of writing and asked if I'd like to read them. There was no name of an author anywhere, so I didn't know who had written them. I said I was no expert but I'd read what he'd given me. The next day, he asked . . .

T. Midday?

C. Oh no. First thing in the morning. Up he comes wanting to know what I thought of it. I told him I wasn't sure what the thing meant but I was struck by what seemed a musical structure—a sort of sonata form with theme, recapitulation, variation, coda and so on. If it's lighted up faces you want, that was when his face lighted up. He beamed all over. After that he told me he had written it.

T. And then he asked you to marry him?

C. No. That was in 33 and we didn't get married until 6 years later in 39.

T. He just began to ask you out?

C. Later that day he said a certain group from the office usually had lunch at a nearby Chinese restaurant and I was welcome to come along if I liked . . . and I did, quite often. It was an interesting group.

T. When did he start asking you out in the evening?

C. He really didn't. I don't believe he went out very much. Once in a while I'd have tickets to a concert and I'd ask him if he'd like to go; and once in a while he would.

T. When did you start going steady?

C. Probably not until 1936 or 37.

T. Three years later?

C. Yes. There at the WPA we struck up a close friendship, rela-
    tionship. But Louis left that project and so did I because I
    got a job working with a fife and drum corp with a Catholic
    school, and oddly enough I went to work for a Yeshiva: that's
    a Jewish parochial school.

T. When did you have your first date?

C. Ah! we became separated because of different jobs but we did
    keep up a correspondence. He would telephone; my parents'
    home had a telephone. Our first date, I think was to hear
    Leonard Bernstein playing a piano piece of Aaron Copland's at
    Town Hall. And I think I invited Louie to come. That is my
    first recollection of being present with Louie at a concert.

T. You invited him?

C. Yes, oh, Leonard Bernstein was an extraordinarily fine pianist
    and also at just about that time Louie introduced me to Tibor
    Serly who had studied with Bartok. I had never met Tibor
    Serly.

T. Had you decided to marry Louie when you invited him?

C. No, no, no! We were just on the higher planes, music and
    literature. I did meet Tibor's sister, Ethel, because she was in
    a Hungarian folk dance group.

T. How long did it take before *he* asked *you* to go somewhere?

C. That must have been quite some time because I was the only
    earning member of the group, but as I said he did introduce
    me to Tibor. He was in the Philadelphia Symphony Orchestra
    at the time and commuting but he eventually gave that up and
    moved to Manhattan.

T. You think it may have taken 3 years before it was fairly clear
    that you and he were going steady?

C. If you want to call it that. But in any case before we had
    really built up a kind of close knit intellectual friendship or
    group. But of course Louie could never understand why I
    had no time: I always had at least 16 jobs, working morning,
    noon, nights, Saturdays and Sundays. There would be this
    folk dance group or that folk dance group or this fife and
    drum corp or . . .

T. And then one day 6 years later, he said, "Let's get married?" or something.

C. No he didn't.

T. Come on, now. Maybe he didn't spread his handkerchief on the floor, kneel down, and do a real Victorian scene, but there must have been a particular moment when he said or did something that settled the matter.

C. I would be making it up if I said "yes." I cannot really remember; I think we sort of arrived at it very easily and very naturally because by that time there were other women whom he not only corresponded with but whom he visited and who visited him in the city. Some of them kept up a friendship [afterwards] : they would come and visit at our house. So . . .

T. You got married in 1939?

C. Yes, August. We were married in Wilmington, Delaware, because in New York City you were required to have a Wasserman test and Louie refused to go thru that. Of course, he refused to have a religious ceremony which is also required in NY. We made several inquiries and it seemed that the state of Delaware was very liberal. You didn't need a Wasserman test and we thought you could just have a civil ceremony.

T. So in Wilmington you didn't have to make arrangements ahead of time?

C. Yes. You could just drive over although we did write ahead, I think, to the county clerk for the marriage ceremony. However, we were told that we did have to have a religious ceremony so we looked in the telephone directory and, oddly enough, found a Rabbi whose name was Henry Tarvel, almost a close spelling to my own name. We telephoned him and he said he would be glad to come and meet us at the county clerk's office and drive us over to his home. He performed the religious ceremony.

T. Sometime before August, Louis must have said "I must take you to meet my parents."

C. Well, yes. I had met his brother probably in 1937 but his sister's family and his father I met probably no more than 3 months before we got married. And I think it was a matter of not wanting them to become too inquisitive: "Is this the girl? what does she do? what does she look like?"

T. Do you remember the day you went and met them? Louie's father?

C. It must have been a Sunday because Louie never went to his father's house on the Sabbath because it would mean he had taken the subway and presumably one was not allowed to travel on the subway on the Sabbath. During the week I worked so it must have been a Sunday and it could not have been earlier than three months before we were married. In fact they were quite certain when Louie announced to them he was thinking about it, that he was marrying a non-Jewish girl. When I did arrive I spoke Yiddish fluently; I speak Yiddish as well as I speak English. I spoke Yiddish, but they didn't believe their ears. They thought I'd just picked up a few Yiddish words to impress them. In fact it wasn't until after we were married that my parents invited Louie's father and his sister, that they were assured, absolutely convinced.

T. How did your father and Louie's father get along?

C. Quite well. My father was a very learned man and of course orthodox. They got along very well. There was no problem. And my mother and Louie's sister (oddly enough they were almost the same age) got along very well. They didn't see each other very much. Louie's sister lived way out, almost to the end of the Bronx. My parents lived at the far end of Brooklyn.

T. You knew in 39 the war was coming?

C. Oh yes, of course. Hitler was very much in the air. Certainly, I think it was probably the war. I was working. I was earning $75 a month; it was something we could rely on, something we could live on.

T. Where did you go for a honeymoon?

C. Nowhere. We came back to Manhattan. Louie had a room in a basement on 111th Street. We stayed there for a few months and then we did find a lovely apartment opposite Bronx park.

T. Did Louie see Pound in 1939 when he . . . ?

C. Yes, Pound had come and left a note in the door; we were away that day. Pound was staying at Ted Serly's house on 58th Street, so Louie went over there.

T. Was it late that year?

C. September. Shortly after we were married.

T. You didn't?

C. No, I had 16 jobs. I preferred it that way. I worked closely with Louie, but I always felt his literary work and his literary friends, those were his, and I'd rather mind my own business, stay out of the picture. I think most people always have the feeling that one, either I knew nothing about it or two, I was Louie's housekeeper. I prefer to go into the kitchen and make the coffee and serve it though I was very aware, very knowledgeable about what he was doing.

T. Did he say anything about Pound at Ted Serly's after he came back?

C. Yes, he and Ezra were arguing—Louie had mentioned the Catholic priest, Father Coughlin (remember he had the radio speeches) and Louie had said to Pound, "Well, if you knew nothing else, if you had heard him on the radio, you should at least be deterred by the sound of his voice." But I don't really remember what Pound's response was. Ted, if I knew where he were, could probably remember since it was in his house. And in fact I never would pry into these literary—"well, what did he say? how did he say it? what was he doing?"—things.

T. But you do remember that they did talk about Father Coughlin?

C. Yes. They always argued about some things they could never agree on: paper money. And Major Douglas! Economics!

T. Did Louie know about Pound's broadcasts [after he returned to Italy in 39]?

C. Oh, yes!

T. What did he say about them?

C. Well, he always felt that Pound's heart was in the right place but that he was always going off on a tangent, getting into business that wasn't his. Bill Williams, you know, would get furious and write Louie about it. Bill was irate because apparently one of the Pound broadcasts mentioned Williams by name and that disturbed him very much.

T. What did Louie think about Pound and Mussolini?

C. He felt Pound was just making the wrong choices in his friends. That innately Pound was a good man if only he would stick to his literature and the good things that he . . .

T. What did he think Pound was up to with Mussolini?

C. Louie thought that Pound was under the impression that he was going to educate Mussolini.

T. About money?

C. About money, about culture, and have Mussolini set up a kind of superior intellectual ruling class or some such thing. But Louie never questioned or doubted the innate integrity of Pound. He felt that Pound—that these were temporary lapses—or he was off on a tangent—

T. Because he was maybe isolated in Rapallo?

C. Maybe isolated. And maybe angry at the reception he was getting by literary critics in the States. It was probably more of a reaction to how he was being treated by people in the States here.

T. The way Pound was being treated?

C. Louie never (for all his so-called neglect)—Louie was never *too* offended. He thought, "Oh well, if they don't like my work they don't like it." People have said "Oh he was bitter." Louie was never bitter. If you could leave Louie alone in a room with a desk and a pencil and a paper in front of him, he wasn't bitter.

T. Long before the 30s came to an end people seemed to want to sign up for some kind of collective action: either socialism, Marxism, communism, fascism or whatever. Even I remember the drama. I would have joined the Communist Party if I'd known how. I vaguely remember being told to forget it, of wanting to know why I should forget it, and getting the answer "You talk too much." In those days the real "salauds" were those who refused to get involved.

C. Everyone took sides. Louie was aware of all this and read his newspapers carefully. But he was mostly concerned with his poetry. All of this political information would appear in his poetry even up until the Viet Nam War. But he did not become an activist politically; he did not join groups; he didn't get into marches or parades.

T. Do you remember anything Louie said about Pound's broadcasts?

C. We never heard any of the Pound broadcasts. Bill Williams apparently did. Now, again, it seemed incredible to Louie that Pound would broadcast this type of material and if he did broadcast it, then either he had a kind of lapse or a temporary form of insanity.

T. After the war and you first heard about Pound's arrest. . . ?

C. Louie was very distressed by it. But again he felt that it would be just like Pound to shoot his mouth off—get himself into all this hot water when he could have been doing. . . . Of course Louie always felt that Pound was the finest poet in the English language of the 20th century. And when he said English language he didn't mean American poets, that included anyone writing the English language, whether he was an Englishman or an American or whatever, or Canadian.

T. Did he think Pound always believed he was telling the truth?

C. Louie never expressed it as you have just put it now. He felt that Pound had very strong convictions about literature and he felt that those convictions were correct; they were *right*. Now his convictions about economics, about politics, about banking, usury, or all of that, Louie felt that if Pound would calm down and just apply the intelligence and the brilliance that he had about literature to these things that he could see the errors he made. Louie didn't feel that everything Pound said about economics was haywire, or that everything he said about Coolidge or Mussolini or Hitler or any of them was absolutely haywire: he just felt that he wasn't thinking clearly. That he was just going off on these weird tangents: if only he would take time out, calm down, and sort his material, then he might see things very differently.

T. I understand. God, do I understand. Couldn't count the number of times I've winced at Pound, thinking does he *have* to say that. *Did* he have to say that! And of course he did. The contradictions are staggering. To come from a position as I did of would-be Marxist, or ultra-leftist, with convictions that "Fascism" is practically obscene and "anti-semitism" is one of the most bizarre aberrations of the human mind; to have the seemingly contradictory conviction that Pound is the greatest poet and man of letters of the 20th century—that does it! That puts one in a position where he has his work cut out for him! Putting the things together results in some kind of education. After 25 years of fussing about it, I no longer find it useful to condemn any of them. The most we can do is try to understand how such things can happen. The upshot is, Pound was a truth teller—that is if he believed something to be true, he would have to say it at the top of his voice. Do you remember the TV interview with Pound when he left St. E's? They caught him on a camera with cane, cape, scarf flowing, hat and the whole bit!

C. No. We've never owned a decent TV set. The bit of junk I have now is waiting to die. Louie hated TV. As soon as you turned it on, he fell asleep. Dope, he called it: marijuana, boob-tube . . .

T. Well, the reporter asked the inevitable question: "What did it feel like to be locked up in an insane asylum for 13 years?" Your story about Paul a little back reminded me of the scene. Pound flipped his cape, jutted out his chin, tipped his head back and said: "Well, if you're going to be in the United States you may as well be there: the whole damned country is insane!" Couldn't he be polite or something? But, of course, he couldn't. He had to be completely himself at all times.

C. Yes. That's what he said when I was worrying about Paul at St. E's.

IV

During his professional life Zukofsky held over a dozen different jobs. None of them paid very much but each paid enough so that the family could get along. Most of them involved either editing or teaching or both. But for a person who preferred to work at his art, none of the jobs was very congenial. To settle the matter now and forever, here is a numbered list of the positions he held starting with the first, which he took after receiving his MA from Columbia in 1927, and ending with the last, which he retired from in 1966. Celia provided the information which she said she took from "his very private little black notebook." She added: "It is possible that one or two of the dates may be incorrect because he often confused dates; but on the whole as far as I could verify from my files I think it is quite correct."

1.	Oct. 1927-March 1928	National Industrial Conference Board, N.Y.C.
2.	1929-1930	Free lance writing (reviews and translations)
3.	Sept. 1930-June 1931	Univ. of Wisconsin, Madison (instructor in English and Comparative Literature)
4.	Sept. 1931-Aug. 1932	To Publishers
5.	Jan. 1934-March 1935	WPA (Columbia Univ. projects)

6. Mar. 1935-Jan. 1936	WPA (WNYC Radio)
7. Jan. 1936-July 1939	WPA (Federal Arts project-Index of American Design)
8. Sept. 1939-Jan. 1941	WPA (NYC Arts project-WNYC Radio scripts)
9. Jan. 1941-Feb. 1941	La France en Liberté
10. Mar. 1941-Apr. 1942	WPA (NYC Arts project)
11. Nov. 1942-June 1943	Substitute Teaching, NYC High Schools
12. June 1943-Oct. 1944	Hazeltine Electronics Corp., Little Neck, N.Y. (editing instruction books)
13. Oct. 1944-Mar. 1946	Jordanoff Aviation Corp., NYC (editing instruction books)
14. Mar. 1946-Jan. 1947	Techlit Consultants, NYC (editing instruction books)
15. Jan. 1947-Feb. 1947	Substitute Teaching, Brooklyn Technical High School
16. Feb. 1947-Aug. 1966	Polytechnic Institute of Brooklyn (instructor to associate prof.)

In 1966, they computed the pension he would receive along with the social security. Paul was by that time launched on a very promising career. It was with a great feeling of thanksgiving and relief that they decided they would have enough to get along on and that Louie could devote his whole time to finishing *"A"* and his other work. Earlier he had taught at some summer sessions. In the summer of 1947 he taught courses in Shakespeare and Renaissance Literature at Colgate University, Hamilton, New York. From Sept. 1947-June 1948 he taught an evening course in creative writing at Queens College, Flushing, New York. In the summer of 1958, he was "poet-in-residence" at San Francisco State College, California. After his retirement, he was guest professor in the graduate school at the University of Connecticut in Storrs. Except for occasional poetry readings, this was it.

A segment from the tapes concerns Louie as a poet at work:

T. I want to ask you about Louie's work habits and his ideas of design in his work as a whole. What time did Louie get up in the morning? Start there.

C. Well he had classes at Poly at nine which means he would get up around seven so he could walk to work. He usually got home around four or five in the afternoon. Two nights a week he had evening classes which usually ran until ten. Then there were papers to read, departmental meetings and so on. But once that was out of the way his free time went to his own work. Of course, he had weekends, holidays and vacations, too. He didn't have any set hours when he sat down at his desk to write, because he always said he wrote all the time which was probably true because these things were going through his mind. However, if he was in the midst of a particular work, nothing could stop him. He would stay up all night and be ready to make his 9 o'clock class in the morning. We kept very late hours; we never went to bed before one or two in the morning. I was always up by six and he was certainly up by seven.

T. Did he rewrite much?

C. Oh, yes. Very often when he had completed a work he would put it aside because he was a great one for picking up something 5 or 10 years later and revising it, rereading it, making changes. Frequently, as in working on *"A,"* if he had an idea for a particular movement, he would start on it, might then go back to an earlier movement, might do a later movement first, yet in the back of his mind he always had a very specific plan.

T. He referred to these things as movements?

C. Yes, musical structures—movements. And he had a very definite plan in his mind so that it didn't matter if for example he worked on *"A"*-17, which is the one he did for Floss Williams, before he worked on *"A"*-14 or 15. Or if he worked on *"A"* -21 before he worked on *"A"*-19. He could synchronize because in the back of his mind he knew just what he wanted and where he was going to go.

T. Did he ever talk to you about the content?

C. No. I worked closely with him, but I worked only if I was asked to do something. I never interfered with what he wanted to do, or told him how to do it or when to do it. I feel the same with Paul. Instinctively the artist knows what he wants to do and I felt the wisest thing I could do was act as a sort of prop if he wanted one. Or a listener, I'm a very good listener. He would read the thing to me. Frequently he would say,

"Now which line, which version of the line do you think is better, this one or the other?" Simply because I picked a particular version did not mean that he used that one at all. Sometimes he might, and other times he might throw out both versions and come out with a third a week or two later.

T. He talked about the Floss Williams one more than the others —*"A"*-17?

C. Yes, but he was reflecting back on his literary friendship with Williams and doing a sort of relationship or synchronization of Williams's work and his own. Perhaps what Williams may have written in 1927 and what Zukofsky may have written in 1928: a kind of thesis and antithesis of two men concerned with the same literary problems.

T. He had a great respect for Bill Williams's work, and Williams had a great respect for his work?

C. Yes.

T. And my impression is that they are totally unalike.

C. Yes and no: their interest in reading or subject matter was quite different, but on the whole they liked each other's work and were very close about how they wanted to work and about what their literary aims were. And since they were very near each other, the correspondence was even thicker and faster than it was between Louie and Pound. They would meet when Williams would come into the city. He knew Floss very well and the Williams boys, young Bill and Paul as they were growing up.

T. Are other movements devoted to a single person?

C. Well, *"A"*-21 is a translation of the Plautus play. When he was curious about transliterating the Hebrew of the book of Job, he used that. No, *"A"*-17 is probably the only one which is intentionally about just one person. But he dedicated *"A"*-21 to his brother and John Gassner, the theatre critic. John Gassner was a very intimate friend of Louie's; they were classmates at Columbia and for a while they were very close friends.

T. When do you think Louie first considered *"A"* would be his *magnum opus*?

C. As soon as Pound used some of the movements in his anthology. Pound apparently saw some of the value of the *"A"* movements immediately; otherwise he wouldn't have printed them. There I feel it was Pound's judgment: he did that right away.

T. Do you think Louie had an idea of how long it was going to be, the dimensions?

C. Yes, right at the start. He knew that he wanted 24 movements. And very often he would put things aside for years, as you can see by the chronology of the dates when particular movements were written or published, 'simply because he was working on other things: he might be working on an essay, he might be working on his play, *Arise, Arise*. Then he had another notion in the back of his head: he wanted to do just one of each particular form, one long poem, one novel, one play, and he did.

T. *"A"* is longer than *The Cantos*.

C. Is it really, I don't think so.

T. What do you think? as long? 800 pages?

C. 800 pages, well *The Cantos* is quite a thick book, but I don't know. It's really of no consequence, what? Any more than saying this man's a better man because he's taller.

T. You are right. It's just a question of time and magnitude—or maybe form. A small love lyric might be exquisite where a symphony might be. . . ? Louie spent 50 years on *"A,"* about what Pound spent on *The Cantos* . . . with about the same magnitude of result. It strikes me as just . . . interesting? What about the novel . . . *Little*?

C. With his novel, he did the first 5 chapters and put it aside and was no longer interested in continuing with it, and I think picked it up 15 or 16 years later and decided to finish it. At the end of the 12th movement in *"A"* he lists a number of things which he thought he might at one time or another want to do: a life of Thomas Jefferson among other things, but he didn't, he discarded all that material. And then the curiosity of translating the Catullus, and that took a great many years to do; he worked very slowly. Louie's method of writing was to write one word and erase two. I think even up to the very end of his life he would look back. Even as he was preparing *"A"* for the UC press edition, he looked back and made slight changes . . .

T. What was the last new work he started?

C. *80 flowers*. After he retired from Poly, he started that. And for that he spent, oh, hours, weeks, months just on research. And when Louie started on research there was no stopping him. Then he just went to the bitter end, every definition, every connotation, every annotation, it just went on and on.

T. What books in his library did he read most . . . that is always go back to?

C. There was Lucretius. That's amusing. Not Lucretius but what happened. Louie never got to teach anything much he liked. Mostly Freshman English and Technical Writing for engineers. But he got to teach Lucretius because the bookstore had all these books they had to sell get rid of. So they got Louie to teach him and he loved it.

T. Others he liked?

C. Aristotle, he was very fond of Aristotle and Plato. Then Aquinas.

T. Pound didn't think very highly of Aquinas.

C. Well, Louie did. That's one of their literary differences.

T. Did they debate it in the letters?

C. I think so. Louie felt right from the very start that Aquinas was not only one of the very great theological minds but also historical minds. No, he equated Aquinas with Spinoza. I think it was in this order: Aristotle, Aquinas, Spinoza, Charles Sanders Peirce who was the one that William James worked with, and Wittgenstein.

T. If I were to say to Louie how can you read a pessimist like Spinoza what do you think he'd say?

C. One: he is not a pessimist! Two: the writing is beautiful.

T. Exactly. Others?

C. I'm trying to think—other things in his library. Oh, his King James Bible. Louie knew his New Testament as well as he knew the Old Testament. It is so annotated, so marked up— the binding is falling apart! It is almost impossible to make out what he has written down. He knew his Bible very well, no question about that.

T. What did he do for fun?

C. Nothing. He was probably the most unathletic person I have ever seen. He was not interested in swimming, he never played ball, not even to throw a ball if he wanted to play with Paul. Walking was probably the only form of exercise. And even that, you know, he'd say, "Oh, I'm so tired I can't." He preferred to go to his room and work.

T. Did he go to the movies?

C. No, not much, unless of course there was something he wanted to see like *The Blood of a Poet*, or *Beauty and the Beast*, or other Cocteau things. He went to see all the Chaplin movies. Some of the Hitchcock things, *39 Steps*. But mostly, he didn't care too much about going to them, nor going to the theatre for that matter unless there was a particular play—some Shakespearean play. We went to see the *Duchess of Malfi*: he wanted to see that Webster play. No, he didn't want to go anywhere. Even concerts! I would go alone and he would stay home and work.

T. What's the meanest thing Louie ever did? that you know of?

C. I think his meanest thing was just to never hear what I was saying. He was oblivious when he was working or thinking about something.

T. Did he ever lose his temper?

C. No, not really. Because he felt that oh well, she'll repeat herself, so what if he didn't hear what I'd say. And very frequently I'd have the feeling that I was talking to myself, you know, like a broken record.

T. Wasn't there a time when you got mad and said "Enough of this! Drop that damn book and listen to me!"

C. No, we never really had knock-down, drag-out fights that way. Probably because I was so occupied with Paul's growing up and Paul's music and his education—after the first three years we educated him at home, you know—and looking after the house and fussing in the garden, and I am a fusspot you know.

T. Yes. I see that. I can see what an extraordinary fusspot you really are.

V

Time and space require that these notes be brought to an end. Thus we conclude with two brief excerpts from the tapes: (1) a dialog about Louie's phantom illnesses and (2) a segment concerning his relationship with younger poets.

T. You say he read to the class and acted out Shakespeare?

C. Yes, he read to them and dramatized for them when he acted. As I said the men who were his students have very fond remembrances of Louie as an instructor. They were very fond of him.

T. Have you seen Louie do something like that for other people?

C. When he would be among friends, yes, he would dance and recite.

T. What kind of a dance?

C. Well, he'd seen the Chinese actor Mei Lon Fong, and he could imitate those lovely gestures. Louie had very long thin arms and long thin fingers, and he was very limber. Just his gestures as he extended his arm or lifted his hand could be a very beautiful thing. Louie and I had gone to see Escudero, the Spanish dancer, and Louie could do an extraordinary imitation of Escudero in his younger days.

T. That seems quite out of character; Louie doing a Spanish dance.

C. Oh, he could even imitate Martha Graham when he was feeling very good. You know the angular kind of dancing, and spreading your legs, well you know how she danced, all this angular gesturing. Louie was very good.

T. Tell me about his hypochondria. When did he start dying?

C. I think Louie was born suffering from hypochondria. I never knew Louie not to complain of drafts: the room was too cold (never too hot), or too drafty.

T. What did he do about it? wear heavier clothes?

C. All the windows, no matter where he was, always had to be shut. Everyone else would just be gasping for breath and he was just about warming up. And you know he never had any major illness, no surgery.

T. Did he ever go to doctors?

C. Yes, and no doctor could ever explain the matter of his being so thin. They all thought it was nervous tension, which it probably was. He could be so tense as he sat there working. He was very abstemious. He did almost no drinking, but he was a heavy smoker for many years. The last ten years he gave up smoking; he smoked no more than about 4 or 5 cigarettes a day, which was quite a feat for Louie. There were times when he could go through two packs a day, but he had given that up.

T. Did he take pills?

C. No. Not even aspirin. He was very—unless he had a bit of a temperature because of a bad cold or flu, no pills, no drugs—

he was very much opposed to any kind of medication. Even when a doctor would prescribe medicine he would take it for one day and say, "Oh, he doesn't know how I react, I feel worse," and just throw the pills out. He took no vitamins. The only medication was an occasional aspirin.

T.   What was his favorite food?

C.   He didn't really have a favorite food. You could feed him anything: he ate anything that you put down. Sometimes I think he wasn't even aware of what was on the plate. If he had some poem or some essay in his mind, he ate because the plate was there in front of him and probably wasn't even aware of what he was eating. Coffee of course was a great favorite with him. That was probably his favorite beverage.

T.   Did he name any diseases that he thought he was going to have?

C.   Oh, he would have all sorts of them and sometimes doctors would get a little angry. He would go to the doctor's office and say, "I think I have meningitis." (At first some doctors would look at him critically as if thinking, "Do you even know what meningitis is?") Or "I have, I'm not quite sure, but it may be just the beginning of TB. I coughed last night." He bought a medical dictionary and he knew the names of lots of diseases. The day before he died I had telephoned Paul to say that Louie had just been taken to the hospital, but to go on to Washington to give his concert because the doctor said it didn't look too serious. Paul decided he would call the doctor and speak to him before he went off and the doctor said, "Don't go too far. I don't think we'll lose your father this weekend." Louis frequently had indigestion and I think the doctor probably thought that's what it was. Paul decided not to go and came over to the hospital where I was and stayed with us and within less than 24 hours it was all over. Over all the years there were many occasions when he complained of indigestion. But he was very cautious about taking any antacids. He could watch other people taking all kinds of antacids; tums, rolaids, milk of magnesia. But not Louie: he was going to let nature run its course though he complained constantly. He'd say in the morning, "Oh, I'm so achey, I just know I'm coming down with something. I have bursitis, I have tendinitis, and I have. . . ."

T.   Reminds me of a colleague whom I shared an office with for years. I figured out finally what made him tick: *Time* magazine. He read the medical section of *Time* and had everything described there in the week that followed.

C. Louie had a medical dictionary for his source, and after awhile even he realized the ridiculousness of approaching a medical man and saying, "I think I have meningitis," or "I know I have bursitis." I think even he became aware of how stupid it was to say that.

Another segment started another train of thought:

T. What was his favorite reading?

C. Poetry. He read very few novels. Thomas Hardy, who was one of his favorite authors: he had to teach a number of Hardy novels in school. He could read and reread *The Mayor of Casterbridge*, although he preferred to read Hardy's *Dynasts*.

T. Did he think the *Dynasts* was good poetry?

C. Yes, he liked the *Dynasts* very much. Oddly enough when he was younger apparently he didn't think too highly of it but came back years later and thought much more of it. I think one of the reasons he was so late in getting to Henry James was that James wrote no poetry. Though Louie would agree with James that James' prose is in a sense poetry.

T. How late was it when he got to James?

C. I'd say that within the last ten years he started to read James very carefully. But the interest in James I think was mine more than his. My interest in James started very young and in the last 4 or 5 years Louie had read *The Ambassadors, The American, Wings of a Dove, The Princess Cassimassima*, and then I think he felt that he should have read James earlier. Of course he read everything that Pound wrote that he could get his hands on, Joyce, Williams, Marianne Moore; he read anything he could lay his hands on of Eliot. He came very late to Wallace Stevens: I think he regretted that he had not known the Wallace Stevens work earlier.

T. Did the family speak Russian as well as Yiddish?

C. No Russian, only Yiddish.

T. Did they read Russian literature or. . . ?

C. No, just Yiddish.

T. He read Tolstoy's *War and Peace*?

C. Oh, yes, but there too, in the matter of novels he usually read

those books which were in the curriculum and he always said
of the curriculum at Poly, "You started at chaos and went to
Beckett."

T. Did he read the young poets?

C. Louie read anything he was sent. And for many years he
would not only thank the young man or woman whose book
he had received but he would indicate what particular poem or
even one line in a particular poem that he liked.

T. They sent him stuff in manuscript?

C. No, most of the time it was published material. He did that up
until the last two or three years, until he no longer had the
energy to continue.

T. Do you remember any poets he encouraged as early as the
40's?

C. Yes, most of the young came to the house: Creeley, Duncan.
Allen Ginsberg came with Peter Orlovsky.

T. That would be later wouldn't it? In the 50's?

C. A little later. But even before that: well, let me name them.
I don't know their ages, so I couldn't put them in any chronological order. As I stated, Creeley, Duncan, Sorrentino, Paul
Blackburn, Rothenberg, Ignatow, Corman, Jonathan Williams, Ronald Johnson; Denise Levertov, though Louie didn't
know her too well. We made her acquaintance rather late. It
was she who accepted Louie's manuscript *All* to be published
by W.W. Norton.

T. Ginsberg you said?

C. Yes. When we were still living at 30 Willow Street, Brooklyn
Heights, he came one night.

T. How young was he then?

C. He was quite young. Bill Williams had told Ginsberg to visit
Louie. Bill Williams also sent Mary Ellen Solt. I hope I'm not
leaving anyone out.

T. We can fill it in later.

C. Oh, and Ferlinghetti. When we were living in Brooklyn, the
Williamses were visiting with us when Ferlinghetti telephoned.
Bill said "Come on over; I'll be at Louie's house." And he
came over. He was quite young.

T. What did Louie think of Ginsberg?

C. Oh, Louie liked Allen and his poetry. All of the material that led up to *Howl*, Allen had probably talked about to Louie first. Allen did not come to the house at first; he preferred to meet Louie at Poly. Oh and Edward Dahlberg. They were both teaching at Poly and he became a close friend.

T. Did Louie talk about the young poets?

C. Yes, he was always interested in reading their poetry.

T. Which ones did he seem most enthusiastic about?

C. Oh, Louie took to Creeley's work almost instantaneously and he has never waivered about Creeley's gift as a fine writer. He liked not only Creeley's poetry, but the short stories, too. He liked one called *The Gold Diggers* very much.

T. Duncan?

C. Louie did not go in for myth as Robert Duncan did. But he liked and respected Duncan's work. Also he liked Jess Collins who is an artist and did some of the illustrations.

T. Charles Olson?

C. We never met Charles Olson. Louie spoke to him on the telephone once. Olson called to ask if he would like to teach at Black Mountain. Now Louie's salary at Poly was nothing to write home about but the salary at Black Mountain would have been even less. And both of us were so attached, addicted in a sense, to living in New York that we didn't want to leave. Too, Louie always felt that Olson's essay on Projective Verse was really a take-off on his own critical writings.

T. What do you mean take-off? You mean redoing what Louie had done?

C. Really a restatement of what Louie had said re the *Objectivists*. He felt about Olson's work that it was too wordy; could have done with editing. But he also felt Olson had a very fine, poetic, rhythmic, melodic flow when he got going. Other sections of Olson interested him less. He felt that the *Maximus Poems* in some sections were very fine poetry and others were not. In the case of men like Williams, Pound or Marianne Moore, he felt there was a very fine consistency about their work, that if there were any sections that ought to be rewritten or deleted, they were few and far between; he felt there was always a development, a growth, with each work as each man progressed. Also Bunting. Basil was not nearly as stubborn and adamant about his work as Louie was. Basil was very gentle about accepting some of Louie's suggestions. Louie was a great one for always making suggestions.

T.   Did Louie continue to subscribe to *Poetry*?

C.   No, after Rego's death Louie had submitted parts of *"A"*-22 which Daryl Hine did print. Then some reader sent a nasty, stupid letter to Daryl Hine asking why do you keep printing this trash. Daryl Hine, thinking that Louie would want to answer, sent a xerox of the letter to Louie. That settled it for Louie. He never answered the letter and he never sent anything to Daryl Hine after that. But that was Louie: he shunned controversy.

T.   Do you remember when the *Pisan Cantos* came out? Did Louie say anything about those?

C.   Louie never felt that any of the Pound material was careless writing. His attachment to Pound was not only respect, it was reverence. And it was reverence for the man as well as the work. He generally felt that Pound was probably the greatest literary mind in the 20th century and the finest writer in English.

T.   One of the controversies now among Pound scholars is that the closer we come to the end of *The Cantos*, the worse they are.

C.   Louie never felt that.

T.   When Pound died and the news came . . .

C.   1972.

T.   Louie was affected?

C.   Oh, yes! It was like losing a father or a very close friend. In a sense Pound was a kind of father image. Louie, the only thing Louie did was go back and read some of his stuff. Louie could not respect the dead by going to a church or a synagogue. I mean Louie didn't respond that way.

T.   He didn't reminisce very much?

C.   No, his only response was to pick up a Pound book and read it. He thought that was the only way he could pay his respect or commune with Pound. Louie was not the type to shriek out: was very quiet by nature.

T.   Not the go-to-the-wailing-wall kind?

C.   No, nor would he beat his breast and say, "I have committed a sin!"

And with these reflections, these reflections must come to an end.

ROBERT CREELEY

FOR L.Z.

It is an *honor* to know men and women of genius and probity, because we live, finally, in a human world and however we would dispose ourselves toward that world otherwise the case, it is the human one which makes the most intimate and significant judgement. For myself and others of my generation, our elders in the art were extraordinary example and resource. Despite a chaos of restrictive generalization, we had nonetheless the active, persistent functioning of example: Ezra Pound, William Carlos Williams, Basil Bunting, Louis Zukofsky—to note those most dear to my own heart.

My first information of Zukofsky was in the dedications of two books crucial to my senses of poetry, Ezra Pound's *Guide To Kulchur* ("To Louis Zukofsky and Basil Bunting strugglers in the desert") and Williams' *The Wedge* ("To L.Z."). It was, however, Edward Dahlberg who gave me my first active sense of Zukofsky's situation and urged me to invite him to contribute to *The Black Mountain Review*, which happily I did, resulting in the publication of a section from "A"—12 (BMR #5), and "Songs of Degrees" and "*Bottom: on Shakespeare*, Part Two" (BMR #6). In the meantime Robert Duncan had arrived in Mallorca and become a close friend and mentor, and it was he who showed me Williams' review of *Anew* as well as texts of Zukofsky himself. Then, in 1955 as I recall, while teaching at Black Mountain and visiting briefly in New York, I determined to meet Zukofsky if possible, and so one evening attempted the subway out to Brooklyn with just twenty cents in my pocket. As luck would have it, I overshot my destination, spent my remaining dime on correcting my error, and finally arrived tentative, confused, and literally penniless.

It's to the point, I believe, that such acts be remembered, especially when they define the possibilities of human responsibility and choice. As I came into the house on Willow Street, to be

met by these extraordinarily dear and tender people, I somehow
determined it would be best for all concerned if I revealed my pre-
dicament immediately, and I tried to. But Louis asked a favor of
me, as he put it, saying that Celia was altering an overcoat for him,
and it would help the sense of fitting required if I would put it
on so that he might see how it looked. I did, and immediately
Louis said, "There, it's yours!" Or words to that effect, because I
cannot remember clearly what literally he did say, being then so
distracted by the generosity of the gift and the fact that I had still
to tell them I was broke. Finally I got *that* said, and their response
was the specific coin required for the subway, *and* a five dollar
bill to go with it, *and* a substantial lunch for the trip back to Black
Mountain next day.

    And it never changed. Always that shy, intensive warmth,
that dear, particular care. In fact, the last time I saw them together
was in New York—we had met the day previous, by blessed accident, in the street—and I had come up to see them where they
were now living in a residential hotel off Central Park. Again, as
luck would have it, there was a torrential thunderstorm through
which I walked a considerable distance, and arrived, dripping and
wet to the skin. My coat was taken from me and hung up over the
bath tub to dry. I was sat down and given hot coffee to warm me
up, etc., etc. When Celia asked me if I'd like cream, I said, yes, if it
were simple—which it proved not to be. So she gave me a spoonful
of vanilla ice cream, to act as cream for the coffee, and then a full
dish of it, in the event I might enjoy it for its own sake. And *then*
we talked.

    If I try to isolate my senses of Louis Zukofsky from those
memories now, I neither can nor can I see the reason to. He taught
me so much, in so many ways. Without the least trying, so to
speak, the measures of person, of conduct, of art, which he con-
stituted, are all of a factual piece. Again I think of that frail man's
walking me late at night to the subway entrance, so I wouldn't
have difficulty finding it, despite the effort it must have been for
him to confront those streets at that hour, and his walk back
alone. I remember "raise grief to music"—"the joy that comes
from knowing things"—"the more so all have it"—"upper limit
music, lower limit speech"—"love lights light in like eyes"—"he
got around . . . ." And if I misquote, then I do—because this is the
practical, *daily* company of Louis Zukofsky for me, the measure
of his father, "everybody loved Reb Pincos because he loved
everybody. Simple . . . ."

    Thankfully, I was able at times to make clear my respect—in

various reviews and notes, in the rather crunky introduction to *"A" 1-12* (New York: Doubleday, 1967) with its several misprints, etc. And, more privately, I could argue the case at times, as Hugh Kenner will remember, apropos "The winds/ agitating/ the/ waters." Which certainly *looked* easy, as he said, but trying, did discover was otherwise—and then wrote the primary review of *"A" 1-12* (in its first Origin edition), in which he rightly qualifies the *art* of Zukofsky's practice as so much the more accomplished than Auden's, whose *Homage to Clio* he was also reviewing. Etc. These 'arguments' will die with us too. L.Z.—never.

CHARLES TOMLINSON

OBJECTIVISTS:
Zukofsky and Oppen, a memoir

'It pays to see even only a little of a man of genius.' Thus Henry
James, of Flaubert. I saw Louis Zukofsky four times, corresponded with him—on and off—for seven years and edited in
1964 what was, I suppose, one of the earliest Zukofsky numbers
of an English review for *Agenda*: I was by no means the first is-
lander to discover Zukofsky—Ian Hamilton Finlay had brought
out over here *16 Once Published* in 1962 and that had given one
something to think about. Indeed, those sixteen poems promised
a way in, whereas the translations from Catullus and the sections
of *"A"* I had already seen in *Origin* had left me more puzzled
than enlightened. Gael Turnbull who early on had confronted
me with Williams, Creeley and Olson, was also puzzled, though
he spoke of Zukofsky the man and also of the holy trinity, Louis,
Celia and son Paul in a way to arouse curiosity. In 1961 Robert
Duncan's poem *After Reading Barely and Widely* had caught
one's eye in the *Opening of the Field* —

> will you give yourself airs
> from that lute of Zukofsky?

But the book was simply not available on which to judge that lute,
and it was not until August 1963 that I came to own No 132 of
the three hundred copies in which edition *Barely and Widely*
was printed—in a facsimile of Louis Zukofsky's handwriting and
published by his wife. 1963 proved in many ways an *annus mir-
abilis*. I met both 'objectivists', Zukofsky and George Oppen.
And those meetings were preluded by two others—with Robert
Duncan and Robert Creeley.

Yet it was not to these previous meetings that I owed my
introduction to Zukofsky's poems: the meetings confirmed what
I was now ready for. What remains difficult to explain in retrospect—in any retrospect—is the way one's scattered awarenesses
suddenly fuse and focus. Perhaps it was further talk with that

indefatigable and indispensable negotiator between cultures, Dr. Turnbull, whom I had last seen in Gloucestershire and who now turned up in Albuquerque where I was teaching at the University of New Mexico. At all events, in the autumn of 1962, I began to realise once more the extent of my ignorance about the work of Zukofsky and about what had been going on when in 1930, as Williams tells us in his biography, 'With Charles Reznikoff and George Oppen in an apartment on Columbia Heights, Brooklyn, we together inaugurated, first the Objectivist theory of the poem and then the Objectivist Press. . . .The Objectivist theory was this: we had had "Imagism" (Amygism, as Pound had called it), which ran quickly out. That, though it had been useful in ridding the field of verbiage, had no formal necessity in it. . . .It had dribbled off into so called "free verse" which, as we saw, was a misnomer. . . .Thus the poem had run down and become formally nonextant. . . .The poem being an object. . .it must be the purpose of the poet to make of his words a new form. . . .This was what we wished to imply by Objectivism, an antidote, in a sense, to the bare image haphazardly prescribed in loose verse.' Present at that meeting on Columbia Heights (the apartment in question had been George and Mary Oppen's) was Louis Zukofsky, and it fell to him to outline in his essays a set of working principles. Since then he had gone on writing but was still largely unread.

Late in 1962 I tried inter-library loan and early in 1963 the system disgorged a pristine copy of *Some Time*. This was the handsome edition put out by Jonathan Williams in 1956 and one thing a quick glance confirmed was that, though this was the seventh year of its existence, no one had ever cut the pages. This realisation blinded me—quite literally as I was to discover in a few minutes—with sudden anger, and rushing into the kitchen for a sharp knife, I carved the pages apart in a crescendo of fury: such was the fate of poetry in a public library—once obtained, it was left unread. When calm returned and I sat down to lose myself in the book, I was surprised to discover that every time I turned the page two blank pages appeared. Anger and surprise, combined, had so reduced my faculties that it was quite some minutes before I realised that what I had carved apart was Jonathan Williams' beautiful intentions, and that the immaculate candour of these backs of pages printed on only one side had never been intended to be read. Shame replaced surprise, then shame too gave way as my eyes were invaded by the lovely and exact pleasure of

Not the branches
half in shadow

But the length
of each branch

Half in shadow

As if it had snowed
on each upper half

—as visually precise as, over the page (or rather over the page and two blanks), the following was aurally meticulous:

Hear, her
Clear
Mirror,
Care
His error.
In her
Care
Is clear

—a weighing of tones to be re-echoed, perhaps, in the 'Ears err for fear of spring' passage from Bunting's *Briggflatts* ten years on.

In these two pieces, one had both sides of Zukofsky's gift, as stated (in reverse order) in *"A"*-6:

The melody! the rest is accessory:

My one voice. My other: is
An objective—rays of the object brought to a focus . . .

I had the clue and so I read on, but it is difficult to disentangle the effect of that reading from the experience of another book which came unexpectedly and almost immediately after to hand. This was George Oppen's *The Materials*—his first for twenty-five years. Was this dual discovery what Breton meant by objective chance? In actuality, it was a treble discovery, for out of the same, largely depressing pile of books that lay on my desk for review, emerged Reznikoff's *By the Waters of Manhattan*. I could begin now to reconstruct what had happened in those far off days in Brooklyn and to see how it was still an active, though temporarily forgotten force in the America of the sixties. Zukofsky and Reznikoff had gone on publishing, but their books had been hard to come by. It was Oppen who was the real mystery—a mystery that has subsequently been explained—since all that one could find out about previous publication was that volume of 1934 ('Oppen's first book of poems' as it said on the cover of *The Materials*) which had earned the praise of Ezra Pound: 'a sensibility . . . which has not been got out of any other man's books.' The existence of that first book—instanced but unnamed on the cover—tantalized more and more as I prepared to write the review. On the track of Zukofsky, I had come upon Oppen whose work showed something of the same terse lineation and exactness I had discovered just before in Zukofsky's 'Not the branches/half in shadow'. On an impulse I wrote to Oppen who, in replying, offered me one of his three remaining *Discrete Series*, that first book of poems, and said of the writing of *The Materials* (his unaffected eloquence struck me as one of the classic statements of modern poetry):

> I was troubled while working to know that I had no
> sense of an audience at all. Hardly a new complaint,
> of course. One imagines himself addressing his peers,
> I suppose—surely that might be the definition of
> 'seriousness'? I would like, as you see, to convince
> myself that my pleasure in your response is not plain
> vanity but the pleasure of being heard, the pleasure
> of companionship, which seems more honorable.

Those last two sentences so held my mind, I wanted in some sense to appropriate them, as one does when learning a passage by heart. They were so close to being a poem, I could both appropriate them to my own need and leave them in the hands of their author, simply by arranging them as lines of verse, changing only the pace yet leaving every word intact. This poem (*To C.T.*) was to appear ultimately in Oppen's third volume, *This In Which*. It drew the immediate response from him:

> I find myself entranced by the poem with which you have
> presented me. I see myself—slightly the elder of the two of us
> —talking to myself—and smoking *my* pipe, which is a shock.
> I congratulate the three of us on the whole thing.

Another letter, in which he outlined for me the history of the objectivists—an account he much amplifies in an interview for *Contemporary Literature* Vol 10, No 2—contains the following:

> We were of different backgrounds; led and have led different
> lives. As you say, we don't much sound alike. But the common
> factor I think is well defined in Zuk's essay.[1] And surely I envy
> still Williams' language, Williams' radiance; Rezi's lucidness, and
> frequently Zukofsky's line-sense.

My mind went back continually to a phrase in that first letter—'I was troubled to know I had no sense of an audience at all'. If Oppen's sense of an audience had been an absence, what was Zukofsky's in the poems of *Some Time*? Occasionally it

---

1. 'Sincerity and Objectification'.

seemed to be almost wholly domestic—as witnessed by those valentines and the frequent family references. But, as I was to learn later, Zukofsky could count on an audience among the circle around *Black Mountain Review*, and its editor Robert Creeley was one of his most convinced readers. When Creeley returned from British Columbia to teach at the University of New Mexico in June 1963, I asked him in a conversation which we taped, what he felt had been Zukofsky's principal lesson for the younger poet. Creeley responded to that question in terms rather different from Oppen's own stressing of the value of Zukofsky's critical sense and the stimulus of his conversation, which were what his letters mainly dwelt upon. For Creeley, Zukofsky chiefly ratified in his poetry one side of the teaching of Ezra Pound:

> What Zukofsky has done [said Creeley] is to take distinctions of both ear and intelligence to a fineness that is difficult . . . .It's extremely difficult to follow him when he's using all the resources that he has developed or inherited regarding the particular nature of words as sound. . . .If you read his translations of Catullus in which he is trying, in effect, to transpose or transliterate, or whatever the word would be, the texture of Latin sound into American language, it's an extraordinary *tour de force*. No, I find that in this whole thing that Pound came into—the tone leading of vowels, the question of measure, the question of the total effect in terms of sound and sight of a given piece of poetry—these aspects are tremendously handled by Zukofsky as by no one else.

A couple of days after talking to Creeley, I set out for Kiowa Ranch, on a mountainside beyond Taos. It had been the gift of Mabel Dodge Luhan to D.H. Lawrence and now belonged to the University of New Mexico. In the period I was to spend there, from June 22 to July 27, I had ample time and quiet to absorb the books Creeley had sent me—Zukofsky's *Anew* and *"A" 1-12*. I copied by hand most of the former and parts of the latter—mainly *"A"-7* and *"A"-11*, which still seem to me Zukofsky's two most impressive sections from that long poem. Kiowa Ranch, the sea-wash sound in its pinetrees, the slightly inebriating sense of height, the long horizons, the slow withdrawals of the sunset to a band of deep orange above the far mesas, all these entered into and penetrated my reading and copying. I found myself composing a poem to Zukofsky and enclosed in my first letter to him

TO LOUIS ZUKOFSKY

The morning
spent in

copying
your poems

from *Anew*
because that

was more
than any

publisher would
do for one,

was a
delight: I

sat high
over Taos

on a
veranda

Lawrence had
made in

exile here
exile

from those
who knew

how to write
only the way they

had been
taught to:

I put aside
your book

not tired
from copying but

wishing for
the natural complement

to all the
air and openness

such art
implied:

I went
remembering that

solitude
in the world

of letters
which is yours

taking
a mountain trail

and thinking
is not

poetry
akin to walking

for one
may know

the way that
he is going

(though I did not)
without

his knowing
what he

will see there:
and who

following on
will find

what you
with more than

walker's care
have shown

was there
before his

unaccounting eyes?

In a letter of 1964, Louis was to suggest emmending '(though I did not)/without/his knowing/what he' to '(though I/did not)/ not knowing/ what he', in order to 'make it even lighter': 'Give it a thought—or more than one—if you reprint in a volume—I may very likely be wrong.' Then he added with characteristic elusiveness: 'I just hope eels will never eat electrons or they might end up in my mad house.' The reply to the poem suggested a meeting in New York on my way back in August. It also told me that he had been reading my work since 1957 'and I find it valid. I can read it—which is to be moved—as Ez used to say. And for the rest Prospero had better shut up about Miranda's accomplishments— just go ahead and prosper.' But he was to continue trying to improve Miranda's accomplishments. A later poem, *Gull*—it emerged from seeing one over Brooklyn harbour—which I dedicated to Louis and Celia, was thoroughly re-lineated and compacted by him from its first version, so that the poem as it now stands is as much a work of collaboration as Oppen's *To C.T.* In fact, it so bears Louis' stamp, I have wondered sometimes whether it ought not to ride one day in his *Collected*:

```
Flung
far down,
as the
gull rises,
the black
smile of
its shadow
masking its
underside
takes
the heart
into the height
to hover
above the ocean's
plain-of-mountains'
moving quartz.
```

The letter which contained his revised version bore the apologetic 'about *Gull*—I probably shouldn't be doing this, but what do *you* say?'—this ran vertically down the right-hand-side of the poem, then vertically down the left: '(And I'm not so sure about alignment, but who's "sure"?)'. And beneath the poem: 'Anyway you moved me to do it fast.' I thanked him. He replied:

> Thank me for? If you hadn't made it in potential, the stroke [axshually, as the weather girl says, I did it very fast] of genius (?) wouldn't have been actual. *No* time wasted, considering you agree—to be perfectly bumptious about it, considering your gratitude makes me happy—and I never take any credit from the prime mover. Don't tell anybody I still do such things, however, or I'll be flooded who knows with rafts of stuff from "pouncers".

I wasn't entirely sure what pouncers within inverted commas implied. The idiom and rhythm of the letter are very much those of Louis' speaking voice. The bits you didn't understand in his rapid patter (he was often extraordinarily comic) left you feeling you ought to have, but there was no ling/ering for regret or greater comprehension, because what he had gone on to say now demanded your whole attention. You couldn't afford to miss it. And just as you had to read his letters at all angles for the tiny parentheses, you often had to strain to hear his low-toned voice. His whisper might be as funny as the minute postscript down the back of an air letter: 'C just bogged in income tax reports calls from downstairs to ask if we can claim for being *blind*'.

I was to hear that voice for the first time in August. To begin with there had been doubts—doubts that made me realise that Louis was already a frequently sick man ('I'm ill so I can't move my head to left or right, but just to say it will have to improve by

August 4, when you pass through'). There were to be several mentions of 'the aches', not further defined, and three years later, in a letter saying that he had refused some teaching at Buffalo, I read the ominous words: 'The emphysema won't bear the traffic.' There had been more than doubts about seeing the Oppens that summer: it was a certainty they would be on Little Deer Isle, Maine. Then, suddenly, their plans were changed and they intended to be in Brooklyn. And, just as suddenly, our postal search for a New York apartment achieved success—that also was to be in Brooklyn. And though Brooklyn is a large place, as we soon knew, it was sufficiently the one place in which we would all coincide, the Zukofskys, the Oppens and the Tomlinsons.

In *Kulchur 5* Jonathan Williams has an imaginary movie cast to play the modern poets—Edward Everett Horton as T.S. Eliot, Lon Chaney Jr., as Robert Frost, Adolphe Menjou as Edward Dahlberg, Cary Grant as James Laughlin. As Louis Zukofsky he casts Fred Astaire. There was an uncanny accuracy about this. Still showing signs of recent illness, Zukofsky had a curious dancing lightness in his build, movement and talk. There was also a touch of elegance, given sartorial precision when ten days after our visit to 160 Columbia Heights, he turned up complete with bow tie at our apartment on Ocean Avenue. What did not fit Jonathan Williams' casting was the densely black thick line of the eyebrows, the continuously re-lit cigarette, the nervous puckering of the forehead as the face flickered from anxiety to humour, the voluble, mercurial, ceaselessly inventive talk. That tenth story of Columbia Heights gave on to a view of the harbour. It was the same spot more or less that had seen the meeting of objectivists—not yet named—on that day in 1930. Through the window, behind Manhattan Bridge, loomed the trajectory of Brooklyn Bridge. You could see it, but only just. The Statue of Liberty rose clear in the sultry August afternoon in the opposite direction. On the balcony the traffic noises floated up from below, often drowning out Zukofsky's soft voice.

We spoke of many things, including the funeral of William Carlos Williams the previous March ('The nicest funeral I ever went to,' said Louis). But what most remains with me is the music of the occasion. By this I do not mean to reduce it to symbolist essence. 'The greatest satisfactions of conversation are probably musical ones,' as Ted Hughes has said. 'A person who has no musical talent in ordinary conversation is a bore, no matter how interesting his remarks are. What we really want from each other are those comforting or stimulating exchanges of melodies.' The music of meeting Zukofsky was exactly right, and one was en-

couraged to play one's few bars of accompaniment with a sense
of satisfaction at having come in at the right place. His stream of
talk was not exactly a monologue—he was too aware of one's
presence for that—but it flowed and flashed and glowed in such a
way that one hesitated to interrupt it. Or, to change the metaphor,
one suggested themes on which Zukofsky variated, very much for
one's benefit and delight. There was a mutuality in this process
which he evidently appreciated and remembered when two years
later he wrote to me: 'Hugh Kenner finally got to see us last
week—just dropped in on a chance that I'd be at home, and we
spent two afternoons together talking, the first talk of its kind I
guess since you and I last talked. (The aches have been such we see
almost nobody.)'

The talk at Columbia Heights gave place to his reading for
us from his Catullus translations. As he did so, one realised that it
was not only Pound that lay behind this venture, but principally
the Joyce of *Finnegan's Wake*. And Joyce came to mind in the
quality of his vocal execution which compared with that light
tenor rendering of the Anna Livia Plurabelle passage on gramo-
phone record. The *Cats* as he called them came over as beautifully comic, though I could not help wondering whether, without
the help of his expert vocalising and extended from half a dozen
to one hundred and sixteen plus fragmenta, these transliterations
could hold the mind and not bring on a feeling of eels eating electrons. Here, he had pushed what he always called 'the noise' of
poetry about as far as it would go. Tune was his other favourite
word:

> The lines of this new song are nothing
> But a tune making the nothing full

Do the tunes of the *Cats* survive in their author's voice? Did the
Library of Congress perhaps tape some of them, when he recorded
there? He would surely have wished them to be heard his way, the
noise bringing to the surface a ghostly Roman gabble. He had
written to Alfred Siegel in 1957 concerning Siegel's transliteration of the Chinese through Canto 97, 'you mean the English
noises[?], that would interest me.'

The Zukofskys regaled us with trifle and cake, washed down
with root beer, then walked with us through the twilight to find
the bus stop. Louis was saying that his last communication from
Ezra Pound was about a rabbi, then went on to define his attitude
to the world of regular publishing from which he, Zukofsky, was
as yet still excluded. 'I don't care,' was his frequent refrain,
though I doubted that. There was a certain undertow of bitter-

ness, though it never dominated the conversation. As we walked through the grimy yet reassuring streets of Brooklyn and finally took up our stand under the pole of the bus stop, it was gaiety that prevailed. We must have talked for half an hour before we realised that no buses intended to halt there and that the notice on top of the pole read 'No Parking'.

George Oppen is a man who came difficultly by knowledge—which makes his Jewishness a very different thing from that of Zukofsky. I recognised the latter's as soon as we had entered his apartment. It had the same flavour that had given point and aliment to my adolescence, when the refugees from Hitler's Germany arrived in the English midlands. Here were people who had records of Bruckner and Brecht's *Dreigroschenoper* at a time when both were unknown to us. Among them I had heard Kant's categorical imperative explained as if it were a fact of daily life, had listened to a description of Thomas Mann glimpsed paring an apple 'with surgical intentness', had discovered that Heine, Kafka, Rilke could still exist among the coal dust and the fumes from pottery chimneys. In this Jewishness one experienced a familial sense at once secretive and hospitable, subtly tenser than one's own involvement in the painful day to day of family bathos, where lack of money and lack of imagination had produced a stale stoicism. That experience of an eagerly tense intellectuality returned as one met the Zukofskys. Not so, with the Oppens.

To gain their apartment in Henry Street, one passed the ground floor window where a pleasant-looking young man sat writing, as George later told me, pornographic fiction. The scarred hallway and stair led up to the top of the house and at the stairhead stood a man with a lined and weathered face like a Jewish sea-captain—a man who, as it transpired, owned a sailing boat but no car. This was George Oppen. Like Zukofsky he saw the humorous side of things, but he listened more. His speech was less fluent, more meditative; it was exact with a pondered exactness like his poetry.

We talked much of Mexico that evening—for we had been there earlier the same year—and of the Oppens' phase of exile in Mexico City and his joinery shop there. In his talk one warmed to a union of the passionate and the deliberate: there was accuracy and there was economy in this, and somehow, in one story he told us, he had managed to carry these to a point where they seemed like miracle or luck. Tired of the way Mexican drivers aimed their cars at you, George, crossing the Zocalo, had once refused to submit to this humiliation and, as the projectile approached, planted his fist square in the windshield: it was not the fist but the windshield that shattered. 'A stupid thing to do,' said George. The owner of the car got out, apparently for the showdown, but looking first at Oppen and then at the shivered glass, could find no way in which *machismo* could account for, admit or take action against such folly, shrugged, re-ascended and drove off. George has a genius for such inevitabilities. They need not always be the fruit of happy violence. In England, nine months after our meeting, the Oppens were at Ozleworth on an afternoon when the vicar called. Conversation turned on the New English Bible and I expended a good deal of wasted wrath on our pastor's admiration for this moribund document. He explained that in order to make sure that its idiom was truly current the committee had consulted a bishop's secretary. George was far more of a marksman than I with my incoherent rage. As the vicar was about to leave, George said with a sort of courteous finality, 'The next time you translate the Bible, call in a carpenter—and make sure he's a Jewish carpenter.' Later, walking down the nave of Wells Cathedral, he gave vent to another unexpected apophthegm: 'I guess I'm a Christian,' he said, 'but with all the heresies.'

The apartment in Henry Street was very much a presence in our conversation on that first encounter. As we sat eating, the evening moved into possession of the scene outside. High above Brooklyn, we watched the sun go down to the right of the Statue of Liberty, swiftly like a coin into a slot. Light shone from the Statue's torch and from the windows of Manhattan—these of a strange greenish hue as if an effect taken up from the water in the summer dusk. Across the bay the Staten Island ferry switched back and forth, a trail of lights above the milky turquoise it was travelling over. The television antennae on the near roofs of Brooklyn looked like ships' masts drawn up before the harbour below. This was a room and a view we were to revisit several times before the Oppens left for San Francisco in 1969 when Henry Street was threatened with demolition. The place seems a cell in a larger aggregate from which memory picks out the building in a street close by where Whitman printed *Leaves of Grass*, now a Puerto Rican restaurant; the commemorative plaque on its wall (stolen, sold and then recovered); what *The Materials* calls 'The absurd stone trimming of the building tops'; the site of the old Brooklyn Ferry and behind its dilapidated stakes the line of Brooklyn Bridge—Whitman superimposed on Hart Crane.

As the shapes of Manhattan hardened into black that evening, I began to realise that all was not well between Oppen and Zukofsky, and the impression deepened on subsequent meetings with them both. I think I may now speak of this, for George's poem with which I shall close, makes no secret of the matter. When I reviewed Reznikoff's and Oppen's books I had wondered why there was no Zukofsky in the series, a joint publication of New Directions (James Laughlin) and San Francisco Review (June Oppen Degnan, George's half sister). His exclusion there clearly rankled with Louis. Even before I had met him, I realised the situation was an uneasy one for, after sending my review to Oppen, I had received the following reply:

> I enjoyed very much reading your review . . . I will have a copy made for New Directions—SF Review for the mention of Zuk . . . . The first year's poetry schedule consists of Oppen, Reznikoff and William Bronk, in which my advice is obvious enough. My recommendation of course included Zuk, but the suggestion—as you see—has not been acted on. It is by now too awkward for me to discuss the matter with Zuk at all, but it is my impression that they would be more likely to do a Selected than a Collected poems, if only for budgetary reasons. I can't really urge Louis to submit a ms. since I have no assurance at all that they would accept it. But you might urge him to try it if you think it worth the risk—to him—of a rejection. If they had a ms. under consideration I could re-open the discussion.

When I arrived in New York, I had some illusory hopes that I might perhaps be able to negotiate on Louis' behalf. As I stayed on, this hope extended to the possibility of somehow reconciling the estranged friends. But the longer I stayed the more I realised that neither project could be easily accomplished. In the first place, not only his self-respect but also Louis' belief that all his life he had been writing *one* poem (and he was very decided about this) stood in the way of my ever persuading him to submit a Selected and secondly, his feelings towards George had curdled to such an extent that any reconciliation must lie far in the future if it were feasible at all. From hints and suggestions, I gathered that he imagined George had simply failed to act for him, which was not the case. Yet one could not simply *state* this to Louis. He did not live in the atmosphere of simple statement and his aggravated nerves pushed him into more suspicion than was good for him. He was a gentle man, yet his own character and long neglect had created a thorny hedge of self-defence and of self-injury. Years of teaching what he called 'my plumbers' at the Brooklyn Polytechnic Institute cannot have helped: 'My own mess of school etc is proverbial,' he wrote, complaining of chalk fights and 'kids of seventeen who cannot sit on their asses'. 'All I need is to be away from the "job" I guess—the eel-lectermonickers, curs, curse.'

Perhaps he even resented the fact that George was at last free from
the job grind. It is hard to be certain. At all events, he made it
clear that no interference however delicate would help repair the
situation. I unwillingly resigned myself to this fact.

On returning home, I set about sharing my new found knowledge of things American with my fellow countryman, or as many
of them as read the little magazines. For *the Review*, January
1964, I edited a Black Mountain number in which Louis figured
as one of the founding fathers. Ian Hamilton Finlay, the editor,
added his own characteristic postscript: 'The editorial motive of
the Review in this project has been a documentary rather than,
necessarily, a critical one. We believe that the movement ought at
least to be known about.' So much for English caution, incapable
of surrendering itself to surprise. The following December appeared the Louis Zukofsky issue of *Agenda*. All this time I kept up
a regular correspondence with Louis and an exchange of books.
He was an excellent critic and immediately perceptive about where
another poet's strengths lay. His method of instruction by letter
consisted of copying out the individual phrases which had struck
him as centrally strong. I mentioned one poem of mine which he
had not touched on and he replied, 'I was trying to point at *that*
in your work which might be more useful to you as "craft", when
you've extended it *past* your forefathers.' On my *Peopled Land-
scape* he wrote: 'As for prosody a little nearer Hardy in impulse
of song rather than for all I revere his integrity the thought metres
of Crabbe—and so on, the old guy's talking too much.' He em-
phasized that it was 'the "pure" of the craft,' he was interested in
revealing to one and on the poem to which I had drawn his attention: ' "Craft" as "invention" etc. In itself the poem is nothing to
be neglected and in a work like my Test of Poetry would do very
well alongside of Crabbe and Marvell . . .' He could respond unexpectedly to poems whose premises were very unZukofskyan, as
when he pointed to one of mine called *The Impalpabilities* and
added '[would be your best defence against *Bottom*]'. His square
brackets managed to be at once intimately playful and also de-
fensive of another's interests, a typical example of the atunement
of his epistolary style and also of his conversation (he was a
man who could *speak* square brackets) to the needs of a friend.
Of friends' needs he was always studious. His caring ranged from
minute, attentive sympathy (on hearing my father was ill, he in-
quired about him for many letters after) to a sense of troubles
taken on his own behalf. It could be simply a question of a meal.
Or it could be a friend's luck that brightened his feelings, as when
Bunting finally achieved publication with Fulcrum Press: 'I hope

Basil gets the garter or sumpin—anything to save him from the dogged silence he's lived. It makes him happy—at any rate he writes cheerfully—to have some attention. *Loquitur* is a beautiful book, and *Briggflatts* is a delayed extension of it.' And there were friends missed. Of Williams he spoke with great affection, for Williams while not quite getting what Louis was at, had always written of him with generosity. One document of their literary relations I discovered while editing the *Agenda* issue—this was a signed statement of Williams' of June 29, 1948 which stated: 'I hereby grant formal permission to Louis Zukofsky to use whatever he wishes to use of my published literary works as quotations in his writings.'

In the winter of 1964 Louis began to talk of retirement. They were to move to two and a half rooms: 'Kitchen, living room with an L for sleeping. We've been living to pay the rent and income tax. The idea is to get down—to something like a bare table top—and maybe something of the feeling of 30 years ago where we wandered the streets of the same neighbourhood, rather young, will come back to us.' By August I heard: 'We're delighted to be in Manhattan again after 25 years . . . the streets have all the interest of a foreign city to provincials.' The same letter contained the news of acceptance by Norton of his poems ('First publication of poetry since they did Rilke in 1938 . . .') and of a further bonus that Reznikoff had just telephoned to read out a long and positive review of *Bottom* in the *TLS*—'very careful and painstaking . . . . So your country gets there ahead of mine.' I hesitated to confess (those were the days of anonymity) that I had written it.

Though Louis continued to feel the loneliness of his position, a period of respite seemed to be ensuing for him. Not that all was plain sailing now. The advance from Norton hadn't, as he wrote, 'covered half the medico's bill.' Yet there was freedom from the plumbers and there was a December visit to Yaddo in 1965 to finish the *Cats*: 'Silence helps—only a handful of reticent respectful guests—so far we can stand the cold. Pines, trails, waterfalls, high views from the foothills of the Adirondacks, and altogether too many good books around with no time to read if I'm to get through with that Guy (Gai).'

In the meantime I had been planning an anthology. If I could not help to reconcile George and Louis, at any rate I could surely get them together inside the covers of one book. And this book would show English readers an area of American poetry with which they were not as yet familiar. The title, *Seven Significant Poets*, embraced the objectivists (Oppen, Zukofsky, Reznikoff and Rakosi), Lorine Niedecker (characterized in *"A"*-12 as 'a rich sitter'), James Laughlin and William Bronk.

I was in New York in the spring of 1966 and so able to speak with Louis about this idea. Our meeting took place at 77 7th Avenue. 'You must come to the biggest Vermeer you've ever seen and you'll find us,' he said over the telephone. The Vermeer proved to be an enormous blow-up of one of his paintings used as a mural decoration for the downstairs vestibule of the apartment building. It still looked solidly composed but uncomfortably stretched. The apartment was overheated, at least for English susceptibilities, and Louis seemed ill, though still full of inventive talk. The meeting was attended by a lingering uneasiness. We were staying with the Oppens a fact not easy to declare, and when the Zukofskys invited us to remain to dinner the awkwardness arose of phoning our hosts from the one room that we would not be back for an evening meal. This I accomplished with absurd secretiveness and put down the phone, having mentioned no names. 'So you're staying with the Oppens,' said Louis. Yet the awkwardness passed and a pleasant meal followed. Louis seemed interested by the idea of the anthology, though he didn't care for the work of Bronk–'All that Stevensian bothering. You either think with things as they exist, or you give up.' 'Is Oppen in it?' called Celia from the kitchen. Louis seemed to accept that fact as inevitable also. I was not so sure that Celia did. But the way ahead looked clear and there was even a sort of geniality in Louis' contemplation of the prospect.

Back in England I put several months' work into the book and Fulcrum expressed their wish to publish it. When they approached Louis for permission to reprint, there came back a firm no in reply. It wasn't entirely unexpected, but one had hoped that, if reconciliations were not possible in daily life, perhaps literary works could still lie down amicably side by side. I never discussed the matter further with Louis, though obviously, without his presence in the book, it must remain a total impossibility. I'd simply spent a great deal of time to little effective end. We continued to correspond with perfect cordiality though we never met again. I should have foreseen the difficulties in the light of George's letter three years before concerning Louis' diatribes against him to innocent visitors: 'But perhaps I had better say that Louis really had no grievance against me, nor has the world, or no greater grievance than it has against anyone in these times of population explosion. And Louis no greater grievance against me than against anyone who "gets printed". Awkward for me, tho.

And overwhelmingly ironic to discuss my position as "a success"
. . . I doubt that I'll produce another book within quite a few
years. Maybe that'll heal things.'

That was after *The Materials*. Other books followed and
finally a *Collected*. But so did books by Louis, including the two
volumes of *All*. Clearly he was right to have resisted a selection.
He got what he wanted, but what a time it took. And time didn't,
in George's words, 'heal things'. When George gave me his *Collected Poems* in San Francisco in 1976 I found in it, towards the
close, a poem I had not read before. I thought perhaps I had
missed it in his previous collection, *Seascape: Needle's Eye* but,
no, it is not there. The title is *The Lighthouses* and the subtitle
'for LZ in time of the breaking of nations':

> *if you want to say no say*
> *no if you want to say yes say yes* in loyalty
>
> to all fathers or joy
> of escape
>
> from all my fathers . . .

and the poem modulates into George's seabord world where light-
houses flash and the coastal waters are rock-pierced. He recognises
the kinship with Zukofsky—for Zukofsky was in a sense one of
his fathers too, a brilliant exemplar and talker in the early days
of objectivism. He recognises also the racial kinship as a motif
returns, previously used in the poem *Semite:*

>   my
> heritage *neither Roman*
> *nor barbarian* . . .

I do not know whether Louis ever read the piece or whether, had
he done so, he would have recognised George's continuing plea for
clarity in relationship. *The Lighthouses* is a final document in a
long and saddening history of misunderstanding, a misunderstanding which a common experience of a time, place and race
might have outweighed but did not. It reminded me of the fact
that from both their windows in Brooklyn they had shared the
view of the same 'lighthouse'—the beam from the Statue shining
back in the dusk towards the windows of Manhattan.

HUGH SEIDMAN

LOUIS ZUKOFSKY
at
THE POLYTECHNIC INSTITUTE OF BROOKLYN (1958-61)

In February of 1958 I left MIT to enter Brooklyn Poly as a freshman in mathematics. Poly's physical plant was spartan, if not grim. It lay on a grassless tract of green cement on Jay Street in downtown Brooklyn near the Myrtle Avenue E1. It boasted the largest graduate evening engineering enrollment in the country and a day undergraduate body of commuters (there were no dormitories) from the depths of places like Queens or Long Island (in my case it was Brooklyn). There were no women and consciousness of the arts was probably minimal extending, for example, as far as the "History of Science" mural that had been commissioned for the front lobby. I recall that the painter labored on it for several years, but that it was still unfinished when I graduated.

Within this fortress of lower and middle class utilitarianism, however, the student of science and technology possessed of more Parnassian interests need not have completely languished. There was *Counterweight*, the literary publication; there were also English courses and a few literature electives. Thus, Louis taught sections of required composition and literature as well as technical writing. Later on we even managed to gather the necessary 12 students (a next to impossible feat) for his poetry seminar using his *Test of Poetry* as a text. He lived on Willow Street in Brooklyn Heights with his wife Celia and their son Paul (the violin prodigy), and presumably the fact that he could walk to work must have been a welcome fringe benefit.

I probably first met him late in 1958 in connection with *Counterweight* of which I was the editor. We had heard of an actual poet! and we tracked him down to ask if he would advise us. Oddly, he agreed—perhaps no one there had ever asked him for such a thing. We also formed a poetry club. As the constitution stated it was meant "to promote a greater interest in poetry among members of the Polytechnic community, to provide an outlet for original poetic expression, and to examine from all directions the art known as poetry." High hopes to be sure! In a picture of the first meeting (January, 1959), Louis' head is turned from the camera and the most dominant things about him are his wonderful bony hands and wrists, and his thinness. He was, in fact, terribly thin and seemed beset by countless physical aches. He once claimed that he sometimes shopped in the boy's department, and this seemed entirely plausible, as in winter when he would appear sunk in his heavy topcoat complaining of the cold and wet.

In general he seemed the perfect examplar of his dictum that, "The poet is interested in everything. He is both an informed person and a sensitive one." He combined an extreme philosophical brilliance with a profound sensitivity that seemed remarkable in one so learned. I was touched myself that he could confess that he had wept over his own lines about his father in *A-12*; and I was amazed that he could be so moved by a reading of Whitman's "Columbus" to our class that he had to dismiss us early. In another regard, the two poles of his character appeared rooted in paradox as when he expressed his love of the simplest folk tune or a Burns song, or when he called for a "common order of speech" (something he did often) in the light of his own work that not infrequently could push a reader to the limits of syntax and meaning.

Whenever possible we took our required English with him. The ground seemed at first mysterious. Conclusions dropped from arguments in a method of oblique reference and private irony. Yet if one followed the game and its repetitions (similar to his contention that the poet wrote the same poem all his life) at some point first principles would invariably resurface. Of course, the student who had not the patience for such tactics might indeed be frustrated. I vividly remember one poor soul who rose angrily one afternoon to grumble that he had been here for months and yet still had not understood one thing that had been said. Characteristically and stoically Louis replied that perhaps in time he would see it.

It might be imagined that such incidents would have embittered him or have driven him to disdain. True, Poly was no Eden ("I've retired as of September of this year [1966] and need all the strength to forget it."—He arrived in 1947), and teaching wore him down ("This is about my most . . . I won't say what at your alma mater yet." [1961]), yet in theory at least he seemed to respect his students. I had heard, for example, that in previous years little Paul had played for his classes just as he had for Pound in St. Elizabeths. (Louis told us that Pound still wrote to his son but had stopped corresponding with him.) And when I asked him in November, 1959 for the college newspaper why he preferred to teach at Poly rather than at a liberal arts college, he joked, "I'm no academician." Then, more seriously, he maintained that the engineer or scientist was closer to his concept of poetry than was the liberal arts student who has less contact with and respect for design, form, and invention and who would perhaps tend to imitate other poets and convention. In the same interview he called poetry and music the most important manifestations of our culture without which culture would not exist. He thought that scientists would someday find a poet to express them, although the best were no doubt writing their own kind of poetry in signs and symbols. Possibly he thought of himself as that new sort of poet who might number in his audience his classes of young technocrats. As far back as 1931, when he taught at the University of Wisconsin, he had translated a book on Einstein written by the son-in-law of the physicist and had written an essay on poetry that began with a definition of "objective" from physical optics. One could also cite his poem about a capacitor (#12 in *Anew*) or the way he could insert technical analogs almost nonchalantly (" . . . Each figure/ is an ordinate of which the axis/ is a peak . . . ." ' "Further than"—' in *29 Songs*) into the body of more literary constructs.

In the poetry club we read our own poems, or Louis read from works like *Bottom: On Shakespeare* and *"A"* his long poem just published by Cid Corman in Japan in a handsome little red-covered edition of 500 (1959). Years later I heard the story that he had been so obscure that Corman had initially thought he was dead. We bought autographed copies of *"A"* for $5 and were thrilled at anything else he might sell like Celia's birthday present *Barely and Widely*, though he was clearly uneasy about taking our money. Subsequently, however, he would write bitterly, "I've stopped corresponding with most people . . . . We're out of 'business' for good . . . . Saves us one embarrassment and the chores —who cares anyway."

In happier days, besides books, he dispensed various nuggets of insight. The key to his beloved Shakespeare, for example, lay in the proportion from *Bottom*: love/reason : eyes/mind. Thus, in the tragedies men thought but did not see while in the comedies they saw but did not think. Only when eye and mind were as one would love flourish with reason. He also apprised us of his poetics from *"A"*-12 represented as an integral with a lower limit of speech and an upper limit of song:$\int_{speech}^{music}$. It will be noted that this notation "repeats" or echoes his critique of music and poetry as the only important vectors of culture. It will also be seen that such highly aesthetic criteria are couched in the "objective" language of mathematics.

At the poetry club we also had visitors. I invited Marianne Moore (also nearby in Brooklyn) whose delicate hand-written note from the hospital explained that she was too sick to come adding that she hoped to be well enough to hear Paul play in Carnegie Hall. In a previous letter she had said, ". . . enthusiastic about the Institute; and Prof. Zukofsky as he knows." Cid Corman appeared in November (1960) on some school grant money and wrote back complimenting our little group and welcoming any poems and/or requests for *Origin*. George Oppen read too and I never forgot his wonderful new poem "Route" with its tragic Frenchman who drives his bicycle into a tree to escape the Germans.

Besides these, and the dead like Whitman, Adams, Aquinas, Catullus, Herrick, Longinus, and the others who lived in his talk like a line-up of all-stars—we grew to know his friends. He described Lorine Niedecker as the best American woman poet after Marianne Moore and broke our hearts with the tale of her scrubbing floors in a hospital in Wisconsin. Reznikoff became heroic composing poems as he walked the miles from Riverdale to his law work in lower Manhattan only to be eventually fired for lateness (I had invited him to read too but he declined). Another time, Louis confided that "Rezzy" was one of the few poets that had ever taught him anything. Subsequently we hounded Frances Steloff of the Gotham Book Mart for Pound, Bunting, Williams, and any and all "Objectivist" poets and bought, for example, all of Reznikoff's beautiful privately printed hard backs for a ridiculous $1 a piece (Miss Steloff seemed to have hundreds in the basement). To an outsider, at least, it seemed a long way from 1959 when Louis paid homage to these colleagues in the essay at the back of Corman's *"A"* to 1967 when their names had disappeared from that same piece ("Poetry") reprinted in *Prepositions*.

Beyond these considerations, I must simply say that I loved him. He was my poetic father who initiated me into the vision of the poem as a sacred and all pervading act. My debt to him is unpayable, and I have never forgotten the lesson of his commitment. More and more I tried to imitate his spare precise style. He was a stern critic and the poems I showed were always liberally corrected. Years later in one of our few meetings at a NYC poetry party he could still tell Clayton Eshleman, "Hugh was my most sensitive kid, but he could never punctuate." I realized too that he could also be hard and pedantic towards others or the "young" as he sometimes called them. Ginsberg, for example, had returned from Paris in 1959 to a triumph at Columbia. When informed that a certain critic had labelled him "the founder of the Beat Generation," Louis replied with a not untypical irony, "I love humanity, but there is just so much I can stand." Another time he acknowledged his influence but denied any real connection, adding that he was absolutely against the poem as an arbitrary expression. He felt that the Beats had potential but that their current work was not yet significant; he thought that they should be more aware of the music of speech and especially of American speech.

At Poly as I listened to such critiques, stories, and misfortunes I thought myself blessed by the gods—often too much in awe to speak much myself. Often he played the role of the old man, the alien, the outsider as epitomized in his anecdote of the poetry conference where a well known figure had asked him, "What are *you* doing here?" One felt that he saw himself as the "guy" (as Paul was the "kid") who "ain't" no academic but who, in reality, is the most learned of all (in the best of senses—the poetic). Yet he implied that some of the other Poly professors tended to be snobbish towards him because he was only a poet with no Ph.D., though he would remind one with some anger that he had done the equivalent of several Ph.D.'s in his work. He lamented the failings of his body with a hypochondriac's zeal: "I'm not a promiscuous old bastard, but it's terrible to be drying up." Or, in a letter, he moaned, "I've been on Cat.—aches not disabling, more my usual ones I can't be 'bothered' by . . . ."

In the summer of the year I graduated Poly (1961) Louis was to read at Les Deux Megots in NYC. Before the reading he wrote:

> . . . So I'll see you and what of the gang at Les Deux Megots (it's not the $10, I just gave into the young's pleas)—and why not bring your parents so we can all feel staid (or "stayed") together. I take it the place isn't a dive once I step into it. Tell your folks it's my first time, too,—no entrance fee or cover charge—everything free I take it except the coffee. Another reason I agreed to read—always careful.

I did bring my parents and he did seem glad of their presence. He even told them not to let me become a poet. At that time I was set for mathematics and physics and thought not at all of being a poet. But perhaps he *was* just being *careful*; as who can imagine a boyish Zukofsky.

After that we mostly lost touch except for a few brief meetings (e.g. a performance of *Arise, Arise* at the Cubiculo in NYC). Yet now as I look over our few correspondences from then and afterwards, I am struck anew by his convolutions and yet also by his compassion and gentleness. When I felt depressed in distant Minnesota at the start of graduate school he sympathized, "No 'answer'—just to say hello to a guy who's feeling . . .what I've been the last 15 years. Chirrup—it'll move." Obviously he himself was not in the best of spirits and seemed to grow more and more weary ("Nothing, nothing new."). He appeared to shed many of his former friends and acquaintances and a reticence that had had a certain charm now turned darker: "Too sick to write letters or see people. Let's leave it at vague 'future' public appearances. . . ." When my first book of poems won a prize (I had left science by that time), I made sure to give him a good credit in the press release. I sent both to him and I think that I did get back a few lines of congratulations but I can't find the communication.

Finally, there is perhaps the urge to analyse or to sum-up. Since I am no psychologist nor critic, I am unqualified on both counts and apologize for any amateurish forays in such directions. This writing is meant to be only what it is: a sort of reminiscence of some things that have stuck with me after almost 20 years about a man I admired, and as I have said, loved. As he says in *"A"* when speaking of his father: "You must, myself,/ As father of Nicomachus/ Say very little/ Except: such were his actions." Also, I hope that he would not be too unhappy with me for touching on what might be called the personal. As he notes in *Autobiography*, he was a man who disavowed the personal: "As a poet I have always felt that the work says all there needs be said of one's life."

FIELDING DAWSON

A MEMOIR OF LOUIS ZUKOFSKY

Susan and myself left town for a three and a half week vacation in the country, on Monday, May 15th. I hadn't read the paper over the weekend, so I missed the news that Louis had died on the previous Friday, May 12th. But when we returned, and I heard the news, that instant I telephoned his wife Celia to offer my regrets and frustration at having just found out—and called her—a month after the fact.

In part I was astonished. I had spoken with him just a couple of weeks before he had died. He sounded okay, a little more tired, and perhaps a little older in his voice, which I mentioned to Celia, and she said it had been true.

It was a difficult telephone call for me to make, being a month late, but death is familiar to me, so late or not I had to, even wanted to—it would have been unthinkable not to—and I felt compelled to know, therefore, to ask her, how did it happen?

On Wednesday, May 10th, she said, he hadn't been feeling well, didn't want to eat anything, but—as Hugh Kenner mentioned in his Memoir (*N.Y. Times Book Review*, June 18), and which Celia corroborated in our conversation (which was before Kenner's Memoir appeared), Louis was such a hypochondriac, forever complaining about drafts and chills, she wasn't alarmed.

*****

This is a personal memoir, and not about Louis's place in literary history, nor about his poems, plays, essays, his novel, and his studies. He was, to me, as famous as Shakespeare, and part of my anxiety about calling his wife, was in perhaps a youthful sense—death can make us feel very young—I felt so humble and sad, I did all I could to say—outright—that I felt terrible, and if there was anything, anything I could do, to please let me know and I'd do it.

We had a long talk, and more details were discussed than need be mentioned here. It turned out, in fact, to be an informative talk. For example she mentioned that the obituaries were long, and flattering, and she had been surprised. In true Zukofsky style, she didn't know anybody knew, or cared.

I didn't quite know how to reply to that thought, and I don't remember what I said, but I (no doubt) said we all had loved him and held him in the highest regard.

*****

I didn't know him well, very few did, because if there was anyone who valued his privacy, it was Louis. So much so that I —as almost everyone else—left him alone. There was something sacred in his being alone, and I for one would never invade it. I sent him my books as they came out, and he never failed to answer—via postcard. His handwriting (as Kenner mentioned), is (I have a couple of the cards) tiny, the line is level, but the letters themselves have serifs that make it difficult to read—difficult! but, after I at last understood it, his message was an unmistakeable delight, always a surprise, and without fail, warm, and brilliant.* His genius—one look told you—was, insofar as my knowledge of him goes, in and on everything he touched and accomplished, with the endemic eccentricities that often accompany true genius. But I never met anyone who had such a skull, such comprehending/steady eyes, and such an incisive continuum of scholarship, music, language and humor. In this sense to me, he had no peers. Thus, which can characterize many thinkers, he kept alone, worked alone, and was alone. Quiet, shy, not gregarious, but firm, yet not difficult to agitate. But he was so shy it made me self-conscious to be in his company, and I often felt a fool beside him.

This truth would embarrass him. He has my apologies!

I tried to draw him twice. The first attempt was in the kitchen of his Brooklyn apartment in around 1958, and the second in his lower 7th Avenue apartment, a decade later. In both attempts, I failed—without fail I failed. There was too much in his face, and skull, his eyes, and those black handlebar eyebrows that seemed to tug him ahead, he had a look, or continuous looking intellect and warmth (music) that took shape into a form

---

*This was true with Olson's letters, too, although Charley's handwriting was far different, but I have a hunch that with Olson it was deliberate, and my guess is, after the reader wrings out the message, the message in that way becomes a discovery, and as such, that much more vital.

I couldn't exact, and though I didn't know it, he was of more shape, of more form—more than line, and it was, is, a paradox indeed, that he, the linear poet of all poets, would be so difficult to draw, by a linear artist such as me.

But I did a great drawing of Celia.

*****

I heard him read twice. One had to listen in a way one was not accustomed to listening for his voice was low, and his eyes were on his text alone. One had to clear one's mind, and settle down to listen, ears out, wide open.

*****

I've quoted Louie in my stories, but in one story I used a whole poem, and felt a little uncomfortable about it—lifting a whole poem out!

It was a Vietnam war story called *Straight Lines*, that later appeared in my book *The Dream / Thunder Road*. But after I'd written it, long before it was published, I sent him a carbon, with a cover letter asking him if it was okay I used his poem. He wrote back—prompt as always—a brief letter attached to the carbon of my story saying I could use his poem, but suggesting two changes, which (amused me no end), of course I made.

But, and I never mentioned it to him, I disagreed with one correction, although I made it. I hadn't then read but precious little of Sappho, so when he suggested I change WCWilliams to Sappho I didn't know the change I was making, but did know—as depicted in my story—that a not very bright young guy would, having read a little of WCWilliams, be more apt to liken that Zukofsky poem to a Williams poem rather than to Sappho, and as I'm reluctant to lay out the plot of the story so you can know what I'm talking about, I should mention it doesn't matter. What does matter was that I made a change Zukofsky *suggested* from his point of view which I obeyed in ignorance. Meaning that Louie wanted himself tied in with Sappho, not Williams, no matter what I, the writer, thought. When Louie drew the line through Williams and inserted Sappho, I followed his wish, and as it stands, there it is in print, it's Sappho.

I like that story, it's a favorite because it reminded me (still does), of an incident in T.E. Lawrence's masterpiece, but from an objective or impersonal view, one might say I also like it because of the exchange with Louie, and though I admit it does give me an extra personal lift, I like it that much more, but not to the degree one might think. I like it yet from another view: something else emerges—from my writer's view.

In his letter to me, requesting the changes, I was pleased, proud, relieved (that I had his go-ahead to use the poem), yet baffled, and disappointed. I liked my story. He said I could use his poem and made two suggestion, but he didn't say *he* liked my story, which in a strange—seeming inextricable way, is a clue to him. And his wit. He would say what he said, and that was it. In my knowledge of him he didn't qualify things, he tended to define them, and his authority, which I respected to the utmost, forbid me to write him back and go into the Williams/Sappho hassle. He didn't like that sort of thing, it made him irritable for he had said what he had meant to say, and that was it. I could have stuck with Williams—I felt it more true—but I would have gone against Louie's grain, and as that grain was definitive I took his word to be the last word—not that he would have thought it so! Not on your life! Never! He had, to himself, made two mere suggestions. Anything else was irrelevant. Of course he liked my story (though that wasn't the point), otherwise he wouldn't have let me use his poem.

This links to Kenner's speaking of Louie's talent and delight with puns in that a master punster with wit would straightface request two changes, and like a slow, but typical Zukofsky curveball, at the end of his letter, he thanked me, for *thinking to use his poem.* Warm genius, warm man.

The way he put things together keeping them apart will always be a miracle to me, and although the words are simple here, it is in this sense that Louie will always be part of my mind. I can't think of anyone except Mozart who did what Louie did—and vice versa—the *way* they did what they did! They had the perfect combination which only the most rare genius can create, and actualize: *the what, and the way.*

So when Lita Hornick asked me to review ALL *The Shorter Poems* for *Kulcher*, I laughed and said you gotta be kidding, me cover Zukofsky? I'm a prose writer, maam. But she persisted, and I did it, and I don't know, but somewhere along the line I heard a soft murmur of pleasure that sounded like Louie talking. I never heard anything definitive, and I knew why. My review was good, and he got praise from me that I wanted him to have, but I think he knew I used his poems to praise him. I love that book, yet it is clear that I also loved the man behind it, who had the what, and the way.

I have no idea what he was like to live with. Warm, but maybe finicky, everything in order his way. How did Celia feel? Or Paul, their brilliant and talented violin-virtuoso son, as shy and soft spoken as his Mother, and his Father. As Paul might have been Louie's pride and inspiration, Celia could have been a source of perception to things Louis might not have considered, as well as she being a translator of him—as he was—to others. Louie might have made omissions she would include, or she might exclude his inclusions. But who knows. Three in kinship. Perhaps a little too quiet, a little too shy.

Louie's novel *Little* is a paradox and not easy to read because, in its classic mode, it works from several approaches. The first two unite in that the story is about young Mozart, and—this is clear—also young Paul. The third is its style of intertwining temporalities and non-spatial effect. I reviewed it somewhere, and used true diplomacy because I knew what Louie had left out, at book's end, and though I was positive Louie didn't know, I compromised, and made the decision to review the book, not what the author left out. I stuck with Louie's perception to the end, added a hint, and ended my review. The novel is classic in form, story, detail, but one feels an insularity that keeps one at arm's length. There were things Louie didn't want to know, or know about. And a couple of those things were serious, and when the nerve was touched, anger exploded.

*****

He didn't know how well his work was known, nor did Celia. They were famous for their collaborations, he was for his own work, and so too Paul with that incredible violin—in short, the family was well known, but as Louie was so often feeling ill, he had a curious double reputation. He was almost as well known for his ill isolation as he was for his work, and in that sense, it is sad to say, he was taken for granted, and in an even sadder sense, he took himself for granted.

Anyone who knew him knew where he was, and how he was. When he moved from 7th Avenue out to Long Island, he cut off his phone, but then had it turned on again because, as I heard, he felt out of touch. He liked to be telephoned, rather than written. He was more than grateful for postcards which said hello, but of himself he was vague, and in conversation in person, on the telephone, or by card, concerning the question asked him: How are things going?

"Oh well," with his small smile, "you know. We survive."

Therefore he became, in the precise understatement, separate from us. Even if he had been the toast and the talk of the town, at every party, or at the bars, he would have been what he was, a genius without peers, but in his isolation he was that same genius, with no peer, and taken for granted.

People and poets, being. what they are, taking things for granted, become rather callous, thus a certain tender amusement concerning Louie circulated among us, we held him in great awe, but this one ironic-seeming eccentricity, his isolating hypochondria, gave charm.

Therefore, two things, both of consequence, come into focus. Neither is amusing:

> *One*: Louie, not aware of the above, and who would have been hurt and angered by it, nonetheless created a situation whereby no one could get to know, in his own specific sense, how he was, or what he was up to. What was he working on? In other words, he created a generalization about himself which in turn became a dangerous paradox: his solitary genius forced a respect and deference towards him that was a reversal, and a direct one, if not a warp, of everything he had done, although that respect and deference was well intended and without fail well deserved. The warm tolerance aimed at high genius missed the mark, created a distortion and without fail, as it does indeed, leaves great gaps. In the face of his unknown (to himself), but international fame, and even the way he was being revered, something is left unsaid and kept in silence, which, as he knew what to leave out, in this sense predicts what the critics will cover—what he left in, and what they won't touch—what he left out. How these gentlemen will do this I'll leave up to you to figure out, it's easy, although reading their results might not be so easy, yet will, because of Zukofsky's lucid genius, be so. He was, is, and will be for many many decades to come, essential in certain academic circles. He used a touch of the fable about him like Eyore.

> *Two*: Everyone knew after W.C. Williams' death—which to me was a personal loss—that Williams was, and still is, my primary figure of influence. But, although Pound was old, he was still writing, so we had The Master, but when Pound died, which held real drama, there was still no threat, because we had Olson, Reznikoff, and Louie—Masters alive and well until Olson died, and that was a shock, for it created an unconscious suspense that left us out on our limbs and when Charles Reznikoff died, something was coming into view, as a spectre through its own fog, that nobody wanted to see, talk about or admit, and with Louie taken for granted his death caused an instant transformation, for that advancing spectre was the fearing body of ourselves with its fog. In Zukofsky's death the illusion of ourselves has vanished. Our Masters have gone, and we have none to look to but our-actual-selves.

Just as those who lived, and died before him, Louie's literary historical importance was and will continue to be staggering, for he will be studied by the academy until God knows when, for their interest *is* historical.

Clear enough.

But what is even more clear are the questions: how are we going to accept our responsibility, and what will we do with it once we accept it? Any poet or writer who makes their art their life must take these questions in a seriousness at Zenith.

Arise, Arise!—Anew!—Bottom—A Test of Poetry, and many other works, two of which I've mentioned here. I speak of *perfect, profound music and scholarship*, who is of us that is that? Duncan —I think of Duncan. We are faced with a mass chaos of such dreadful, ignorant, pretentious and selfish *sameness* in poetry and prose today, one shuts one's eyes, ears, and mind, and shudders under the avalanche. It is unbearable, an absolute horror to consider, although of course, we have much good work being done. Maybe too much.

Louie, in his last act, has, in his innocence, forced us to be the best we can be, and do the best work we can, for the alternative is unthinkable—but not untenable, for it makes no difference that thousands and thousands and thousands of poets and writers have never heard of Louie much less read his work. But it makes every difference that Louie's not here any more.

There's nobody Great we can take for granted.

Thus Death has given us all the space and energy each of us has, to be the best we are, and do the best we will. We have no one to turn to, our Masters aren't around—no. In this sense, Death holds hands with God: we are Their gift.*

*****

I sent Louie a copy of my novel, *A* Great *Day for A Ballgame*, bang, his postcard back, thanking me for thinking of him, and in that handwriting made an allusion to something that took me a couple of days, with a couple of my friends' help, to figure out, and we got it—*Sterne*? And what was that next line? something about a sentimental journey, a *Sentimental Journey*—? A Sentimental *Journey*? I knew Louie's puns, etc., my book couldn't have reminded him of that old song, but then, somewhere in town

---

*Creating a most amazing irony. Death took the last great Poet, and leaving us one more, leaves *two critics* as his peers: Kenner, and Guy Davenport. Somehow, this has got to be a first.

somebody told me yes Sterne wrote Tristram Shandy but also a short novel, called, *Sentimental Journey*. I went zip to the bookstore, got the book, came home, sat down and read it, closed the book after the last page, put my head in my hands and *couldn't believe it.*

I couldn't believe it.

Talk about dancing on the ceiling, I danced down the walls, across the floor and out the door and around town for a few days, dazed and happy out of mind.

Only Louie would say that. No one else except maybe Kenner, but even then, in that way, that one single way, it was Louie. That wit, warmth, scholarship, music, that Mozart-humor, would make that connection. That contact, which sparkled and shone, in his generous starlit mind and music.

*****

The afternoon I made my second attempt at drawing him, and failed, but did a beauty of Celia, we were in their living room, in the apartment house on 7th Avenue, and after I finished drawing we talked, and if you think I was proud to be likened to Laurence Sterne, listen to this.

I'd been thinking about the response structure in Williams' poems, those so-called simple little poems which are anything but simple, or little, and Louie agreed. I said they were in fact the form Williams used to achieve his *response to his perception*: that the plum poems were Williams' way to bring form as well as completion to perception, and as if in a wild *viola*! no sooner had I said that, Louie jumped up, gestured for me to follow, and we walked—cool fast—into his study, and he began searching through his wall of books until—he moved his hand with care, but quick! he too was eager, and he found it, a little magazine published in 1928 (he said), turning into the book so fast I didn't see the name of the magazine, and without checking the table of contents, he found his essay, turned the page bam, the next page bam, the next page and ran his index finger down, stopped at a line, handed the magazine to me, and with his index finger still there, said read that.

I stood by his side, holding the magazine with him, and read what he had written—two or three sentences—and it was what I had said, in different words not all that different, four minutes before, that he'd written forty years before.

"You're right, Fielding," he said, soft-spoken as always, putting the book back in its place on the shelf, and we returned to the living room, me in a kind of tailspin. I knew what he meant, but wasn't he—reversing things? But then, wouldn't he, in his generosity, compliment me, instead of saying he was right, he'd written it forty years ago, etc., but no. What he enjoyed was I had agreed with him, and standing for a moment, as in tableau I was speechless, but then I cried—

"That's—GREAT! *Louie*!"

He was—he was great, and it was fantastic—incredible that I had said something that reminded him—what a memory he had! yet it was also clear he was enjoying it too, that it was terrific in just that exact single sense: what had happened had happened with us.

*****

On Thursday, May 11th he had difficulty getting out of bed, but did, halfway, using the end table as support, yet he became stuck, could go no farther nor go back—Celia got him back into bed and called their doctor who said bring him over in a taxi, but when she returned to get Louie, she being a bit confused about taxis, doctors and—Louie, she saw—no need for details—that he was far worse than she had thought, so she called their doctor again, an ambulance came fast, he was taken to the hospital, put in isolation and given full and finest treatment. Paul cancelled an important performance in Washington D.C., so was with his Mother at Louie's bedside, when Louie went into coma, and died the following night, Friday, May 12th, of cardiac arrest. He was seventy-four years old, and God I'll miss him.

BARRY AHEARN

THE ADAMS CONNECTION

> child 'tasted *A*'
> (Hen Adams) *schlissel* to *key*, H.J. intensely in
> New York the year that I was born.
> 60 gone . . . .   *"A"*-18

> Next to smell came taste, and the children knew the taste of
> everything they saw or touched, from pennyroyal and flagroot
> to the shell of a pignut and the letters of a spelling-book—the
> taste of A-B, AB, suddenly revived on the boy's tongue sixty
> years afterwards.
>
> *The Education of Henry Adams*

The divisions of time and birth that separated Louis
Zukofsky from Henry Adams were sufficiently vast. As a child
Adams took it for granted that he would grow up to be President.
The young Zukofsky, nurtured in a different world, should have
anticipated a career as a pants presser. Or perhaps he might have
aspired to eventual proprietorship of a haberdashery. Somewhere,
however, the laws of cultural probability flickered out just long
enough to throw together the most educated American of the
nineteenth century and the precocious son of an illiterate immigrant. Time and again Zukofsky tended to see himself as Adams'
successor. "Just re-read Education H.A. What a book! I believe he
had buzzin' in his head my Bottom but didn't bother to tell anyone."[1] Zukofsky was usually much more circumspect about his
relation to Adams, partly out of a natural modesty, partly because
the relation was complex. Accurate statements about the Adams-
Zukofsky connection necessarily grew complicated, and so less
and less explicit. This was true even as early as Zukofsky's Columbia days, which were crowned by the 1924 essay "Henry Adams:
A Criticism in Autobiography."

1. Letter to Lorine Niedecker (n.d.). Quotations from Zukofsky's unpublished letters
and essays appear through the courtesy of the Humanities Research Center, The University of Texas at Austin, and Celia Zukofsky.

In 1924 Henry Adams was only six years dead. Brother Brooks still occupied the family home in Quincy. Yet, Zukofsky notes, as if forecasting his own future difficulties, "works that he published in the seventies and eighties, and even the *Life of George Cabot Lodge*, which appeared as late as 1911, are now out of print and forgotten."[2] The young scholar found himself entering a field untrodden by previous researchists. The files of the *North American Review* had lain idle until Zukofsky took the trouble to cull them for contributions by Adams. Those fortunate enough to discover such unmediated contacts sometimes identify with their subject to excess. It is a pardonable sin, and readjustment of focus comes easily. But the reader should keep this in mind when considering Zukofsky's essay.

Zukofsky begins by defining two "actuating forces of his [Adams'] nature: poetic intellect is its continual undertow and detached mind the strong surface current in the contrary direction."[3] These polar elements, suggestive of Adams' own tendency to speak in terms of "forces" and "motivation" when defining his and others' characters, reflect on Zukofsky. He also was accustomed to juggling opposites and arranging "hidden paradox not in the least to be dispensed with by a wit."[4] Just as Henry Adams tended to depict historical crises in terms of antinomies (see his scrutiny of the divisions within the British cabinet during the Civil War, or the remarks on the march of Science ca. 1900, "evidently the new American would need to think in contradictions, and instead of Kant's famous four antinomies, the new universe would know no law that could not be proved by its anti-law"[5]) Zukofsky's works swarm with opposites: objective/subjective, thought/music, autobiography/reticence, and a formula he found in Spinoza, "natura naturans, natura naturata" (nature as creator, nature as created). For Zukofsky these phrases served as a convenient shorthand. They encapsulate a double-edged law that guides *"A"*'s formation. The artist is both product and molder of his age. All sorts of influences: social, economic, literary, philosophical, will mold an inquiring nature. That mind in turn will alter its own, and succeeding, generations. Henry Adams seems to have subscribed to a version of this dialectic; it bears a resemblance to his late interest in "the reaction between mind and nature."[6]

---

2. *Prepositions: The Collected Critical Essays of Louis Zukofsky* (London: Rapp and Carroll, 1967), p. 80.
3. *Prepositions*, p. 80.
4. *Prepositions*, p. 91.
5. Henry Adams, *The Education of Henry Adams* (1907; rpt. New York, The Modern Library, 1931), pp. 497-498.
6. *Prepositions*, p. 117.

At several points in his essay Zukofsky suggests that, given slightly altered conditions, Adams would have found his true vocation as a poet. We may be inclined to reserve judgement, but can at least assent to Zukofsky's argument that Adams was gifted with "precise phraseology and order of thought—two prerequisites not the least important for a poet . . . ."[7] At the time he wrote those words Zukofsky had yet to produce poetry worth preserving, but hindsight, reading between the lines, detects a large ambition complementing the deft prose. A bit of that ambition surfaces with Zukofsky himself (though not by name) as occupant of a point on a line of development predicted by Adams. "And those who look around them and see the product of the age—the child, as Adams called him, of incalculable forces yet undetermined—seeking with his own disillusion to avoid repetition—can sense the desires behind Adams' 'ocean of potential thought, mere consciousness, like static electricity'."[8] This is as close as Zukofsky comes to overtly proclaiming himself as Adams' heir. But in another respect he shows that the torch has been passed—in terms of style. "The *Life of Gallatin*," he points out, "was more than half quotation."[9] The same is true of Zukofsky's "Criticism."

The quotation method of presenting material insures, in one sense, "precise phraseology." Any faithful copying can be said to be precise. Since a poem is not made merely by stringing together correct copies of other texts (some would argue this point), another power—"order of thought"—must presumably command the degree, type, and placement of quotations. The *Life of Lodge* can be recommended as a masterpiece of judicious selection and arrangement.

Zukofsky went one step further. Most quotations in *"A"* undergo subtle alterations. The tampering was necessary to align the quoted bits with the entire fabric of the poem. When done well, as Zukofsky demonstrated in case after case, the result was one brilliant job of editing and assemblage after another. His success, however, tends to obscure the considerable risk involved. The words chosen have some worth: truth, wit, pungency, bathos, etc. Altering or deforming those words in order to enhance their value, while laying them into the poem's design, is a delicate business. It requires lapidary finesse, as *"A"*-8 demonstrates.

At the close of his *Education* Adams speculated that he, Clarence King, and John Hay might be allowed a glimpse of the

---

7. *Prepositions*, p. 91.
8. *Prepositions*, p. 118.
9. *Prepositions*, p. 92.

state of the world in 1938, their centenary. *"A"* was composed between 1935 and 1937: perhaps Zukofsky had the centenary in mind, for the movement contains his greatest tribute to Adams. The quotation method advances to new heights of intricacy and versatility, and the entire Adams clan participates. (How could one define Henry, after all, without including his ancestors?)

The story of *"A"*-8 really begins in 1927/28, when Zukofsky was first charting *"A"*. At that time he jotted down, in meticulously tiny script, a list of 24 parts for a projected poem. The list comes complete with section titles and brief notes on what might be included.[10] Item X on the plan was dubbed "Tombeor." Adams retold the story of the "Tombeor de Notre Dame" in Chapter Thirteen of *Mont-Saint-Michel and Chartres*. Zukofsky was clearly intrigued by the story, as his comments in the "Criticism" indicate.[11] Between 1928 and 1935, however, Zukofsky changed his mind and the lively tumbler disappeared. No trace of the story remains in *"A"*. Further, material from *Chartres* is conspicuously absent. It may be that the Adams who yearned for unity was too alien for Zukofsky's tastes. "The child born in 1900," Adams had predicted, "would . . . be born into a new world which would not be a unity but a multiple."[12]

On the reverse of the ur-plan for *"A"*, which Zukofsky thriftily saved, are jumbled notes dating from 1934 and 1935. Among them we can barely trace out this sentence (question marks in brackets stand for illegible words); "The Valley [?] by the [?] was called in Washington's gener[?]."[13] In *"A"*-8 we discover some lines that are plainly a development of the note.[14]

> The valley bridged by this viaduct is
> The Hollow Way of General Washington's time—   (77)

About ten lines further on a quotation from John Quincy Adams appears. Why are viaducts, Washington, and the Adamses brought into conjunction? The connection lies in Zukofsky's presentation of the role of the Adamses in American history and how they perceived that role. Brooks Adams, in *The Degradation of the Democratic Dogma* (1919), offers this version of early America.

---

10. MS. courtesy the Humanities Research Center, The University of Texas at Austin.
11. *Prepositions*, p. 111.
12. *Education*, p. 457.
13. MS. courtesy the Humanities Research Center, The University of Texas at Austin.
14. Page references to "A"-8 are from *"A" 1-12* (Garden City: Paris Review Editions, Doubleday, 1968).

> In his wanderings in early life in the western wilderness, Washington conceived the principle that a consolidated community which should have the energy to cohere must be the product of a social system resting on converging highways . . . .[15]

> Washington's conception of a national capital corresponded in magnificence with his plan for the concentration of the nation. Built on converging avenues, it was to be adapted at once to military, commercial, administrative, and educational purposes, for at its heart was to be organized a university which was to serve as the brain of the corporeal system developed by the highways.[16]

Tantalized by the notion of unity, Brooks stresses that coherence is achieved by centralization. There was sufficient precedent for thinking so; the Roman Empire knew the value of excellent roads leading to and from the central authority. The Adamses confessed themselves products of the Age of Reason; hence the model city and state are based on a conception of the body that puts the brain at the center. Their premises were classically elegant, and totally unsuited to the times.

Zukofsky writes in his "Criticism" that "the general reader will perhaps give 'the cake' to the introduction" to *The History of the United States During the Administrations of Jefferson and Madison.* The introduction minutely details the rigors of travel at the beginning of the nineteenth century. Adams indicates that

> Nature was rather man's master than his servant, and the five million Americans struggling with the untamed continent seemed hardly more competent to their task than the beavers and buffalo which had for countless generations made bridges and roads of their own.[17]

Adams implies that the main issue confronting the young nation was whether man could subdue the wilderness or whether the wilderness would absorb and bestialize man. Zukofsky follows that quote in his essay with another that serves to hone the point.

> A traveller on the levee at Natchez, in 1808, overheard a quarrel in a flatboat nearby . . . 'I am an alligator,' cried the other, 'half man, half horse . . .' 'I am a Mississippi snapping-turtle,' joined the second, 'I have bear's claws, alligator's teeth, and the devil's tail . . .'[18]

---

15. Henry Adams, *The Degradation of the Democratic Dogma* (1919; rpt. New York: Capricorn Books, 1958), p. 14. This edition retains the pagination of the original Macmillan edition.
16. *DDD*, p. 17.
17. *Prepositions*, pp. 99-100.
18. *Prepositions*, p. 100.

Who would flourish in America, the Adamses or the Mike Finks?
Henry answers the question in *The Education* by comparing himself to a wilted begonia.

Henry and Brooks, looking back at Washington's generation,
read into the effort at building a "consolidated community" a
naive faith on the part of the founding fathers that good communications would ensure government by the best. John Adams
and his son trusted that the foremost men would be working at
the center of a republic made strong and monolithic by internal
improvements. In *The Degradation* Brooks could only helplessly
recount the betrayal of the hopes which they held for the nation.
Referring to John Quincy Adams, Brooks writes;

> He alone among public men of that period appreciated that a
> nation to flourish under conditions of modern economic com-
> petition must organize its administrative, as well as its social
> system upon scientific principles.[19]

The "period" was that following the deaths of John Adams and
Jefferson, when "scientific principles" still meant Newtonian
physics. As the last great exponent of Enlightenment doctrine,
J.Q. Adams was left alone to discover that

> in 1828, democracy would not permit the ablest staff of officials,
> to be chosen by him, to administer the public trust. Democracy,
> on the contrary, has insisted on degrading the public service to a
> common level of incapacity, thereby throwing the management
> of all difficult public problems, such as the use of railroads and
> canals, into private hands, in order that they might escape ruin,
> and thence has come the predicament in which we, in particular,
> and the world at large, now stand.[20]

So, according to a latter scion of the Adams dynasty, the forefathers had staked all upon centralization, but in order to main-
tain prosperity were forced to turn control of communications
over to those unscrupulous robber barons thrown up by the democratic system. One hardly knows whether Brooks refers to the
nation or to the Adamses when he uses "we" above.

Brooks dwells on the unfortunate last years of his grandfather as if he were Roderick Usher contemplating the effigy of
an illustrious ancestor. His ruminations provide a good part of the
Adams material in *"A"*-8. The last quote serves as the source for

> Democracy would not permit John Quincy Adams
> The ablest staff of officials, to be chosen by him,
> To administer the public trust (79).

---

19. *DDD*, p. 61.
20. *DDD*, p. 121.

If we pursue the thesis that the founding fathers based the national welfare on a network of roads and canals, and assume that this lies behind portions of *"A"*-8, some puzzling passages begin to make sense. Consider, for example, the following litany of discomfort.

> As cold as Nova Zembla.
> In the morning awakened by the hail—the
> Train frozen to the rails
> Could not be broken free for an hour.
> I felt as if I were incrusted in a bed of snow.
> Four of us slept, feet to feet
> Next to a stable bulging with horses,
> The boat staggered, a stumbling nag (78).[21]

This is Zukofsky's arrangement of the account of a journey made by J.Q. Adams in 1843. The story of the ordeal can be found in *The Degradation*; Brooks dwells at length on the rigors of the trip and how they almost killed the old man. He does so with surprising relish, as though entertaining the notion that it was all a punishment inflicted not by God, but by Adams' own commitment to centralization, communication, and—worst of all—democracy.

For Brooks and Henry, and for *"A"*-8, J.Q. Adams represents faith in science as an ameliorating influence. Science, education, and rational self-government by the masses all went hand-in-hand. So we are shown Adams taking an interest in scientific pursuits with the public welfare in mind. The "forest of live-oak near Pensacola" (79)[22] was one of his projects. His plan for preserving the forest was scrapped by the Jackson administration. The effect of the new democracy coming to power in 1828 was to destroy "everything of which I had planted the germ" (79).[23]

Adams' scientific interests were not limited by gravity. Pages 77-78 of *"A"*-8 are a capsule condensation of his desire to encourage astronomy. "Light-houses of the sky" (77) was his colorful locution for observatories. Brooks adds one more detail to a portrait of his grandfather struggling vainly against public apathy.

> The phrase "light-houses of the sky"
> Probably brought more ridicule on
> Mr. Adams than anything he ever said.[24]

Adams made that terrible journey in 1843 to speak at the groundbreaking for America's first observatory—in Cincinnati. Brooks

---

21. Cf. *DDD*, pp. 68-69.
22. Cf. *DDD*, p. 53.
23. Cf. *DDD*, p. 53.
24. *DDD*, p. 61.

concludes his sketch of the tribulations of J.Q. Adams by claiming that the philanthropist died thinking his life had been a failure, doubting himself, doubting science and education, and even struggling not to doubt his God.

The sad odyssey of John Quincy Adams serves as a prologue to the history of his grandsons. By 1869 public and private morality had declined considerably, and in the chronological section of *"A"*-8 for that year we find some quotations from Henry and Charles Francis Adams, Jr.'s *Chapters of Erie*—their joint diagnosis of financial chicanery in the Gilded Age. The railroads are in the clutches of crooks.

> Ten o'clock the astonished police . . panic-stricken
> railway directors . .
> In their hands . . files of papers . . and their pockets
> Crammed . . assets and securities . . One,
> Captain, in a hackney-coach . . with him . . six
> millions in greenbacks.
> Under cover of night . . to the Jersey ferry.
> Some . . not daring publicity . . in open boats
> Concealed by darkness and a March fog . .
> A majority of the Executive Committee
> Collected at the Erie Station in Jersey City
> Proceeded to the transaction of business. (82)[25]

Zukofsky silently makes a few alterations in the text that render the case against these scoundrels even more damaging. "Captain" here is short for "captain of industry," Zukofsky's favorite designation for predatory capitalists. (His favorite probably because the phrase carries military overtones.) But in *Erie* the word used is simply "individual." Zukofsky had to change it since, for him, those thieves are hardly individuals. Stamped from the same rotten mold of selfishness, Vanderbilt and Gould are as different as Tweedledum and Tweedledee.

In *Erie* the brothers Adams had laid bare the shame of the railroads. What then was the result? *"A"*-8's chronology tells the tale. It skips to 1871 and shows the "captains" even more brazen.

> By means of this simple and smooth machinery,
> Which differs in no essential respect from
> roulette or rouge-et-noir . .
> I went down to the neighborhood of Wall Street . .
> And to my Newport steamer . . Mr. James
> Fisk:
> In blue uniform, broad gilt cap-band,
> Three silver stars on coat-sleeve,

---

25. Cf. Charles Francis Adams, Jr. and Henry Adams, *Chapters of Erie* (1886; rpt. Ithaca, New York: Cornell University Press, 4th printing, 1966), p. 30.

> Lavendar gloves, diamond breast-pin
> Large as a cherry, stood at the gangway,
> Surrounded by aides bestarred and bestriped
>   like myself . .
> And welcomed President Ulysses Simpson Grant. (84)[26]

The account of the welcoming committee combines several different portions of *Erie* for special effect. At first we assume that the "simple and smooth machinery" must be some kind of trolley or other public transportation. But how does this fit with the references to gambling? Aside from the continued use of the communication motif, and the mention of roulette ("chance" is one of Zukofsky's interests in *"A"*-8), what are we to make of this gaudy scene? A glance at *Erie* reveals that the "machinery" is the process known as "buying on margin."[27] In other words, the anonymous captain arrived at his bad eminence by speculation—gambling. One important distinction: with these operators it is not gambling. The founding fathers' plan for an internal binding network now constitutes a rigged game.

> Three distinct railways, with all their enormous resources, became the property of Cornelius Vanderbilt, who, by means of their credit and capital, again and again swept millions of dollars into his pocket by a process curiously similar to gambling with loaded dice.[28]

The most promising child of the Enlightenment, the United States, has turned into a crooked casino.

After the passage recounting the flight of the captains across the Hudson to Jersey, the movement passes another judgement on them.

> Doll said: "A Captain!
> God's light . . the word as odious as
>   the word 'occupy' . .
> Excellent . . before it was ill sorted (82)."

As is so often the case in *"A"*, we are reading a quotation of a quotation. In *Erie*, C.F. Adams, Jr., calls on Doll Tearsheet to comment on the titles Vanderbilt and his cronies adopted.[29] Doll complains about the word "Admiral" and how it has been debased by those unworthy of the title. Adams only quotes her to put the barons of Wall Street in their place, but Zukofsky continues his denigration of "captains." Following Doll's commentary comes a medley of quotations from *Erie*, in which Charles Francis

---

26. Cf. *Erie*, pp. 102, 116.
27. *Erie*, p. 102.
28. *Erie*, p. 103.
29. *Erie*, p. 95. See also *II Henry IV*, Act 2, scene 2.

speculates on the future evils corporate octopi have in store for the nation.

> The old maxim of the common law,
> That corporations have no souls.
> Corporate life and corporate power
> As applied to industrial development,
> . . yet in its infancy.
> It tends always to development, —
> Always to consolidation . .
> Even threatens the central government.
> It is a new power, for which our language
> Contains no name (82-83).[30]

If the corporations have no souls there can be nothing individual about them. Huge and amorphous, they cannot be located and held to account for their crimes because they are de-centralized. Still more ominous, "it is a new power, for which our language / Contains no name." Language is called into question, and Zukofsky immediately inserts a surreal scene whose source, if it is a quotation, remains hidden. It does bear a resemblance to visions of desolation found in some of Thomas Cole's landscapes.

> (a river that would seem to hang from a tree
> Flood valleys, the sky between hung trees and
>   caved arches,
> Thru crashed firs red radish half-plugged). (83)

The chronic American anxiety that the westward expansion of the nation would one day conclude with the nation's dissolution helped produce Cole's series *The Course of Empire*, which hangs in the galleries of the New York Historical Society. Comparisons of the United States with Rome in its decline trouble the rest of C.F. Adams' text.

> It, perhaps, only remains for the coming man
> To carry the combination of elements
> One step in advance, and put Caesarism
> At once in control of the corporation and of the
>   proletariat. (83-84)[31]

Zukofsky succinctly comments on the parallel of Rome and America in a parenthetical aside; "Him to—hymn to—Latinity" (83). We see converging the "deline of the West" syndrone, Henry's attraction to the Church of Rome (a centralized organization if there ever was one), the Adamses late interest in entropy, and the increasing alienation of the family from its surroundings.

---

30. Cf. *Erie*, pp. 96-98.
31. Cf. *Erie*, p. 99.

After documenting the gross corruption of the post-Civil War period, the chronology of *"A"*-8 leaps suddenly from 1871 to 1893. Zukofsky, monitoring the age through the Adamses, chose to keep step with Henry. The twenty-year hiatus coincides with the twenty years of which Henry says nothing in *The Education*. (He skips from Chapter 20, "Failure"—1871, to Chapter 21, "Twenty Years After"—1892.) A score of years drops out because, according to Henry, during that period his education ceased. 1871 also seems to be the year that Henry and his brothers lost hope that their exposures of corporate greed would have immediate impact. They retreated to other pursuits. Charles went to work on the railroad; Henry vowed to study the situation more thoroughly and publish a few works which might guide the rising generation. He later concluded in *The Education* that during those two decades he worked in vain.[32] The portion of *The Education* which follows 1892 has no faith that the forces of history will be stayed by any man's books.

The Degradation represents the last gasp of the family's pessimism. Though published in 1919, it supplies some of the material dated 1893 in *"A"*-8.

> Henry, like the good brother he was . .
> Stayed with me in Quincy . . (85)

> Hot August . . and talked endlessly of panic.
> If I live forever, I shall never forget
> that summer. (86)[33]

The Panic of 1893 was a severe jolt to the Adamses. Henry and Brooks were together that summer keeping a close eye on the family finances. As Henry drily observes in *The Education*, the collapse meant that "the community was bankrupt and he was probably a beggar," or so it seemed at first. The manuscript under discussion in Quincy was Brooks' *The Law of Civilization and Decay* (1895). Its thesis: civilizations rise by accumulating capital, but eventually capital becomes "the controlling social force."[34] This marks the beginning of the end for any civilization.

The Adamses were, as Henry and Brooks saw it, a product of the dead past. Their ideas and energies were suited to a fixed conception that had grown obsolete, or so they thought. The theory of entropy they flirted with, in which the universe becomes a closed system running down like a complicated watch, happens to be an agreeable notion if one's personal capacities, great as they

---

32. *Education*, p. 315.
33. Cf. *DDD*, pp. 90, 94.
34. Brooks Adams, *The Law of Civilization and Decay: An Essay on History* (London: Swann Sonnenschein & Co., 1895), p. viii.

may be, are geared to problems and opportunities that existed a century earlier. Though Henry and Brooks said nothing about the relation between entropy and the family character, *"A"*-8 invites us to make the connection.

The last stage of entropy would be an undifferentiated mass at a temperature of absolute zero, and at several points in *"A"*-8 the family members suffer from freezing chills. For example, the passage

> "To sponge in a brook
> Before sunrise with the thermometer
>   at thirty
> and a bracing breeze blowing,
> tries the epidermis" (64)

is Henry laconically describing the rigors attending cleanliness out in the Wild West.[35] We have already reviewed the journey west of J.Q. Adams during which he almost froze to death. The quotations from the family conclude with Henry's Baltic and Russian journeys, where images of icy cold abound: "Uniformity of ice and snow" (87), "The glacial ice-cap" (88), "Ice-cap of Russian inertia . ." (88).[36] Another bout of cold afflicts someone in *"A"*-8, but he (or she) is not identified.

> So cold . . the freezing of the ink on . . my pen
> Renders it difficult to write . . (106)

Perhaps another of the Adamses—a family noted for their voluminous writings—struggles with dropping temperatures.

In only one instance does the family suffer from the heat.

> Hot August . . and talked endlessly of panic.
> If I live forever, I shall never forget
>   that summer (86)[37]

"A"-8 presents the Adamses sweltering when their money is threatened by the Panic of 1893. The legacy of Peter Chardon Brooks had put the Adamses on easy street in the third generation. Perhaps they would have been better off coping with straitened means, as did John Adams and his son.

It is not the business of *"A"* to speculate on what might have been. Instead it suddenly veers to suggest that the decline of the Adamses comes to its conclusion just as another cycle of growth begins in Russia. *"A"*-8 seems to view Lenin and Stalin as new Adamses in the right time and place: quotations from

---

35. Worthington Chauncey Ford, ed., *Letters of Henry Adams: 1858-1891* (Boston: Houghton Mifflin, 1930), p. 215.
36. Cf. *Education*, pp. 409-411.
37. Cf. *DDD*, p. 94.

Henry and Stalin are juxtaposed on page 84. On page 86 Brooks
calls it quits.

> "It is now full four generations since John Adams
> Wrote the constitution of Massachusetts.
> The world is tired of us
> We have only survived because our ancestors
> Lived in times of revolution."

The source of this passage indicates more clearly why the American and Russian revolutions are rhymed.

> Here have I, for years, been preparing a book
> to show how strong hereditary personal characteristics
> are, while the world changes fast, and that a type
> must rise or fall according as it is adjusted to
> its environment. It is seldom that a single family
> can stay adjusted through three generations.
> That is a demonstrable fact. It is now full
> four generations . . . .[38]

"A"-8 intertwines the decline of the Adams family with new beginnings. Zukofsky elsewhere observes that Henry's theory of the
acceleration of history (which Henry thought of as the rush of
disintegration), may have anticipated the Russian Revolution.
That a Russian uprising might be heir to the Spirit of '76 is further developed in *"A"*-8 by the last of the Adams quotations. As
Henry's voice fades out, diminuendo, in the frigid darkness of
northern Europe, we read;

> Nothing to say.
> For him, all opinion founded on fact must be error,
> Because the facts can never be complete,
> And their relations must be always infinite.
> Very likely, Russia would instantly become— (88)[39]

At the moment in *"A"*-8 when Henry Adams falls silent, an inter-
ruption—

> Then feed, and be fat,
> Come we to full points here; and are etceteras nothing? (88-89)

The lines dismiss an overstuffed generation and look to a new
people. The source is the same play, act, and scene, in which we
heard Doll Tearsheet expostulate earlier. Here Pistol has the floor;
the points to which he refers are "stops." In short, the end of the
Adamses is not the end of all. What continues are some immigrants
—uprising Russians—from Eastern Europe (mere "etceteras" to
patrician Adams?), among whom are the Zukofskys.

---

38. *DDD*, p. 93.
39. Cf. *Education*, p. 410.

In his preface to *The Law of Civilization and Decay* Brooks saw only one remedy for a senile civilization.

> The evidence seems to point to the conclusion, that, when a highly centralized society disintegrates, under the pressure of economic competition, it is because the energy of the race has been exhausted. Consequently, the survivors of such a race lack the power necessary for renewed concentration, and must probably remain inert, until supplied with fresh energetic material by the infusion of barbarian blood.[40]

It makes perfect sense, according to the "blood" scheme, that Henry's musings should cease just as the poem picks up the earliest memories of Louis Zukofsky. (The tapering off of Adams followed by Louis' infant recollections may have helped Pound organize his long poem; the Chinese cantos conclude in the eighteenth century, and are followed by the Adams cantos.)[41] Just as he hinted in the "Criticism," Zukofsky plugs himself into a spot one step removed from the Adamses.

With the "Criticism" and *"A"*-8 behind him, Zukofsky had said enough about the Adamses—except for one brief postscript. Poem 26 of *Anew* has for its title "1892-1941." A visit to a cemetery provides the setting, and our first assumption tags those years as birth and death dates. The conclusion is logical but wrong. The poem tests, in a small way, any American reader's familiarity with the history of Henry Adams. In 1892, Adams, just back from wandering with La Farge in the South Sea, returned to Washington and for the first time inspected the St. Gaudens memorial erected over the grave of Mrs. Adams. His reactions form a page in *The Education.*[42] Line 24 of the poem—"The cemetery known as Rock Creek"—quotes from that page. Recognizing 1892 as Adams' first acquaintance with the enigmatic figure permits us to guess 1941 as Zukofsky's first visit.

The title, brief as a riddle, suggests a particular balance. It puts Zukofsky and Adams in close alliance, denoting as it does a shared point in physical and mental space, yet there is a gap of fifty-nine years. Two generations cannot be so easily dismissed. This tension between alliance and division is the friction that generates the poem.

It produces, for example, a syntax of contradiction that crops up in almost every line. "Shrubs, close to hands" are evergreens near the statue's unchanging hands, but they are also

---

40. *Decay*, p. viii.
41. When the possible influence of "A"-8 on the *Cantos* was brought up, Zukofsky responded with, "Possible, but small comfort in 1977" and "Ezra always thought he had the hambone."
42. *Education*, p. 329.

bushes seen as the hands of a clock, since their growth marks the passage of time. "Cast, the statue rests, stopped" demands that we recognize "cast" as both "projected" and "solidified." The memorial shrouds from view the joys and sorrows known only to Adams and his wife, yet passes this emotional tangle on to the future as a solid puzzle.

This poem, too, is an artifact holding many opposing tendencies in suspension. Its form is slow, stately, serious, and on one level it is an examination of clues to be found in the setting and details of a gravesite. But this cannot be the poem's motivation or aim. Where or from whom could the sleuthing visitor expect response? The questions, never specified, are unanswerable: why did Mrs. Adams kill herself? What were the relations between Adams and his wife? When confronted by a puzzle the historian has no recourse but to stick to method. "1892-1941" has a thoroughly methodical air, and it is in part about being methodical.

Any historian worth his salt has, since Herodotus, cultivated his talents for observation. The poem is full of observation: of people (tourists, a mysterious woman, the poet), plants, stone, benches, a statue, and itself. Few observations end in answers, whether the object of interest be a tomb, the significance of a dead man's life, or Time—guardian of all secrets.

Time is the historian's great adversary. To see Time whole is the historian's El Dorado. Henry Adams once dreamed of Time as a series of layered transparencies.

> One's instinct abhors time. As one lay on the slope of the Edge, looking sleepily through the summer haze towards Shrewsbury or Cader Idris or Caer Caradoc or Uriconium, nothing suggested sequence. The Roman road was twin to the railroad; Uriconium was well worth Shrewsbury; Wenlock and Buildwas were far superior to Bridgnorth. The shepherds of Caractacus or Offa, or the monks of Buildwas, had they approached where he lay in the grass, would have taken him only for another and tamer variety of Welsh thief. They would have seen little to surprise them in the modern landscape unless it were the steam of a distant railway. One might mix up the terms of time as one liked, or stuff the present anywhere into the past . . . .[43]

Time will not contract itself into a convenient ball. Historians must grudgingly settle for the scattered contacts available. If the historian has a bit of the poet in him he might even develop some contacts. Not the least of the poem's triumphs is that its last words—"One's instinct abhors time"—are, by that stage of the poem's development, as much Zukofsky's as Adams'. Fifty-nine years and a cultural abyss are momentarily cancelled. We hear one voice.

---

43. *Education*, p. 228.

NEIL BALDWIN

ZUKOFSKY, WILLIAMS, AND THE WEDGE:
Toward a Dynamic Convergence.*

I have always been proud of this book.
—William Carlos Williams,
speaking about *The Wedge* in 1958.[1]

William Carlos Williams was convinced that "nobody ever saw" his experimental collage of prose and poetry, *Spring & All*, when it was first published in 1923: "It had no circulation at all," he recalled years later.[2] But at least one reader at the time, nineteen-year-old Louis Zukofsky, was impressed by Williams' daring attempts. In one of his earliest critical essays, he made special mention of the "terrifically sensitized American intellect" which produced "that perfect piece in *Spring & All*, 'The pure products of America/ go crazy.' "[3]

The poem does indeed represent basic affinities shared by these two poets, because it is primarily on and about "things," an itemized cataloguing in a condensed Whitman mode. And at its conclusion, Williams asserts that "It is only in isolate flecks that/ something/ is given off."[4] Perhaps Williams' clearly-etched form appealed to Zukofsky's "delight in spareness,"[5] or to his conviction that "Poems are only acts upon particulars."[6] Its surges of feeling through compression and its inherent sympathies with the people and objects described placed "The pure products . . ." in tune with Zukofsky's nascent theories of poetry.

*Excerpts herein from unpublished manuscripts and letters by William Carlos Williams Copyright ©1979 by the Estate of Florence H. Williams. Permission to quote from the letters of Louis Zukofsky has been granted by Celia Zukofsky.

1. William Carlos Williams, *I Wanted to Write a Poem*, ed. Edith Heal (New Directions, N.Y., 1958), p. 70.
2. Williams, *ibid.*, p. 36.
3. Louis Zukofsky, "Beginning Again With William Carlos Williams," *Hound & Horn*, IV.2, January-March, 1931, pp. 261-264.
4. Williams, *Spring & All* (Frontier Press, N.Y., 1970), p. 70.
5. Hugh Kenner, *The Pound Era* (University of California Press, Berkeley, 1971), p. 319.
6. Louis Zukofsky, " 'Recencies' in Poetry," Preface, *An "Objectivists" Anthology* (TO, Publishers, N.Y., 1932), p. 25.

Twenty years after *Spring & All*, Williams asked Zukofsky to help him shape and bring to readiness another important, threshold collection of poems: *The Wedge*. This essay examines certain aspects in the development of a relationship which laid the critical groundwork culminating in Williams' act of faith and acceptance; then takes a close look at the nature and influence of Zukofsky's editorial stance, and Williams' wholehearted integration of his friend's advice.

I

Of course, as he had done with so many others, it was the great catalyst and fulcrum Ezra Pound who brought the two men together in 1928. "I'd like greatly to see you since you came with an introduction from my old friend," Williams wrote, on March 23.[7] By Easter-time they had shared work and ideas: "What meeting you meant to me," the older man confided, "was at first just that Pound had admired your work . . . . I was happy to find a link between myself and another wave of it . . . . The thing moves by a direct relationship between men from generation to generation."[8] Zukofsky was 24 at the time, Williams was 45. Both were struggling for recognition, not soon to come for either of them.

Throughout the summer and fall of that year, they exchanged letters, and met either on the weekends in New York City, or at Williams' home in Rutherford, New Jersey. Williams seems to have very much wanted to encourage the younger poet, was especially excited by the prospect of passing along some kind of poetic "legacy," even if not articulated at that point. He staked out a territory for each of them, so that there would be a complementary atmosphere: "Eyes have always stood first in the poet's equipment. If you are mostly ear—a newer rhythm must come in more strongly than has been the case so far."[9] Williams, the poet of *vision* honed to perfection, things "narrowed to a point," valued Zukofsky for his *musical* sense of metric figure which he would rely heavily upon in years to come.

Zukofsky had just begun work on *"A,"* his lifelong project, which he sent to Williams in fragments as they were completed. Williams went further in his encouragement: "Your thesis shows a grain and selective power of thought which is unusual . . . . You

7. Williams, *Selected Letters*, ed. John C. Thirlwall (McDowell, Oblensky, N.Y., 1957), p. 93.
8. Williams, *ibid.*, p. 95.
9. Williams, *ibid.*, pp. 101-102 (July 5, 1928).

seemed to hold the damned subject up from the table with clean hands . . . . You have power that is real, penetrant, and (so far) flexible . . . ."[10]

Williams was "testing" Zukofsky's conformity to his own standards of poetry. Pound also interjected from his base in Rapallo, encouraging Williams to help "yr eminent friend ZUKofsky . . . [and] contribute to benemerito support of the man (or ??famille?) Zukofsky," by recommending his work to Harriet Monroe at *Poetry*.[11] In four short months, then, a bond had been constructed between all three. Some years later, Pound agonized to Williams about the propriety of inviting Zukofsky to Rapallo: would "Yourup" pollute the younger man's American aesthetic?[12]

During the 'twenties, 'thirties, and 'forties, Zukofsky kept close track of Williams' published works, responding quickly to them, monitoring Williams' progress and encouraging him constantly. For example, Williams' novel, *A Voyage to Pagany*, based upon his travels in Europe during 1924, was published on September 7, 1928. Zukofsky reviewed it, praising the intrinsically American spirit of the book, just one month later, on October 9. These were his first remarks in print on Williams.[13]

Zukofsky, Williams, Charles Reznikoff, and George Oppen created the Objectivist atmosphere of the 1930's—and then proceeded to operate within it, albeit hermetically. However, although it died down quickly, its members going their own ways to pursue diverging ideas on the poem, the Objectivist movement cannot be underestimated with respect to its adhesive workings on the shape of *The Wedge*, later on.

Zukofsky assembled a special Objectivist issue for *Poetry*, XXXVII.5, February 1931, and brought Williams into it: "The need is for the best in you—and to pick that one must start from a point of vantage."[14] He chose "The Botticellian Trees." Its sparse, clipped, two-line stanzas, and its musical conclusion appealed to his conviction that "the more precise the writing, the purer the poetry," and to his sense of the poem as "a context associated with musical shape."[15]

10. Williams to Zukofsky, July 12, 1928. *See* Neil Baldwin & Steven Meyers, *The Manuscripts and Letters of William Carlos Williams in the Poetry Collection, Lockwood Memorial Library, State University of New York at Buffalo: A Descriptive Catalogue* (G.K. Hall & Co., Boston, 1978), item no. F1181.
11. Pound to Williams, August 31, 1928. *Ibid.*, item no. F525.
12. Pound to Williams, November 22, 1931, in Louis Simpson, *Three on the Tower* (William Morrow & Co., N.Y., 1975), p. 70.
13. Zukofsky, "Beginning Again . . ." *op.cit.*
14. Zukofsky to Williams, September 26, 1929, *Descriptive Catalogue* item no. F756.
15. Zukofsky, " 'Recencies' . . ." p. 16.

In the poem, Williams synthesizes the shift of seasons: leaves renew after winter has passed and the potential for spring is imminent—to be displayed under the encompassing metaphor of the tree, itself a manifestation of language hidden from the poet. It is his duty to bring out the "alphabet of / the trees," the language built into the objects of the world around him, releasing thereby "the song . . . above the muffled words—."[16]

Objectivism was not all austerity and distance and phenomenology; Zukofsky may have chosen "The Botticellian Trees" for its organicism: "A poem as object—and yet certainly it arose in the veins and capillaries, if only in the intelligence."[17] Zukofsky's introduction to the *Poetry* issue was indeed direct and serious. But it also called for the *ideal* in poetry. In the "desire for what is objectively perfect, inextricably the direction of historic and contemporary particulars,"[18] objectivism acknowledged possibilities for perfection in the poem.

For the subsequent *An "Objectivists" Anthology*, which appeared in summer 1932, Zukofsky chose a broad group of poems by Williams, not reprinting "The Botticellian Trees," but including that poem which had first caught his eye, "The pure products of America . . ." with sixteen others. That same year, TO Publishers, also formed by the Objectivist group, brought out Williams' *A Novelette and Other Prose*. These books were followed soon after by *Collected Poems 1921-1931* (Objectivist Press, January 1934): "Louis Zukofsky did most of the work of making the collection," said Williams in an interview.[18a] "The pure products . . ." made another appearance in this volume.

II

During the late 'thirties, Zukofsky sent parts of *"A"-8* to Williams periodically, as their mutual critiques continued. One evening, Zukofsky heard Williams reading from his poetry over radio station WOR, and, with characteristic restraint, wrote him that "with a little more emphasis here and there on selection of material, contrast, rather than understatement" the broadcast would have been that much more effective.[19]

Williams respected that kind of deliberation, priding himself on being able to achieve it in his best moments, content in

16. Williams, *Collected Earlier Poems* (New Directions, N.Y., 1951), pp. 80-81.
17. Zukofsky, " 'Recencies' . . ." p. 15.
18. Zukofsky, *ibid.*, p. 14.
18a. Williams, *I Wanted to Write a Poem*, pp. 51-52.
19. Zukofsky to Williams, February 22, 1937, *Descriptive Catalogue* item no. F791.

later years to acknowledge it as the primary quality in Zukofsky's writing: "speech pared to its essentials, to the salient pertinences."[20]

Again, with characteristic vigilance, Zukofsky seized upon Williams' *The Complete Collected Poems*, published by New Directions in November 1938, with these quick comments in December: "What struck me especially at this time is not only yr eminent readableness which very few of us have, but the music—the total movement of each piece, as well as the detail . . . ."[21] That very ability which Williams had so admired in Zukofsky—to convey the "music" of the verse—he now assigned to his friend reciprocally. The drive toward "particulars" was also something they shared, Williams believing that only through such exactitude could the "universal" be revealed.

At the same time that Zukofsky was beginning to break into print with two collections of poetry, *First Half of "A"-9* (self-published, New York, 1940), and *55 Poems*, (James A. Decker, Prairie City, Illinois, 1941), Williams was drawing together his previously-uncollected poetry, "details," and improvisations, into two groups: the first unpublished (*Detail and Parody for the Poem Paterson*) and the second published (*The Broken Span*, New Directions, 1941).

Both collections were actually "build-ups" to *The Wedge*, and (less-obviously) Williams' way of hedging a commitment to more definitive work on the long poem *Paterson*, which had been preoccupying him since the 1920's. *Detail and Parody* was "separately arranged . . . for James Laughlin as a beginning on the *Paterson* poem in 1939 . . . . The reason I haven't gone on with *Paterson* is that I am not able to—as yet, if I ever shall be," he admitted in a note in the manuscript.[22] Many of the poems in *Detail and Parody* found their way into *The Wedge* manuscript by way of *The Broken Span*—a collection focussed upon works from 1939-1941. Poems such as "Sparrows Among Dry Leaves," "Raleigh Was Right," "The Last Turn," "To Ford Madox Ford in Heaven," and others are also in *The Wedge*. But Williams was far from satisfied. He spent his energies on collecting and "arranging" work that he felt should be seen by a broader audience, avoiding the *Paterson* drafts, amassed into long, discursive

---

20. Williams, "A New Line is a New Measure," review of Zukofsky's *Anew* (1946), in *The New Quarterly of Poetry*, II.2, Winter 1947-8.
21. Zukofsky to Williams, December 12, 1938, *Descriptive Catalogue* item no. F796.
22. Williams, *Detail and Parody* manuscript, item no. D4.

columns of verse with no discernible shape.[23]

He also managed to write a brief dramatic "dialogue" called *Under the Stars*, which tells us more about his developing relationship with Zukofsky.[24] The scene is the evening after the Battle of Monmouth in 1775. George Washington, the older general and statesman, and Lafayette, his young ally, share a blanket under a tree near their slumbering troops. Lafayette is trying to build up Washington's confidence in his abilities generally. There is a deep bond of comradeship between them, as Washington confesses, "What I need was what you've given me, better than sleep, peace of mind again . . . . Some instinct kept you at my side. I needed your support . . . ." But Lafayette cautions him to be "more reserved" in his speech.[25]

Williams gave this manuscript to Zukofsky to read and critique during his work on *The Wedge*. The parallels with the Washington/Lafayette configuration are obvious: Williams/Washinton depends upon Zukofsky/Lafayette to keep him going through the struggle for survival. The older man expresses his debt to the younger, who is by contrast more restrained in his words and emotions. So it is not surprising to see that Zukofsky places in "brackets" many of Washington's excessive, overtly-emotional statements. Williams then goes back to Zukofsky's pencilled emendations and crosses out each bracketed phrase in blue ink, definitively heeding each and every correction.

This relentless push toward economy—even in a written situation where life and art seem to mutually imitate each other—is demonstrated even more dramatically in *The Wedge* manuscript.

III

Williams began assembling work for what was to become *The Wedge* in 1938. He wanted it to be "A New Summary—Recent and other poems heretofore unpublished in book form."[26]

The manuscript he sent to Zukofsky for his perusal and commentary in March 1943 was a hefty 115-page typescript entitled, "The (lang) WEDGE": a diffuse pot-pourri of 83 titles, including poems going back to 1905 ("Acrostic for H.D."); stories; improvisations (experimental, free-associative prose-

23. Williams, *Paterson* manuscript, item no. E1.
24. Williams, Under the Stars, *University of Kansas City Review*, XI.1, Autumn 1944. *See* also manuscript, item no. B116.
25. Williams, *Ibid.*, manuscript, item no B116 (a), (b).
26. Williams, *The Wedge*, manuscript, item no. D6. All citations from MS transcripts follow.

pieces written during the 1920's); and "details" (verse dialogue-fragments abstracted from daily-life encounters).

Zukofsky's corrections and deletions throughout the manuscript are all in very light pencil, "so [they] can be erased," as he tactfully told Williams later. However, although the manner of his corrections is subtle, their intent is clear.

Zukofsky begins to cut immediately, with Williams' proposed epigraph for the book's title page:

The (lang) WEDGE
With the tip of my tongue
I wedge you open
My tongue!
the wedge of my tongue
between those lips parted
to inflame you . .

"The first three lines are enough," Zukofsky writes, bracketing the last three neatly in pencil. The idea is to avoid repetition—but perhaps, also, to defuse the sexuality of the passage in deference to absolute (literal) linguistics. In any case, Williams' sense of the aggressive powers of poetry comes through clearly enough in the word-play. He abandoned the entire poem, and it does not appear in the published volume, or anywhere else in print.

Redundancy falls prey to Zukofsky's keen eye in three subsequent poems, again, in understated but crucial ways. "Paterson: the Falls,"[27] which is a "plan" in ten stanzas for the structure of the long poem, begins, in manuscript:

What common language, [what] to unravel?

a line which surfaces again in *Paterson I.*[28] Zukofsky has bracketed as shown above, and writes, "Dont repeat yrself" in the margin. The published version of the line respects his comment. One word can upset the delicate ecology of the poem. Williams was a much more *insistent* writer than Zukofsky, who shows how the line could have been pushed too far.

Thus, "Writer's Prologue to a Play in Verse," (pp. 13-15) is footnoted: "The verse is excellent. But I think it would gain if the ideas it presents were not frequently repetitious." Notice the praise comes first, to make certain that a measure of respect is preserved. Then the advocacy of economy as positive—"it would *gain*"—the ideas would be displayed to their best advantage if the

---

27. Williams, *Collected Later Poems* (New Directions, N.Y., 1963), p. 10. Page references to this edition cited in the text of essay for comparison with MS versions.
28. Williams, *Paterson* (New Directions, N.Y., 1963), p. 15.

excess were cut away. A close comparison of the manuscript with the published version shows that Williams observed all deletions.

Zukofsky's attention to the minutiae of poetic construction can be seen in his approach to the longer poem, "Burning the Christmas Greens," (pp. 16-18) which he calls "a little ornate, albeit Shakespearian." Near its conclusion is the passage:

> . . . ash and flame and we, in
> that instant, lost [!]

and Zukofsky's comment, "comma would be enough." The admonition to temper excess, even typographically, accepted into the poem as changed, makes for a smoother transition into the last stanza:

> . . . lost,
>
> breathless to be witnesses . . .

and a "breath" is indeed taken there, to bridge the space between lines.

Zukofsky is in tune with Williams' unique metaphor-system. In the manuscript, the last line of "The Cure," (p. 23) reads:

> and opened fragile to my hand

Zukofsky suggests changing "fragile," but offers no specific replacement. It becomes, more characteristically,

> and opened flower-like to my hand

in the final version of the poem.

Turning to "Three Sonnets," (pp. 30-31), we find a somewhat unwieldy opening stanza, words bracketed by Zukofsky:

> I
> As the eye lifts, the field
> is moving—the river [ruled
> by an ungovernable determinant,]
> slowly between the stones . . .

And at the beginning of the second sonnet, he points out a similarly elaborate moment:

> II
> The silent and snowy mountains
> do not change their [hieroglyphs
> of] poise—

In both instances, Zukofsky wants to allow the "thing itself" to proceed on its own terms, free of any superimpositions.

The original version of "Figueras Castle," (p. 35) possesses a revealing conclusion, which Zukofsky prefers to suppress:

[Rhyme that
up right for us, will yuh
Williams, ol' keed?]

Here the poet is unable to keep traces of bitterness to himself—
which goes back to early passages of *Spring & All*, in which Williams disdainfully imitated the disparaging remarks of those who
did not understand his poetics of non-rhyme and non-rhythm;
how could this be poetry?[29] The implication in "Figueras Castle"
is poet-as-standardizer: bring everything into resolution. The stanza is omitted from subsequent versions.

   "Perfection," (p. 40) is quintessential Williams:

          O lovely apple!
   beautifully and completely
          rotten,
   hardly a contour marred—

          perhaps a little
   shrivelled at the top but that
          aside perfect
   in every detail! O lovely

          apple! what a
   deep and suffusing brown
          mantles that
   unspoiled surface! No one

          has moved you
   since I placed you on the porch
          rail a month ago
   to ripen. No one. No one!

Zukofsky notes, "If the last 4 lines mean the perfect rottenness
of one's isolation—I wonder if the last 5 lines arranged as follows
wouldn't make the sense clearer:

          has moved you
   since I placed you on the porch
          rail a month ago
   to ripen.

          No one. No one!

And he notes in the right margin between "ripen" and last line:
"Space as between other stanzas." The thing, partly in nature,
partly domesticated, left to its own devices, is undisturbed—admired not only for inherent properties but even more for what
it *becomes* in the world. Its original "use" transcended, it is

---

29. Williams, *Spring & All, op. cit.,* pp. 1-2.

metamorphosed by the infinitely-adaptable poet into a focal-point for praise.

Zukofsky's empathetic footnote reminds us of his *own* keen sense of isolation at this point, removed—by his insistence on a certain poetics—from prevailing trends. As so often earlier, the "opening of the field," (to use Robert Duncan's term, himself aware of affinities with Zukofsky) accomplishes the desired dramatic space. The penultimate line then falls short, marring the symmetry of the three preceding stanzas, moving the very subject of "perfection" into a more organic context, because the poem's perfection is likewise disturbed.

By dropping those four words down, Zukofsky demonstrates the eloquence of space as silence. He could advocate equally a more fully-realized approach, as in "The Last Turn," (p. 44) where Williams catches a fragmentary event glimpsed (as was so much of the world for him) from his car stopped "behind a red light / at 53d and 8th": a woman hit by a car. Her body is mutilated by passing traffic, and she becomes an abstract chaos of colors and shapes. In manuscript, the poem concludes by acknowledging

> the genius of a world,
> artless but supreme

in which such transformations occur constantly. But Zukofsky feels that "the last line doesn't seem inevitable enough," taking a larger view of the situation presented. Williams then inserts a line bringing his presence into conflict with what has occurred:

> . . . the genius of a world,
> against which rages the fury of
> our concepts, artless but supreme

The man and his universe of perceptions are fused.

Zukofsky leaves the actual *text* of "Raleigh Was Right" (p. 52) alone. But he takes issue with line-breaks and what they represent. "I think if you would realign this so that the lines end on the spoken cadence rather than a metrical one, the really new meter of speech *in it* would be shown off better." This addresses one of Williams' central concerns, that the poem be an "elevation" of everyday spoken language, a fine but discernible boundary between speech and artifice being maintained. As do many of Zukofsky's criticisms, the statement contains praise: the poem is seen as "new," a quality they both pursued, had difficulty defining, yet could recognize immediately. Williams saw it when he praised Zukofsky's poems several years later as, "a crevice, letting in the light—but it is *the light*!"[30]

The matter of isolation occurs again in "Another Year," (p. 56) where Williams begins by addressing the reader directly, and attempts to develop a mutual experience by inviting him in:

[Come walk with me] in the rose-garden
in the park

Zukofsky disagrees with those first four words: " 'Come walk with me' does not seem to be the *theme* of that composition." The poet has to risk "fierce singleness'; let an undeniable thread of solitude run through it. If his record of what happens can then be of significance to others, so much the better.

"There is some of your finest writing here embedded in a discursive form which still doesn't form a setting . . . ," Zukofsky writes in a comment on the poem, "History," dating to 1917. "I don't know exactly where [it] would fit into this arrangement . . . ." He felt much the same about eleven other poems, which he categorically advised Williams to omit for much the same reason: they simply did not conform to the overview he had in mind. He also advised Williams to "type out as verse" the nine experimental prose "improvisations." Otherwise, Zukofsky seems at a loss to understand why they would belong in the collection.

IV

Zukofsky returned the manuscript to Williams on April 6, 1943, with a covering note:

Dear Bill,
    Here y'are! Don't accept the detailed criticism in the manuscript unless it verifies your own misgivings, doubts etc. I've written in the MS. lightly so it can be erased & you can still use the copy.
    There's a big book in it (in size and more) & if you mean it as summary, there's no reason why it shouldn't be an *inclusive* collection. As that, it arranges itself in my mind in an order along the lines outlined on the attached sheet. If you prefer to be more serious about the title, perhaps you might call it (simply) *The Language*. In any case, it's your summary of what you've done with, & to, it over some time—or in your life . . . .

What began as The (lang) WEDGE, an amorphous, retrospective wide-ranging collection of 115 pages and 83 titles, was now (more simply) trimmed to *The Language*: 86 pages, 69 titles, in four

---

30. Williams, "A New Line . . ." *op. cit.*

sections arranged by Zukofsky.[31]

More changes were quickly to come. First, on May 11, Williams "cut the prose bits entirely,"[32] no doubt reading between the lines of Zukofsky's hesitant remarks. This reduced the manuscript further, by seven titles. Over the course of the next several months, he cut 17 more poems, and added five new ones which Zukofsky had not previously seen: "To All Gentleness," "These Purists," "A Plea for Mercy," "The Monstrous Marriage," and "The Clouds." The first four poems were all written in 1943. "The Clouds" began in 1918 (it touches upon the death of Williams' father at Christmas of that year), and continued with expansion and revision in 1943. Mathematics concluded, the final manuscript stood at an even 50 poems, all of them written and/ or published in periodicals between 1938-1943.

The focus had been achieved, as we have seen, sometimes by Zukofsky's marginal admonitions ("chisel down," "don't repeat yrself," "wordy," "confused metaphors," "is the cadence there?"); and at other times by his piercingly-subtle, astute, miniature critiques, sincerely and judiciously applied. Poetry was indeed, as Pound had said, "compression." Zukofsky stood by his similar belief that "Condensed speech is most of the method of poetry."[33]

All was apparently in readiness. Publication seemed inevitable. However, both Simon & Schuster (which Williams approached first) and New Directions were suffering from the same wartime syndrome: a paper shortage. "I have a new book of poems . . ." Williams wrote, with a mixture of pride and impatience, "but try as I may all I get from the publishing house is, Sorry, no paper."[34]

Williams composed an "Introduction" for his book, first presented as a speech at the New York Public Library on October 26, 1943, in which he complained further: "Who isn't frustrated and does not prove it by his actions—if you want to say so?"[35]

Finally, toward the end of that long year, he found "two

31. Williams, *Wedge* MS, item D6 (c) 1.
32. Williams to Zukofsky, May 11, 1943, in Emily Mitchell Wallace, *A Bibliography of William Carlos Williams*, (Wesleyan University Press, Middletown, 1968), p. 54.
33. Louis Zukofsky, "A Statement for Poetry" (1950), in *The Poetics of the New American Poetry*, ed. Donald M. Allen and Warren Tallman, (Evergreen, Grove Press, N.Y., 1973), p. 143.
34. Williams, "Paper Shortage, Poets, and Postal Rates," in *The New Republic*, CIX.8, August 23, 1943.
35. Williams, "Author's Introduction to *The Wedge*," in *Selected Essays*, (New Directions, N.Y., 1954), p. 255.

young men, . . . associates of the Cummington Press"[36] in Massachusetts, who "were interested in publishing small volumes of poetry . . . . They manned their own press . . . and they decided to do the book for [him]."[37] *The Wedge* was printed from hand-set type during August 1944, and was finally published in a limited edition of 380 hard-bound copies on September 27, 1944, dedicated, appropriately enough, to "L.Z."

V

Williams' remarks in his "Author's Introduction" resonate well with Zukofsky's *Objectivist Anthology* essay. Where Zukofsky referred to "the components of the poetic object,"[38] Willaims insists upon his "machine made of words," going so far as to say that "there can be no part, as in any other machine, that is redundant." The poem must be "pruned to a perfect economy."[39] Zukofsky's reading of the manuscript for the book certainly reinforces this austere view.

The Wedge can be seen as a threshold work, opening the way for Williams to *Paterson I* (published in 1946); perhaps a "wedge" was needed to be driven into the momentarily-stalled epic poem, before it could progress. The "war" that Williams refers to in the introduction may also have been his inner struggle with the materials—one which Zukofsky helped him win. A sense of defiance pervades the book, in such aggressively-lyrical poems as "The Cure," and "To All Gentleness," where he refers to "that gentleness which harbors all violence" (p. 29).

"This book is brilliant through an overall consciousness of its own warmth, its own despairs, its own indifferences to anything but its own excellence in the writing."[40] Williams had briefly reviewed the *Objectivists Anthology*[41] and *55 Poems*[42] upon publication;· however, he went to much greater lengths in the *New Quarterly of Poetry* of Winter 1947-48, conferring high praise upon Zukofsky when *Anew* appeared in 1946: "Zukofsky has asserted the bare possibility of anything's being a poem—

---

36. Williams, *Autobiography* (New Directions, N.Y., 1967), p. 306.
37. Williams, *I Wanted to Write a Poem*, pp. 70-71.
38. Zukofsky, " 'Recencies' . . ." p. 20.
39. Williams, "Author's Introduction . . ." *op. cit.*, p. 256.
40. Williams, "A New Line . . . ."
41. Williams, "Review of '*An "Objectivists" Anthology*' " in *The Symposium*, IV.1, January 1933, pp. 114-116.
42. Williams, "An Extraordinary Sensitivity," review, in *Poetry*, LX.6, September 1942, pp. 338-340.

today. (In today's terms.)"[43] Williams appreciated the pacing, control, and exactitude of Zukofsky's poetry, singling out "42" in particular as an example of Zukofsky's gift for distillation and sparseness.

Just as Zukofsky had shown consistent respect for the textual integrity of Williams' poems in *The Wedge* manuscript, Williams reciprocated by looking at Zukofsky's poems "objectively," in the sense that they were "sincerely" integral unto themselves, "compressed with feeling."[44] In *"A"-17* (1963), Zukofsky remembered Williams' praise:

> You three:—
>   Poem 42 from *Anew*
> ". . . this poem, all Z's art, that is to say,
> his life . . ."
>   W[45]

Concluding his laudatory summary of *Anew*, Williams becomes proudly paternal toward Zukofsky, as if the younger man—first by giving firm yet deferential critical assistance, then by coming forth with a fully-fleshed manifestation of his own talents—had passed through a rite of passage, emerging successfully and stylistically mature: "Suffice it to say that I have accepted these lyrics of Zukofsky as adult, a development, and an accomplishment."[46]

---

43. Williams, "A New Line . . . ."
44. Williams, *ibid*.
45. Louis Zukofsky, *"A"* (University of California Press, Berkeley, 1978), p. 380.
46. Williams, *op. cit.*

THE POET

L.Z., Bellajio, Italy, Dec., 1972

LOUIS ZUKOFSKY

DISCARDED POEMS

Preamble

*While conversing recently, Hugh Kenner, in a characteristic ges-
ture, took his pipe out of his mouth and said: "One of the interesting things about Louis is that he came to complete maturity
in poetry so quickly and so young." Kenner suggests that by the
time he was twenty-four, he had almost perfected his art, and by
the time he was twenty-six, the rest of his life's work had been
roughly laid out. Thus these poems, which he discarded from his
canon because they fell below his exacting standards, are published here for comparison purposes only. The poems are published by the kind permission of Celia Zukofsky and the Humanities Research Center, the University of Texas at Austin,
which provided Xerox copies of the texts.*

*The first poem is in typescript except for the title which is
written in ink in parenthesis above a canceled one word former
title which is not now readable so that the title now is "(The Master Aristippus)." One line in the poem has been partly re-written
in ink so that we now have over a deleted phrase: "the skies which
bent over." A 4-line stanza following "Regretted his work?" has
been deleted in ink. A word following "He" is deleted from each
of two lines in the three line stanza which now reads: "He did
this/ For love, my friend?/ He did this for love?—" The excised
word cannot be read. Just before the last two lines in the poem,
the word "Damn!" is written over an unreadable deleted word so
that the line reads: "Damn! I,".*

*The remaining poems except for the final translations are
ink transcripts in Zukofsky's hand. The first eight have never been
published and all date around 1923. The next one called "(Collaboration)" is a collaboration. It is dated May 10, 1932. Zuk's note
says: 'lines 1-8 J[erry] Reisman. line 3 "leaving"–G[eorge] Oppen. line 9–L.Z.' The poem called "The Gathering" has a note*

which says "Used Arise." All of the lines, except for the last two
of the next to the last stanza, are used at various places in the play,
either separately or two lines together. They are also used in "A,"
pp. 748, 749, 750, 751, 758, 759. The last two poems are in type-
script. They are translations of Alain Bosquet done in 1943, while
they were living at 202 Columbia Hghts in Brooklyn, and dis-
carded some years later.

(The Master Aristippus)

What shall I do for money, my friend,
What shall
I do for money?

The master Aristippus
Owned but one silver mina,
And kept it a curio —
As women keep their china.

But I, what shall I
Do for money, my friend,
What shall I do for money? —

What did he do for land, my friend,
What did
He do for land?

He left the Cyclados
And settled in Cyrene;
He had enough space all his life
To save him from being spleeny.

But I, what shall I
Do for land, my friend,
What shall I do for land? —

What did he do for housing, my friend,
What did
He do for housing?

He built a hut and sowed
His garden to the river;
When the roof of his hut became too low
He trusted the skies which bent over.

But I, what shall I
Do for housing, my friend,
What shall I do for housing? —

Where could he bring his friends, my friend,
Where could
He bring his friends?

They dined at the foot of his door
And splendidly they talked;
And by the river the sun fell
On the hematito whenever they walked.

But I, where can I
Bring my friends, my friend,
Where can I bring my friends? —

What did he do for love, my friend,
What did
He do for love? —

He said pleasure is Good, my friend,
And Virtue is the norm;
And sometimes went to Athens
For a particular form.

He did this
For love, my friend?
He did this for love? —

And had he time to read his books, my friend,
And had
He time to read his books?

The master Aristippus
Said, we never have time
To read all we want
And lived with Homer all his prime.

But I, where shall I
Find time to read my books, my friend,
Where shall I find time? —

Aristippus never regretted his work, my friend?
Never
Regretted his work?

Sometimes, you know, I think
I might have written music, my friend,
Sometimes I think I might have written music, you know. —

Aristippus never regretted his life, my friend?
Never
Regretted his life?

He did for a while, but after
Forgot his regrets in living;
He said, he never has anything
Who lives on misgiving.

Damn! I,
Am an exceptional case, my friend,
I am an exceptional case!

Sept. 19, 1923

[*Untitled*]

Seeing, the eyes
Grow black with dancing.
Hearing, the heart
Beats lost upon the ribs,
Graced, the eyes
Grow black with dancing.
The antic ends.

1923?

[*Untitled*]

Graced — graced,
Deathward are we dancing,
Graced — graced,
Deathward are we dancing,
Graced — graced,
Deathward are we dancing,
Astral — flame

Night
Ravishes the valleys.
Night
Stalks above the gullies.
Night
Shadows all the waters,
The astral downs.

[*Untitled*]

And they rest: the manifold light rays —

Misty my elbows press in the shore grass:
In dew, in thru blades risen before me,
My eyes look into night:

And they take in breakers in moonlight —
Moonlight white in the breakers —

The same which is said to deflect to the source of
    its coming —
(after an age it is found the light of our sphere
                          travels finite,
The boundaries of our dawn are finite) —

And they glance far out, down the shore line,
The changing furrows; —

Purling, as from wells near
    households mornings —

        Bird not only for me I feel
        Beginning to fly speckling the ocean —

The sea near, falling, crickets single.

                Long Beach
                June 15-16, 1925

[*Untitled*]

The people change and the birds in the air,
And the air itself. In the town
None stirs till real summer is there;
We pass it, we feel a way down
Broken asphalt to cold floods on the sand.

Long Beach
May 25, 1924

[*Untitled*]

The movements of clouds have not a mind's precision
But the infinitude of things that last
Awhile and go as wind, or music passed
Into transient being by the chance collision
Of winds among poised leaves.

Yet the mind can be mutual with clouds —
Even as it can build on an earth of shifting
Nature, — trace feelings in their still drifting
Of changing light and texture — sad or elate,
And when they sweep out gravely.

May 3, 1923

Song 11

And the least see
your ministry

and the least sea
beside me

S.F., Calif.
May 27, 1932

[*Untitled*]

"whose life has been a broken arch."
H[enry] A[dams]

Their shapely throats breathe as of song!

Stay where the casement suns unapproachably
high,
See where over its aerial arch
trees appear.

Force sleeps in motionless space,
And space, to thought, lights.
Shut the eyes,
the heart has grace.

No hurt comes here, as blind derision:
Only the sense of children, who once touched
hearts
With their living divinity, attaining
Still forms perfected in vision.

Nov. 22, 1923

(Devotions)

Would what oppresses a night
Should go with a night,
And a heart that vexes till day
Accept the day.
As reaches of lowly earth
A sunbeam comes to survey:

And that which plots in the dark
Should hide with the dark, —
As a horse that crops and is blind
It reaches a wall, is blind —
Then step thru the dawn like the steed
Lifting its host who is kind.

Dec. 23, 1923

(Collaboration)

The water lifted me
in daylight

leaving my
ears

but your
breath

your fingers touch
an eyelash

even the water is dry now

> (lines 1-8 J. Reisman)
> (line 3 "leaving" — G. Oppen)
> line 9 — L.Z.
>
> *May 10, 1932*

The Gathering
(Guillaume Apollinaire)

We came to the garden aflower for the gathering.
Beautiful, do you know how many tea-roses, fling
Flower pale, with love, as towards your head in a ring
        Petals after the spring?

Their stems bend to the great wind which rises.
The petals of rose are a ruin in the way.
O beautiful, gather them, — flowering of surmises
        Fades after today.

Put them in a cup — when each gate closes —
Zest lost and cruel, reflect what days consume —
We will see the amorous agony, the roses'
        Fences of perfume.

An expansive garden is nipped, my egotist,
Day's butterflies have fled to other flowers,
Henceforth remains only the garden's night-mist,
        Butterflies of its hours.

The flowers are doomed for the rooms — unholy.
Our roses each by each strip of their grief.
Beautiful, sob . . . Each pale corolla
        Is love's brief.

Nov., 1931

Belly Lox Shnooks Oaky

Belly Lox Shnooks Oaky
Went for a walk with a stokey
They were so doped
They could not have hoped
But to sink down to poke-pokey.

1088 E. 180 St.
N.Y.C.
April 7, 1941

Conversation

No road!
— No.
Idiot!
— What difference does it make!

1088 E. 180 St.
N. Y. C.
April 28, 1941
(Orig. 1/1/41)

TWO POEMS
[Translated from Alain Bosquet]

To Begin Again With Your Body
(From "Recommencer Avec Ton Corps")

By degrees foundered seeing ourselves lonely
Like books too subtle and dusty,
We will grow thirsty for a magnanimous prayer,
And our sick forehead at last will own
Its harmony, that sidereal panther
On the point of recoil, and then, quite gently
Its equipoise, that other more rigorous cat
That scents music about our fever.
Then, in this new trial of eternity,
How merciful and how prophetic we shall become!
A shock will be enough to create our speech,
And the words "good morning" or "good night"
                    will make us
Guilty of feeling or joyous being moved
Like rain transformed into a cathedral.
All will be clear to our fool's impenitence,
We shall go on to discover the starry sceptre,
The crown of the birds, the purple of stinginess,
And, from appearance to appearance, we shall
                    reach
The dazzling conquest of our grave sorrows.
Then I shall recall our frantic body
— That magician reduced to submissiveness —
So that the verb "see" be sweet under our
                    eyelids,
So that our fingers touch our viny hands,
So that your breasts cause my warm lips to die,
So that your fear invent that unique pitching,
So that in the evening — our seeds soldering
                    our shape —

We know how to find again, in a gesture more
                    simple
Than decency or divine lassitude,
A daily promise of life
And so that at last, alas! despite our endow-
                    ments
We cry in the dawn — yes, cry! — to be
So tenderly a bit of comprehensible flesh!

                                        February 2, 1943

To Go On
(From "L'Image Impardonnable")

The south will be in our shoulders,
let us rejoin it so that it will dazzle us
and give us the world to find again.
There the earth is naturally warm,
with its believing hands, its patient ways,
and its uneasiness of old standing dew
that one names a height or a hanging.
Don't show your fear of the grand tour:
nothing is more sweet, more close
than the antelope that looks for a smile.
Blue will be the natural and calm
order to our bodies of the moment.
Some words, some miraculous phrases
will fill our laughing sails,
and to turn pale, dear insensible wound,
to turn pale will be a thing so fresh
                    in its train
of flaming crystals and anemones!
Be still, don't speak to me before drinking
some mouthfuls of poisonous seasons,
meditate in those quiet shawls
that will unroll you under the tempest,
then seize me sweetly with your breath
like the friend who cannot conjure
false departures or uncertain love.

                                        1943

DON BYRD

THE SHAPE OF ZUKOFSKY'S CANON

> —Our world will not stand it,
> the implications of a too regular form.
>
> "Mantis," An Interpretation

I

Much can be said for close examination, of course, but large things must be seen from some distance if we are to have a sense of their shape and size. Some of Louis Zukofsky's poems escape from unrelieved detail because the city is seen from an upper-story apartment window.

In my effort to propose a view of Zukofsky's canon, I have the precedent of Zukofsky's himself in *Bottom: On Shakespeare:* "It is simpler," he writes, "to consider the forty-four items of the canon [Shakespeare's] as one work, sometimes poor, sometimes good, sometimes great, always regardless of the time in which it was composed, and so despite defects of quality, durable as one thing from 'itself never turning,' so growth is organic to decay and vice versa."[1] In the space I have I can only make some assertions about such a large, complex, and largely unstudied canon as Zukofsky's. So I will make my two assertions forthwith and then try to make them plausible or at least comprehensible.

1) Zukofsky's work proposes a unique and useful approach to the central formal problem of the twentieth century, a problem so pervasive that several possible formulations suggest themselves. Pound's terms are probably most familiar to readers of *Paideuma.*

---

1. (Austin, 1963), 13. Hereafter, Zukofsky's works are cited in the text with a short title. In the few cases where a work has appeared in more than one edition, I have used the most recent.

"An 'Image,'" Pound tells us, "is that which presents an intellectual and emotional complex in an instant of time."[2] Elsewhere, he says that Dante's *Commedia* is one immense image. The difficulty we face comes when we try to map the fragmentary images—Pound's "apparitions of faces in a crowd" or Williams' "red wheel barrow/ glazed with rain/ water"—onto the universal image. Pound's juxtaposed images of Odysseus, Dionysos, Sigismundo Malatesta, Confucius, and so forth do propose currents of coherence, which the careful reader can follow, but not closure. The evidence of *The Cantos* seems to suggest that the poem articulates an order which perpetuates itself. Ultimately we learn from it that experience is unfinished (unfinishable?). It was only Pound's life-long habit of reading experience in terms of archetypes which led him to expect his design to arrive at equilibrium. Similarly, in *Paterson,* "To make a start,/ out of particulars/ and make them general, rolling/ up the sum" leads only to continual addition, leaving a snarl of fragments, written and unwritten, to be accounted for.

It is not solely an aesthetic problem. In other contexts, it can be seen as alienation or lack of cultural coherence.

2) The Zukofsky canon is a single work, no part of which can be fully understood without reference to the whole.

All: The Collected Shorter Poems begins with the assertion of a definitive order, with "Poem beginning "The."" "The," here, is the definite article of what can be called perhaps, taking a cue from Eliot, the impersonal lyric. Such a poem seeks to find unified structures in experience, structures imposed *by* experience, not the personality. It is a motive which unites Imagism, Objectivism, and Eliot's search for the objective correlative. Although "Poem beginning "The"" is a travesty of Eliot's and Pound's insistence upon *the* tradition, Zukofsky also recognizes that cultural order is necessarily one context of all and *All*. Against the multiple voices and the tentative musical organization of "Poem beginning 'The,'" he poses in the first of "29 Poems" the theoretical and practical clarity of Lenin. These two possibilities, as premises of the volume, nearly cancel one another out, and Zukofsky finds himself near ground zero: "Not much more than being,/ thoughts of isolate, beautiful/ Being at evening." The remainder of *All* is an effort to trace a way through the immediate and local to an inclusive vision from a single point of view. The book is not a miscel-

---

2. "A Retrospect," in *Literary Essays of Ezra Pound,* ed. T. S. Eliot (New York, 1968), 4.

lany, a mere collection of pieces which do not fit elsewhere in the design, but a carefully organized—even carefully argued—poem which is nonetheless fragmentary. The book ends with the section, "After I's," a term which can be taken in one sense of the complex pun as a translation of "metaphysics." In section five of "The Old Poet Moves to a New Apartment 14 Times," Zukofsky offers some measure of how far he has come: "After all—/ *nothing*/ interests me/ when it is full of being." The volume ends, however, with a frank admission that it is not, in fact, all:

> There is
> a heart
>
> has no
> complaint
>
> better a-
> part
>
> than
> faint
>
> so the
> faintest
>
> part of
> it
>
> has no
> complaint
>
> a
> part.

"A," Bottom: On Shakespeare, and *Catullus* are the ABC of another order which arises from the fragmented whole. These three works, taken together, are a critique of and are critiqued by *All. All* is an inquiry into the dialectical nature of objectivity; *"A," Bottom*, and *Catullus* are inquiries into the dialectics of intersubjectivity. Tentatively, and to avoid temporarily matters which could become very complex, I will suggest these three books are related to one another after the order of three principles which Charles Sanders Peirce calls simply, First, Second, and Third:

> First is the conception of being or existing independent of anything else. Second is the conception of being relative to, the conception of reaction with, something else. Third is the conception of mediation, whereby a first and second are brought into relation. . . . In psychology Feeling is First, Sense of reaction Second, General conception Third, or mediation. In Biology, the idea of arbitrary sporting is First, heredity is Second, the process whereby the accidental characters become fixed is Third. Chance

is First, Law is Second, the tendency to take habits is Third.
Mind is First, Matter is Second, Evolution is Third.[3]

Peirce—in whom Zukofsky takes interest on more than one occasion—tells us that these terms can be derived from Hegel. They
are obviously first-cousins to more unwieldy terms which could be
derived from Marx. In Zukofsky, intersubjectivity is First; mastery
of the other is Second; immersion in the other is Third. *"A,"Bottom*, and *Catullus* represent the intensive or analytic dimension
of impersonality against the extensive dimension of *All*, in which
simultaneity is the rule.

II

O head, think, how climbing you would be.

"A"-5

In 1930, Zukofsky, reviewing the poetry of the previous
decades, offered some insights which criticism is only now beginning to incorporate. For the lack of them, we have failed for almost fifty years to distinguish clearly between the poetry which is,
as Zukofsky says, in the direction—"and so good for the next age
and the next"—and the poetry which is a sentimental glance in
the mirror of decorous complacency. It is small wonder that
poetry is so little valued.

Whatever happened in the latter-half of the nineteenth century and first flowered in the second and third decades of the
twentieth, *still* inhabits the cultural arena tentatively, and we
still do not know much about it. In his preface to *The American*,
Henry James writes, "The balloon of experience is in fact, of
course, tied to the earth, and under that necessity we swing,
thanks to a rope of remarkable length, in the more or less com-
modious car of the imagination." And he goes on to say, "The
art of the romancer is 'for the fun of it,' insidiously to cut the
cable, to cut it without our detecting him."[4] As a matter of fact,
most art before the middle of the nineteenth century—much of it
still—is romance in precisely this sense. Since James, since Melville,
since Whitman, a few writers have found themselves climbing
down the rope to question its condition and the location of its
anchor. All of the evidence we have collected indicates that the
modern vision is staked in a point of perpetual crisis. No single
imaginative act can contain all of the complexities and contradictions which rise from the ground. Thinking of the life of

---

3. "The Architecture of Theories," in *Philosophical Writings of Peirce*, ed. Justus Buchler
(New York, 1955), 322-23.
4. *The Art of the Novel: Critical Prefaces* (New York, 1934), 33-34.

Henry Adams, and the contradictions to which it bore witness, Zukofsky quotes this passage from *The Life of George Cabot Lodge*: "In the last half of the nineteenth century, the poet became everywhere a rebel against his surroundings. What had been begun by Wordsworth, Byron and Shelley, was carried on by Algernon Swinburne in London or Paul Verlaine in Paris or Walt Whitman in Washington, by a common instinct of revolt" [*Prepositions*, 121].

Zukofsky does not give a resounding formulation of how the nineteenth-century instinct of revolt produced in this century a poetry of perpetual crisis, but in 1930, he was very early, and what he does say is clear enough. He speaks of "Joyce's sense of simultaneity" and its opposite in "the work of Gertrude Stein in its analytical aspects" [*Prepositions*, 129]. Although he never focuses on this distinction, it informs the entire essay, and, through it, he invokes a dialectic which continues to hold sway not only in the best of our poetry but in the culture at large. He manages to clarify his point a good deal by contrasting the "modern" situation to the one which it replaces: "The diction which is dead today is that of poets who, as someone said of Matthew Arnold, have put on the singing robes to lose themselves in the universal" [*Prepositions*, 139]. These insights are the germ of a poetic under the full burden of dialectical thought, and, as far as I am aware, the only one which does not defeat itself with either confusion or simple-minded ideology.

Not until Zukofsky's canon was more or less complete could we begin to see how thoroughly modern poetry and modern criticism have a common origin in the romantic questioning of knowledge, and the crisis which arose from the Hegelian recognition that knowledge cannot be grounded in a critique of knowledge. In *The Phenomenology of Mind*, Hegel demonstrates that knowledge which has its origins in epistemology can never overcome the doubt that motivates its first question.[5] Knowledge, if there is to be any, must take knowledge itself as its basis: ". . . just because consciousness has, in general, knowledge of an object," Hegel writes, "there is already present the distinction that the inherent nature, what the object is in itself, is one thing to consciousness, while knowledge, or the being of the object *for* consciousness, is another moment."[6] The first object and our knowing it always implies that there is more. The first conception always encounters the remainder, the object in its aspects

---

5. Zukofsky addresses himself to a similar critique of epistemology in *Bottom*. It might be called *The Phenomenology of the Eye*.
6. Trans. J.B. Baillie (New York, 1967), 4.

to which the first conception is inadequate. Dialectical thought discovers the non-identity in every identity. In the *Aesthetik*, Hegel describes the disappearance of the epic world in which life is the practice of forms thoroughly integrated with themselves. In the "world of prose" which follows the epoch of poetry, he writes:

> . . . the individual is no longer able to maintain that appearance of autonomous and complete vitality and freedom which is the very foundation of the notion of beauty. It is true that neither system nor a totality of activities are lacking in the immediate human reality and in the undertakings and institutions of the latter; yet that whole is but an aggregate of individualities, its occupations and activities are split and fragmented into innumerable parts, so that only tiny particles of the whole fall to various individuals.[7]

In this tightly limited condition, the critic's task is to arouse consciousness to fuller experience of its objects and reveal their untruth, their limitations as concepts, the ways in which our world disallows too regular forms. The poet, on the other hand, traditionally denies the fundamental distinction, and, if he cannot demonstrate the identity of appearance and essence, he undertakes to create the illusion.

The antagonism between poets and critics, then, is understandable. It is not lessened by the fact that so many of our poets have possessed fine critical intelligences. This internal conflict, intense ever since the time of Coleridge, accounts for many of the salient features of our poetry: its largely fragmentary condition, its rambunctious power, its frequent desperation. It also accounts for one of the two primary poetic undertakings of the past nearly two centuries: to write a poem about which nothing can or need be said, a poem so fully articulated that the gap between literary creations and *the* Creation closes, a poem which leaves the critical intelligence no toe-hold. As a poetic strategy, it can be traced almost from the beginnings of the romantic movement. It is a possibility which troubles Coleridge throughout *Biographia Literaria*, it is clearly implied in Keats's letter on negative capability, it leads Shelley to claim that poetry is "at once the center and circumference of knowledge." The romantics, however, stay within the idealistic and subjective moment of the dialectic and, so, arrive with Mallarmé at the book as the only object which can be retrieved from alienation.

---

7. Quoted in Frederick Jameson, *Marxism and Form: Twentieth—Century Dialectical Theories of Literature* (Princeton, 1971), 353.

The idealistic destruction of the other, however, manages to control the devastating effects of alienation only by annihilating life, an option which seems, to say the least, extreme. If one primary undertaking of poetry has been to silence criticism by perfection of form, the other has been to silence it by all inclusiveness. The second movement of the modern dialectic can be shown, I believe, to have its literary roots in *Leaves of Grass*—in which subjectivism becomes so thoroughgoing as to burst its bounds—and in *Moby Dick*, but that would require lengthy argument for which I have no space. Suffice it to say, there were emerging literary means equal to the Marxist critique of Hegelian idealism. In *The German Ideology*, Marx and Engels write: "In direct contrast to German philosophy, which descends from heaven to earth, here we ascend from earth to heaven. That is to say, we do not set out from what men say, imagine, conceive, nor from men as narrated, thought of, imagined, conceived, in order to arrive at men in the flesh. . . . Life is not determined by consciousness, but consciousness by life."[8] Thereafter, the critic could not longer content himself by questioning the objects of consciousness; his task was to carry criticism into practice, not merely to interpret the world but to change it. Likewise, the poet could no longer be satisfied with an ideal reconciliation of appearance and essence, rather he demanded a renewed material world to which he could give evidence. The epic possibility was not something irreparably lost but something to be created in the present. Whatever political changes have been rung on the theme, such are grounds from which imagism, objectivism, and the related poetics grew.

After the futility of aestheticism became apparent, after the revolution failed to materialize in the West, after Futurism was suppressed precisely because it would become an index of the failure of the Marxist promise in Russia, it was the task of the poets to criticize poetry itself. In a superb essay, "Modernism and Post-modernism: Approaching the Present in American Poetry," David Antin traces the series of wrong turns which were made in the attempts to satisfy that task and the resultant trivialization of the moral space which poetry occupied.[9] In place of the poem which is motivated by the tensions which Zukofsky located between Joyce and Stein, the New Critics offered a poem which gives with one hand and ironically takes away with the other.

---

8. In *Marx and Engels: Basic Writings on Politics and Philosophy*, ed. Lewis S. Feuer (Garden City, N.Y., 1959), 247.
9. *Boundary 2*, I, 1 (1072-73), 98-133.

Consequently, the poetry which we have been most frequently offered from the years between 1930 and 1960 has been what Antin calls "a kind of poetical Episcopalianism."

Perhaps now, with Zukofsky's entire canon before us, we can begin to understand something of the opportunity which he recognized nearly fifty years ago. This lag will not surprise readers of Pound.

Writing of William Carlos Williams, who seemed to him the central figure of the 1920's, Zukofsky says, "The aesthetics of his material is a living one, a continual beginning, a vision amid pressure" [*Prepositions*, 140]. To allow vision to arise from the complex interactions of physical space, logical space, social, historic, economic, and moral space, as they all bear on the space of the poem, where desire, feeling, fact, form, and language enact their destinies of coincidence and conflict, was to experience fully the exhilaration which the "modern" offered. Williams' poetry, as Zukofsky reads it, is a poetry without presuppositions, a poetry of pure inquiry. Everything, it had been discovered, bears on everything else. To keep pace with a reality which was not mediated by linear conventions required an eye that could follow the magician's impossibly quick hands. Nothing could be stopped or isolated or framed. Study and meditation could find no still object. After quoting some short passages from Williams' *The Great American Novel*, Zukofsky writes, "Such things are seen and recorded not as notes, but as finished, swiftly trained deliberations of the mind between leaps to other work or the multiplicity of living scenes" [*Prepositions*, 141]. This discipline, which does not exaggerate the significance of any phase of the process by which sight passes to vision, is the sole guarantee against life's forming to patterns of unshakeable habit. It requires the quickness of the living present to create a history, otherwise things settle down into repetition and tiresome justification of the status quo. Zukofsky's sole commitment is to the *clarity* of the process of history. He objects to the exaggeration of the formal in Wallace Stevens: "The poetic emotion is lacking," he says, "and the product is 'intellectual' rhetoric; blurred disjointed tangibilities" [*Prepositions*, 131]. In Hart Crane, he objects to the exaggerated value placed on the ecstatic moment and the inevitable divorce from the process in which the ecstasy finds its relation to other experience: "The result is an aura—a doubtful, subtle exhalation—a haze" [*Prepositions*, 131]. Of Pound, Eliot, Williams, Marianne Moore, and Cummings, he says, "The things these poets deal with are of this world and time, but they are 'modern' only because their words are energies which make for meaning" [*Prepositions*, 139].

Zukofsky was writing in the immediate wake of a historical rupture—a world-wide collapse of the economic system—and the single assurance to be derived was that, while history could not be arrested, it might offer its ruthless kinetic energy to certain kinds of responsive form. In another essay, this one from 1946, he seems perhaps to be paraphrasing Eliot's "Tradition and the Individual Talent." A thoughtful reading will indicate, however, that his emphasis is directly opposite: "Poetry if anything has a sense for everything. Meaning: without poetry life would have little present. To write poems is not enough if they do not keep the life that has gone. To write poems may never seem enough when they speak of a life that has gone. The poet may visibly stop writing, but secretly measure himself against each word of poetry ever written" [*Prepositions*, 11]. Zukofsky does not seek to frustrate or short-circuit history but to enter it fully, not only as a poet but as a person (when he *stops* writing). There is an implicit willing acceptance of historical change, even though the changes which had occurred during the previous two decades had left almost no one untouched by the suffering. History, as he understands it, does *not* offer an order which transcends the immediate and the personal. Even the relationship of father to son—one of the central themes in *"A"*—is itself historical and dialectic. Zukofsky closes the essay with an address to his son: "Writing this, Paul, for a time when you can read, I do not presume that you will read 'Me.' That 'me' will be lost today when he says good night on your third birthday, and not missed when he says good morning as you begin your fourth year. It took all human time to nurse those greetings" [*Prepositions*, 31].

It is true, of course, that the major poets of this century have given overwhelming evidence to arcane structures which inform history. Yeats, Joyce, Pound, Eliot, Lawrence, Crane, even the later Williams found or expected to find patterns of recurrence which are fundamentally narrative, mythic. Their sources have been the insights of mediums, the lore of lost ritual, dreams, and direct intuition of almost-knowable epiphenomena. Although they have felt themselves to be at odds, therefore, with the dominant modes of western thought, which insists upon finding logical (i.e. non-temporal, non-narrative) structures in experience, they have no less proposed a reading of history in which the experience is guaranteed by a form embodied roughly in this or that narrative situation but never itself realized. The heroic archetype, for example, is only somewhat more immediate than geometry or a Platonic Idea. In its numerous embodiments, it does run a historical course, before it is regathered into eternity; it does share itself with us as creatures in time; but it does not satisfy the intuition that the *inherent structure* of history itself might change. The submerged possibility, which appears in *Leaves of Grass*, in the unclosing *Cantos*, is that the structure of history is not to be found in logic or mythologic, these informants of language, these skeletons, but in language and the complex web by which language is involved with perception. Zukofsky is almost alone among poets in this realization.

Zukofsky was raised in precisely the kind of tradition Pound and Eliot looked to for relief. Although the Judaism of New York's lower east side may have been provincial in comparison to the European tradition of high culture, it did not need to be patched together like a crazy-quilt to give it coherence. *"A"*-4 opens with a short lyric, typical of the lyrics which appear in "55 Poems." The voice of Zukofsky's community responds in these terms:

> Wherever we put our hats is our home
> Our aged heads are our homes,
> Eyes wink to their own phosphorescence,
> No feast lights of Venice or The Last Supper light
> our beards' familiars; His
> Stars of Deuteronomy are with us,
> Always with us,
> We had a speech, our children have
>   evolved a jargon.

At the time his contemporaries were in a desperate search for the logos or mythos of history (the Speech), Zukofsky was under a contradictory impulse, to explore the jargon, as a way beyond the repetitious ritual reenactment of the forms of eternity. His work neither refers to nor embodies an arcane structure as its source of meaning or as the guarantee of its ontological claim. He writes: "The poet wonders why so many today have raised up the word 'myth,' finding the lack of so-called 'myths,' in our time a crisis the poet must overcome or die from, as it were, having become too radioactive, when instead a case can be made out for the poet giving some of his life to the use of the words *the* and *a* both of which are weighted with as much epos and historical destiny as one man can perhaps resolve" [*Prepositions*, 18]. In the interplay of the definite and the indefinite—the poem beginning "the" and a poem beginning "a"—we are in the condition of history as present, history as destiny, rather than as transcendental order.

Although the imagined epic possibility is never forgotten and inheres quietly in Zukofsky's poetic process throughout, it is always tentative. In the book of *All* which follows "Poem beginning "The," " "55 Poems," he explores the dilemma of the poet as public figure—the keeper of the epos—vis-a-vis the lyricist. The correspondences between "29 Poems" and "29 Songs" need to be studied in detail. He implicitly suggests that the poem, addressing political or philosophic themes, has trans-personal significance in its content, while the lyric is ideological only in its consequences. It is worthwhile to observe that after "29 Poems," Zukofsky's use of political and philosophic material is rarely thematic in the strict sense.

It is the lyric or the lyric *moving toward* the poem which, almost from the beginning, attracts Zukofsky's primary attention. It is partly a matter of temperament, but he is also clearly aware of the difficulties—impossibilities?—under which the modern poet labors. In the first of "29 Poems," he writes, "Single we are, the others still *may be* with us/ and we for others." The sad fact is that the poet holds his office by public permission, and Zukofsky is perhaps the first poet whose work is written in the knowledge of the public's withdrawal of permission, indeed its disappearance as an audience for poetry. The fourth poem of the sequence records the vertigo which attends Zukofsky's recognition of his situation:

> Of course, commerce will not complete
> Anything, yet the harbor traffic is busy,
>   there shall be a complete fragment
>
> Of—
>
> Nothing, look! that gull
> Streak the water!
> Getting nearer are we,
> Hear? count the dissonances,
>
> Shoal? accost—cost
> Cost accounting.

Obviously any poem which becomes an object of such a world must find some grounds beyond "a complete fragment of nothing." There is no darker or more devastating indictment of capitalism's destruction of reality to be found anywhere in Marx.

In the penultimate section of "29 Songs," Zukofsky takes stock in prose of the dissonances which arise from the process in which he is engaged: "Specifically, a writer of music," he writes. "The composite of notes proceeded with assumed qualities in a definite proportion. But, as dreamed, they controlled the nature of plants, bodies, etc., and the elements of the notes became not easy to separate." As he is beginning to discover, however, the relationship between the notes and things is not as simple or as direct as he had dreamed. There is some contradiction at the very heart of his undertaking. He has a vision of dancing donkeys, and "the ever falling stomping of their hoofs, now following the range of his notes, were imparting to him clearly: 'Sir, not only a mathematique point flowers into every line which is derived from a Center, but our soul which is but one, hath swallowed up a negative.' " In his continuing consideration of this mock visionary revelation, I can only feel that he is working toward a concrete understanding of the dialectic which will inform his entire work:

> If his notes could not extricate themselves from this complicated mass, they would be to his tactility like meeting at a point without further coincidence or intersection. If they did extricate themselves, they would, moving toward a definite shape, become capable of being apprehended, themselves their own existence in the plain of surrounding existence, tactility of materials become tangible.

It is difficult to know *how much* consciousness to attribute to Zukofsky. Without doubt, he was one of the most totally conscious artists who ever lived. Could it be that Psalms 18, 38, 66, and 68, which are given as references at the end of the poem, correspond to *All*, *"A,"* *Bottom*, and *Catullus*? I am not prepared to make that argument, though I can see some grounds for it. Given what we know about the way Zukofsky worked, it is not wholly unlikely.

It is at least clear that the dilemma which the donkeys announce is exemplified in "Mantis" and "Mantis: An Interpretation." They establish the crisis in which *All* develops. Refusing to commit himself to a vision of unity which does not inform the whole of life, Zukofsky must inevitably deal with images and melodies which are frankly arbitrary. The central Zukofskyan value, therefore, is sincerity. It seems a weak word; we tend to be embarrassed by it. As a matter of fact, however, what other appeal is there to be made in the face of an arbitrary existence? "In sincerity," he writes, "shapes appear concomitants of word combinations, precursors of (if there is continuance) completed sound or structure, melody or form" [*Prepositions*, 20]. The poet *can* achieve music or an approach to music, form so perfect that it begins to sing, but there is always something more. The perfections of "Mantis" are conventional and arbitrary, almost. Three lines hang over at the end of the sestina, out of place, like a mantis in a subway station. It is a sestina and a twelfth, but, Zukofsky tells us in "An Interpretation," "The ungainliness/ of the creature needs stating." In sincerity, the subject finds its form and then, caught up in "the battle of diverse thoughts," exceeds it by three lines and, then, carries over into another poem which is almost six pages long. Looking at both the poem and the process of its making, Zukofsky recognizes that a mantis in the subway station—even something this small—presents an insoluble problem. He objects to the only interpretation by which the "meaning" of the poem might be enforced. But lacking the advantages of symbolism, as a technique for universalizing the particular, he can only bring together "the simultaneous/ the diaphanous, historical together in one head." It is at this point that *"A,"* *Bottom*, and *Catullus* are grafted onto *All*.

By putting Zukofsky's work in a context of Hegelian and Marxist thought, I intend to emphasize its timely character. It is not a poetry of thought but a direct response to what *can be* thought at a given time. In response to the question, "what specifically is good poetry?" Zukofsky says, "It is precise information on existence out of which it grew." Image, that is, is a historical claim, a poem's stake in the word and its guarantee of producing consequences in the world. And, he goes on to say, that "good poetry . . . is . . . information of its own existence . . . , the movement (and tone) of words" [*Prepositions*, 28]. Against the temporality of image, he poses not mythos or logos but language and especially the physical production of language, its closeness to the voice and the voice's body, the lips, tongue, lungs of speech. In an interview, he speaks of the word as "a physiological thing."[10] Poetry has to do with the organism in which people have their daily living, as much in their bodies as in time, and the human organism is remarkably constant, despite the transience of given bodies. It is this fact which allows even the person "who does not know Greek to listen and get something out of the poetry of Homer: "to 'tune in' to the human tradition, to its voice which has developed among the sounds of natural things, and thus escape the confines of time and place, as one hardly ever escapes them in studying Homer's grammar" [*Prepositions*, 28]. The interaction of image and sound, finally, allows a poetry of precise inquiry: that is, experience can be measured. It is not thought, but thought is frequently hovering around. There is, Zukofsky says, an "interplay of concepts."

It is hardly an exaggeration to say that, since the rise of the Greek lyric, image, sound, and the interplay of concepts—these

---

10. *Contemporary Literature*, X, 2 (1969), 205.

terms I take from Zukofsky's "A Statement for Poetry"— have become increasingly identified as functions of the individual and the individual alone. By the beginning of the twentieth century, the poet arrived at a point where it seemed almost impossible to speak of anything but himself. In Zukofsky's criticism, however, these terms are restated as precise foci of almost two centuries of radical poetic and philosophic thought. In his careful understanding of the situation, he establishes a practice which relates the poem-object not to poet alone but to experience at large and to other individuals.

III

"too full for talk"
"A"-11

Zukofsky's work may never be as widely read as Williams' or even Pound's. The reader of *Paterson* or the *Cantos* who loses track for a time still possibly maintains an interest in the anecdotes, the sharp images, and so forth. Much of Zukofsky's work offers nothing, nothing at all, to the attention that is not wholly on edge. Consider this more or less randomly chosen passage from "*A*"-22:

> 64 guesses at order in
> mist early insatiate resigned to
> the season, what's fortunate what's
> calamitous creating created treads the
> tail of a tiger and
> it may, may not bite.
> Stuck in a rut? try
> a flagstaff pry the wheel
> then horses may travel light
> get on with less.

Even the sharp reader, who recognizes—with few clues—that the "64 guesses at order" refer to the hexagrams of the *I Ching* and who also gets the puns on "treads" and "rut," which imply a sexual order in the couplings of fate, may still feel ill at ease with the passage. Why are there five words—regardless of syllables or stresses—in each line? How can the voice speak the second line and still hew to the rhythm proposed by the first and the third? And, for that matter, why are we reminded of *hex*agrams in this passage of the poem which is obsessively concerned with quincunxes?

Part of the problem is simple ignorance of the text. Our collective ignorance is immense. I expect, however, that no amount of information, as useful as it will be, will solve the fundamental problem. Reading Zukofsky we are athwart a fundamental aesthetic problem, and Zukofsky is unwilling to allow himself any of the formal ploys which seem to offer a way beyond it. We are lyricists, one and all, in all we do, no matter how poorly we sing our parts: poets are lyricists in poetry; doctors are lyricists in medicine (such is the state of the science); lawyers are lyricists in law; businessmen in business; politicians in politics; priests in religion. Yet, after five-hundred years of feeling the strength of ourselves as individuals and the magnificence of self which we are heir to, we begin to sicken of our individual souls, both because they are *still* limited ("only tiny particles of the whole fall to various individuals") and because the free-play of a multitude of individuals creates situations in which the simplest and most necessary human activities, living together in cities, for example, become nearly impossible. The other alternative, the *imposition* of order, is equally repugnant and leads only to its own kind of chaos.

Zukofsky's art has a strong sense of limits, in the mathematical sense, of a function approaching a limit, and, in the human sense, of how much *can be* done. Zukofsky's tone is quiet, and it might be mistaken for understatement. It can be safely said, however, that he never understates. In a quiet way, he always lets more into a passage than can be resolved. Even when he is simplest, in those passages which we expect to present some sufficiency, some haikku-like sense that enough has been said, we generally feel a quantum of poetic energy only because it presents a measure of what can be said against what cannot be: "See:/ My nose feels better in the air" [*All*, 126].

In a well-known passage in *"A"*-12, Zukofsky writes:

I'll tell you.
About my *poetics*—

$$\int \begin{matrix} \text{music} \\ \text{speech} \end{matrix}$$

An integral
Lower limit speech
Upper limit music.

It is possible to establish three senses of musical limits which are relevant to Zukofsky's work:

A. Lyric. A poetry in which fragmentary images approach simple melody, a poetry of image and sound, the poetry of the single voice. In Zukofsky's work the lyric is an expression of an idiosyncrasy which is valuable for the reason we value any concrete thing.

B. "Harmonic" music. A poetry of sound and the interplay of concepts, the poetry of multiple voices, a community or a movement. It is useful to distinguish three kinds of "harmonic" music to which Zukofsky's work has some reference: 1) aleatory music, the music of happy accident, a "harmony" of voices speaking together without intentional concert; 2) atonal music (see, most specifically, *"A"*-20), a "harmony" of arbitrarily organized elements; 3) traditional polyphonic music, a music which usually suggests transcendental harmony.

C. *Mousike*. The poetry of total musical organization, the epic music, a music of image, sound, concept, and tradition, all thoroughly integrated.

Music, mathematics, and magnetic fields offer about the only images of order to be found in the twentieth century. For Zukofsky only music and mathematics seem especially persuasive or important. We do not have recourse to "nature" as an image of order in the nineteenth-century sense or to the "universe" in the eighteenth-century sense; we do not have the great chain of being or St. Thomas. Our images of order are without content.

To make a *simple* analogy between poetic form and musical form (I am not prepared even to speculate about Zukofsky's use of mathematics), however, is for the present discussion beside the point: Stevens' "Peter Quince," Williams' "The Clouds," and the several other attempts to adapt the sonata form to poetry, for example, make only the too obvious point that poetry is *not* music or even musical in that sense. The poet may produce something analogous to melody but not harmony, not counterpoint, not within current conventions anyway; harmony and counterpoint imply multiple voices. Since the seventeenth century, even most of the innumerable poems entitled "Song," to say nothing of the more elaborate analogies between poetic and musical forms, are references *to* music, not music as such. I can think of only a few instances in which it is not clear that the poet is talking, and the reader is being asked to imagine that he is singing or playing the harmonium.

Zukofsky does not try to appropriate music for poetic use. It is too important to him to allow a relatively cheap ploy. Rather, he poses the question, if the poet can produce an effect which can be legitimately called "melody," can these atomic units—these small catches—be extended, combined, developed, to produce larger musical forms? Is it possible to take a lyrical theme, laden with meaning, remove it from the limitations of the single vision, let it create dissonances and energies to be resolved and used, let it become something like the empty notes which are the composer's theme or tone-row? Is it, in short, possible to create a music of *content*?

Zukofsky remains essentially a lyricist, a fact he underscores with the title of his collected lyrics. *All* is a collection of "objective" lyrics, which infinitely expanded would produce a single vision. If the mathematical limit of speech is music, however, its human limit is time. Consequently, neither of the two primary musical strategies of the twentieth century—Stravinsky's and Schoenberg's—are directly relevant to Zukofsky's undertaking. While Stravinsky and Schoenberg offer solutions to the problem of form, Stravinsky by cannibalizing forms from the past and Schoenberg by declaring the radical perfection of his own subjectivity, both produce objects which are problematic in their relation to time. *"A," Bottom*, and *Catullus* are inquiries into stragegies which engage the lyric voice with other voices in time. They are extended, intersubjective lyrics, the various voices involved all reaching beyond the lyric moment in an effort to establish a community. *"A"* investigates the intersubjective play of image, sound, and concepts; *Bottom*, of tradition and concepts; *Catullus*, of image, tradition, and sound or "breath," as Zukofsky says.

In these works, we witness the re-founding of the tradition of secular choral poetry, which had its very brief day in the age between the decline of the epic and the rise of the lyric of the single voice. I do not mean simply that Zukofsky gives us an instance of choral poetry in *"A"*-24. The whole of *"A"* is an investigation into the inadequacies and limitations of the single vision and the single voice. In *"A"*-9, Marx and Cavalcanti sing a duet which Zukofsky conducts; *"A"*-21 is a drama; *Bottom* is a lengthy discussion between Aristotle, Spinoza, Wittgenstein, and Zukofsky on the subject of Shakespeare; in *Catullus*, Zukofsky sings a close-harmony duet with the Roman poet, while all of the dead speakers of Latin hum back-up. We are witness in these three works to the creation of a music of content. It is a music controlled not by mythos as in Stravinsky, or by logos, as in Schoenberg, but by the actual, temporal, melodic, *and* semantic content of the language itself.

I mentioned in the previous section the passage of *"A"*-4, where Zukofsky interfaces his own lyric jargon with the Speech of his community. As I have the space here to take only a glance at Zukofsky's texts, perhaps I can show quickly, with an abbreviated reading of *"A"*-1, how Zukofsky's masterpiece takes its initial impulse from images which spill-over from the lyric.

We are introduced, at the beginning, not to a concert but to the aftermath of a concert. Not until *"A"*-24, when Handel's *Pièces pour le Clavecin* contribute to the intersubjective collage, will we hear actual music. The incidents which attract Zukofsky's interest seem almost inconsequential. He is struck by the contrast between the audience of which he is a part and Bach's original audience, for which Bach was as remarkable as the father of twenty-two children as for his music. It was not an abstract crowd but a community. The poet in the modern audience is only one of the crowd, and to the extent he cuts a figure at all, it is almost ludicrous. Nothing in the situation seems to provide the occasion of a poem, especially not one which will prove to run more than eight-hundred pages. The reader might reasonably expect to be instructed in these lines how to read the poem. Long poems typically offer the reader this service, either directly or indirectly. If it does, however, it doesn't underscore the instructions so they are immediately recognizable. If anything we seem to be given miscues. "O Lamb of God most holy!"—the ninth line—might well arouse expectations which will not be satisfied. It is not a religious occasion either for Zukofsky or for the part of the audience which is presumably Christian. If there is a lyric crisis, it is associated so completely with the scene that it doesn't appear either personal or immediate: "The lights dim, and the brain when the flesh dims." Is it, then, a confrontation with mortality? Or is that just one of the many impulses which arise from the crowded scene? The image is likely to be missed. The modern crowd is no longer either the shock it was for Poe and Baudelaire or the exhilaration it was for Whitman. In the face of it, however, what is the value of the lyric voice? What can one lonely person say or do that makes any difference at all? It is from this scene that *"A"* takes its rise.

The poet is lost in his own subjectivity, carried away by the music, and starts out the wrong exit. He discovers when he tries to respond to the usher that he is speechless:

> And as one who under the stars
> Spits across the sand dunes, and the winds
> Blow thru him, the spittle drowning worlds—
> I lit a cigarette, and stepped free
> Beyond the red light of the exit.

Through the next fifty or so lines, he continues to have difficulty focusing on the immediate situation: the usher fades through the smoke, a tramp's face appears, "and suddenly/ Nothing./ About me, the voices of those who had/ been at the concert." The "nothing" breaks the syntactical bounds, negating everything around it, and we are into the silence, perhaps Mallarmé's silence justified. The poem will take another turn toward the end, but as he listens to the post-concert chit-chat, we are given a precise portrait of one kind of aesthetic response. If anything, we are being instructed in how *not* to respond. Although he is wholly taken up by it, "Desire longing for perfection" is a potentially destructive emotion. He feels the city and all of its bustling life being reduced to inconsequence. The bitter irony of the lines beginning "Such lyric weather" is not typical of Zukofsky, nor is the aesthetic rapture of the passage which follows:

> The blood's tide like the music.
> A round of fiddles playing
> Without effort—
> As into the fields and forgetting to die,
> The streets smoothed over as fields,
> Not even the friction of wheels,
> Feet off ground:
> As beyond effort—
> Music leaving no traces,
> Not dying, and leaving no traces.

To this point the poem might be a lyric in a manner which became typical in the wake of Eliot's criticism. The irony is simple: aesthetic perfection judges less exalted experience as trivial; for a time, a visionary moment, the city itself is leveled. In a neo-metaphysical touch, the train is implicated in the effect.

The poem, then, opens with a tribute to a possibility which Zukofsky will not allow himself, a possibility which may indeed not be available to any legitimate artist at this time. The turns which the poem takes through the closing passages are dizzying. Without warning, Zukofsky breaks the lyric illusion by reminding us that this is not a "speech overheard," as J.S. Mill said of the poem, but writing: "Not boiling to put pen to paper/ Perhaps a few things to remember." Even as the lines, "Music leaving no traces,/ not dying and leaving no traces," are still ringing in our ears, he starts making notes for the poem, the poem we are reading: the time of the poem catches up with itself. The sense of eternity folds in, and we are in the fragmentary present. It is an admission of *literacy*—something one rarely finds in poetry. It calls us to attend to the actual process, the *tracing* of the poem (because, unlike the musician, the poet leaves traces). In terms of

music, if there is to be an analogy at all, we are nearer Schoenberg than Bach. Schoenberg is possible because we are musically
literate or we have access to a phonograph. When musical performances are rare and expensive, the composer must give us
something we can take home, a tune we can whistle. With the
phonograph, it is possible to have musical performances which
can be repeated at will. It is indicative of the conservative nature
of literacy that nearly five centuries passed before poets began to
appreciate the advantage which the printing press offered them.
The poet is no longer required to write memorable lines or to present neatly simplified structures, some story or point, which can
stand in the memory in place of the poem itself.

In the next twelve lines of more or less disconnected notes,
the intimations of immortality fade, and Zukofsky is recalled to
the city. The noted fragments now, unlike the fragments of conversation earlier in the poem, are not part of a ritual design. They
are rather directly pertinent to the act of the poem itself, the
actual work being done, the poet himself, like the trainmen,
working far into the night:

> "There are different techniques,
> Men write to be read, or spoken,
> Or declaimed, or rhapsodized,
> And quite differently to be sung";
> "I heard him agonizing,
> I saw him *inside*";
> "Everything which
> We really are and never quite live."
> Far into (about three) in the morning,
> The trainmen wide awake, calling
> Station on station, under earth.

This harshly realistic image might seem a sufficient corrective for
the airy mood into which he had fallen. Zukofsky, however,
pursues his responses into the next day:

> The next day the reverses
> As if the music were only a taunt:
> As if it had not kept, flower-cell, liveforever,
>   before the eyes, perfecting.

The vision of immortality is replaced in the closing lines of the
poem with images of, with the evidence of, the decay of the city,
the exploitation of the population, the ruthlessness of the rich
and the powerful. It reads like a condensed and modernized version of Engels' *The Condition of the Working Class in England*. In
the face of these actualities, a fragment from the Bach, now
wholly divorced from its original context, can enter the inter-

subjective design of the poem's beginning: "Open, O fierce flaming pit!"

"A"-1 presents a case of the personal dialectic at work. We are witness to the development of an identity and the discovery of non-identity. It concludes with the energy charge of the new information to lead into the subsequent sections.

In the poems which follow, other voices enter the process. In *"A"*-2 Kay (otherwise unidentified) objects to Zukofsky's fundamental strategy, doubting that the self-referential quality of music—"itch according to its own wont"—is appropriate to poetry, and, although he has an answer for her, he feels the force of her argument enough to pick it up again in *"A"*-6: "The song-omits? No, includes Kay, Any body." In *"A"*-3, Zukofsky identifies with Arimathaea, but not in the sense that Pound identifies with Odysseus; it is only one of the many equations to be tested in the on-going process of the poem. In *"A"*-4, the identity of father and son is called into question; bits of song, a complete Japanese lyric enter the dialectic. To trace out the complex relationships is to trace the entire fabric of the poem. Perhaps it is sufficient for now to note that the process of *"A"* is not, in Pound's sense, ideographic, image *added to* image, rather it is analytic and negative. *"A"* is not resolved in a final metaphoric ration of Zukofsky to Handel. The juxtaposition of material from Zukofsky's canon (arranged by Celia, incidentally, the process having become so thoroughly intersubjective) with the music brings the poem to a point at which the continuing dialectical tensions are clarified. The Handel harpsichord pieces are not, in other words, the musical limit toward which the speech has been reaching: Handel, rather, lends his "voice" to the community of voices which constitute the intersubjective lyric. He joins Zukofsky, characters Zukofsky has created, and other writers Zukofsky quotes and refers to. Its structure is as much dramatic as musical. *"A"*-24 is choral drama or dialectical choral lyric.

The coincidence with which *"A"* concludes, however, like any dialectical occasion, resolves into contradictions, despite the apparent harmonies of the moment. The possibility of intersubjectivity implies at once the subject's mastery of others and the subject's submission to others. I want to suggest that these alternatives are explored in *Bottom* and *Catullus*. If my argument has been at all cogent, these points should not require lengthy discussion.

For most readers, trained in a tradition in which Shakespeare is almost beyond criticism, *Bottom* is a rather shocking book.

David Melnick, in his excellent essay, is obviously ill at ease with the heavy-handed treatment Shakespeare receives. Zukofsky, however, does not pare Shakespeare down to his philosophic nubs because, as Melnick suspects, "He shares with [Spinoza and the early Wittgenstein], as with Shakespeare, fears of chance and change, i.e. time itself,"[11] but because the intensity of the experience of time in *"A"* requires a likewise intense experience of immutable reality or law. Zukofsky tells us that *Bottom* is "A long poem built on a theme for the variety of its recurrences. The theme is simply that Shakespeare's text throughout favors the clear physical eye against the erring brain, and that this theme has historical implications" [*Prepositions*, 159]. Unlike *"A,"* which might be called a poem with a strategy, *Bottom* is a poem with an argument. In fact, in one of its dimensions it can be taken as a justification of the strategy in *"A,"* an effort to discover in Shakespeare an authority for his own procedures. The premise of the book, therefore, requires a certain ruthlessness.

In *Bottom*, the reader finds himself at one of those centers of dialectical reversal where language seems to turn against itself. In his discussion of Zukofsky's remark that "the theory of knowledge . . . is done away with in *Bottom*," Melnick very precisely explains the dialectical twist involved: ". . . the form he has chosen permits him, in the very act of putting *all* epistemology into his book, to contain, negate, and transcend it. Thus Zukofsky has done away with the theory of knowledge, and returned us to the eyes themselves."[12] By doing so, as Melnick fails to see, by recovering his truth—this eternal principle—he returns us to a dependence upon the physical eye, to the point at which we have our most reliable stake in the temporal and the historical. His mastery of Shakespeare—some might say his rape of the Shakespearean texts—returns us to our physical eyes with which, among other things, we can read Shakespeare in all of his rich profusion.

In his treatment of Shakespeare, Zukofsky discovers the dialectical rule that the master becomes subject to the subject he masters. In *Catullus*, Zukofsky investigates the other dimension in his theme. "This translation of Catullus," he writes in his preface, "follows the sound, rhythm, and syntax of his Latin—tries, as is said, to breathe the 'literal' meaning with him." He is assuming a persona with a vengeance, or, more exactly, he proposes to assume not Catullus' person but his body. In part, he does so for the reason Guy Davenport explains: "Contemporary New

---

11. "The 'Ought' of Seeing: Zukofsky's *Bottom*," *Maps*, 5 (1973), 58.
12. Ibid., 55.

York is probably as close an historical rhyme to Catullus' Rome as we are likely to find, unless you would like to think of medieval Kyoto or Berlin in the 1920's."[13] Again, however, it is a point of dialectical reversal: the very act of making like is making differences. By submitting totally to Catullus' language, he is remaking his own. If *Bottom* is an attempt to make us *see* a physical world which is in danger of becoming transparent, *Catullus* is an attempt to make us hear an English which is in danger of becoming silent. It is certainly an English such as we have never heard before:

> Seek or record then the benefactor—pree or voluptuous
>   is the meaning, come say cogitate essáy pious,
> no sanctum will owe loss—so feed him, not foiled there in all he
>   divined not falling those numina abusing no man's
> mull to be rapt there manning a long ah high tide there, Catullus,
>   sort from ingratitude good and from more a to be.

The central demand which Zukofsky's art makes on him in *Catullus,* as in the other books, is to keep the historical process alive at the roots, where image, sounds, concepts, and traditions combine and recombine in their restless incongruence. It is an art which calls attention to the deadliness of habit and the possibility of change. It does not seek resolution—and certainly *Catullus* resolves nothing—but it can bring us to those moments of intense vital awareness when resolution seems unnecessary and even undesirable.

---

13. "Zukofsky's English Catullus," *Maps*, 5 (1973), 75.

HUGH KENNER

TWO PIECES ON "A"

Of Notes and Horses*

(In medias res) . . . when what was put on the page collaborates with what readers understand in its presence. The former is constant (more or less, despite editors' tinkerings), the latter mutates with time, and given enough time, as with Homer, a spectacular inventory of mutations will accumulate. An *Iliad* totally (radically?) unlike ours glowed in the mind of Socrates. Until the collaborative process is moving the poem exists only as an unperformed score exists, and Zukofsky's "*A,*" forty years in progress, has only begun to exist.

The text, for one thing, has been barely accessible: installments in scattered magazines at scattered times through several decades, and eight years ago an edition of "*A*" *1-12* published by Cid Corman in Japan and limited to 200 copies. Of "*A*" *13-24* bits have appeared but much is still unwritten. But at last there's a trade edition of *1-12*, offset from the Japanese letterpress, with typos corrected and the format enlarged just enough to ease reading. Though two appendices to the Kyoto edition are lacking, a 1946 essay by Zukofsky and a 1957 statement by Dr. Williams, the reader who wasn't so blessed as to be in touch with Cid Corman at the proper time may now feel that he has in his hands what is necessary.

Like *Leaves of Grass*, like *The Cantos*, it's a poem-in-progress to encompass the poet's life; but unlike Whitman and Pound, who knew at the start what kind of texture they wanted and little else, Zukofsky began about 1927 with a formal plan, a plan of the form, which means in practice (1) an intuition of the poem without any words in it, a silent structural eloquence; and (2) a sequential table of difficulties to be overcome. I picked up this information from Basil Bunting, who doesn't know, nor do I, how closely the plan has been stuck to; but even if it presides over the written poem only in the way of a slowly fading ghost, it gives our

---

*Reprinted with permission from *Poetry*, January, 1968.

attention some pointers.

The eloquence, around and under the words, of some structure that holds them in their relation; the poem as testimony to difficulties overcome: these principles permeate Zukofsky's poetic. In the version of Catullus, for example, which has not yet located a bold enough publisher, the translator's normal quest for semantic equivalence has been complicated by a determination to make the result *sound like* the Latin—

> Irascere iterum meis iambis
> Immerentibus, unice imperator

yeilding

> Irascibly iterating my iambics—
> unmerited, unique eh—imperator.

Here the structural eloquence is phatic, the Latin treated not only as a source of "meanings" but as a graph of breathings and intonations; the achieved English is irremediably strange; and the strangeness is accepted and turned into a virtue by the sheer scale of the enterprise, which (difficulty overcome) offers not just a few compliant instances but Catullus whole, subdued after unimaginable trouble. A mad enterprise? yet it carries Pound's way with *The Seafarer*, or Joyce's with what you like, to its logical term.

Bilingual printing yields the key to this fairly quickly. It takes Hebrew scholarship, or a tip from the author, to explicate the opening of *"A"*-15 (*Poetry*, September 1966), and to disclose that in reading aloud

> Wind: Yahweh at Iyyob
> Mien His roar 'Why yammer
> Measly make short hates oh
> By milling bleat doubt?
> Eye sore gnaw key heaver haul its core
> Weight as I lug where hide any? . . .'

we are more or less pronouncing Hebrew passages from the Book of Job. I hope Zukofsky's taut, low-keyed reading of this has been recorded by somebody; being exposed to it is a memorable experience. But the bare text is richly suggestive, and loses less than we'd think without the key, if only because we don't expect Yahweh to sound urbane and so don't look round in dismay as an unclued reader of the Catullus might well do. One can imagine this tour de force being greatly admired for decades without anyone discovering what it really is.

But would anyone discover, without prompting from the privately circulated *First Half of "A"-9* (New York, 1940) that *"A"*-9, for five strophes and coda, in following precisely the rhyme scheme of the *Donna Mi Prega*, not only adapts from *Das Kapital* (Everyman edition) the phrases it sets to this tune, but also governs the distribution of "n" and "r" sounds according to the formula for a conic section? Almost certainly not (who would think of counting the n's and r's?); yet the poet's "intention to have it fluoresce as it were in the light of seven centuries of inter-related thought" has chosen that rigorous and hidden way of impressing itself upon the language. What we *can* hope to notice, what can challenge our response, is a surface turbulence, as in the Catullus, as in the derivations from Job:

> . . . Broken
> Mentors, unspoken wealth labor produces,
> Now loom as causes disposing our loci,
> The foci of production: things reflected
> As wills subjected; formed in the division
> Of labor, labor takes on our imprecision—
>   *("A"*-9, p. 112)

—just so much departure from naturalness as will betoken language responding not only to semantic sequence but also to formal laws, though we cannot say unaided what those laws are.

Such hidden laws, presenting a different face to the poet and to us, not only prevent him from dashing things off without thought, they also suspend the whole poem on some plane other than the plane of unresisted discourse, much as musical laws, though we may not know what they are, yeild effects we do not confuse with random sonority. For Zukofsky's fondness for mathematic form parallels Bach's, who is often invoked in *"A"* as the active presiding spirit. Some structural principles, corresponding, say, to the parts of a sonata, we can discern without difficulty: that *"A"*-11, for instance, the shortest movement, five richly textured stanzas in polyphonic feminine rhymes, brings us almost exactly to the mid-point of the volume, its concentration therefore expanding at once into the last and longest movement, which in turn counterbalances (since it's half the book) everything that has led up to it. Counterbalances, that is, by page-count; there are fewer words in the second half, because more passages that, on the analogy of the solo violin, propel their thought through brief twinkling phrases, line by line by line:

> A sound akin to mosaic:
> A rhythm of eyes
> Almost along a line
> Looking into and out of the frame —
> Empress Theodora and court ladies
> Moved to the East

> Where the sun begins.
> Unearthed catacombs
> Brought into the sun
> Whereto is playing
> A good shepherd's song
> Amidst plenty of sheep. . . .
>   ("*A*"-12, p. 191)

Fewer words, shorter lines, more tension: a verse tense (like a string) but nearly weightless, as against

> Horses: who will do it? out of manes? Words
> Will do it, out of manes, out of airs, but
> They have no manes, so there are no airs, birds
> Of words, from me to them no singing gut.
> For they have no eyes, for their legs are wood,
> For their stomachs are logs with print on them;
> Blood red, red lamps hang from necks or where could
> Be necks, two legs stand A, four together M.
> "Streets closed" is what print says on their stomachs; . . .
>   ("*A*"-7, p. 45)

—polyphony, tricky rhymes, a playful difficulty unafraid to look clumsy; and the horses are sawhorses guarding an excavation. More: "*A*"-7 is made of seven sonnets, arranged like a canzone, giving and receiving themes and sounds: this in anticipation of "*A*"-9, which *is* a double canzone. Each sonnet, if we tabulate rhyme-schemes, has a regular octave, *ababcdcd*, but only the third and fifth (which are Shakespearean) have identical plans for the sestet. The diction, the rhythms, the objects handled, are comically inappropriate to these Renaissance formalisms, but the formalisms, and the dexterity with which forms mutate make the clumsy words and objects tumble as though weightless through an intricate juggling act.

—Weightlessness again: precisely as in music, where there isn't a burden of "meaning" and playing can seem like play. It's play that gets from sawhorses to manes to "out of manes, out of airs" by way of the Latin *manes* (ancestral spirits); and that ties "airs" to "words" ("I made x out of a mouthful of air," said Yeats) but also to tunes by way of "singing gut"—both the fiddlestring and the insides wooden horses lack—and that brushes against "out of manes" some such locution as "out of gas." And these clumsy Pegasi serve not only for empiric degradations (what's a Brooklyn poet got to work with?) but also for Renaissance emblems, since "two legs stand A," the name of the poem, and when four together make M they calligraph AM, the name of God.

This is a game of alertness to possibilities, single words floating loose to attach themselves to simultaneous contexts.

We're forced to follow them—in this they depart from Empsonian "ambiguities"—if we want to see how the poet makes his transitions. It's a game that commences at the top of the first page,

> A
> Round of fiddles playing Bach.

—where "A" is the title of the poem, and its first word (as of the alphabet), and the indefinite article, and the note musicians tune by. (On page 70 Vitamin A enters the dance.) "A case can be made out for the poet giving some of his life to the use of the words *the* and *a*: both of which are weighted with as much epos and historical destiny as one man can perhaps resolve," wrote Zukofsky in the 1946 essay that is unfortunately missing from this reprint. "Those who do not believe this are too sure that the little words mean nothing among so many other words."

It is a curious possibility that the whole poem may be an exegesis of the indefinite article, and so of cases standing for kinds, and so of a tension between the kind of reality kinds have and our stubborn pragmatic intuition that our need for a filing system has merely devised them.

> I grant no one is deceived
> In so far as he perceives.
> The imaginations of the mind
> > in themselves
> Involve no error,
> But I deny that a man
> > affirms nothing
> In so far as he perceives—
> > SPINOZA
> > (*"A"*-12, p. 195)

And as to little words being weighted with history, we may note Charles Williams's speculation (*Witchcraft*, p. 83) that the inability of a Latin devoid of articles to distinguish between "the" and "a" malign spirit may have hastened the conception of the devil, whence *La Chambre Ardente* and Salem.

But back to Zukofsky's aside on little words, in context a dissent from those who have "raised up the word 'myth,' finding the lack of so-called 'myths' in our time a crisis the poet must overcome or die from." Myths stand between facts and words, and Zukofsky is pleading the case of words that suffer no need of such intermediaries, being free-floating. Against such levitation the makers of syntactic boxes seek to legislate, but all they achieve is existence "entirely in that frozen realm without crisis that Dante called the 'secondary speech.'"

Myths stand between facts and words. Thus Pound in Canto

II rehandles Ovid's myth of a kidnapped Dionysius who transformed his captors' ship into a rock and the captors into non-men.
Pound's words give us the myth directly, taking its events as
actual—

> The back-swell now smooth in the rudder-chains,
> Black snout of a porpoise
>   where Lycabs had been,
> Fish-scales on the oarsmen.
>   And I worship.
> I have seen what I have seen.

This "I" is both E.P. and Ovid's Acoetes, addressing King Pentheus
who proposed to outlaw the revels; and Pound, by way of the
myth, is both building his poem and addressing (yes he is!) the
American legislature which in 1919 had committed the Republic
to what a much later Canto calls "the constriction of Bacchus." In
Canto II no word mentions Congress; it is the myth, not the word,
that reaches in many directions including the direction of newspaper events, events it doesn't bring onto the page. The words
stick to the business of rendering sensations, so that the myth, the
radiant event, will be handed over to us actual.

Which is a way to work, but not Zukofsky's way. Though the
miraculous verbal transaction, shaped and shapely words by their
joinery achieving meaning, is central for both poets, *"A"* is devoid
of structural myths, though probably crammed as full of facts as
The Cantos. Zukofsky's facts—for instance sawhorses—are light-
ened and loosened by play, in all senses of "play," with the words
that denote them; and many kinds of horses, classical, Biblical,
zoological, consorting with other facts and themes, canter through
the intricacies of *"A"* -12 without symbolizing anything, or
assembling themselves into an equine myth:

> —Look Paul, where
> The sawhorses of "A"-7
> Have brought me.
>   (*"A"*-12, p. 234)

—as though they were ridable!

Some of the poem's facts are public—the Great Depression,
the labors of Marx; some are private—the death of the poet's
father, which is the principal episode of *"A"*-12. They interact
endlessly, intersecting and counterplaying on the plane not of
myth but of language. The father, for example—

> "They sang this way in deep Russia"
> He'd say and carry the notes
> Recalling the years

Fly. Where stemmed
The Jew among strangers?
As the hummingbird
Can fly backwards
Also forwards
How else could it keep going?
Speech moved to sing
To echo the stranger
A tear in an eye
The quick hand wiped off—
Casually:
"I loved to hear them."

Then a space; then an unspoken answer from the poet-son:

As I love:
My Poetics.

Are what I love? Are the fact that I love? The colon will have it
either way. The devotion the poem has so long commanded contains (by incorporating it) filial and paternal devotion, and also
supplies a measure for it. Much earlier it had contained the sorrow
of the immigrant elders:

   ... His
Stars of Deuteronomy are with us,
Always with us,
We had a Speech, our children have
     evolved a jargon.
             ("*A*"-4, p. 18)

"My poetics" is one mode of that "jargon," incomprehensible to
the old man whose mind darted back like a hummingbird and yet
bore the heavy notes from "deep Russia": such notes as (in "*A*"-4)

We prayed, Open, God, Gate of Psalmnody,
That our Psalms may reach but
One shadow of Your light,
That You may see a minute over our waywardness.
Day You granted to Your seed, its promise, its Promise,
Do not turn away Your sun.
Let us rest here,
        lightened
Of our tongues, hands, feet, eyes, ears and hearts.

Against which, secularized children ("Deafen us, God, deafen us to
their music") set up cosmopolitan exercises, flouting the Heritage:

"Rain blows, light, on quiet water
   I watch the rings spread and travel
Shimaunu-San, Samurai,
   When will you come home? —
     Shimaunu-San, my clear star . . ."
             ("*A*"-4, p. 19)

—and three more stanzas, an anthology-piece, and from other points of view than that of the elders "a jargon," in this poetic of continual measured change, change specifying its measure, that excludes anthology pieces as rigorously as graven images.

For change, as in music, here specifies its measure, its laws, internal laws, often hidden and mysterious. All moves, and without the movement we could not guess that laws were there, as without the moving water we could not discern the curled form of the waves, let alone compute their determining dynamics. And as nothing is more ridiculous, if we close our ears, than what a violinist or a bassoonist does with his time and his fingers, so nothing is more trivial, from one point of view, than what goes into a poem (even the *Iliad*). A lit cigarette on page 8, a Valentine on page 135 (and home-made at that), domestic anecdotes throughout the 12th movement, each brings its quantum of attention on taught affection into the intricate *perpetuum mobile*. And as the collaborating mind of the listener alone justifies an Oistrakh's absurdly difficult stunt—scraping Bach's harmonies out of catgut—so in the minds of readers willing to let the poem teach them its appropriate modes of attention the forty years' enterprise called *"A"* hopes for its justification. Bach played on the notes B, A, C, H for no Olympian reason; *"A"*-12, correspondingly, on the words:

> Blest
> Ardent
> Celia
> Happy

also for no reason except that the formal problem, as for Bach, is a pretty one, and the domestic feeling of Louis for Celia, an encompassing and compelling one. Domestic feeling, like simple good will, commonly wears in poetry a chasuble of myth. Freed of that —set in little words—it is light, it can play, it can compel a structure.

> Music does not always
> Call on the human voice
> Only free (often wordless)
> Men are grateful to one another.

A wordless poem? It hung that way, in the poet's mind, during the forty years he was finding words to make it audible.

Too Full for Talk: *"A"*-11*

Your impression may well be that if *"A"*-11 would go by more slowly you could follow it. (With experience you almost can.) So a fiddler might feel that, forced less rapidly, his fingers could subdue all the notes; but at a slower tempo they are no longer the same notes.

> River that must turn full after I stop dying
> Song, my song, raise grief to music
> Light as my loves' thought, the few sick
> So sick of wrangling: thus weeping,
> Sounds of light, stay in her keeping
> And my son's face—this much for honor.

For the voice to rhyme "few sick" with "music," pronouncing the one word as one and the two as two, for the mind meanwhile to comb out and braid the syntax, putting for instance on "weeping" the proper rising pitch that will attach it to "sounds of light," both of them epithets for something addressed, in fact for "song, my song" (and likewise for "river")— this exacts a considerable athleticism of attention. Having swung the pitch of "thus weeping" upward, you pause; then after its rhyme-word "keeping" you must not pause, whatever the pull of rhyme, but must keep the integrity of the two-lobed phrase "in her keeping and (in) my son's face." You must isolate two main verbs, both in the imperative, "raise" and "stay." Your mind must, though your voice can't, make "loves'" a possessive plural, silently linked to the dedication, *"for Celia and Paul."* And you've little manoeuvring time, for only the compaction of a crisp pace will keep those rhymes audible, or hold together a syntax of appositives: of elements pressed together, not strung out. . . . By contrast, the first elements of *Paradise Lost* are strung along tension members secured to great emphatic stanchions by grappling-hook prepositions and conjunctions: *Of, and, whose, with, till, and:* SING! If you slow Milton down, those syntactic liaisons still direct expectation forward and memory backward. If you slow down Zukofsky's verse it falls to pieces.

And you must hold yourself a little back from the language, alert to watch where something may jump; it's not an idiom you

---

*Reprinted with permission from the author from *Maps*, No. 5, 1973.

can quite trust. Two elements in this stanza,

                                                            raise grief to music
                    Light as my loves' thought

        and

                                                            thus weeping,
                    Sounds of light,

both pair "grief" with "weeping" and "music" with "sounds," but
they do not pair "light" with "light," not exactly, since the first
"light" is an alleviation, offsetting "grief," while the second "light"
is a luminance, synaesthesizing "sounds." Less absolutely, "sick"
changes when it enters the idiom "sick of," and "my song" isn't
quite identical with the apotheosized "song."
  . One thing we come to sense is this poem's custom of moving
by means of dualities that (like Celia and Paul) aren't quite dual.
"River" and "turn" in line one of the first stanza will recur, after
long absence from the dance, in line one of the last stanza, and
both changed: "river" a little, "turn" (as we'll see) profoundly.
    Though nowhere before *"A"*-11 has so compact a cluster
been set twinning and twinkling in so compact a space, the long
poem has been using this principle among others ever since

        A
            Round of fiddles playing Bach

got it started. That first word, "river," is repeated from the opening of *"A"*-4:

        Giant sparkler
        Lights of the river,

        (Horses turning)
        Tide,

        And pier lights
        Under a light of the hill,

        A lamp on the leaf-green
        Lampost seen by the light

        Of a truck (a song)
        Lanterns swing behind horses,

Their sides gleam
From levels of water—

—which is where a number of *"A"*-11's elements are first collected.
It's where "river" first enters the poem, and while "light," "leaf,"
"song," have all been present earlier they have not been present
together. A phrase in *"A"*-1, "the blood's tide like the music,"
forsaw motifs in *"A"*-4 and helps sponsor *"A"*-11's river turning
full that is also song. Many other details in *"A"*-11 repeat little
verbal sequences from the previous 123 pages. But caught all at
once like fireflies on the fine grid of *"A"*-11 itself, its compact
two pages, 46 lines, 425 syllables, they enact an intricate rite of
local repetition, interlocking in pairs, trios, sixes, sevens, whose
pattern hints at an order just beyond our capacity to grasp.

Two *songs*, two *sicks*, two *lights* in the first stanza might be
embellishments; but when its last word, "honor," is featured in
the opening line of the stanza that follows, we commence to
intuit a poetic structure of pairings, and grow alert, amid still
more intricate syntax than before, to spot further binaries. Two
stars reveal themselves, two *golds*, another *song*, and yet another
"honor."

Freed by their praises who make honor dearer
Whose losses show them rich and you no poorer
Take care, song, that what stars' imprint you mirror
Grazes their tears; draw speech from their nature or
Love in you — faced to your outer stars — purer
Gold than tongues make without feeling
Art new, hurt old: revealing
The slackened bow as the stinging
Animal dies, thread gold stringing
The fingerboard pressed in my honor.

This too ends with "honor." Do all the stanzas? Yes, they do.
Does "honor" launch all of them? Only one more, the next, the
central one, which runs straight from "honor" to "honor." What
other symmetries do we approach? A succession of similar stanzas
(the first alone is atypical). All are rhymed ABABBCCDDE. (Con-
spicuous rhyming is another mode of pairing.) All the rhymes are
disyllabic. The lines ABABB have, without fail, 11 syllables each,
as though to sign *"A"*-11 with a rigorous count. The lines CCDDE
hover around 8 syllables, though no two stanzas are patterned
quite identically: 87889; 87899; 77777; 87777. These are 10-line
stanzas. The atypical first had six lines, rhymed ABBCCD, with
the syllable pattern 12-8889.

More symmetries? Yes, in the texture of the idiom. Not only
do words pair and cluster, there are theme-words, constantly

recurring. So we encounter "love" 8 times, "honor" 7, "song" 7 also, "light" (including "lights," "delight" and "lighting") 6, "leaf" (only in the final stanza) 5, and "music" 3. *Love, honor, song, light*, average out to 7 apiece, and may be the "four notes first too full for talk" that the final stanza specifies.

Reading in the normal sense—collecting a sequential meaning —is all but out of the question, so impacted are the formalities and the syntax. The first impulse is simply to listen, as to violin music, while intricate recurrencies sound and tease. It's as if the poem *approximated* human speech, the way a fiddle does when the fiddler "makes it talk." If we try to force our minds to follow the sense, our first discovery, amid many vanishing nuances, will likely be that *"A"*-11 is built on the convention of the Envoi, the entire poem addressed to song, to *a* song, in fact to itself; and commencing four lines into the penultimate stanza we discover a speech that has been composed for the song to deliver to the poet's son. This speech serves for the poem's exegesis, addressed to Paul, not to ourselves; though we share it, we are outside it. At its clearest, *"A"*-11 is still an enclave, its full import for family ears. And the poet is imagining himself dead. The poem perpetuates his voice, vibrating in the grief-filled void left by his absence.

One more formality: the difficulty is graduated. Stanza 2 is difficult, stanza 3 more so: positively impacted. Stanzas 4 and 5 grow suddenly clearer without being simpler: a sustained speech alight with formal brillance, a long syntactic trajectory undoing knots, gathering up motifs, a-dazzle in its final moments with light on turning leaves, resolved in a last 20-word cluster both musically and semantically penetrable.

En route to this triumph, we must pick our way through the densities of the second and third stanzas, possibly assisting ourselves with paraphrase. "Take care, song"—that's the syntactic germ of Stanza 2. Take care that "what star's imprint you mirror/ Grazes their tears." Take care that your reflection of the distant, scintillant stars will not draw you away from two people's human grief. From their nature or love you are to draw speech; the speech will be gold, purer than the speech/gold made by tongues that are bewildered by hurt as though it were a novelty, and are unimpressed by art because art's deliverances are after all commonplace. No, it is hurt that is commonplace ("old"), art that is made new. That is one way to unfold the stanza's syntax, one notation for the system of words paired and equated. And as the song, faced toward stars, draws speech from human passion, we shall find it

> revealing
> The slackened bow as the stinging
> Animal dies, thread gold stringing
> The fingerboard pressed in my honor.

A terminal "-ing" from "feeling" and "revealing" pulses through "stinging," "stringing," "fingerboard," to exemplify "art new" and move speech toward violin music. (Bow and fingerboard specify violin.) "As the stinging/ Animal dies" seems a simile for the suggestion that he, the poet, on some plane other than poetry, accuses himself of being "the stinging animal." There will be more of this in stanzas 3 and 4, where we shall learn that he "offended [his son] with mute wisdom," a father's most irritating offense.

> Honor, song, sang the blest is delight in knowing
> We overcome ills by love. Hurt, song, nourish
> Eyes, think most of whom you hurt. For the flowing
> River 's poison where what rod blossoms. Flourish
> By love's sweet lights and sing *in them I flourish.*
> No, song, not any one power
> May recall or forget, our
> Love to see your love flows into
> Us. If Venus lights, your words spin, to
> Live our desires lead us to honor.

This is in every sense the poem's *selva oscura*. "Ills," "hurt," "poison," prolong the suggestion of "the stinging/ Animal," that in the world where the poet merely lived he is conscious of having caused hurt. If I follow rightly, the song is first told what the blest sang, that honor is the delight we have in discovering we overcome ills by love. The song is then instructed what to do in case of hurt: "nourish / Eyes, think most of whom you hurt." (This is novelty, that a song as much as a person can suffer hurt, not only cause it.)

> For the flowing
> River 's poison where what rod blossoms. . . .

The careful space in front of the apostrophe designates a contraction, not a possessive: "river is." The flowing river—which is the song, we remember—whose business is raising grief to music, is poison if it dwells on hurt and not on persons: is poison "where what rod blossoms." What does *that* mean? The clue to Tannhauser's flowering staff leads me nowhere. Rod, an instrument of chastisement? This is the darkest part of the most embriared stanza. The rest of it is intricate but (with good will) transparent, till the final words:

> If Venus light, your words spin, to
> Live our desires lead us to honor.

I can think of three possible syntaxes, none really satisfactory. "Your words, spin," that would seem to be the nub. This whole dense stanza is a bewildering spinning.

Out of the spin emerge, like a sheet of light, two stanzas, two sentences, gravely eloquent though surface intricacies abound and twinkle:

> Graced, your heart in nothing less than in death, go —
> I, dust — raise the great him of the extended
> World that nothing can leave; having had breath go
> Face my son, say: 'If your father offended
> You with mute wisdom, my words have not ended
> His second paradise where
> His love was in her eyes where
> They turn, quick for you two — sick
> Or gone cannot make music
> You set less than all. Honor

> His voice in me, the river's turn that finds the
> Grace in you, four notes first too full for talk, leaf
> Lighting stem, stems bound to the branch that binds the
> Tree, and then as from the same root we talk, leaf
> After leaf of your mind's music, page, walk leaf
> Over leaf of his thought, sounding
> His happiness: song sounding
> The grace that comes from knowing
> Things, her love our own showing
> Her love in all her honor.'

"I, dust" is perfectly explicit: when I am dead. And the song, which has been told to raise grief to music, to take care, to nourish eyes, to flourish, is now told to go an errand to the dead poet's son. This is the traditional Envoi: *Go litel boke.* "Raise the great hem of the extended/ World that nothing can leave," the world of pure music that is not the world I have left but a world you (song) are capable of unveiling. This is the mirror of "his second paradise," where "his love was in her eyes."

"Honor," as always the stanza's final word, for once does not close the stanza. It launches, this time, the final flight of the poem:

Honor

> His voice in me, the river's turn that finds the
> Grace in you, four notes first too full for talk . . .

Here in the opening line of stanza 5 is the "river's turn" repeated from the first line of stanza 1. But as so often in this poem, a word on its second appearance has a second sense. "Grace" is not the "graced" of stanza 4, nor "turn" quite the same as the "turn" of the opening "turn full." The dictionary can help us by providing the musical sense of "turn":

> *Mus.* An ornament consisting of four tones, the first a degree above and the third a degree below the principal tone which comes in the second and fourth positions. When the auxiliary tones are reversed in order the grace is called an *inverted turn.*

(A "grace," by the way, is "an embellishment not essential to the melody or harmony, as the trill, turn, etc.")

We may wonder if *"A"*-11, in Zukofsky's own rabbinical way, has contrived to do what this definition stipulates. I'm unable to decide, though I do note that "love" occurs once oftener than "song" and "honor," but "light" once less often, which may mean that these are the tones a degree above and below the principal tone. This kind of clue is more tantalizing than useful. If we had only the information that the formula for a conic section is imbedded in *"A"*-9, would we guess that the way to go about locating it is to count the n's and r's? Yet that was Zukofsky's way of working it in.

Uncertain what mathematic Zukofsky may be pursuing here, we may content ourselves with the climate of musicality, an immediate delight as the quick movement incorporates run after run of rapid notes:

> ... leaf
> Lighting stem, stem bound to the branch that binds the
> Tree, and then as from the same root we talk ...

—from leaf down to the father's and son's common root, and their talk will be

> leaf
> After leaf of your mind's music, page, ...

"Page" elucidates "leaf" with perhaps a glance at Dante's leaves of the universe love has bound into a volume. "Page" is perhaps also one way the song is being enjoined to address the son, calling him by the title of a youth preparing for knighthood. And you, son, the song is to say, are to "walk leaf over leaf of his [the father's] thought," "sounding his happiness," apparently on your instrument, as from a score. And his happiness as you sound it will be a new song,

> sounding
> The grace that comes from knowing
> Things, her love our own showing
> Her love in all her honor.

—Celia's love now ours, the song's and Paul's; her love, moreover, "our own showing [forth of] her love in all her honor." All the syntax floats. Her love inheres in her honor, we shall be showing her love in honor of her . . .; triumphantly, the syntax of enjambment that knotted the third stanza yields overlaid planes of clear meaning in the fifth.

For sense, we may at last discover, does inhere in *"A"*-11's progress from word to word. An appositive syntax leaves us many times choosing, and bewilders us when we don't see possibilities, but normally it guides univocal choice. But—here we loop back to where this discussion started—our attention is apt to be so overloaded by multiple choices that it loses track of its criteria for choice, and then the rich polyphony supersedes: light, leaf, song, honor, love, light. Mallarmé, who receives homage in *"A"*-19, may have been the first to explore a poetic of information overload, the sentence diagrammable but just too intricate in its system of digressions for the mind to grasp it whole. This is a procedure to be carefully distinguished from entanglement into which the poet has strayed by mistake. The reader of *"A"*-11 might profitably spend an evening with "Toast Funèbre," concentrating on the 9-line sentence that commences "Moi, de votre désir soucieux . . . ." And the troubadours and Guido Cavalcanti are relevant too, for their fostering of the ritual poem compact with subtle doctrine. The shape of Cavalcanti's great canzone, twice iterated, gave the armature for *"A"*-9. What is new in *"A"*-11, apart from the newness of every great feat of execution, is the use of the closed family unit, husband, wife, son, as echo-chamber, so to speak, for what had been traditionally public ceremonies. In their roles—he father and poet, Celia wife and musician, Paul son and violinist—they quicken the never explicit possibility that she will set this song and Paul will play the setting while she listens. Bound by love, talent, and musicianship, each person mirrored in the other two, they are terms in a metaphysic of endless relationships. Intent on their private understandings, the poem need not seek excuse for its closed quality, for its habit of curving away from readers of the book. The late mediaeval metaphysicians of love voiced a bravado of hermeticism, the song comprehensible (it asserted) only by men fit to comprehend it. *"A"*-11 is more tactful. If we do not wholly comprehend, it is not that our understandings are unfit; it is merely that we are not of the family, and are overhearing family conversation.

PETER QUARTERMAIN

"NOT AT ALL SURPRISED BY SCIENCE":
Louis Zukofsky's First Half of "A"-9

> A man should be learned in several sciences,
> and should have a reasonable, philosophical,
> and in some measure a mathematical head, to
> be a complete and excellent poet.
>
> *John Dryden*[1]

In November 1940, Louis Zukofsky published in a mimeograph edition of 55 copies (40 of them for sale) his *First Half of "A" -9*.[2] It sold slowly: he could send a copy to Edward Dahlberg in January 1951, and he still had one left to send to Cid Corman in December 1958.[3] Here is the opening strophe of the poem:

> An impulse to action sings of a semblance
> Of things related as equated values,
> The measure all use is time congealed labor
> In which abstraction things keep no resemblance
> 5   To goods created; integrated all hues
> Hide their natural use to one or one's neighbor.
> So that were the things words they could say: Light is
> Like night is like us when we meet our mentors
> Use hardly enters into their exchanges,

---

1. John Dryden, "Preface to *Notes and Observations on The Empress* of Morocco," *Works*, ed. Sir Walter Scott, 2nd edition, Edinburgh and London, 1821. XV, 411.
2. *First Half of "A"-9*, New York, 1940. Further references will be identified parenthetically as *First Half* only when the material cited is peculiar to this edition. The poem itself, without the apparatus included in *First Half*, is in *"A" 1-12*, London, 1966, pp. 112-114, and in *"A,"* Berkeley, Los Angeles and London, 1978, pp. 106-108. All references to the text of *"A"* appear parenthetically in my text as *"A,"* followed by two page numbers: the first refers to *"A" 1-12*, the second to the 1978 edition of the whole of *"A."* Other work by or referring to Zukofsky is abbreviated as follows: *Bottom: On Shakespeare*, Austin, Texas, 1963, as *Bottom*; *Prepositions*, London, 1967, as *P.*; Marcella Booth, *A Catalogue of the Louis Zukofsky Manuscript Collection*, Austin, Texas, as Booth. When *"A"-9* was printed as a broadside ("Futura 9," Stuttgart, 1966) Zukofsky reiterated his earlier (and in my view deeply regrettable) decision that *First Half* is "not to be reprinted."
3. The correspondence between Zukofsky and Dahlberg and Corman relating to these copies is at the Humanities Research Center, University of Texas at Austin.

10   Bought to be sold things, our value arranges;
        We flee people who made us as a right is
        Whose sight is quick to choose us as frequenters,
        But see our centers do not show the changes
        Of human labor our value estranges.

Fourteen lines, an upside-down sonnet, revolving round the "sold"
of line 10, where the difficult syntax, in its compression, brings
the voice up short amidst mellifluous lines whose tune lulls the attention, where rhymes sound changes almost like English church
bells. If you read it aloud without paying attention to the sense it
sounds gorgeous, unlike any other poem in the English language.
Then your ear seduces you into figuring out what it says, and you
pause, and consider. Should the voice pause for breath, for example, at the "when" in line 8, and then run on into line 9? or do
we runover the "when" to take a breath between the two lines?
Is "sold" in line 10 an adjective? or is it the passive verb, "to be
sold"? The antecedents, in any case, are elusive, and our confusion over these apparently muddled parts of speech is reflected in
the broken rhythms of the last four lines of the strophe. The language is very abstract, and it looks something like Marx, contrasting "sold things" with "made things," talking (after Aristotle)
about proper use and unnatural use, about value, good, and labour.
And in fact the sense of the strophe is fairly straightforward.

    When he published *First Half of "A"-9* in 1940, Zukofsky
included a prose "Restatement" of the poem. It summarises the
first strophe as follows:

> The poem sings about things embodying a common denominator
> of past work, tho this abstract evaluation of them hides the fact
> that things are goods made to be used by people. If things could
> speak, they would point out that those who buy to sell them in
> the exchanges withdraw them from their proper owners who
> work in order to enjoy them (*First Half*, p. 40).

Voicing the sense, we fight against the tune: the syntax is so compressed, so difficult, that—drawn into thought by the demands of
the ear—we are forced continually to rephrase or re-emphasise our
speech, and we discover, tracking the complicated second sentence
through, paying attention to the verse, that our thought is—like
the syntax—perpetually shifting from one perspective to another:
ideas and thoughts come and go the way the sound comes and
goes, the way parts of speech in this language modulate one into
another. Not only do these lines bring voice to crisis, they bring
thought to crisis too: we tend to bewilderment, for we are (as is
customary in Zukofsky's poetry) left off-balance, with only the
music of the verse to hold us steady, and we are forced into a state

of perpetual alertness and concentration where we remain open to possibilities of meaning and relationship.

In his 1946 essay on "Poetry," Zukofsky describes rhetoricians as "responsible for the rule that a clause introduced by the word 'that' is not preceded by a comma, whereas a clause introduced by the word 'which' is." One wonders what they would make of the unpunctuated eighth line. Zukofsky accuses them of existing "entirely in *that frozen realm without crisis* that Dante called the 'secondary speech' " (*P.*, p. 18. Italics added). And what might that crisis be? If you read the rest of page 18 of *Prepositions*, it might be syntax, or punctuation, or rhythm:

> A dog that runs never lies down—and of the dog who if not mythical has rhetorical distinction, having been stopped by commas—
> A dog, *that* runs, never lies down.
> All this about dogs may be learned from a study of quantity and from the fact that both prose and poetry, if they are that, are meant to record and elate for all time.

Or there is "Julia's Wild" (*Bottom*, p. 393), where that crisis might, as well, be repetition, recurrence. And if you read Henry Adams, on whom before he was twenty Zukofsky wrote a book[4] (if anybody would print it that way), then *this* is crisis:

> Of all the elaborate symbolism which has been suggested for the Gothic cathedral, the most vital and most perfect may be that slender nervure, the springing motion of the broken arch, the leap downwards of the flying buttress—*the visible effort to throw off a visible strain*—never let us forget that Faith alone supports it, and that, if Faith fails, Heaven is lost. The equilibrium is visibly delicate beyond the line of safety; danger lurks in every stone. The peril of the heavy tower, of the restless vault, of the vagrant buttress; the uncertainty of logic, the inequalities of syllogism, the irregularities of the mental mirror—all these haunting nightmares of the Church are expressed as strongly by the Gothic cathedral as though it had been the cry of human suffering, and as no emotion had ever been expressed before or is likely to find expression again. The delight of its aspirations is flung up to the sky. The pathos of its self-distrust and anguish of doubt is buried in the earth as its last secret.[5]

Zukofsky quotes this paragraph in his work on Adams (*P.*, p. 110), and omits what I omit: the opening sentence, which talks of

---

4. *Henry Adams: Detached Mind and Poetic Undertow* was substantially complete by May 7, 1924, and was Zukofsky's M.A. thesis at Columbia University. Not only was it, as Zukofsky himself noted, the first full-length study of Adams; it was written within six years of the publication (in 1918) of Adams' *Education*.
5. Henry Adams, *Mont-Saint-Michel and Chartres*, Introduction by Ralph Adams Cram, Boston, 1933, p. 377. Emphasis added. Further references are abbreviated *MSM*.

"*apparent* instability" (italics added). The omission is interesting, for it points to what might that crisis be.

Michel Foucault locates that crisis in *thought*, which he calls "a perilous act";[6] Robert Duncan, in an essay on Olson, has spoken of *language* as risk, "the conquest of babble by the ear."[7] And Henry Adams, in *Mont-Saint-Michel and Chartres*, finds that crisis expressed in *structure*, in architecture, in building. "Look with delight," he enjoins us, "at the theatrical stage-decoration of the Gothic vault":

> the astonishing feat of building up a skeleton of stone ribs and vertebrae, on which every pound of weight is adjusted, divided, and carried down from level to level till it touches ground at a distance as a bird would alight. If any stone in any part, from apex to foundation, weathers or gives way, the whole must yield . . . (*MSM*, pp. 107-108).

An *apparent* instability: the Cathedral at Chartres, a twelfth- and thirteenth-century building, "as solid," Adams notes, "as when it was built." Contemporary with Cavalcanti's precursor, Arnaut Daniel, whom Dante called *il miglior fabbro*. As airy, aerated, as light. An apparent instability.

And crisis? To record and elate for all time. Such crisis, that the line should bound from the page (yet still, perhaps, be the "bounding line" Blake wrote of in *A Descriptive Catalogue*, "distinct, sharp, and wiry"): like a spring, wound, wound up. "A mason will tap a pillar to make its stress audible," says W.R. Lethaby. "We may think of a cathedral as so 'high strung' that if struck it would give a musical note."[8] In *"A"*-6, written in 1930, Zukofsky talks of

> Forms only in snatches,
> Words rangeless, melody forced by writing, ...
>
> (*"A,"* p. 28; p. 22).

These are difficult lines, and I shall come back to them. From their context I take them to signify a breakdown of a larger system from which the writer once drew. Words rangeless, I take as words with nowhere to go—like lost cattle—or unable to go, like penned ones. I take Form to be intermittent, and melody to arise

6. Michel Foucault, *The Order of Things: An Archaeology of the Human Sciences*, London, 1970, p. 328.
7. Robert Duncan, "Notes on Poetics Regarding Olson's Maximus," *The Poetics of the New American Poetry*, edited by Donald M. Allen and Warren Tallman, New York, 1973, p. 190.
8. William Richard Lethaby, *Architecture: An Introduction to the History and Theory of the Art of Building*, with a new Preface by Basil Ward, 3rd edition, London, 1955, p. 153. Partially quoted in *Bottom*, pp. 183-184.

from thought rather than from song or felt impulse. A breakdown of forms and a loss of resource.

In his essay on Adams, Zukofsky wrote that "Adams had not the faith which makes of its thoughts a system to be put forward as text" (*P.*, p. 111). He might be talking of himself, for whatever the text *"A"* might be, it is no system ("A" is, after all, the *in*-definite article): *"A"* might be *rangeless*: *"adj rare . . . .* That has no range or limit" (*OED*). Words rangeless might be words which can go anywhere, then: making forms only in snatches, such forms being songs (snatches), melody forced by writing: an intermittency, perhaps, but hardly a system. Hugh Kenner reports, of *"A"*:

> Zukofsky began about 1927 with a formal plan, a plan of the form, which means in practice (1) an intuition of the poem without any words in it, a silent structural eloquence; and (2) a sequential table of difficulties to be overcome. I picked up this information from Basil Bunting, who doesn't know, nor do I, how closely the plan has been stuck to . . . .[9]

Melody, *forced* by writing. There is no clear single thematic content of *"A,"* though there are intermittent themes; there is an *intended* structure, "a table of difficulties," a sequence, no matter how loosely one might think of it.

Such sequence has some coincidences—or rather, some elements that are hardly likely to have been planned from the beginning in 1927 (the last movement of the poem, after all, was finished in 1974).[10] There is, for example, the matter of dates: *"A"*-7, written in 1928-1930; *First Half of "A"-9* in 1938-1940; and second half of *"A"*-9 in 1948-1950. At ten-year intervals. *First Half of "A"-9* is a canzone (which, says Pound, Dante set as "the grand bogey of technical mastery"),[11] about "labour" and "value." The second half is, as any reader can see, a "reply" to the first half, "love" replying to "value." Each half copies exactly the rhyme-scheme and form of Cavalcanti's *Donna mi priegha*; each half is 75 lines long: five strophes of 14 lines each (but hardly sonnets) and a coda of five lines. The whole of *"A"*-9, then, is a *double* canzone.

And *"A"*-7? In 1928-1930, at the beginning of those ten-year intervals, Zukofsky wrote this cycle of seven sonnets (that is,

---

9. "Of Notes and Horses," *Poetry*, CXI (November, 1967), p. 112.
10. Of the 24 movements of *"A,"* the last completed were *"A"* 22 & 23; the manuscript at the Humanities Research Center, University of Texas at Austin, is dated April 17, 1974.
11. Ezra Pound, *Literary Essays*, edited with an introduction by T.S. Eliot, London, 1954, p. 170. Further references abbreviated *LE*. Ezra Pound's *Gaudier-Brzeska A Memoir*, New York, 1970, will be referred to as *G-B*.

half a sonnet cycle, if ideally the sonnet cycle consists of fourteen sonnets). And in his essay on Cavalcanti, written by 1931 and in its final form published after Zukofsky had written *"A"*-7, Pound says this:

> The sonnet was not a great poetic *invention*. The sonnet occurred automatically when some chap got stuck in the effort to make a canzone. His 'genius' consisted in the recognition that he had come to the end of his subject matter. (*LE*, p. 168)

The sequence is of difficulties for the *writer*, and the compositional methods are opportunist; that is, Zukofsky seizes the difficulty when and as it presents itself. In *"A"*-9, for example, the letters "r" and "n" are distributed in the first five strophes according to a mathematical formula: "the first seventy lines," says a note on "The 'Form' " (*First Half*, p. 37), "are a poetic analog of a conic section." When asked why, Zukofsky replied that "the formula for a conic section was a friend's suggestion I used with my usual impulse to overcome something, as a resistance for work or working out" (which is to write by impulse: a push against, a counterthrust). "During the work it may after a while come easy, or at least must look that way to the reader" (for such is to sing), "and when it's done it can all be scrapped."[12]

"A"-7 is a sonnet cycle which, as it progresses, gradually breaks down: the predetermined form slowly collapses. The lines are almost all uniformly decasyllabic (though the syntax breaks up the iambs early in the sequence), and there are some notable exceptions which mainly cluster toward the end of the final sonnet (one line is a thirteener). The octets are in their rhyme scheme perfectly regular, but the sestets vary considerably, playing variations on a basic Shakespearean pattern until, in the final more-or-less Miltonic sonnet (which is itself run-on from the sixth so that the two sonnets together make a single rhythmic statement) the rhyme scheme collapses, rhyming "words" with "care" as it does (!), in lines of ten and eleven syllables respectively. At the same time, the decasyllabics of the sonnets move, in the final one, towards hendecasyllabics—i.e. toward the line of the canzone in *"A"*-9, Arnaut Daniel toward Cavalcanti. Through the turbulent rhythms of *"A"*-7, where quantity comes gradually to dominate, the form slowly collapses until the writing is scarcely recognisable as sonnets, is perhaps *sirventes*. *"A"*-7, that is to say, is responsive to something other than its predetermined form, its overt plan. It is form subject to outside interference which generates crisis:

---

12. Letter to Peter Quartermain, October 18, 1968.

it may well, indeed, have been written to demonstrate Pound's proposition that the sonnet "marks the beginning of the divorce of words and music" (*LE*, p. 170). (I might perhaps note in passing that the whole of *"A"* is—among other things—an exemplum of most poetic forms familiar to an English ear: tercets in *"A"*-13, for example, or Roman comedy in *"A"*-21, elegy in *"A"*-3, ballads, folk-songs, even anthologies, elsewhere. As Zukofsky wrote to Cid Corman on 11 July 1960, "despite the Cavalcanti yoke of *"A"*-9, plus the mathematic etc—it's still L.Z. & not a prosody book."[13] But the notion of "prosody book" is a strong formal element overall, in *"A."*)

At any rate, in *"A"*-7 the form (i.e. sonnet cycle) slowly collapses, and such collapse is followed by *"A"*-8, whose burden is "For Labor, who will sing . . . ?" (and labour surely includes writing), and *"A"*-8 slowly and laboriously works towards song. Quoting extensively from the correspondence of Marx and Engels, and from Henry and Brooks Adams, on the problem of "value," occasionally parodying Spinoza, breaking forth sporadically into more-or-less crude Proletarian Song (such as "March Comrades" on pp. 54-55; pp. 48-49)[14] quoting snatches—odd lines and phrases—from poems, folk-songs, and plays which Zukofsky was gathering in *A Test of Poetry* (which once again suggests that *"A"* is, amongst other things, a text-book of poetry), quoting bits of interviews, newspaper reports, and "history," the rag-bag collage-pastiche of *"A"*-8 struggles through its disorders, at the last, into song: the "Ballade" of 36 lines which ends *"A"*-8. In that struggle, *"A"*-8 has recourse to formulaic elements: among Zukofsky's papers at the Humanities Research Center at the University of Texas at Austin there is Zukofsky's chart of the "r" and "n" patterns in what he calls the "Calculus Section" of *"A"*-8, which immediately follows the crude Proletarian Song of "March Comrades" (*"A,"* pp. 55-58; pp. 49-53): the number of "r's" and "n's" accelerates or decelerates in varying ratios in each stanza, treated in groups of three lines.[15] The "Ballade" itself, with its three ten-line stanzas followed by a six-line Coda, draws heavily on formulaic elements with its careful sequence of rhymes (which are the same for each stanza), its varied refrain (which in the Coda reads "Labor light lights in earth, in air, on earth" − p. 111; p. 105), and a scrupulous distribution of "r" and "n" according to formula.

---

13. Letter to Cid Corman, *Origin, Second Series*, No. 1 (April 1961), p. 46.
14. Published in *New Masses*, XXVII, 6 (May 3, 1938), 14 as "March Comrades. Words for a workers' chorus."
15. Described in Booth, p. 52, item C8a. There is also a balancing of patternings amongst the nine stanzas. I, V, and IX, for example, are almost identical.

In the mid-nineteen-thirties Zukofsky had, with Jerry Reisman, been discussing and experimenting with the possibility of writing poetry according to various mathematical formulae (the manuscript notes on *"A"*-8 illustrated on p. 88 of Booth are largely in Reisman's hand), and after he had determined his plans for *"A"*-9 Zukofsky rewrote the "Ballade" to conform to "the analogy to the calculus":

> the ratio of the accelerations of two sounds (r, n) is equal to the ratio of the accelerations of the coordinates (x, y) of a particle moving in a circular path for nine symmetrically located points on the path. (Booth, pp. 53, 88)

However, the full complexity of song toward which *"A"*-8 struggles is achieved not in the "Ballade" which brings it to a close, but in the complex formulaic double-canzone of *"A"*-9, where the form of the canzone, although hendecasyllabic, reflects both the sonnets of *"A"*-7 and the stanzas of *"A"*-8's close. *"A"*-9 is followed, after *"A"*-10's elegy (an inverted Mass) on the fall of Paris in 1940, by *"A"*-11, whose stanzaic form is almost an exact mirror-image of the closing thirty-six lines of *"A"*-8 (though the writing is no longer formulaic), and which is devoted to the domestic life of Zukofsky's family.[16] In *"A"*-11 the more-or-less turbulent surface of *"A"*-9 is smoothed out into the clarity of Bach's music, and of a lyric voice more subdued, less overtly virtuoso, less public. The whole sequence of *"A" 1-12* is progressively a more and more urgently felt struggle toward *form* and struggle toward *song*, in which traditional forms break down, somehow to recur, recognisable, broken, crabbed, but nevertheless lurching towards music until, the music of *"A"*-11 clear, *"A"*-12 is freed to go its own way, speech into song. "A noble structure is not a thing of will, of design, of scholarship," writes W.R. Lethaby. "A true architecture is the discovery of the nature of things in building."[17]

So, let us go back to Henry Adams. For as I read Louis Zukofsky, I see more and more of Adams' presence. Adams is discussing twelfth-century stained glass:

> The French held then that the first point in colour decoration was colour, and they never hesitated to put their colour where they wanted it, or cared whether a green camel or a pink lion looked like a dog or a donkey provided they got their harmony or value. Everything except colour was sacrificed to line in the large

---

16. See Hugh Kenner, "Too Full For Talk: *"A"*-11," *Maps*, No. 5 (1973), pp. 12-21, for a careful discussion of this poem. Reprinted herein pp. 195-202.
17. *Architecture*, p. 159.

sense, but details of drawings were conventional and subordinate. So we laugh to see a knight with a blue face, on a green horse, that looks as though drawn by a four-year-old child, and probably the artist laughed, too; but he was a colourist, and never sacrificed his colour for a laugh. (*MSM*, p. 138)

Henry Adams is discussing an art which is close indeed to Zukofsky's, though I do not think that the details in Zukofsky are conventional—or, if they are, they are not conventionally treated. Whether or not they are subordinate is another matter. Adams' point, though, is that the artists never hesitated to put their colour where *they* wanted it—yet the whole tenor of his argument is that the artist was subservient to the Muse (who, at Chartres, was the Virgin): everything is done to please Her. The work, the worker, the artist, is without intention—or, if there is an intention, it is to please the Muse, not the World or the Self. "Value," says Karl Marx, "does not wear an explanatory label."[18] I shall have occasion later to quote a story Guy Davenport tells, about "mg. dancer." It is hard to believe that "mg. dancer" exists to please anyone but the Muse.

Secondly, Adams says in this passage that *content* is subordinate to *form*: or, rather, that whatever it is that the stained glass does, it does not seek to state propositions about the world. It seeks rather to have an *effect*.[19] It is also implicit in Adams' argument that the artist *may* not have known what the effect would be, ahead of time: we cannot know, for as Adams says "we have lost many senses" (*MSM*, p. 129). Whether the artist knew or not, one thing is clear: *form* is, as Adams discusses it, something to be *felt*. And one's feelings, though they may be intent, are hardly to be spoken of as having intentions. And, as Adams describes it, or as I have talked about it in terms of crisis, form is a *force*, itself generative. Somewhere around A.D. 1300 Lawrence of Aquilegia, presenting a collection of letters to be used as models in writing (formulae, then), asserted that "it is better to work from form rather than material."[20] Robert Creeley commented in 1966 that Zukofsky "feels form as an intimate presence, whether or not that form be the use or issue of other

18. Karl Marx, *Capital*, Translated from the Fourth German Edition by Eden and Cedar Paul, introduction by G.D.H. Cole, addendum by Murray Wolfson, London and New York (Everyman's Library), 1974. Further referred to as *Capital*.
19. Of course, a "sought effect" might indeed be *per se* a proposition, and "effects" might well generate "propositions" anyway. The matter is discussed *passim* in *Bottom*.
20. Lawrence of Aquilegia, *Speculum Dictaminis*; quoted in James J. Murphy, introduction to *Three Medieval Rhetorical Arts*, Berkeley, 1971, p. vii. I am grateful to Meredith Yearsley for showing this to me.

feelings in other times, or the immediate apprehension of a *way* felt in the moment of its occurrence."[21] That apprehension is a force which makes its own form or takes it as it finds it, ready made.

"Probably the artist laughed, too; but he ... never sacrificed his colour for a laugh," Adams says. The poetry is not—any more than is a stained-glass window at Chartres—a proposition about the world. It is a play, a play of words, a play of content, where play becomes song, becomes colour. Melody, *forced* by writing.

> Forced: *"ppl. adj* .... Compelled, imposed, or exacted by force; enforced, compulsory; not spontaneous voluntary, or optional .. .. Produced or maintained with effort. Strained .... In literary usage: strained, distorted .... Of actions, affected, artificial, constrained, unnatural .... Of plants, made to bear, or produced, out of the proper season." (*OED*)

The *Oxford English Dictionary* tells us, too, that "to force" is "to put a strained sense upon (words). Also, to force (words) into a sense." And a forced march is "one in which the marching power of the troops is forced or exerted beyond the ordinary limits." Guy Davenport once asked Zukofsky what the "mg. dancer" is who dances in *"A"*-21, "a milligram sprite, a magnesium elf, a margin dancer, or Aurora, as the dictionary allows for all of these meanings. 'All,' he replied."[22]

Hence—or thus!—the lines from *"A"*-6, a visible strain:

> Forms only in snatches,
> Words rangeless, melody forced by writing, ...

"I take Form to be intermittent," I wrote earlier, but there I had in mind Form as a noun, when it could be verb. A "snatch" is a short space of time; it is a song or tune—or part of one; it is a sudden grab. "In snatches": by fits and starts, in hasty unsustained efforts. And "snatch" is also slang for what, in another poem ("The Translation"), Zukofsky calls *"malakòs leimown,"* a soft grassy meadow, *pudenda muliebra.* Zukofsky has a book called *Thanks to the Dictionary* (unfortunately long out-of-print) which gives us a clue: go to the dictionary and these lines from *"A"*-6 come to reveal what William Blake found, not in "Grecian mathematic" but in the Gothic: "living form."[23] Words rangeless, conveying not one meaning, but a play of meanings; the form not a system but a *way*. Words slip and slide in their syntactic bounds.

---

21. Robert Creeley, *A Quick Graph: Collected Notes & Essays,* edited by Donald Allen, San Francisco, 1970, p. 130.
22. Guy Davenport, "Zukofsky's *"A"-24,"* *Parnassus,* II, 2 (Spring-Summer 1974), 19.
23. William Blake, "On Homer's Poetry & On Virgil."

Rangeless, words strain and threaten to crack, but the delicate balance holds.

"Writing," both as an *object* (the writing on the page) and as an *act* (the man writing), becomes *a* force: shaping, pressuring, bringing to *crisis* (the point, the dictionary reminds us, in the course of events which is decisive of recovery or death), bringing to crisis the LANGUAGE, forcing *melody*, perhaps as a plant might be forced. A range is a limit while it is at the same time an extent (a range of mountains), and like Wittgenstein's boundary suggests what lies beyond. It is only through boundary, I think Wittgenstein says somewhere, that we can imagine a beyond, a sense of further. And "strain" is an air is a tune. "To throw off" is to produce, or can be. And I come back to the by now inevitable Henry Adams, talking of "the visible effort to throw off visible strain." Which is to say,

> melody forced by writing.

And if this is the nature of the content, then how can the poet have intentions about what the poem will *say*? How can *"A"* remain, was it Zukofsky who called it, in 1938, "an epic of the class struggle"?[24] Or, what may be more to the "point," how can one know what the poem will say until it says it? What kind of content might such poem have? No predatory intent will serve; no theory or presupposition can account for the poem, or bring the poem to account; there can be no expectations of *that* sort. The poem is, as Robert Duncan asks, adventure, or discovery, or both: an act of crisis. And it is the outcome of a great deal of concentrated thought, like "the great cathedral" as W.R. Lethaby described it in a book Zukofsky read:

> a balanced structure of stone which found its perfected form at the limits where men could do no more. Thus it was that a cathedral was not designed, but discovered, or 'revealed.'[25]

II.

"We have lost many senses," said Henry Adams. Ezra Pound, in his essay on Cavalcanti, provides an instance: "We appear to have lost the radiant world where one thought cuts through another with a clean edge, a world of moving energies . . ." (*LE*, p. 154), which is Adams' world of the Gothic, almost contemporary

24. "Notes on Contributors," *New Directions, 1938*, Norfolk, Conn., 1938 (unpaginated).
25. *Architecture*, p. 159.

with what Pound calls Cavalcanti's "scholastic definition in form" (*LE*, p. 161). One thought cuts through another; concentrated thought. Of the 41 pages of *First Half of "A"-9*, only two are taken up by the poem. The rest, as the one-page "Foreword" tells us, consists of the materials that went into the writing of the poem. They are as follows:

> Cavalcanti's *Donna mi priegha* (2 pages)
>
> extracts from Karl Marx's *Capital* (Everyman's Library edition), chapters 1-13, and *Value Price and Profit* (22 pages)
>
> extracts from Herbert Stanley Allen's *Electrons and Waves: An Introduction to Atomic Physics* (3 pages)
>
> four translations of Cavalcanti's canzone: two by Ezra Pound, and two in slang, by Jerry Reisman (the first two strophes only) and Louis Zukofsky (8 pages altogether)
>
> a note on "The 'Form' " (1 page).

The poem itself, titled *"A" - 9 (First half)*, is followed by a prose "Restatement" of the poem's "content" (two pages). The note on the form quotes Pound's analysis/description of the rhyme-scheme and structure of *Donna mi priegha* (*LE*, p. 168), and explains that

> the first 70 lines are the poetic analog of a conic section—i.e. the ratio of the accelerations of two sounds (r, n) has been made equal to the ratio of the accelerations of the coordinates (x, y) of a particle moving in a circular path with uniform angular velocity. I. e. values of
>
> $$\frac{\dfrac{d^2y}{dt^2}}{\dfrac{d^2x}{dt^2}} = \tan \theta \text{ where } \theta = \text{arc tan } \frac{y}{x}$$
>
> are noted for five symmetrically located points. The time unit in the poetry is defined by 7 eleven-syllable lines. Each point is represented by a strophe. Mr. Jerry Reisman is responsible for this part of the "form." The coda is free. (*First Half*, p. 37)

Thus, in the second strophe for example, there are 13 n and 13 r sounds in the first seven lines, and 14 n and 13 r in the second ("ng" combinations are not included in the count): "n" thus has an "infinite" acceleration over "r," which does not increase-frequency at all in this strophe.

All this sounds like—and is—very complicated formulaic writing. The formulaic element of the poem is increased by the fact that the poem itself is a version if not exactly a translation of *Donna mi priegha* (which means that the "content" or "material" of the poem is provided) written under the formidable constraints imposed by specific vocabularies (Marx and Allen). By providing

the matter of the poem, the formula can be said to guarantee coherence of thought, just as by providing letter-frequencies and
rhythms (to say nothing of complex rhymes!) it guarantees a coherent sound-pattern: the occurrence of a similar sequence of
sounds in each strophe unifies the strophes into a coherent structure: a complex song.

"For Labor, who will sing . . .?" asked *"A"*-8. And the coda
to this poem provides the answer: no-one; *Labour* can sing—as it
does here—of its own accord. For inspired by the abstraction
"time congealed labor" (line 3), the poem has in the course of its
writing been *forced* to turn from the abstraction to the actual and
specific labour which the words themselves, in the song, embody:

> song's exaction
> Forces abstraction to turn from equated
> Values to labor we have approximated. (lines 73-75)

That is what the coda tells us, and it tells the truth, for in the
course of the poem the writing works against so much, the formula demands so much; it is only through song's *exaction* in this
way that the poem can work at all. Thus the abstract (like the
word "value," for instance) becomes concrete, specific, in the
activity—the action—the labour, which the form of the song embodies, and which the form of the song calls forth in the reader:
concentrated thought. And the poem itself, *"A"*-9 *(First half)*,
becomes—how shall I put it?—an act of incarnation, where the abstract is *bodily* put forth. On page 79 of *Bottom: on Shakespeare*,
Zukofsky talks of the three terms, "sense (the *universal* term for
singular feeling), essence (the *universal* for singular *being*), and
nonsense (i.e. non-sense, the *universal* for universal being uncon-
cerned with singular *feeling*)" as having "always made up the arguments of logic and metaphysics." The language of *"A"*-9, abstract (the first six lines of the poem, after all, summarise the
opening chapters of *Capital*), *essence*, is converted into the *sin-
gularity* of sense, singular feeling, by the very act of writing the
poem, or by the act of reading it. The intense concentration of
the poem demands much the same of the reader as it did of the
writer: the method of composition forces labour, and the poem
offers a kind of proof-by-experiment. In the act of understanding
the poem, wound-in as it is, the abstractions of language, the
things which are words, become singular, turn to the particulars
of their existence—something which Spinoza always insisted
upon. They act out, one might say, the Revolution they call for,
and the reader participates in the activity of their incarnation:
an idea is thus experienced, *felt*, and the words of the poem are

immediate to our senses. "Were the things words," says line 7. By the time we reach the coda, they are—or rather, the words are things.

And we should not forget that the poem is a version/translation of Cavalcanti's poem which is, Ezra Pound tells us, "a struggle for definition" (*LE*, p. 177). The poem begins with a question, and then seeks to answer it, in rational and philosophical terms, as well as in a densely musical form. And Zukofsky's stage-Irish/Brooklynese version dismisses the question, almost, by beginning "A foin lass bodders me I gotta tell her," reminding us of the sound, the *speech*, of it, and forcing our attention on the patterns which emerge, the rhymes and echoes. It is a careful and comic debunking of the literary or "pretty," like Jerry Reisman's, whose first stanza insists on the flat matter-of-fact nature of the question the poem treats, with fine irreverence. It is called "A Dame Ast Me":

> It's so hot an' proud comin' so often, dough
> A natural freak, I'm itchin' to speak becuz
> A dame ast what wuz love. Wut is it? I t'ink
> A heel in a crowd is not too dumb to know -
> It may be all greek, a lot of cheek or fuzz
> To wise guys - it does no good to teach a gink
> Who'll never ever be high's a Georgia pie
> Yet git by fine widout no experiments.
> I don't wanna, gents, nor am I apt 'a prove
> Where it wuz born, how it begun to move,
> What its good points are an' how it gits in high
> An' how by an' large it is its own movements
> An' de pleasin' sense of what it feels "to love"
> An' if guys see it clear's a t'ing in a groove.

> *(First Half, p. 34)*

Cavalcanti's answer, says Pound, "shows leanings toward . . . the proof by experiment" (*LE*, p. 149). Zukofsky's answer (*"A"*-9, that is), sticking to Cavalcanti's form, drawing on a mathematical formula for a conic section, takes a vocabulary drawn from Karl Marx and modern physics as well as from Cavalcanti so that, concentrated, one thought may indeed cut through another, Marx through Cavalcanti through physics. Discussing Charlie Chaplin in 1935, Zukofsky talked of "*inventive* existence interacting with other existence in all its ramifications" (*P.*, p. 54, emphasis added), and in his "Foreword" to *First Half* he speaks of his "intention to have the poem fluoresce as it were in the light of seven centuries of interrelated thought." Fluorescence occurs, I recall, "when a substance is excited to fluoresce" by radiation or impulse, and is, of course, itself a source of light. Ezra Pound talks of a "radiant world" which we have lost, talks of "magnetisms that take form, that are seen, or that border the visible, the matter of Dante's *paradiso* . . ." (*LE*, p. 154). I notice, incidentally, that in 1896 Edison, "by coating the interior surface of a Crookes' tube with crystals of a new fluorescing substance," caused "X rays to change to light." (*OED* 1933 Supp., "Fluorescing.") Later in his essay, Pound remarks of Cavalcanti's poem that it is "quite possible that the whole of it is a sort of metaphor on the generation of light . . ." (*LE*, p. 161). "Light is/ Like night is like us," things sing in lines 7 and 8 of *First Half of "A"-9*. Things *sing*.

The formula for a conic section Zukofsky uses to determine the distribution of "r" and "n" is a second degree equation derived from Descartian or Analytical Geometry, in which, says Pound, "space is conceived as separated by two or three axes (depending on whether one is treating form in one or more planes)" (*G-B*, p. 91). In his 1921 essay on Brancusi, Pound talked of "form as free in its own life as the form of the analytic geometers" (*LE*, p. 444), while seven years earlier, in his essay on "Vorticism," he had written that "the difference between art and analytical geometry is the difference of subject-matter only" (*G-B*, p. 91). Pound is discussing sculpture, but it sounds remarkably like a discussion of formulaic art (the music of Bach was especially attractive to those who would find mathematical procedures for composition during these years) and later in his essay Pound applies his geometrical analogy to writing. It is quite clear that in *"A"-9* the three vocabularies, Cavalcanti, Marx, and physics, are to be treated as planes which intersect. As the documents presented in *First Half of "A"-9* show, the poem has a base in mathematics, and in *"A"-12* Zukofsky states emphatically that "A poet is not at all surprised by science" (*"A,"* p. 192).

"Everyone who has lived since the sixteenth century," says Henry Adams, "has felt deep distrust of everyone who lived before it" (*MSM*, p. 139). Which is to say, somewhere in the sixteenth century something happened which most clearly separates the thirteenth century (Cavalcanti) from the twentieth (modern physics). In *Capital*, Marx found it necessary to remark that "*value* does not wear an explanatory label" (p. 47). The necessity he felt to say so reflects a world which has departed from *felt* ethical forms, that has lost the *singular* feeling, the particularity, of value; it instead finds its surety in empirical observation and verification: the proof by reason and the proof by experiment —value is an abstraction. The shift between Cavalcanti and Marx is more than a shift in language, it is a shift in thought, in the *forms* of thought, a shift, if you like, from the divine to the secular, where ethical authority has moved from Church to legal fiction of State, and has perhaps lost Author. To ask "Wut is it?" in 1290 is not to ask the same question as in 1939. For one thing, Bishop Thomas Sprat, who published his *History of the Royal Society* in 1667, stands in between, as does Marx, whose thought Sprat (or what he reports) in-forms, and Sprat's answer to the question (and Marx's) would be in a language designed to register observation, to convey verification. Sprat's is not a language of affirmation so much as it is a language of counters, approximating mathematics. The members of the Royal Society, he wrote, have

> a constant Resolution, to reject all the amplifications, digressions, and swellings of style: to return back to the primitive purity, and shortness, when men delivered so many *things*, almost in an equal number of *words*. They have exacted from all their members, a close, naked, natural way of speaking; positive expressions; clear senses; a native easiness: bringing all things as near the Mathematical plainness as they can: and preferring the language of Artizans, Countrymen, and Merchants, before that, of Wits, or Scholars.[26]

"Were the things words," says line 7 of *"A"*-9. And, Zukofsky reminds us in *Bottom* (p. 104), in Hebrew "the word for *word* is also the word for *thing*." The seventeenth century dreamed of establishing an identity, in men's minds and in the world, between language and things. "Though we cannot comprehend the *Arts* of men without many praevious *Studies*, " Sprat wrote, with such an identity in mind,

> yet such is the indulgence of *Nature*, that it has from the beginning, out of its own store, sufficiently provided every man, with all things, that are needful for the understanding of itself. (*History*, p. 344)

The world Sprat proposes is a world subject to analysis, and capable of being understood, accounted for, controlled, in terms and in ways scarcely recognisable to Cavalcanti, to whom for example the word "impulse" might, Pound guesses, rest on "A Neoplatonic gradation of the assumption of faculties as the mind descends into matter through the seven spheres, *via* the gate of Cancer" (*LE*, p. 184). Yet to Clerk Maxwell, the great nineteenth-century physicist, "impulse" is "the product of the average value of any force multiplied by the time during which it acts" (*OED*, "impulse"). Maxwell's notion of it is a long way indeed from the

---

26. Thomas Sprat, *The History of the Royal-Society of London, For the Improving of Natural Knowledge* (1667), edited by Jackson I. Cope and Harold W. Jones, St. Louis, 1959, p. 113. Further references abbreviated *History*.

Latin from which the word derives: a "push against." With the Latin in mind it becomes easy to see how "impulsive behaviour" might be the result of "a force or influence exerted upon the mind by good or evil spirits." Whatever the language of Maxwell does, it does not remind the reader of the mysteriousness (or of the mysteries) of the universe, for Maxwell's world, like that of his near-contemporary, Marx, is subject to exegesis and explanation in terms which are verifiable, *measurable.*

First Half of "A"-9 begins:

> An impulse to action sings of a semblance
> Of things related as equated values.

The material from Marx which Zukofsky quotes as one source of the poem's vocabulary is, in part, concerned with the *Value* of a *Product*—both, I notice, terms which occur in Maxwell's definition of *impulse.* "An impulse to *action.*" Pound ascribes "impulse" in the second strophe of *Donna mi priegha* to Mars, "spirited"; he does not use the word "action" at all in either of his translations of the poem, though anyone answering or thinking about the question "what is love?" might well begin by calling it "an impulse to action." For "action" is another word from Latin, from the participial stem of *agere: to do.* An action is a doing. Spinoza, the great seventeenth-century philosopher, lens-grinder, and opponent of Descartes, whose presence and words march and sing through nearly all of Zukofsky's work (and, notably, through the vocabulary of the *second* half of *"A"-9*), Spinoza, writing in Latin his geometrical propositions to prove the existence of God, affirms that "*esse = agere*," to be is to act or to do; and he discovers, deduces, proves—what you will—that God is a verb (a notion argued somewhat forcibly some centuries before by Thomas Aquinas). Action, then, "*sb*," is a verb, retains its verbal residue; it is *a doing,* a *process.* Yet on the other hand there is H. Stanley Allen, whose *Electrons and Waves* is another of the sources of Zukofsky's vocabulary in this poem. Allen calls the quantum "an atom of action,"[27] and defines "action" as "the product of energy and time" (a definition quoted in the coda of the poem; the "Restatement"—*First Half,* p. 41—ascribes that definition to "Applied mathematics") so that "if we consider the action during one complete period of vibration we find it equal to h [i.e. Planck's constant]" (*E&W*, p. 45). Here an action is *a done;* action is a noun, measured. Its verbal residue has vanished, absorbed into *product.*

---

27. H. Stanley Allen: *Electrons and Waves: An Introduction to Atomic Physics*, London, 1932, p. 43. Further references abbreviated *E&W*.

In 1879 action was defined in a physics textbook as "proportional to the average kinetic energy which the system has possessed during the time from any convenient epoch of reckoning, multiplied by the time" (*OED*).

One might conclude that definition—or, rather, the kind of definition which assumes, as Hugh Kenner puts it,[28] that "the natural operation of the mind" is "a sequence of assertions" entirely devoid of figuration—arises out of a world of appearance, and can find *value* only in appearance. Thomas Sprat found it a praiseworthy endeavour "to separate the knowledge of *Nature*, from the colours of *Rhetorick*, the devices of *Fancy*, or the delightful deceit of *Fables*" (*History*, p. 62), but he failed as a result to see that he was pinning his faith on *semblance*: "a person's appearance or demeanour, expressive of his thoughts, feelings, etc., or feigned in order to hide them" (*OED*). An impulse to action sings of a semblance. *Semblance*: "a likeness, image, or copy of." Not, then, necessarily the "real" thing. The difficulty of definitions of the sort given by empiricists is that they freeze the world into a closed system of *nouns*, locked as they are into a world of appearance known only to the senses. Known only to the senses, H. Stanley Allen is careful to emphasise, at "an instant of time at a point in space" (*E&W*, p. 59 n.): the world of semblance, the world of Newton and of Marx which moves from action into reaction and back again until it reaches equilibrium. (The second law of thermodynamics asserts it will reach inertia, entropy.) "All systems will their own closure," says Hugh Kenner (*Counterfeiters*, p. 167), for all systems seek the sure, the safe, the secure, the explicable: they seek clarity, for they seek to predict. Their aim, then, is to avert crisis, to avoid risk.

So, Marx.

Marx, in the pages from which Zukofsky draws, speaks of *value*. It is "a jelly of undifferentiated human labour" (*Capital*, p. 35). Henry Adams tells us that for some three hundred years, from 1000 to 1270, the French spent ten million dollars a year (at the 1840 worth) building cathedrals and churches. In one hundred years (from 1170 to 1270) they built 80 cathedrals and nearly 500 churches; such "intensity of conviction" has never been reached, he says, "by any passion . . . except in war." Such intensity of conviction, for three hundred years, "prostrated

---

28. Hugh Kenner, *The Counterfeiters, An Historical Comedy*, Bloomington, 1968, p. 129. Much of the argument in this paragraph is indebted to this book, hereafter cited as *Counterfeiters*.

France. The efforts of the bourgeoisie and the peasantry to recover their property, so far as it was recoverable, have lasted to the present day" (*MSM*, pp. 92-97). Marx would call that effort, those things, those buildings, "congealed labour time" (*Capital*, p. 8), and such definition, more abstract even than Henry Adams' millions of dollars, becomes a mere *datum*, redolent of neither passion nor trouble, but simply *there*. To Cavalcanti, as to those Frenchmen his contemporaries, it would be a statement of No Value. "How much does it cost," Williams asks at the beginning of *Paterson* III, "to love the locust tree/ in bloom?"

The *Oxford English Dictionary* does not include, among its definitions of "value," one which incorporates "labour" in its terms. It lists neither Marx nor Engels among its sources. Marx, like the Dictionary, was engaged in the Promethean task of bringing order to the world; balance, stability, prediction, and above all clarity. A clarity of *sense*, that is, of what is accessible through the senses: the feelings have been left behind, along with all the passions save the social or the political, rolled out of the language.

> Value: "*sb* . . . That amount of some commodity . . . which is considered to be an equivalent for something else; . . . The material or monetary worth of a thing . . . . The relative status of a thing." (*OED*)

Henry Adams reports that in Cavalcanti's time "a good miracle was in its day worth much money—so much that the rival shrines stole each other's miracles without decency" (*MSM*, p. 278). The shrine, Adams says, "turned itself into a market" (p. 104): an impulse to action? a piece of the action!

Value? In mathematics, "the precise number or amount represented by a figure, quantity, etc."; in music, "the relative length or duration of a tone signified by a note." A *measure*, then for counting, for counting time perhaps—or, in physics, temperature, or the strength of an impulse. H. Stanley Allen, discussing the emission of electrons from hot wires, talks of "the value of the saturation current from a metal [which] increases very rapidly as the temperature of the filament is raised" (*E&W*, p. 32). Henry Adams, in a passage I have already quoted, talks about the primacy of colour in twelfth-century stained-glass windows. The French, he says, never "cared whether a green camel or a pink lion looked like a dog or a donkey provided they got their harmony or value" (*MSM*, p. 138). The dictionary puts it somewhat differently: "Painting: Due or proper effect or importance; relative tone of colour in each different section of a picture; a patch characterised by a particular tone" (*OED*). And for Henry Adams, dear to Zukofsky? Value = harmony. "Things related as equated values," says line 2 of the poem. Harmony is to be felt; definition, to be perceived. The poem, through the interplay of actions, of semblances, of values, generates feelings.

One might well ask, then, what Marx is doing in this poem. Why does he fill so many (22) pages of this text? Yet one should not have to ask, any more than need ask about the Cavalcanti. The question that needs to be asked is how so many readers can see *First Half of "A"-9* as a Marxist poem. Jacques Roubaud, for example, says that it is "Marx in verse."[29] Which it is. But it is also physics in verse, and whatever else the dictionary might bear. (One effect of the formulaic "r" and "n" is to make abstract the language of the poem.) Roubaud says that the Marx in verse of the *First Half*, which talks of "value," is answered by the second half, which talks of "love." (It would be more accurate to say that the second half poses the vocabulary of Spinoza against that of Marx —the vocabulary of the Spinoza who tried to prove the existence of God, a task by the way which, Henry Adams tells us, both Saint Bernard and Blaise Pascal thought impossible [*MSM*, p. 129].) Eric Mottram, in a kind of street-corner or soap-box rhetoric, dismisses *First Half of "A"-9* as "strained versifying" which "operates as a trite statement of art taking its place as labour in 1938-40," as a "virtuosic rhetoric which, although it refuses the cruder excesses of 'proletarian poetry,' verges on . . . extravagant games."[30] That the poem is, in other words, a *failed* Marxist work. But writing about *"A" 1-12* in 1957 to William Carlos Williams, who was then contemplating his preface to the whole work, Zukofsky cautioned that "those who do not read the poem carefully may call me 'Communist' " (Booth, p. 248).

The vocabulary drawn from Marx misleads the unwary reader, for readers (and indeed some writers!) of poetry in this century have been in the habit of supposing that a poem addresses itself to one frame of reference only, and that if there is any ambiguity in a poem, then that ambiguity serves to intensify and render more complicated a "central theme" of the poem, or to reveal a covert theme or "point" of the poem which must then be "reconciled" to the overt statement/s the poem makes. Talking of

29. Jacques Roubaud, "Poétique comme exploration des changements de forme," *Changement de Forme: Révolution Langage*, edited by Jean Pierre Faye and Jacques Roubaud, Volume I, *Change de Forme: Biologies et Prosodies*, Paris, 1975, p. 75.
30. Eric Mottram, "1924-1951: Politics and Form in Zukofsky," *Maps*, No. 5 (1973), pp. 98-99.

the "resolution" of tensions and ambiguities in the poem, such readers have often identified that resolution with what they also call the poem's (and the poet's!) "integrity." It is easy to assume that the finished composition, the poem, when we finish reading the last line, is "composed," i.e. at rest, and that such composure is a means of putting the poem to bed, like a dictionary definition set in printer's type. The anticipation of "coherence" that many readers thus bring to their reading is a result in part, in Henry Adams' words, of taking for granted that there is an object to be reached at the end of [man's] journey" (*MSM*, p. 339); in part from the assumption, fostered by the schools, that "the mind of man is not satisfied with a conception of the physical universe which requires a number of different elements for its formulation" (the words are H. Stanley Allen's, *E&W*, p. 47); and in part from the notion that, since language is used to "formulate" a conception of the universe, then the language of the poem is a *vehicle* for the content of the poem, such content being, of course, the poet's "beliefs" or "ideas," which can be verified. Such language, used to transport content rather than readers, is the language of Bishop Sprat, where words are linked directly to things. Men speak, and men write, to record their observations and to communicate them, in a cautious, rational language.

Yet any poet, surely, and certainly Zukofsky, knows that such a view of language is absurd, and what coherence the poem might have is to be found elsewhere than in the poem's "themes" and "statements." For when words *are* things-in-themselves, immediate to the senses, then they have no more "content" than has a chair, or a vacuum-tube. In 1935, Zukofsky emphasised that "What Mr Charlie Chaplin (himself) thinks should be nobody's business" (*P.*, p. 51). It is not the content of the scene in *Modern Times* that is so important, but the "relation . . . that has the amplitude of insight impelled by the physical, to be found in the actual events themselves" (*P.*, p. 55). I take the matter of "relation" here to be a matter of "form," and it is irrelevant whether Zukofsky is a Marxist or a Buddhist. It does not matter at all. The Marxism, like Cavalcanti, like the physics, is the pretext of the poem: the pre-text. The poem itself, the TEXT, is not concerned with the content, which came before: "Thinking's the lowest rung," says the close of *"A"*-12; "No one'll believe I feel this" (*"A,"* p. 266; p. 260). The Text is a movement of languages, of *a number of* frames of reference, held in the language of the poem simultaneously, *at once*. And it is a *felt* world, which is not, therefore, to be interpreted; one's feelings are not subject to exegesis. As

Robert Creeley has remarked, *First Half of "A"-9* is "the *exper-ience* of valuation."[31] Zukofsky does not judge Allen or Marx against Spinoza or Cavalcanti, and find them wanting: *things*, in the poem, do the judging. Henry Adams, describing mediaeval art, says that

> anyone willing to try it could feel it like the child, reading new thought without end into the art he has studied a hundred times; but what is still more convincing, he could, at will, in an instant, shatter the whole art by calling into it a single motive of his own. (*MSM*, p. 177)

The poem is an attempt to voice, call it "the world out there," by following Marx's notion: "If commodities could speak, they would say: 'Our use-value may interest human beings; but it is not an attribute of ours, as things. What is our attribute, as things, is our value. Our own interrelations as commodities proves it . . .' " (*Capital*, p. 58). *"A"-12* expresses it "Actions things; themselves; doing" (*"A,"* p. 162; p. 156).

And like Henry Adams' cathedral, "if any stone in any part, from apex to foundation, weathers or gives way, the whole must yield" (*MSM*, p. 108). Isolate out from the text one element, one thread, one vocabulary only, treat the poem as "Marx in verse" say, and it does indeed as Eric Mottram says look like an extravagant game. One sees one stone very thoroughly indeed, and the verbal cathedral has vanished from the mind, from the ear, and from the eye. For the language of *"A"-9* is remarkably abstract, derived as each word is from three separate contexts at once, working—as Zukofsky is—with at least three things at once. Given the intentions Bunting reported for the poem, it is not surprising that at times we feel, reading *First Half of "A"-9*, that just as there may have been "an intuition of the poem without any words in it, a silent structural eloquence" (which I take to be also, then, a tune struggling for words), so too there is abstraction struggling for particularity. The particularity is found in the *collage* of contexts which accrete to the words "value," and "impulse," and "action," and so forth, and the tune, shaped as it is from Cavalcanti's form, re-inforced as it is by the formulaic "r" and "n," itself arises from impulse—melody, forced by writing. The tune, in its complex musicality, makes of those contexts, those vocabularies, disparate as they seem to be, a family. Value = harmony. The tune, the text, the poem, become a family of words, all singing together. A family. Henry Adams, describing his beloved

31. *A Quick Graph*, p. 141.

Chartres Cathedral, continually stresses—with some wonder—that it is a church of the Holy *Family*, of Mother and Son. A human place, where the best human value erected great stained-glass windows, the finest, he says, that the world has ever seen. Seen in different lights, seen as the light changes through the day and through the seasons, such stained glass itself changes, the values of the colours change. The light itself becomes the source and centre of attention, light becomes something *seen*, a thing itself, rather than instrument. So too with this poem, its words: "the *experience* of value," as the poem "fluoresces" in "the light of seven centuries of interrelated thought."

Exegesis should not be necessary.

M. L. ROSENTHAL

ZUKOFSKY: "ALL MY HUSHED SOURCES"

A good deal of nonsense has been written about Zukofsky—that is, since people began writing about him at all. You won't find him mentioned in early books on modern American poetry like Kreymborg's *Our Singing Strength* (1929) and the Gregories' *A History of American Poetry 1900-1940* (1946), or in Millett's *Contemporary American Authors* (1943). The most intelligent comments remain those by William Carlos Williams, appended to the 1959 edition of *"A" 1-12*. They are intelligent because Williams sweetly respects Zukofsky's talents and interests without exaggerating his accomplishment. "There was always a part of this poet which would not blend. . . . I for one was baffled by him. I often did not know what he was driving at."

Williams speaks with deferential interest of Zukofsky's involvement with musical structure, of parallels between his work and the *Cantos*, of his careful, "meticulous" art, of his intellectuality, and of the Jewish dimension of his writing. But the sense of bafflement is pervasive: "The concentration and breaks in the language didn't add anything to my ease in the interpretation of the meaning." Also, "an obscure music, at least to me obscure, related to the music of . . . Bach, has dominated the poet's mind, beliefs, and emotions." Yet Williams can also say: "It is amazing how clean and effective Zukofsky has kept his composition . . . [he is] a poet devoted to working out by the intelligence the intricacies of his craft; he is imbedded in a matrix of his art and the multiple addictions which govern him, make him, of this time."

These apparently self-contradictory observations pretty much sum up the situation. As a fellow poet with certain affinities, Williams could appreciate the tonal delicacy and attenuated music of many passages in Zukofsky. He saw him, too, as sharing his own relationship with imagism; that is, the movement had had a necessary impact, inseparable from the Pound connection, without making either of them a complete imagist. Williams, the more robustly vivid and emotionally direct of the two poets, nevertheless sympathized with Zukofsky's kindred effort to deploy a precise, subtly associational poetic speech, weighted melodically. Subtlety can sometimes produce warping, however, and Williams was too honest and too normally human to pretend to love the extended monologues, full of tangential and muted rhetoric and going on forever in pretty much the same tone, that Zukofsky often indulged in. That is, Williams found Zukofsky's mentality and methods more interesting than his poetry, but distrusted his own instinctive reaction.

In the world of grown-up poets and critics one can feel this way and say so and be showing genuine regard at the same time. Williams' essay sustains Zukofsky's reputation as the unqualified praise of some of the Black Mountain poets, who have borrowed his mannerisms, does not. The play with grammatical ambiguity, the introduction of highly private references, the identification as essential poetic process of one's own halting movement into clarification of emotion and perception, and the extreme academicism of a poetry larded with literary puns and allusions— all these provide poetic opportunities and obvious pitfalls of preciosity at the same time. The most damaging instance of the latter that Zukofsky provides comes in his Catullus "translations." Robert Creeley's introduction to the 1967 edition of *"A" 1-12* suggests—if I understand the opaque prose correctly—that Zukofsky has caught a special music in these translations. Creeley has at this point been quoting, without commentary, a passage to illustrate the musical character—that is, the intimate music of poetic composition in action—of Zukofsky's method. He introduces the Catullus reference as a further instance.

> Thus to *hear*, as he would hear Catullus, in the translation he has made with his wife—"fact that delights as living hint and its cues" being "facit delicias libidinesque"—"which is much more simple in the Latin. It has to do with pleasures and desires . . . ."

Creeley has a little trick, throughout his introduction, of suggesting a commitment to admiration of Zukofsky while in practice quoting him almost all the time and avoiding clear statements of his own—as in the odd sentences just cited. But I think it is necessary to point out that the Catullus "translation" is merely spiritless bilingual punning. Anyone can do it who sets himself the task of doggedly transliterating from one language into another, wringing words out of the sounds of the original that make a certain strained sense. The passion, the wit, the art of the original are replaced by a display of low-level ingenuity, just as when some verbose wag breaks up serious conversation by turning everything other people say into material for puns and jokes. The inner music of Zukofsky's method was not always worth hearing. Take, for another sad example, two candidates for the worst lines of verse ever written: the opening lines of his serious poem "Peri Poietikes":

> What about measure, I learnt:
> *Look in your own ear and read.*

But. The other side of Zukofsky was the true poet. I shall risk the wrath of those who think that to have an ear is a positive hindrance to poets and their readers (unless the ear be a purely visual object), and shall cite a lovely early poem:

> Not much more than being,
> Thoughts of isolate, beautiful
> Being at evening, to expect
> at a river-front:
>
> A shaft dims
> With a turning wheel;
>
> Men work on a jetty
> By a broken wagon;
>
> Leopard, glowing-spotted,
> The summer river—
> Under: The Dragon:

Like Williams, and not—a shared mode of sensibility, but with a modulation toward philosophical reverie that arrives like a glow of insight, finds the quiet particulars out of which it emerged, and then notices more encompassing instances as well, remaining open and entranced throughout. "Not much more than being" finds an echo over thirty years later in the more active "The Ways," whose movement is similarly widening and whose absorption is similarly keen but which introduces an altered idiom in its second half (not unlike the closing stanza of the earlier piece in its shift of emphasis but much more freely handled):

> The wakes that boats make
> and after they are out of sight
> the ways they have made in water:
> loops, straight paths,
> to do with mirror-like,
> tides, the clouds the deep day blue
> of the unclouded parts of the sky,
> currents, gray sevens or darker shadows

against lighter in and out weaving
of mercurial vanishing eights,
or imaginably sights
instantaneously a duration and sun,
and the leaping silver
as of rain-pelted nipples
of the water itself.

After reading, a song

a light snow
a had been fallen

the brown most showed
knoll trunk knot treelings' U's

The Sound marsh water

ice clump
sparkling root etc

and so far out.

The contradiction between beautiful Z and tiresome Z is simply a given of the man's artistic life, of interest mainly because of the continuum between the extremes we have been observing. A fair amount of the work falls somewhere between Z^b and Z^t; that is, it has elements of both. One might suggest a curious doubleness related to a confusion of traditions, a possible result of Zukofsky's immigrant family background and of Jewish traditions of the display of cleverness and subtlety for their own sakes. An infatuation with thought-process (apart from its aims and content), with the tone of linguistic ingenuity (apart from whether the play of speech is sparkling or not, penetrating or not, pointed or simply continuous), and with the pleasures of just feeling intelligent because one is articulating something keeps Zukofsky going as a kind of secular talmudist even when the poet is fast asleep. (Samuel Greenberg, although much less developed than Zukofsky, seems to have had the same verbal proliferativeness.) The influence of Pound's allusiveness and constant show of learning must have fed this side of Zukofsky's intellectual personality. But Pound's psychopathology—his projection of the role of hero-leader and visionary summoning a civilization to its salvation —was not Zukofsky's. It could not convert the younger man's complex of thought into poetry of power. Many of the poems, including the innumerable personal messages and valentines in verse, are coy exhibitions, counting heavily on the recipient's affection for their acceptance.

Yet the poetry is full of strong political interest and specifically Jewish memories and preoccupations. Here we are not speaking of cultural nuances but of the most familiar kind of alienation—and struggle for recognition—and superimposed on that the equally familiar and natural reaction to the outrages of the Nazis. Zukofsky was in his early 20's when Pound accepted his "Poem beginning "The" " for *Exile*. Heavily saturated with *Mauberley, The Waste Land*, and *Ulysses* (and associated works and authors, including Vachel Lindsay and Virginia Woolf), the poem showed revolutionary sympathies and the poet's conflict between being a "Jewish boy" and his need to depart from home ties and give himself up to mastery of the dominant literary culture. The young man's self-consciousness and hostility are striking, especially in the section called *"FIFTH MOVEMENT: Autobiography"*:

> Assimilation is not hard,
> And once the Faith's askew
> I might as well look Shagetz just as much as Jew.
> I'll read their Donne as mine,
> And leopard in their spots
> I'll do what says their Coleridge,
> Twist red hot pokers into knots.
> The villainy they teach me I will execute
> And it shall go hard with them,
> For I'll better their instruction,
> Having learned, so to speak, in their colleges.
>> It is engendered in the eyes
>> With gazing fed, and fancy dies
>> In the cradle where it lies . . .

The notes from *Hamlet* and *The Merchant of Venice* suggest self-irony toward the speaker's own feelings. Elsewhere in this most indicative poem we find an apparently hostile reference to Mussolini and a sentimental address to the speaker's mother, alluding to her childhood in Russia and recalling (and distorting) a Yiddish folksong:

> Speaking about epics, mother,
> How long is it since you gathered mushrooms,
> Gathered mushrooms while you mayed.
> It is your mate, my father, boating.
> A stove burns like a full moon in a desert night.
> Un in hoyze is kalt. You think of a new grave,
> In the fields, flowers.
> Night on the bladed grass, bayonets dewed.
> It is your mate, my father, boating.
> Speaking about epics, mother,—
> Down here among the gastanks, ruts, cemetery-tenements—
> It is your Russia that is free.

We find echoes and developments of these deeply felt motifs in a number of Zukofsky's later works, among them "A Song for the Year's End," "Song of Degrees: 3," "The Old Poet Moves to a New Apartment 14 Times: 10," passages in the "A" sequence, and "Anew: 14." The motifs—strong emotional currents, rather—surface very effectively at times and yet are never fully explored or resolved. They are not *assimilated*, either psychologically or artistically, and seem at odds both with the weaker rhetorical stretches in Zukofsky and with the gentler intensities of his most successful writing. Somehow the touching manifesto of the clever and boisterous boy who speaks in "Poem beginning 'The' " has been carried through at the level of a word-game rather than of the most highly realized art. The poem "Anew: 42," written in his early 50's, reveals to a rare degree Zukofsky's potential power but also his innate secretiveness of manner and ultimate inability to mobilize his efforts into an original poem of tragic force. It is a poem that starts out with an intriguing combination of Dantean and colloquial idioms, grave and compelling despite some lapses, and passionately cumulative in its charge. Later, it somehow slips into the idiom of Marianne Moore, gaining a certain wry humor and personal appeal but losing its true affect in the process. At its height the poem promises:

> like the devil in the book of *Job*
>
> Having come back from going to and fro in the earth
>   I will give the world all my hushed sources
>   In this poem, (maybe the world wanted them)
>
> I will be so frank everyone
>   Will be sure I am hiding—a maniac—
>   And no one will speak to me.

And the poet mocks his own cleverness, his tendency to be one of Job's comforters rather than a Job (let alone "the devil"!), to clear the way for something finer and greater:

> (I am, after all, of the people whose wisdom
> May die with them)

In the wake of the Holocaust, the double thrust of these lines is irresistible. But moving as the inner pressure is in "Anew," and pure-spirited and clear as its conclusion is, the poem remains but a promise to develop what it has begun. The "hushed sources" remain so. A fierce energy of pathos, engaging our affection but never resolved, is the most advanced point of arousal in Zukofsky's most serious vein. Yet notes of genius remain notes of genius, even if unresolved. Zukofsky's poems are full of love and need, reverberating perceptions and keen awareness of their own process, and idiosyncratic formations that compel us although they often lose us at last.

HAROLD SCHIMMEL

ZUK. YEHOASH DAVID REX

"... I dedicate this poem to Anyone and Anything
I have unjustifiably forgotten"

Someone must have said it. William Carlos Williams did in a quirky
essay at the back of the Kyoto edition of *"A"* 1-12: all of Zukofsky's themes were there at the start in a *Poem beginning "The"* —
his card file for a lifetime of sequent days on *"A"*.

He was true to himself. He leaned to his bent playing on the
resistancies of poetry like a gull sinking into an air current and
rising on it. The most American of all Jewish poets (may he be
accorded no place in parochial anthologies!); the most Jewish of
all American poets. His loyalty to Paul (Pinchos)-Celia-Poetry as
radical, eloquent, traditional as Mishima's suicide. He sided with
life—L.Z. did—is what all of *"A"* is about.

When Guy Davenport wrote recently that Zuk. was engaged
on a finite series of flower poems projected into an unending future (only flowers he knew firsthand of course) I didn't stop to
think that this was the ploy of a man who smelled his end. Now it
seems just possible. A poet's device, like Yehuda Amichai at fifty-
four saying, "If the Angel of Death happens to stop by my door
and hears the voice of an infant, perhaps he'll think "Ah here
there are young children!" and move elsewhere. So Louis Zukofsky's flowers:

> ... as
> Blaise Pascal's
> candle pleaded
> 'no one
> is offended
> at not
> seeing everything'

Poem beginning "The" appeared in the heyday of Yiddish
poetry in Ezra Pound's *Exile*. Paperhangers, pressers, waiters, the
New York School of Yiddish poets flourished. They stuck

together buoyed on their young years and a passionate, totally partial love of their city. They read Mikhail Kuzmin's "Fujiyama in a Saucer" alongside Sologub, Heine and Old English ballads.

But *they* were immigrant poets and Louis Zukofsky was a born American. It was his fate neither to attend NYU Law writing free verses in Yiddish (as Glatstein and Minkoff did) nor to suffer the brokenness of a Samuel Greenberg who penciled phrases like ". . . for the very day of fairness itself was enough to educate a lizard" or, ". . . all that was the East Side history became a laurel of use" on the gaps of his knowledge of English. Still, a poem like "Ferry"

> Gleams, a green lamp
> In the fog:
> Murmur, in almost
> A dialogue
>
> Siren and signal
> Siren to signal.
>
> Parts the shore from the fog,
> Rise there, tower on tower,
> Signs of stray light
> And of power.
>
> Siren to signal
> Siren to signal.
>
> Hour-gongs and the green
> Of the lamp.
>
> Plash. Night. Plash. Sky.
>
> *55 Poems* (1923-1935)

uses the indicativeness of Yiddish syntax—a gestural thumb which dips, in guise of a verb-form. "Ferry" would rest comfortably in Mani Leib's little anthology (Inzel, 1918), *New York in Verses.* Maud's diminutive india ink decorations (not unlike the insets later adopted by *The New Yorker*) suit it. Moreover the music is Yiddish, not yet contrapuntal, not yet Bach; Jewish Folk Song despite the typically New York School-Yiddish modernism, "Plash. Night. Plash. Sky.". There is a blurring of the visual and the musical which has its affinities in American neo-impressionism (Abraham Walkowitz comes to mind). It lacks the recognizable voice which, played against a keenness of eye, quickly emerges as Zukofsky's earmark.

II

"Blood and desire to graft what you desire"

"A"-1

How did young Louis Z. come upon S. Bloomgarden (pen name Yehoash)'s two volumes of verse, *In the Web*? Was Reb Pinchos (his father) a reader of Yiddish verse? Not unlikely, if only via the daily Yiddish press whose poetry (circa 1905-1930) was more advanced than that of the *N.Y. Times*. Was he conscious of the tremendous jump Yehoash had made from his first volumes? Did he know that Yehoash was printed and sold in numbers exceeding most contemporaneous American poets?

How do we account for the fact that 60 of the 330 lines of *Poem beginning "The"* are translated from the Yiddish (49 of these from Yehoash's *In the Web*, printed just five years before Ezra Pound's *Exile* number appeared)?

In part the answer is the casually accurate one of any artist and especially of the poet at twenty-two—namely, the artist builds with the materials at hand. Things fit as he makes them fit. Eliot's posited poet gets in the morning egg as he has had it for breakfast. The truly astounding thing about Zukofsky's debut poem in *Exile* is that the territory he flipped his penknife at and sliced out neatly at twenty-two is the same ground he inhabits at his death at seventy-four. The major themes and personages—horses, the Ricky elegy motif (linked by the epithet "lion-heart"), sun, Yehoash, to name a few—reappear as sections or fragments of sections of *"A"*.

Even Heine's German spelling, "Kadish" (1. 269), is maintained twenty-four years later—in preference to the accepted American transliteration "Kaddish"—both for its greater loyalty to the Hebrew and to point the reference backward in time.

> Had he asked me to say Kadish
> I believe I would have said it for him.

"A"-12, p. 149

The stubborn accuracy in spelling is matched by the cautious syntax and phrasing. Reb Pinchos being Reb Pinchos *would not ask*. "Had he asked," Zukofsky would like to think he would have complied; for Kaddish may be recited only with a quorum of ten (therefore, in synagogue) for the 365 mourning days at morning, afternoon and evening prayers.

The late nineteenth century formula which appeared on Yiddish translations and adaptations, "Translated and Made Better" (this, even for Shakespeare), is valid for Zukofsky. His versions comb the originals not out of cockyness, but in so much as they subtly alter sense to suit his immediate needs. He does not render the Yiddish, he addresses it—both speaks it and speaks to it, much as Pound does with the latinized Greek in the first Canto.

The homage to the original is essential. Not transference from language to language but regeneration as the materials move from man to man. Thus Yehoash's adaptation of Arab lore for Yiddish readers (1920) becomes the moving coda for that ur-version of Ricky's elegy in *Poem beginning "The"*, two years later emerging as *"A"*-3. It is this recycling that embodies one man's need for another man's work:

> "And out of olde bokes, in good feith".

A glaring example of the hazards of translation without re-presentation is William Carlos Williams' version of Theocritus' first Idyl in *The Desert Music* volume of 1954. All too altruistic, Williams abandons his own voice for the nineteenth century niceties of C.S. Calverley, whom I suspect he uses as a crib. No one would guess "dainty", "plashes", "yonder", "snood", "fair-haired youths", "Love's/ long vigils" or "Labors/ all in vain" to be the work of Zukofsky's old friend. Not true to himself Williams falsifies the ancient. The real Theocritus is to be located of course in *Paterson Four*, "The Run to the Sea".

Sidney Morgenbesser's retort, "If you don't quote the whole thing anything you quote is 'out of context' " is exactly to the point, a defense of all shrewd poetic liftings.

III

> "Tenderly the season...Spared the petted flowers
> that the old world gave the new"
>
> O.E.D.
> Bryant, 3rd November 1861

"A"-4, the little homage to Yehoash, "roots" and "The courses we tide from", stands as an early model of a technique later used in the William Carlos Williams "coronal", *"A"*-17. "On the third floor/ Of our Brooklyn brownstone," writes Zukofsky in *"A"*-12 (p. 239), "Is my fetish for building,/ A collage". The amazing thing about the Yehoash fragments of *"A"*-4 is the close parallel they bear to the coronal of translated sections of two years before in *Poem beginning "The"*.

In both cases Zukofsky chooses to exhibit Yehoash first by a piece of exotica (a Bedouin lyric in *"Poem"*, Samurai in *"A"*-4), some folk motifs, and a hymn to the sun. The strangeness of intro-ducing foreign materials via Yiddish is apparent and allowed under the banner of "Song's kinship". Still, "Shimaunu-San, my clear star" as an illustration of "The courses we tide from" is not without some irony.

Yehoash succeeded in baffling his readers by this conscious internationalism but gained the admiration of the younger Yiddish poets (personalists who wrote homey imagistic poems), stimulating their impulse toward translation. Yehoash was also close to Zukofsky's own feelings about the Hebrew-Yiddish dichotomy. He compiled an excellent dictionary of Hebrew and Chaldaic elements in Yiddish with Dr. C.D. Spivak, emphasizing native connections between the two languages. His translation of the Bible into Yiddish was a lifetime task—a labor of love.

For Zukofsky Hebrew was "Speech" and made possible such elements of a historical past as "Temple", "Wall", "Psalms" and "the Land" itself (L.Z. accords these words their majuscule). The accepted epithet for Yiddish was "jargon" (minuscule), that is, not "Speech" with its national-historical implications but a bastard lingua franca. Still, Yiddish was the language of simple human communication, the language father and mother used around the kitchen table, and Zukofsky's first language (Guy Davenport, "Zukofsky's English Catullus", see pp. 365-370 herein).

At the end of the nineteenth century Yiddish, the spoken medium, was in process of becoming a codified language with a grammar of its own, and a rapidly developing modern literature. Hebrew, on the other hand, with a long and distinguished literature, was being revived as a spoken language. When Yehoash visited Palestine in 1914, he met the local antagonism to Yiddish with the wisdom of distance. "Hebrew speak Hebrew" was the slogan, embossed in a circle on the tea glasses, while Alexander Harkavy's popular "The English Teacher" (N.Y., 1924) had this confusion in translating "Ich bin a yud": "I am a Hebrew (a Jew, an Israelite)".

Ideally Zukofsky would like to tie himself as Jew and poet to the Hebrew past. Realistically he accepts "roots" as Yiddish and unabashedly transliterates bits and pieces of jargon throughout *"A"*, as he feels inclined. His Hebrew has undergone a long exile and, shored on New York's East Side, is rendered as the lion beneath the mangy pelt. He delivers it as he received it from his father, through the garment of the Yiddish vernacular—as Theocritus his Greek through Sicilian sunglasses—with this only for apology: "(the Sephardim speak it differently)" and, "We had a Speech, our children have evolved a jargon".

Zukofsky is conscious of the Greek past as an alternate and sometimes simultaneous possibility, and sets up this contrast:

for the Jews' portable ark—wood, for "Aphrodite's drapery" (i.e. temple architecture)—marble. Greek columns, as he reads them, are abstracted from the plain wood of the Hebrew ark:

> . . . from the trunk trimmed
> Set up for one day and moving tomorrow

> *"A"*-12, p. 147

Like Yehoash, no Zionist (the Zionists and the Yiddish Bundists were traditionally at odds) Zukofsky's loyalties lean out to "the Land". His little apologia for the modern Delaware-sized State draws to its close with a running pun on Callimachus' minimalist plea: "a great book great mischief". His oblique reference to "the People of the Book' is theoretical and defends also his own Alexandrian art. Like the latter-day Greek, Callimachus, Zukofsky glances playfully (therefore, seriously) over the sacred hymns, and his great work is built on microscopic particulars (swarming, elastic amoebae on the new Smithsonian's tele-screen). The Zukofskies (unlike their old friends, the Oppens) never actually visited the Land but its majority status is firmly embedded in *"A"* 's architecture and distinguished from "4 Other Countries" in *Barely and widely*:

> In the flagrate of cold
> theatre of the world the
> wren and hindsight nest—an
> architecture honors a people's obstinate
> valor ages thru infinite changes,
> cold, caldron run over, scattered
> congregate, their sanctuary the Land:
> the blood's motion—arteries to
> veins and back to the
> heart: come at last into
> ample fields sip every cup
> a great book great mischief
> perched dwarf on a giant
> may see horse race or
> hidebound calves out to pasture:

> *"A"*-22, pp. 25-26

Zukofsky's absenteeism is defended along with his exile as he builds-in a little remembrancer—a missing word in his five-word sequence:

> 'I have loved you, yet
> you say *wherein*. Return, I
> return' A coast unseen.

This stands like the traditional unfinished detail in any Jewish structure "in remembrance of the Destruction" (i.e. of the

Temple) as Zukofsky compounds his own American exile with the great Babylonian exile:

> By the river sat down
> remembered the harp on the
> willow required a song a
> song in a strange land
> the score a right hand
> the back of a tongue.

"A"-23, p. 46

One notices and admires how the lines in *"A"*-22:

> twigged heart flounce the Land
> be not fought—greatness remains

link up with *"A"*-23's lines:

>   . . Heart's nubile
> trees,wordless,horses draw from
> the isles new earth . . not
> desolate . . from new moon . . another . .
> rest . . sowers-wage-rages . . harassed nations . .
> good *will* covet,desire redeem:

But Zukofsky's native affections and family loyalties cannot undermine his basic humanist stand:

> The sound in the Temple built after exile
> Is never worth the sound
> At the earth where no temple stood
> And on which no law of exile can fall.

Here, the Land of his People is poet's ground ("the earth where no temple stood") and "land"—like "temple"—retrieves its minuscule as in Yehoash's hymn, "To the Sun", quoted in *"A"*-4.

IV

"stolen apples spur running"

"A"-22&23, p. 59

Very much like MacDiarmid's technique in "A Drunk Man Looks at the Thistle" (1926), Zukofsky lights on the translated lyrics in *Poem beginning "The"* partly to keep things going, partly to vary texture and tone and almost always opportunistically. There is no question of trying to preserve the integrity of the original. Neither MacDiarmid nor Zukofsky are particularly interested in hawking the poets they engage. True to the *satura* both employ a form broad enough to include singsong, banter, and colloquial outbursts alongside elegiac, didactic and lyric poetry.

Zukofsky emphasizes the separateness of individual lines by his running numbers. These are referential (the prologued index is essential to the manner of the poem and one wonders whether its omission in *A Controversy of Poets* had Z.'s approval) but also serve as a test of poetry, a young man's gauge for reviewing his lines individually. If MacDiarmid's poem was said to have been put together from haphazard sheets assembled on a living room floor, Zukofsky's draws attention to its random matter by its appended numerals. Transitions are often absent or absent-present in the mode of vaudeville ("I've changed my mind, Zukofsky,/ How about some other show—", (130-131).

The Ricky section (76-129) is one of the ample stretches in *Poem*. It seems to come of a long breath despite the Yehoash inset. In fact Zukofsky disguises the traces of the borrowing by running Yehoash into his own lines and breaking Yehoash's stanza. With the two exceptions of the Yiddish of Yehoash and the Yiddish of Jewish Folk Song most of Zukofsky's references are slapstick or parody. The only sequential lines of any significance truly quoted are those from the Yiddish. They are the solid matter of the poem and if I dwell on them in sombrous detail it is because Zukofsky himself returns to them taking up *"A"*.

Yehoash's poem (110-129) transliterates the Arabic word for "mirage" (translated literally, "the devil's sea") as its title. Sa-idi, a young Bedouin, is ruled and beaten by the desert sun; his kingdom comes at night. Zukofsky uses the pattern for Ricky's temporal death followed by a prayer for his release and resurrection. He picks up Yehoash mid-poem, custom tailoring as follows:

112   But his eyes <u>no longer</u> blink
113   <u>Not even as</u> a blind dog's.
114   With the blue <u>night</u> shadows on the sand
115   <u>May</u> his kingdom return(s) to him,
116   The Bedouin leap(s) <u>again</u> on his *asila*

Zukofsky's contribution to the succeeding stanza is mainly in way of padding to keep Yehoash's meter. Translation follows syllable for syllable; "Lighter than the storm wind, dust or <u>spray</u>" to satisfy a rhyme with "prey" is unfortunate. "Younger yet his gay, wild wife" is justified in trying to imitate the two-syllabled *vilde* in Yiddish.

A foretaste of the late Zukofsky and the verbal marksmanship of *"A"*-22&23 is there in the lines:

127   Some new trappings for his steed,
128   All the stars in dowry his meed
129   From the Desert-Night.

Both "steed" and "meed" are perfectly matched Old English words (Yehoash has no rhyme); they underline the folk borrowing—albeit secondhand—and support the fable. Another matched historically placed word is "trappings". Three lines early-on in *"A"*-1 seem to get their impetus from the two year old Sa-idi passage. Here Zukofsky takes up the guise of Yehoash's young Bedouin:

> And as one who under stars
> Spits across the sand dunes, and the winds
> Blow thru him, the spittle drowning worlds—

> *"A"* 1-12, p. 8

The specific vocabulary and chivalric setting return in the uncannily moving Ricky elegy, *"A"*-3:

> Ricky,
> Coeur de Lion.
>
> Lion-heart,
> A horse bridled—
>
> Trappings rise,
> Princelet
> Out of history.
>
> Trappings
> Rise and surround
>
> Two dark heads

But Kenneth Cox informs us (AGENDA, Winter-Spring 1976, p. 127): *"A"* was "foreseen" in 1926, when Zukofsky was 22, as a "curve" to be plotted in 24 movements at unforeseeable points of time.

Yehoash's neo-folk song, "Cheshvan" (the Hebrew calendar month corresponding approximately to October), sounds surprisingly like the Pound of the Confucian Anthology:

> 205 Winged wild geese, where lies the passage,
> 206 In far way lands lies the passage.

Once again Zukofsky fills in the missing syllable of the Yiddish, *vilde,* in translating "Winged wild geese" but here the adjective is musically and visually equivalent. The brilliance of Zukofsky as translator of Catullus is anticipated in such word-choice as "cobalt stream" (214) for the Yiddish, "lead-blue". The adjective supplies exact dictionary-meaning and reminds us that a good Unabridged will be the best commentary on difficult Zukofsky.

Often Zukofsky sets himself squarely in the tradition of the Aramaic *Targum* (literally, "translation") of the Bible. *Targum Onkeles* was not only intended to be read aloud interlinearly but incorporated a built-in commentary or translator's-gloss to "make it clear". The *Targum*, for its usefulness, frames the text of almost every Hebrew Bible. Zukofsky' "steed" (127) for Yehoash's "horse" is pure Onkeles, as is the brilliant gloss, "jaded sheep" (219), for Yehoash's "tired". Any Zukofsky reader would recognize "jaded" as Zukofsky's word just as he'd spot "My petted birds are dead" (*"A"*-4, p. 21), where "petted" translates the Yiddish diminutive, "birds", but also picks up on the next unquoted line:

> And why do I fondle the nest?

To give Yehoash his due, a passage like,

220   An old horse strewn with yellow leaves
221   By the edge of the meadow
222   Draws weakly with humid nostrils
223   The moisture of the clouds.

is beautiful writing and Zukofsky's English follows exact syntax word for word, almost a mirror image in another language of the original. It must be said that Zukofsky singled out these poems in 1926 whereas two generations of Yiddish critics have yet to deal with their excellence.

"Finale, and After" opens with some stanzas (from many hundred versions) of the most well-known of all Yiddish folk songs, "Raisins and Almonds" (270-280). The refrain, "Ai-li lu-li lu-li lu", which Zukofsky's Mother may have sung is rendered:

275   Lullaby, lullaby, lullaby, lullaby.

The "movement" closes with Yehoash's Sun-song, *Oif di Churvos* ("On the Ruins"), and Zukofsky is content to end his *Poem* on this note. The word "wrack" (318) as a translation of *churvos* (with backward reference to the destruction of the Temple) is Onkeles-like. Similarly, "Comrade" (323) for *chaver* (Yiddish like Hebrew has no system of majuscules and minuscules) is on the mark, for *chaver* (from the Hebrew) is "friend", "companion", "brother" and, in Eastern Europe, "Talmud partner". Yehoash writes shortly after the revolution in Russia and Zukofsky's gloss keeps this resonance. But the whole section (318-330) is adaptation rather than translation. Zukofsky has had to tone down its messianic fervor partly by changing "I" to "we" and partly by careful rewriting, for English will not tolerate the same range of oratorical high jinks as home-country Yiddish.

"A"-4 continues the couplets and tone of the Ricky elegy (*"A"*-3) using bits and pieces of no less than five Yehoash poems for its collage. The closing lines,

"I will gather a chain
Of marguerites, pluck red anemone,
Till of every hostile see
Never a memory remain."

transform the Yiddish phrase, "all false thrones", using the archaic
noun "see" (ME *se*, related to seat) and introduce "chain"—happy
innovations inspired by Zukofsky's loyalty to the rhyme scheme.
All in all one is impressed by just how little Zukofsky had to tam-
per with the Yiddish of his "courses".

"A"-5, *"A"*-6 and *"A"*-7 (the 1930 *"A"*s) echo the *"A"*s of
1928 as *"A"*-4 itself picked up from previous *"A"*s and *Poem beginning "The"*.

The song—omits?
No, includes Kay, Anybody.
Ricky's romance
Of twenty-three years, in
Detail, continues

"A"-6

. . . no one's cut out, pump a-
Ricky, bro', Shimaunu-Sān . . .

"A"-7

The footwork's all there on the page like Fred Astaire's black sole
and heel tracks in his popular handbook. No Sherlock Holmes is
needed where eyes and ears are clear:

"Taste" we say—a living soul.

"A"-12, p. 132

Or as David rex spelled it:

Taste 'n See
that the Lord's   Good

Psalms

—*abi*
gesunt abi

"alright" my
father'd say

"A" 13-21, p. 77

JOHN TAGGART

ZUKOFSKY'S "MANTIS"

The question that matters for reading "Mantis" and Zukofsky's own twisting interpretation of the poem is: what form should that take? "That" being five or six thoughts' reflection (pulse's witness) of what was happening without transitions, the actual twisting of many and diverse thoughts (the coincidence of the mantis lost in the subway, the growing oppression of the poor), the contents of "the simultaneous,/ The diaphanous, historical/ In one head." That is, what shape best fits or suits them, what shape do they in themselves define? Zukofsky's answer is the sestina with its repeated end words that wind the lines around themselves as continuously as the mind winds the sensorium's information.

It may be objected that this choice forgets to mention the villanelle, which, with only two rhymes and several repetitions of the first and third lines, would also allow for the suggestion of simultaneous winding motion. To this, Zukofsky might reply that repetition, after all, is static; the first and third lines are not twisting or weaving; they simply reappear throughout the poem, each time the words of the lines in identical order with their first occurrence. The end words of the first stanza in a sestina, in comparison, are in motion (transformation), which then forces the poem as a whole to be "moving." So "leaves," the end word for the first line of Zukofsky's sestina, occurs on the second line in the second stanza, on the fourth line in the third stanza, the fifth line of the fourth stanza, the third line of the fifth stanza, the sixth line of the sixth stanza, not repeating again in the first line position until the three-line coda stanza. Too, the use of the end words in other than end positions, e.g., "it" in the third stanza, carries the poem's motion even closer to the originating "thoughts' torsion."

Other repeating French forms, the rondeau or the rondel, might be mentioned. Yet they share the villanelle's static countermotion and, besides, almost always imply a playfulness that is out of keeping with the seriousness of the "poor's helplessness/ The poor's separateness/ Bringing self-disgust." That the sestina is in concert with the poet's seriousness is made clear by Karl Shapiro, a poet whose own practice obviously and radically differs from Zukofsky's, in his reflection on the form:

> The sestina seems not necessarily to be a mere curious exercise or virtuoso showpiece, but at least ideally to be a form designed to encourage and express a meditation or reverie upon certain thoughts or images. If such an obsessive vision or reverie-like impulse does not in fact exist or come into existence as the poem is written, the six key words will seem unmotivated and the whole poem will turn out to be an academic exercise. *The sestina would seem to require the poet's deepest love* and conviction, involve his deepest impressions as these take on a rather obsessive quality. . . .[1] [my italics]

The poet's deepest love and conviction equal an attitude of sincerity. The choice of the form or shape of the sestina for "Mantis" manifests something more than the passive recognition of what sort of form many thoughts' torsion outlined.

And as Leslie Fiedler realizes in an essay on Dante's sestina that begins *"Al poco gior no e al gran cerchio d'ombra"*—the model, as several references in the interpretation indicate, for "Mantis"—the great sestinas of literature remain faithful to the metaphysical implications of the form itself.

> It is only too easy to make the sestina an embodiment of ingenuity rather than necessity, to give the impression that the word at each line ending is sought and prepared for, a prize rather than a trap. On the contrary, the successful sestina must make it seem that each mono-rhyme is seven times fled and seven times submitted to; *that the poet is ridden by a passion which forces him back on the six obsessive words,* turn and twist as he may.[2] [my italics]

The question remains whether Zukofsky actually fulfills the sestina shape "sincerely," i.e., as a force and not wicker-work. The poem's source is the coincidence of Zukofsky seeing the mantis with begging eyes, which then flies at his chest as he stands at a subway station. In the act of seeing the mantis, the poet—without transitions—immediately has several thoughts' reflection, one on another, which connect the mantis' desperate situation with that of the poor. The combination of his multiple reflection and his

---

1. Karl Shapiro and Robert Beum, *A Prosody Handbook* (New York: Harper & Row, 1965), p. 120.
2. Leslie Fiedler, "Dante: Green Thoughts in a Green Shade" in *No! In Thunder: Essays on Myth and Literature* (Boston: Beacon Press, 1960), p. 24.

interest in stating the creature's ungainliness lead him to choose the sestina as a suitable form for this collective. The question may now be sub-divided and rephrased: is this situation and its attendant associations described, "written" with adequate care for detail, is Zukofsky's complex emotion as reported in his interpretation—surprise, curiosity toward the creature, sadness toward the condition of the poor, outrage at those responsible for that condition, resolution to help the mantis and the poor—, is all of this "emotion" sufficiently objectified?

The poem's first stanza begins with a startled recognition of something that is totally out of place; hence the surprised, exclamatory naming: Mantis! praying mantis! A logical sequence is then set up with "since" (logical and causal: since you have done this, I will do that). But the sequence is left seemingly incomplete in the first stanza. Since the mantis' wings' leaves and terrified eyes beg the poet to take it up: "it," by lines position, would seem to refer to the parenthetical thoughts' torsion. If this is the case, Zukofsky would be depicting the mantis begging him to take up what he alone can be expected to be conscious of, the contents of his own forgetting and remembering head. Or, following the interpretation ("That this thoughts' torsion/ Is really a sestina"): the mantis urges the poet to take up the sestina, save it from the ravages of inattention or misuse.

Such readings are torturous and silly. I prefer "it" as referring back to the mantis itself, thoughts' torsion being a parallel (correlative, an aside as in drama) speech from Zukofsky's "conscience" as a distinct third person voice saying "within" him "Look, take it up, save it!", an admonishment to himself. The logical-causal expectation aroused by "since" is gone through with, though not in the anticipated orderly fashion; since the mantis begs *and* since the poet can't bear to look at it or touch it, the mantis may be rescued by an anonymous nearby "You"—"You can"—. But no one sees "you"—the mantis—lost in the cars' drafts on the lit subway stone. There will be no rescue of "you" by a non-seeing (or caring) "You." The poet, alone, is forced to return, despite himself, to what he alone has apparently cared to see, the mantis. The upper case-lower case you distinction returns in the third stanza with the "You" indicating those, collective singular, surrounding the mantis and the poet—the public crowd—, while the "you" is once more the mantis, now being asked by the poet where the newsboy as representative of the crowd would put "him."

Another series of questions, in the second stanza, precedes this, which—from the poet to the mantis—serve to identify the mantis with the poor by their shared position (the stone) and, by extension, shared emotions of terror, being lost and "not seen" by those of the public crowd around them. ("The mantis, then,/ Is a small incident of one's physical vision/ Which is the poor's helplessness/ The poor's separateness.") The stanza ends with what Zukofsky's interpretation accurately describes as "pun, fact, banality." The shops' crowds—the public crowd(s)—are a-jam and offer no food or any attention to the mantis or, by association, to the poor.

The first line of the third stanza returns to the multiple references of "it." What even the newsboy sees is "it" as the mantis *and* "No use, papers make money, makes stone, stone,/ Banks", i.e., even the crowd's representative is somehow aware that the economic system will not alter itself, that the poor will continue as they are. The newsboy says it, the mantis, is harmless, a painfully unconscious pun revealing his real non-sight in relation to the double reference of "it." Then "You?": are You, the crowd, harmless? And: where will he, its representative, put the mantis? For there are no safe places as the spinning syntax of "here, here's" indicates in ending one "thought" and instantly turning to another in the smallest of spaces. Here=the subway station; here's news=perhaps the newsboy's papers, their characteristically inaccurate and superficial reporting, as opposed to the lover-poet's, *is* too poor to save the poor; they offer no information which their readers could reliably use as a basis for positive action. The poem's reader's own remembering head then recalls, from the second stanza, "the poor/ ...who rising from the news may trample you—". In their anger with the unreal or unreliable news, the poor may trample a mantis; there is no shelter for it or for any of the separate poor when "the times" have made the massed poor sightless in their rage with a condition that continues "steadying lost."

In the fourth stanza the poet overcomes his fear to allow the mantis to light upon his chest, an item of his shame and of the poor who laugh at his fright: shame at his non-caring for the creature itself and as an emblem of the separate poor (as opposed to the laughing mass). The mantis is described through three images: spectre, strawberry, a stone that "leads"—as a sign—lost children through the close paths left by men. What do these mythic images (see Zukofsky's interpretation for these lines), compacted by alliteration, signify? Possibly, that the mantis as sign is part spiritual entity, part sweet and infrequently obtainable fruit; it is as a delicious fruit to the lost, a delightful succor, and a reminder as spirit that men, like thorns in the paths they leave, can kill, that other men are in fact dangerous.

Notice that "(once men)" in the fifth stanza's first line functions similarly to "(thoughts' torsion)"; both are, while in the line, removed by the parenthesis from the line's development of the poem's larger on-going movement. These removals register the poet's on-looking consciousness of the composition process without greatly disturbing the lines' motion. The poet is in the poem as actor-speaker and as the reflective maker of the poem itself. If, according to myth, the mantis was killed by thorns that were once men, the poet asks who can possibly save "you" now, "what male love bring a fly, be lost/ Within your mouth, prophetess, harmless to leaves/ And hands, faked flower"? That is, not only who can save you—if no persons, as another mantis—"care", but also who, in view of your devouring love, could want to? These questions, though,—as indicated by the dash following "flower" in the fourth line—are false; for the "myth is: dead, bones, it/ Was assembled, apes wing in wind." The answer to the poet's questions are given by himself back to the mantis that is told he will not be saved, will not be killed either by mythic thorn-men, but *will* "die, touch, beg, of the poor." Zukofsky's use of "of the poor" is unclear, particularly for "die" and "touch." Going back to the previous line, it is "on stone" that this will happen to the mantis. He will die on the subway platform's stone, die of the poor's inattention—caused by their despairing anger with the news of banks and money that are "beyond" them—(and the inattention of the shops' public crowd, those with at least some money) in spite of the mantis being near enough to touch them, in spite of "her" begging eyes.

The sixth stanza's first line connects back with the fifth by a number of close associations: "android" with "apes," "loving beggar" with "love" and "beg" from separate lines, "dive" with the likely outcome of apes winging in the wind, "poor" with—as printed—"poor" immediately above it on the preceding stanza's last line. And the connections function beyond the formally desirable binding of the poem, which in itself is again only wickerwork, to what the poet now requests of the mantis: to attempt to restore the sight of the poor ("Save it!") by sacrificing itself before them. The connection between the two stanzas must hold if the sacrifice is to count for anything: if the mantis is to die of the inattention of the poor as given in the fifth stanza, then the poet's request really does ask sacrifice by the mantis.

In the interpretation's language, the mantis *can start* history. In exchange for such sacrifice, the poet affords the mantis a magical speech:

> Say, I am old as the globe, the moon, it
> Is my old shoe, yours, be free as the leaves.

Reading it, the reader's own however intuitional head remembers Zukofsky's "poets measure by means of words, whose effect as offshoot of nature may (or should) be that their strength of suggestion can never be accounted for completely."[3] Perhaps the exchange is fair, as fair as it ever could be. What the mantis gains is passionate oration as

> ...speech, language, utterance, tongue moved for a time to sound; barring confusion as the push of *this* animalcule—as against *that*—curving a lobe of itself around food particle or dust; or a humane red showing thru a translucent film of cells of one life, or the sallow green of another—follicles hairing views—spectra. *Or they see* as eyelashes flicker; or come out one by one, air without hairs, *eyes—round, unfringed.*[4] [my italics]

And to alter the direction of another statement by Zukofsky, the mantis is given a measured order of words moving to a visual end, a product of the poet's love, that demonstrates loving compassion for the poor (from the mantis, from the poet) so that they may see with round, unfringed eyes. The poet's hope is their restored sight, restored from the non-sight of the newspaper will permit them to see themselves, each other, as they are, the separate individual poor. With that seeing, there is a chance of truly being saved, by each other, and not by the banks.

What remains after the joint exhortation of the mantis and the poet to the poor to be as free as the leaves is a three-line coda, which is the

> only thing that can sum up the
> jumble of order in the lines weaving
> 'thought,' pulsations, running commentary, one upon the other,
> itself a jumble of order
> as far as poetic
> sequence is concerned:
>
> > the mantis
> > the poor's strength
> > the new world.

As a summary, the coda is complexly addressed to the mantis and to the poor. The mantis is again urged to fly upon the poor, whose armies' strength will arise like leaves from a stone on stone

3. Zukofsky, "Poetry" in *Prepositions: The Collected Critical Essays of Louis Zukofsky* (London: Rapp & Carroll, 1967), p. 15.
4. Zukofsky, *Bottom: On Shakespeare* (Austin, Texas: the Ark Press for the Humanities Research Center, the University of Texas, 1963), vol. I, p. 369.

accretion (cf. the second line of the third stanza) to build the new world "in your eyes."

> Fly, mantis, on the poor, arise like leaves
> The armies of the poor, strength: stone on stone
> And build the new world in your eyes, Save it!

I cite the coda entire to emphasize the complexity of the poet's appeal ("a jumble of order"), and especially the final "Save it!" For with this the reader is referred back to the third line of the first stanza where "it" is read as a pronoun for the mantis; now, in the coda, "it" may again refer to the mantis, which the poet wishes the new world-building armies of the poor to save; but there is the additional reference, gathered from the shared stone, of all the separate poor. The two references co-exist in "it" somewhat separately. The point is that, while separate, both references are at once within "it": the saving is an interdependent act by the mantis and the arisen armies of the poor, who now see beyond the newspaper generalities to real particulars (individuals) and presumably act upon their vision: first the mantis saves the poor by forcing them to sight, which then permits them to see the mantis' plight and save it.

This paraphrase no more than prepares for questions of rhythm and style. While it, along with the poet's own interpretation, does indicate that Zukofsky faithfully attends to the shape of his several thoughts' torsion in choosing the sestina for the poem's form, it may be claimed that "Mantis" is merely another instance of inherited form writing. That is: if Zukofsky had been listening to himself and writing in accord with what he heard, why was he not content to let the poem's form (shape) reveal itself as it moved toward its own completion?

Zukofsky's interpretation, in response, makes it clear that he *has* listened, is conscious of himself, the equivalent of Charles Olson's breath-registering. As evidence:

> Thoughts'—two or three or five or
> Six thoughts' reflection (pulse's witness) of what was happening
> All immediate, not moved by any transition.

> Feeling this, what should be the form
> Which the ungainliness already suggested
> Should take?

And

> Consider:
> '(thoughts' torsion)'
> la battaglia delli diversi pensieri...
> The actual twisting
> Of many and diverse thoughts

> What form should *that* take?

Typically, or so Olson would have us believe, the non-projectivist or closed poet begins with the form and ends with a poem determined by the form; his actual subject, in effect, is the form itself; what the closed poet "expresses" is himself as the possessor of literary acumen; he is an illusionist reproducer of items of past —what may come to be known as tradition—writing; he can, after all, produce recognizable "literature."

Zukofsky, though, begins with his poem's originating thoughts (and even before them, with what his eyes see, i.e., "a small incident of one's physical vision"), reflects on what they define, and then proceeds to select a form in accord with his many and diverse thoughts' cumulative shape definition, the sestina. His position is analogous to the projectivist poet who finds to his surprise (alarm?) that what his listening directs him toward is a sonnet. There is a certain degree of admirable courage in Zukofsky's resolve to stick with the sestina as "the only/ Form that will include the most pertinent subject of our day—/ The poor—." Zukofsky *is* conscious, awake: for there is no demand that he cite the objection contained in Williams' "—Our world will not stand it,/ the implications of a too regular form" in his interpretation. And as Olson comments from the context of his projective verse essay: "is it not the PLAY of a mind we are after, is not that that shows whether a mind is there at all?" Active and sympathetic consciousness, in respect to the seriousness of Zukofsky's subject, may be substituted for Olson's play. The point is that an audience does want to know a mind is there—as opposed to a form filling tradition-alert automaton—as some indication of the poet's love, of his sincerity. That a mind is active in the poem's shape (surface) can be seen from Zukofsky's treatment of rhythm in "Mantis."

Given the poet's convoluted thoughts and a recalcitrantly convolute form, what should the sound-shape, the *belleza*, be to fulfill and not just fill the sestina and the "pledge" of the sincere poet's love? It should participate in and be, in effect, a growing definition of that convolution. As such a definition and as the product of a pattern of stanzas rather than a single stanza arrangement, the poem's rhythm emerges from binary comparison. I read the first two lines as hendecasyllabic patterns. Thus:

Mantis! | praying mantis! | since your | wings' leaves
And your | terrified eyes, | pins, bright, | black and poor

The remainder of the lines in the first stanza may be read similarly, though with internal variation and a syllable count that varies from nine to twelve. The unitive rhythmic contour of the first stanza does sound convolute, i.e., the first two measures of the above two lines—and of the following lines in the stanza as well—are made up of short repeating duple co-ordinates that tend to sound more quickly, despite the stacatto effects in the second line, than the longer and more distinct sounds of both lines' latter two measures. These measures do not resolve the rapidity of the first two measures so much as they repeat them, but, generally, more gradually. This enlargement or gliding effect is achieved in the fourth line, for example, by the vowel sounds in "cannot touch, —You—" and by the delaying-holding of punctuation.

Further reading shows that all six lines in the other five stanzas may also be read as hendecasyllabic patterns with a tendency for a faster-slower (many smaller-fewer longer) line sound organization. The relevance of this sameness is that an even closer internal line analysis is needed to decide how densely the lines' and stanzas' rhythms operate in relation with one another.

The second lines of the first three stanzas with their similar choppy alliterative effects immediately present themselves as instances of close relation (pins-prop-prey-papers), but in place of an infinitely regressing analysis of each line's words, I shall examine only the end rhyme words, the *parola-rima*, and their reappearance at other points on the line. The end rhyme words in their first stanza order are: leaves, poor, it, You-you, lost, stone. The occurrence of these words on different lines in later stanzas is controlled by Zukofsky's model, Dante's *rime petrose* sestina (itself based on Arnaut Daniel's *Lo ferm voler*), which follows a scheme known in medieval Latin treatises as *retrogradatio cruciata*. By this scheme the sixth and last rhyme word of each stanza becomes the first of the next stanza, the fifth and fourth become the third and fifth, whereas the first, second, and third become the second, fourth, and sixth; the poet takes one from the end of the preceding stanza, then one from the beginning alternately. All the possible combinations are exhausted in six stanzas and the poem, as mathematical unit, is complete. To that Dante adds a *congedo* of three lines in which he uses all six rhyme words, one at the end and one in the middle of each line. With the exception of "lost," Zukofsky's coda follows Dante's practice, including the connection between four of the rhyme words by assonance (poor, you, lost, stone in Zukofsky: *donna, ombra, petra, erba* in Dante).

Except for "leaves," all of Zukofsky's rhyme words appear at more than their predetermined end positions throughout the poem. Thus "Poor" appears ten times (most emphatically in the coda with two repetions in three lines), "it" appears nine times, "you"—and the related "your"—appears twenty-one times, "lost" appears seven times, and "stone" appears ten times. The result is a heightened fugal complexity of very few words with the repeated rhyme words occurring as a constant "leaf around leaf" growing subject, their other line appearances acting as counter-subjects and episodes caught up in and resonating, by repetition of exact and near same sound equivalents, against the sounds made by non-rhyme words (voices).

Zukofsky's preoccupation with music, particularly that of Bach, is well known. But, as Kenneth Cox has noticed, Zukofsky's work, including "Manits," is not musical as that term is conventionally applied to poetry, which has more to do with imitative "sound effects" than anything else. For Zukofsky "is concerned for the pitch of vowel and duration of syllable which fit verse to be sung and it distinguishes song from declamation and declamation from recitative. . . ."[5] The pitch of vowel and duration of syllable: "poor" in the first stanza ends a series of rim-shot "sprung" monosyllabic words. There, in alliteration with the relatively closed sound of "pins," it is open—longer held, though not stressed—; its pitch, coming after the crackling "bright, black" is descending, lower, suggesting that it is (as it in fact is) the most crucial element of the series. "Poor" appears only once, the end rhyme for the fourth line in the second stanza, but is extended by earlier alliteration with "prop, prey" in line two. "Papers" likewise carries the p sound in the third stanza. Here "poor," in the fifth line, again has lower pitch and comparatively longer syllable duration by the juxtapositioning of "too," ascending and open. In the sixth line, these qualities are played off against the expanisve "too" with "Like all the separate poor *to* save the lost." "To" is the extreme opposite of "too," signifying the seeming paradox of the newspaper which in its contents' blurring generality is inadequate for any particular problem or its solution in the case of the separate poor: the poor get poorer.

The close repetition (lines two and three) in the fourth stanza creates a just delayed trip hammer effect that underscores the non-seeing of the poor. "Poor" is again at the climax of a serial movement in the next stanza: "On stone,/ Mantis, you will die, touch, beg, of the poor." And again, with the anticipation made by close comma partition and the specifying preposition phrase "of the . . .," "poor" is low pitched and held. In this case, however, pitch and duration are virtual. What lowers and holds them is the ruthless meaning that all of these things will happen

5. Kenneth Cox, "The Poetry of Louis Zukofsky: *'A,' " Agenda*, IX-X (Autumn-Winter 1971-1972), p. 82.

to the mantis as a result *of the poor*. In direct opposition—further stated by the lines' literal closeness—, the first line of the sixth stanza has "poor" as the end-object of the mantis'—now become "loving beggar"—dive "*to the* poor." Thus the final line of the preceding stanza declares the mantis to be victim of the poor's non-seeing inattention and the very next line implores the mantis to sacrifice itself to the poor, to force them to see, as a loving beggar. The space constriction involved is not coincidental.

It may seem odd that the poet's voice, which heretofore in the poem is undeviatingly grim, suddenly becomes compassionate. But the change is of the nature of the act required; it would be "irrational," as love may be thought irrational facing the equations of individual gain, for the mantis to give itself to the poor. The immediacy of the change in the appearance of "poor" sub-stantiates ("sounds") the genuine disinterest the poet would have the mantis embody, i.e., his own, as an urged "idea." "But the mantis *can start*/ History." The coda maintains the prepositional focus upon "poor" through the poet's final urging. "On the poor" is a variation of "to the poor"; both are *for* the poor (directives to the mantis) as "of the poor" is not, a stage at which (strength) the mantis' sacrifice is not needed. The second "of the poor" (the first was in the last line of the fifth stanza) is crucial; for while in both places there are indications of power, it is the poor's strength, which now sees, that will save the mantis.

In each of the coda's first two lines, "poor" lies precisely in the center of the line, stopped there by commas. The pitch and duration are quite similar, though meaning developing out of syn-tax makes them utterly different. The first "poor" remains in need of the mantis' loving sacrifice; the second "poor" comes, pre-sumably the effected result of that sacrifice, as armies whose strength will build a new world. "Poor" ranges throughout the poem, weaving the poem by sound and what might be called "position associations" with other words, the sound of the word never allowed to leave the reader's forgetting and remembering head, to come down twice, again and again, the central insistent subject of "Mantis."

What does this single word, watched and listened to through its changes, sound like? What, in the words of Robert Duncan's poem "An Essay at War," is the "hidden thing/ revealed in its pulse and/ durations"? It is a fugue, a principle, a process, one voice contrasting and joining with others. Or as Bach has written: "the parts of a fugue should behave like reasonable men in an orderly discussion." Yet the poet's voice in "Mantis" is anything but reasonable—his reason *is* rational, but frantic, without

syllogistic manners—; his discussion with the insect is passionately
disorderly. How can such things be identified with fugue as defined by its great master? But before trying to answer that, I
would cite Zukofsky's own description of fugue as made in a discussion of Shakespeare's *Pericles:*

> And if that intellective portion of mind that is music can make
> poetry and prose interchangeable, because there is a note always
> to come back to a second time—sung to the scale the 'subjects'
> of speech are so few and words only ring changes one on another,
> the differences perceived by their fictions are so slight music
> makes them few. Up, down, outwards—for even inversions and
> exact repetitions move on—are the melodic statement and hence
> the words' sense: or after syllable have been heard before in
> contiguity, they may also be augmented or diminished, or brought
> to crowd answer on subject in a great fugue. . . .[6]

There is no real discrepancy between Bach's understanding (and
practice) of fugue and Zukofsky's. A reading of *"A,"* which cites
Bach's definition, only serves to notice Zukofsky's continuing
attentive sympathy for Bach's music, which, in fact, is used as
one of that poem's modes of organization.

And however casual that reading may be, it is impossible not
to notice

> What stirs is
>   his tracing a particular line,
> Tracings of lines
> Meeting by chance or design.
> With him *ornament,*
>   acquires
> A precision of appeal—
> Let no one think it
> Unnatural.

This appreciation of Bach's skill in renewing the use of the ara-
besque is followed three pages later by the poet's account of his
own work.

> This imagined music
> Traces the particular line
> Of lines meeting
>   by chance or design.

Bach's music and the poet's consciousness of his own art exist in
shared words, shared so that, much later in *"A,"* Bach's quoted
voice and Zukofsky's active composing voice become a single
voice without trace of heavy-handed joinery:

---

6. Zukofsky, *Bottom*, p. 432.

> old man and close lady as one August gust on another stop
> speaking in pretty ears: B's *Notenbuch* compiled by both: her
> copy has her initial no other signature: 'between order and
> sensibility in its power at once to suggest all complexity and
> keep every form each form taking up the same theme': not by
> 'association' it is *so* things come to me.

"Certainly," as Robert Creeley writes in his introduction to the
American edition of *"A" 1-12*, "Zukofsky *hears* Bach . . . ."

Still, it remains true that "Mantis" outrightly violates the
reasonable and the orderly. And still, again, the sestina reveals
itself as a mathematically unforgiving form, forcing those without great surety of technique to become its enthralled manipu-
lators: the form *is* orderly. Here, though, lies the clue. For if a
sonnet as an instance of received or inherited form may be said to
be orderly, then the sestina is demonically so. Or as two of Dante's
commentators write with admirable brevity: "The form in itself
renders an obsession."[7] "Poor" in "Mantis" sounds an obsession
with "the most pertinent subject of our day—/ The poor—". But
the ways "poor" is sounded—exact repetition, augmentation,
dimunition—*are* the ways of fugue process. "Mantis" is a fugue,
but speeded up, a film made blurred and "jumbled" by being run
at more than usual speed, quarter notes all transposed to eights
and sixteenths, without transitions.

The rhythm of "Mantis" does fulfill the shape chosen for the
poet's torsioned thoughts, the relentless sestina experienced as
fugal drive and not wicker-work. The realization grows, however,
that the poet's emotion, no matter how apparently genuine, can
never, despite the attractions of biography, be known beyond the
necessary remove of the poem itself, a construction of language,
with its own special tests for sincerity, style and technique.

Style acts as a corrective, critical template of adjustment
(judgment) upon patterns of expectation developing from the
poet's word combinations. Its judgments, based on awareness of
good continuation, are expressed as in or out of style. In the case
of "Mantis," the governing style is the obsession of the sestina
form in the right relation with the subject of the poor. It is accordingly never enough merely to exhibit one more contemporary
reproduction of the form.

How a test of style for "Mantis" comes out depends on the
functioning of individual words. For it is there that the patterns
of expectation inhering in shape either organically contribute as
"minor units of sincerity" or simply act as a form's required

---

7. K. Foster and P. Boyde, *Dante's Lyric Poetry*, Vol. II: *Commentary* (London: Oxford
University Press, 1967), p. 266.

identifying place-holders. "Wind-up" in the second stanza, for instance, is curious, but not incomprehensibly arbitrary: a combination of wind's motion and that of mechanical toys can easily be "applied" to the mantis as insect and sharer of the terror of the lost poor, who are controlled at will by the banks and newspapers. A part of the coda—". . . arise like leaves/ The armies of the poor . . .", wrenches the syntactical expectation made by "Fly, mantis, on the poor. . .", but such inversion is suitable for *la battaglia* and for additional stress upon the inextricably tied fate of the mantis and the poor. These instances appear to stick out in relief from the poem, but are then seen to resolve themselves into its larger shape.

Less easily resolved are the three parentheses: (thoughts' torsion), (is it love your raised stomach prays?), and (once men). I have already pointed out that Zukofsky uses the parenthesis to remove or disengage his voice from the flow of the poem to comment upon it as an actor might use an aside to his audience. This comparison's involvement of audience is not without interest, though any consideration is made difficult by the anonymity of the modern mass art patron audience (what is "out there" according to Stravinsky) and by the serious poet's own insulation from a dictating audience while in the act of composition. Who is Zukofsky talking to? Perhaps to himself—"While you're partly right you're all wrong—/ I speak to myself most often."[8]—,perhaps to anyone out there.

The point remains that, for however momentary a time, the energy of the sestina is made to pause, then plunge on in its convolutions. The parentheses are delays, disruptions of the poem's musical shape. In measuring the disruption more precisely, it must be admitted that the parentheses are of some aid as landmarks in the otherwise blurring speed of the sestina. And their very aid uncovers their difficulty: that they are somehow outside the poem which does not possess the larger space of drama. A further distinction can be made between the parentheses themselves. (Is it love's food your raised stomach prays?) represents another level of the poet's voice *in* the poem, addressed to the mantis, whereas (thoughts' torsion) and (once men) are essentially exterior explanations. Yet no satisfactory link can be found for (thoughts' torsion) and "it" of the same line, and the reader is forced to assume that the parenthetical torsion, though perhaps in a more impersonal manner, represents another level, distinct from the passionate voice level of most of the poem, even to the extent of

---

8. Zukofsky, *"A" 1-12* (London: Jonathan Cape, 1966), p. 136.

interior admonishing "mind-voice" conscience. Likewise, (once men) may be taken as spoken by the poet, but it is spoken to neither the mantis, nor to the poor—nor to the poet himself—. Its lack of "local" direction is a sign for its explaining connection with "the paths men leave" and the mantis' death by thorns with the mythic explanation— Cadmus reversed— which helps in turn to connect with the later flat reference to "the myth."

Arguing for Dante's Donna Pietra as a symbol of a poetics, Leslie Fiedler remarks in passing that "if there is a 'true love' behind the *rime pietrose*, it is the love of Arnaut Daniel."[9] I at first read this to refer to Daniel's own "real" romances in comparison with Fiedler's *idée fixe* description of Dante as a member of university homosexual society more concerned with finding a subject to justify a new style than with the unrelenting charm of a historical maiden. A later reading is that whether Dante's sestina was written for an actual female or not, what "*Al poco giorno*" inescapably demonstrates is a love of language as embodied in the practice of Arnaut Daniel, *il miglior fabbro*, the best smith of language. To repeat, the poet's emotion can never be directly warranted, however contemporary he may be with his readers. (So the pretty dilemma: what if Zukofsky—asked if he were really passionately concerned with the poor—were to say "yes," but in an unconvincing manner?) Similarly, reversing analysis cannot be expected to lay bare anything like the full dynamics of the composition sequence. The emotion that can be indicated through analysis is love of language from the treatment of style and technique. There is at least the implication that, by virtue of his treatment, Zukofsky successfully objectifies his complex emotion toward the poor in "Mantis."

That is to say if the poet's personal love or compassionate emotion for the poor cannot be finally determined, it nonetheless can be inferred from his love of language, his consciousness of word combinations and their construction to the extent that, in Eric Mottram's phrase, "technique is mythicized." The poem is an emotional object made of words. The emotion is objectified—held for the inspection of others—if the poet has sufficient technique, the particular point to point (not to suggest military march music regularity) realization of the shape to rhythm to style sequence. The undeniable obsession of Zukofsky's sestina, his "successful" consciousness and realization of technique, all these "facts of practice" ground the extensions I have made of his understanding of sincerity as the care for detail founded on love that sees with

---

9. Fiedler, *No! In Thunder*, p. 27.

the eyes (with the justly co-ordinating mind), the "engenderer" of his composition sequence. Such care may come to exist for language well constructed—not pure—, for language seen as an object of delight in the eyes of the sincere poet who desires to witness his love.

THE THINKER

LOUIS ZUKOFSKY

[SINCERITY AND OBJECTIFICATION] *

Q. I know that "objectivism" was short-lived as a movement, if it ever existed at all, but your essay in the February 1931 issue of *Poetry* does seem to suggest a particular way of looking at reality. In fact, you actually use the term nominalism in connection with André Salmon. Wouldn't you say that your own poems from the beginning attempted to get away from normal generalization and theme to present an experience of the object or of nature directly?

A. Well, I don't want to get involved in philosophy. I might as well say that *Bottom: on Shakespeare* was written to do away with all philosophy. Naturally you can't do it without getting involved in their blasted terminology. In the first place, objectivism . . . I never used the word; I used the word "objectivist," and the only reason for using it was Harriet Monroe's insistence when I edited the "objectivist" number of *Poetry*. Pound was after her; he thought the old rag, as he called it, was senile, and so on. He had had his fights with her; he couldn't get across the people he wanted, and in one of his vituperative letters he told old Harriet the magazine would come to nothing, that there was this youngster who was one of the best critics in America . . . well, I'm reminiscing. In any case, Harriet was fond of Pound and after all she was enterprising. Well, she told me, "You must have a movement." I said, "No, some of us are writing to say things simply so that they will affect us as new again." "Well, give it a name." Well, there were pre-Raphaelitism, and dadaism, and expressionism, and futurism—I don't like any of those *isms*. I mean, as soon as

*Reprinted from "The 'Objectivist' Poet: Four Interviews," conducted and reported by L.S. Dembo in *Contemporary Literature*, 10 (Spring, 1969), pp. 155-219. Just the Zukofsky section (pp. 203-19) are given here. We are grateful to Professor Dembo for permission to reprint. The title in brackets has been added for indexing purposes.

you do that, you start becoming a balloon instead of a person. And it swells and a lot of mad people go chasing it. Another word I don't want to use is "reality." I try to avoid it; I use it in *Bottom*, I think, only because I had to quote some text. Occasionally, a really profound man—a Cardinal Newman, for example—can use the word; there isn't any word you can't use if you have enough body to make something of it. Anyway, I told Harriet, "All right, let's call it 'Objectivists,' " and I wrote the essay on sincerity and objectification. I wouldn't do it today. (I've sworn off criticism after *Bottom*, after nineteen years of going through all that.) In any case I wouldn't use the same terminology anymore. But looking back at that essay, and as it was revised in *Prepositions . . .* what I did in this volume of criticism was to get it down to the bare bone. Granted that there are certain infelicities of style in the original. Actually, I don't think I changed ten words in editing the collected criticism. I omitted a great deal though, and that made all the difference.

But let me explain what I meant by "sincerity" and "objectification." Any artist lives with the things as they exist. I won't go into the theory of knowledge. I don't care how you think about things, whether you think they are there outside of you, even if you disappear, or if they exist only because you think of them. In either case you live with things as they exist. Berkeley's table that exists only in the mind, Plato's table that couldn't exist without the idea of a table, or Aristotle's table that was a table because you started with wood and had a purpose to make something for the good of society —you're still talking about a table. The theory of knowledge becomes terribly dull to me unless somebody like Wittgenstein, who really saw what the word game was, writes about it. Then it becomes very moving, because of the life, the fact, that goes on in your head no matter how evaporated the body becomes, no matter how much "gravity" you have (what Lawrence Sterne defined as the mysterious carriage of the body to betray the defects of the mind).

But getting back to sincerity and objectification: thinking with the things as they exist. I come into a room and I see a table. Obviously, I can't make it eat grass. I have delimited this thing, in a sense. I call it a table and I want to keep the word for its denotative sense—as solid as possible. The only way it will define itself further will be in a context. In a way it's like grammar; only grammar is more abstract. In traditional grammar, you start with a *subject*. "I'm going to talk about *that*," says Aristotle. "What are you going to say about *it*?" "Well, what *can* I say about *it*?" says Aristotle: *"It* is, *it* exists, or *it* acts, or sometimes you hit *it* on the head and *it* seeks an action, a change in voices as we call it. Grammar is that kind of *thing*. The object *is*. Now what objects *aren't*?"

To the human being with five senses. . . . (How many more is he going to get when he goes up there beyond gravity? Probably lose them all.) Some senses are more important to some people than to others. To the cook, I suppose taste and smell are the most important; to the musician, hearing (the ear); to the poet, all the senses, but chiefly, sight (the eye)— Pound said we live with certain landscapes. And because of the eye's movement, something is imparted to or through the physical movement of your body and you express yourself as a voice.

Let's say you start with a body, the way a kid does when it's born, and it cries almost immediately. It takes a long time for its eyes to focus, a month I suppose. But anyway, the eye concerns the poet; the ear concerns the poet because he hears noises, and like the kid he's affected. And you can do all sorts of things with the noises. You can imitate natural things, and so forth. I like to keep the noises as close to the body as possible, so that (I don't know how you'd express it mathematically) the eye is a function of the ear and the ear of the eye; maybe with that you might feel a sense of smell, of taste even. So much of the word is a phsiological thing. I know all of the linguists will say I'm crazy. In fact I think there's a close relationship between families of languages, in this physiological sense. Something must have led the Greeks to say *hudor* and for us to say *water*.

But the word is so much of a physiological thing that its articulation, as against that of other words, will make an "object." Now you can make an object that is in a sense purely image and, unless you're a great poet, it can get too heavy. You will become one of those painter-poets who are, really, too frivolous; they exist in every generation. You know, they look at something and they immediately want to write a poem. That's not the way to make an image; it ought to be involved in the cadence—something very few people realize. What I mean is the kind of thing you get in Chapman's "the unspeakable good liquor there." Obviously, the man who wrote that knew what it was to gargle something down his throat. So body, voice, in handling words—*that* concerns the poet.

The last thing would be, since we're dealing with organs, the brain or intellect. That's very abstract. The parallel in physics would be the gaseous state. Now gas exists, but it is awfully hard to write the gas-stuff unless you have a very clear mind.

The objectivist, then, is one person, not a group, and as I define him he is interested in living with things as they exist, and as a "wordsman," he is a craftsman who puts words together into an object .

I tried in *A Test of Poetry* to show what I meant by giving examples of different poets writing—colloquially, not philosophically speaking—on the same subject. People are free to construct whatever table they want, but if it's going to be art, you had better have some standards. I at least want a table that I can write on and put to whatever use a table usually has. Well, this is all the answer to one question, and I don't really like to discuss these things. . . .

Q.   Please go on.

A.   Well, I'd prefer a poem that embodied all I have said here, a poem which said them for me, rather than the criticism. They say my poetry is difficult. I don't know—I try to be as simple as possible. Anyway, I have a poem that shows what I've been talking about, "The Old Poet Moves to a New Apartment 14 Times" [*All*, 1956-1964, p. 78]. Let me read some of it:

> The old poet
> moves
> to a new apartment
> 14 times

> I
> "The old radical"
> or surd—

> 2
> *I's (pronounced eyes)*
> the title of his last
>
> followed by *After I's.*
> "After"—*later* or
> chasing?

> 3
> All the questions are answered with their own words. . .

[Interrupting:] What was your question?

Q. "All the questions are answered with their own words." Why don't you continue?

A. All you have to do is say "yes" or "no." That's about all we have ever done as far as action is concerned. The trouble is most people just won't be that definite. [Continues reading:]

> All the questions are answered with their own words
> intellect the way of a body a degree "before"
> soughed into them

[Commenting:] I'm thinking of boiling off water so that it becomes vapor.

> if the words say silence suffers less
> they suffer silence
> or the toy of a paradox
> a worth less worth
> than that *shall* will be said
> as it is

[Commenting:] There is something that exists and the "shall," well, I don't know; it's up to the scheme that seems to be running everything, God, whatever you want to call it.

4
Aleatorical indeterminate

[Commenting:] Are we determined or not determined?

> to be lucky and free and original
> we might well be afraid to think
> we know beforehand exactly
> what we're doing

[Commenting:] It sometimes helps not to know "exactly," and no one knows exactly. How can he know "exactly"? I think we might as well be honest about that.

> rather let it happen
>
> but the 'illogical' anticipation,
>
> music, has always been explicit
> as silence and sound have

[Commenting:] What have you? What does this art consist of? Well, with poetry as with music, I go on, with silence and sound, "how long is a rest to rest." All right, according to John Cage, sometimes it's all silence. You want it that way? Doesn't make very much sense to me. I don't see why you should call it music. Maybe it is. That's the intellect part of it. John Cage is an intellect; I think that's the trouble with him.

Otherwise, he's very wonderful, does some marvelous "things"
to evoke silence.

> in the question
> how long is a rest to rest.

> In the 'old' metered poetry
> the Augustan proud of himself
> jingle poet as he says it

> freedom also happens
> tho a tradition precounts

[Commenting:] He may think he's writing a line in iambic
pentameter, but is he? Does he control every bit of it? It's a
question: are you going to write by chance? Are you going to
be absolutely rational about it? All conventional poetry . . .
poets have the idea that they're in complete control of what
they're doing. Sometimes it happens that the jingle poet has a
marvelously metrical line that somebody else may do consciously for that effect. Or he can't help himself; it's in the language that two stressed syllables will come together. He's already determined by the speech that exists. It's one of the
functions that the poet, if he's entirely honest, will realize.

> freedom also happens
> tho a tradition precounts

> but someone before him
> is counting for him
> unless it happens

> that the instant has him
> completely absorbed in that someone:

[Commenting:] Sometimes you may like Shakespeare so
much you may, as Emerson says, turn out to be as good as
Shakespeare for a minute

> a voice not a meter

[Commenting:] That's what I'm emphasizing.

> a voice not a meter

> but sometime a meter's a voice.

[Commenting:] Sometimes you discover what you think is a
measure and it's the same as that objectivist voice. And it's
nothing "new"—that is, hankering for the new in the sense of
novelty. I'd say this of Chaucer, of Wyatt at his best. You
can't carry the poetic object away or put it in your pocket,

but there is a use of words where one word in context defines the other and it enriches so that what is put over is somebody's reaction to existence. That's all I was going to say.

Q. What about the relation between "sincerity" and "objectification"?

A. Sincerity is the care for the detail. Before the legs of the table are made, you can see a nice top or a nice grain in the wood, its potential, anyway, to be the complete table. Objectification is the structure. I like to think of it as rest, but you can call it movement. I cut out things from the original essay because I wanted to avoid all the philosophical jargon. Actually, looking back at it, it wasn't bad for a guy of twenty-five or twenty-six; it's certainly clearer than parts of Whitehead. I don't mean the mathematical Whitehead; I couldn't even kiss his toe there. I don't know whether it was as good as Peirce. . . .

Q. Concerning this phrase, "thinking with the things as they exist," doesn't one man make them different from another, or doesn't what existence means to one man differ from what it means to another?

A. That's true. But I'm thinking of only one person, the poet. Anyway, there's a certain amount you've got to get across to the next man or there's no sense in talking about art—we'll have bedlam. If you're talking about art, you want to give it to at least one person—that's your audience. Otherwise, unless you're talking to yourself, you probably set up a person. I mean, if we can't agree that this is a table, then, all right, you can use it to sleep on, but you're messing up uses. I'd say the business of writing is to see as much as you can, to hear as much as you can, and if you think at all to think without clutter; then as you put the things together, try to be concise.

Q. Well, what is involved in thinking without clutter? I don't think it's as simple as it seems to be.

A. It depends on how long or how deeply you've lived; after all, it's thinking or, if you wish, sensing with the things as they exist. I said in the essay—perhaps it isn't explicit—that it depends on the depth of the person. Everybody, some time in his life, wants to write poetry for reasons that have nothing to do with poetry. A kid falls in love and he wants to write a poem; it might turn out to be a good one simply because he's so innocent. But it's not likely. That is, if you want to be a good carpenter, you either know something about your craft or you don't. Each poem is in a sense its own law; I mean the good poem always is and there's no other like it. But if you're talking about at least a minimum of human value, humane value, you better have some kind of standard, especially if you're going to be true to your language, if you really want to affect people, and so on.

Q. Still, doesn't the "clear physical eye" see in a different way from the eye working with the brain or influenced by abstractions? For example, there's a poem in *All* that goes:

> Not much more than being,
> Thoughts of isolate, beautiful
> Being at evening, to expect
>   at a river-front:
>
> A shaft dims
> With a turning wheel;
>
> Men work on a jetty
> By a broken wagon;
>
> Leopard, glowing-spotted,
>   The summer river—
> Under: The Dragon   [*All*, 1923-1958, p. 24]

It seemed to me the poet here was seeing as an objectivist, in terms of particularities rather than wholes. He seems to be literally thinking with things as they exist and not making abstractions out of them.

A. But the abstract idea is particular, too. Every general word is particular, *as against another*—glass, table, shoe, arm, head . . . "reality," if you wish. Individually they're all, apart from their sound, abstract words. I'd like to keep them so that you don't clutter them with extra adjectives, extra adverbs; the rest is just good speaking. It might turn out to be crabbed rather than being glib, but if you're good, maybe you'll be blessed by some grace. But this poem is an example of what happens if you deal mostly with sight and a bit of intellect.

Q. Yes, that's what I meant. And doesn't this mean that the poet sees in terms of individual details—with "sincerity," in your sense?

A. But it all mounts up. I suppose there's a general statement: "Not much more than being," whatever that is. The opposite would be non-being. And then I go ahead and say a little more about it; that being becomes isolate being, a beautiful being. These are all assertions. Where is this? That's the first tangible thing, a river-front; the one I saw was probably the Hudson or the East River. But the point is that the river-front becomes more solid as against the general flow of intellect in the beginning. The first part is intellective, "gaseous"; the second part would resemble the "solid" state.

Now what kind of being? There is a shaft with a turning wheel; there are men on the jetty, and a broken wagon. It could have been a good wagon, but I wanted it to be broken. And above this, the sky. So actually I suppose the guy who was doing this was trying to get the whole picture, instead of saying as a "romantic" poet, "Now I'm seeing, now I'm being; I see the jetty; this wagon was once pretty."

What really concerned me in these early poems was trying to get away from that kind of thing—trying to get away from sounding like everybody else. We are all dealing with the same things. Someone makes a table, a bad one; someone makes one that is new and hopefully not to be thrown out the next day.

Q. Where do the leopard and the dragon fit in?

A. That's the constellation. "Leopard, glowing-spotted, / The summer river— / Under."

Q. Why do you refer to the constellation?

A. There I'm . . . I'm not for metaphor, unless, as Aristotle says, you bring together unlikes that have never existed before. But they're in words; they're in verbs: "the sun rises." My statements are often very, very clipped.

Q. Well, the colon in the last line after "Under" would seem to imply that the dragon is under the river.

A. "Summer river— / Under: . . ." There is a question of movement and enough rest; notice the space after "Under." The dragon is also reflected in the river—inverted. Of course, that kind of thing has already been done by Mallarmé—not that I knew as much Mallarmé then as I do now.

Q. Well, to continue this matter of seeing, it seems that many of your poems—for example, "Immature Pebbles"—are based on "the unsealing of the eyes bare," as you put it in "her soil's birth." Isn't this kind of vision associated with what you have called the "spontaneous idea," which seems to be the mental activity that corresponds to "thinking with the things as they exist"?

A. Yes. I would hope so. All poetry is that. Suddenly you see some thing. But what was I doing in "Immature Pebbles"? [Thumbing to the page and looking at it. *All*, 1923-1958, p. 46:] I start with a quote from Veblen. *"An Imponderable is an article of make-believe which has become axiomatic by force of settled habit. It can accordingly cease to be an Imponderable by a course of unsettling habit."* Well, this was Veblen's way of writing; it amuses me sometimes. But it was always very difficult. Actually, Veblen was the kind of man who'd give you a bag of bees and walk off. All right, I started out with that: an imponderable is an article of make-believe and it's associated with settled habit, the ordinary, the mundane, and so on. The only thing is to unsettle it. This particular spring, in the poem, happens to be the kind of thing that you see on any beach, but I observed certain very particular things. Notice that the spring is still too brisk for water suds, and I've even defined it, "bathers' dirt."

(All you can say about this poem is . . . it doesn't even have to be me, but the person will result from the poem. That's why I think it's useless to try to explain one's poetry. Better that it explain itself after the poet is gone. One way of its explaining itself is by your reading what's there: 2+2=4 does not say 2+2=5. Now where the difficulty may come in is that sometimes you get an equation that is so condensed, it is good only for the finer mathematician. I don't say that to compliment myself, but, you know, mathematicians have standards of fineness, the more condensed the equation, the "nicer" it is.)

Well to go on, "ripples / make for . . . An observer's irrelevancy / of April." May follows. Obviously, he's not very happy about it because it is "objectless / of inconsequence" and brings "the expected to the accustomed / in this place." How happy can it be? Obviously, this man who is looking at the "shivering" bathing suits and "the mandrill's blue and crimson / secret parts" is looking at things the "wrong" way and he wants to get away from the scene. But at the same time he has rendered it, "In our day, impatience / handles such matters of photography / more pertinently from a train window." I think you can gather that the man who wrote this poem isn't interested in photographing people bathing on a beach. That's it.

All right, is it as good as Seurat's painting? It may have rendered as much as Seurat in words. Obviously, Seurat was happier with his points of paint than I was with my words. But I've certainly rendered much of these "immature pebbles," in the sense that one may give another the (perhaps undesirable) gift of a table. These kids are pebbles; they're a part of nature, they're "nice," but I'd rather see them through a train window. I didn't want to make a photograph and yet I did. It's an ironic poem, but irony is one of the ways of saying things. I prefer singing to this type of thing, but there it is.

Q. I wonder whether you'd mind also commenting on "Mantis," and the poem interpreting it [*All*, 1923-1958, pp. 73-80]. You seem to be concerned here with the sestina as the ideal expression of the "battle of diverse thoughts" or associations arising in the poet's mind upon his encounter with a mantis.

A. I never said it was the *ideal* form of expression. You have to be careful with this sapless guy, you know. Actually, I was trying to explain why I use the sestina, and there are a lot of old forms used. I suppose there are two types of natures. One is aware of the two-hundred-year-old oak, and it's still alive and it's going to have some use to him; the other one is going to say cut it down and build a supermarket. I'm not inclined to be the latter, nor do I want to imitate a traditional form, but if that thing has lasted for two hundred years and has some merit in it, it is possible I can use it and somehow in transferring it into words—as I said in *"Aleatorical indeterminate"*—make something new of it. And the same for the form of the sestina. Musicians have done that with fugues; there are some today who try to do counterpoint or traditional harmony, but most won't even talk in that terminology. Ultimately it'll come down to silence or sound, words or no words. And where are you going to get them? Where does language come from? Are you just going to make it out of a mouthful of air? Sometimes, but most of the time you don't; there's a world already there; it might be a poetic form that is still useful.

Now the so-called "modern" will say you cannot write a sestina anymore, that Dante did it and it's dead and gone. But every time I read Dante, it's not dead. The poet is dead, but if the work is good, it's contemporary. There's no use in writing the same sestina as Dante, because in the first place, you couldn't do it, except by copying it word for word and believing it's yours—an extreme case. What is possible is that L.Z. or somebody else could write something as good as it.

Well, Williams came along and said, "No, we've got to get a new poetic foot," and while he did wonderful things instinctively, I wish he had omitted some of the theory. Pound was more sensible. What kind of meters can you have? Well, what we've had throughout the history of poetry: you can count syllables, or your language is stressed and so you will count accents, or else you have a musical ear and know when so much sound approximates so much sound and there's a regularity of time. You want to vary the time or have no time signatures . . . whatever the case, it'll have to hold together. So there's no reason why I shouldn't use this "old" form if I thought I could make something new.

" 'Mantis,' An Interpretation" is an argument against people who are dogmatic. On the other hand, I point out that as it was written in the nineteenth century (and some "contemporaries" are nineteenth century), the sestina was absolutely useless. It was just a facility—like that of Sunday painters, who learn to smear a bit of oil on canvas. They're not Picasso; Picasso has used every form you can think of, whether it came from Greece, Crete, or Africa. But what I'm saying in " 'Mantis,' An Interpretation" is not that the sestina is the ideal form; rather that it's still possible. Williams said it was impossible to write sonnets. I don't know whether anybody has been careful about it. I wrote five hundred sonnets when I was young and threw them away. Then I wrote A-7 and a canzone, which is quite different from the sonnet, as Pound pointed out. A very intricate form.

Q. I didn't mean to imply that the sestina was the ideal form of expression *per se*. I thought that for the particular experience that the poet was having with the mantis on a subway, his undergoing a process of "thought's torsion," the sestina was most appropriate.

A. Someone else might have done it differently, but for me that's what it led to. I have that kind of mind. Somehow, you know, the thing can become kind of horrible—to connect a thing with everything. But how can you avoid it? And it's not that I want to be long-winded; I want to be very concise. And when I've done it the long way, as in *Bottom: on Shakespeare* or *A*, which is unfinished, then I want to make it very short. For anybody who is interested in the theory of knowledge, which is done away with in *Bottom*, here is the short way of doing it:

> I's (pronounced *eyes*)
> Hi, Kuh,
>
> those
> gold'n bees
> are I's,
>
> eyes,
>
> skyscrapers. [*All*, 1956-1964, p. 71]

A man can't help himself, any more than Shakespeare could help himself, from saying the same things over and over. The idea is to say them so that people always think you're saying something new. Not that I'm always conscious that I'm doing it. It isn't that I have this concept in my head, that I must say this. God knows, when I was through with doing away with epistemology in *Bottom*. . . . (And I don't see why Wallace Stevens ruined a great deal of his work by speaking vaguely about the imagination and reality and so on. He can be a wonderful poet, but so much of it is a bore, bad philosophy.) I was trying to do away with all the things the Hindus avoid by saying, as in *"A"*-12: "Before the void there was neither / Being nor non-being / Desire, came warmth, / Or which first? / Until the sages looked in their hearts / For the kinship of what is in what is not." They had no trouble with non-being, you see.

I said solid state, liquid, gas; as a matter of fact you can word it sense, essence, non-sense. As to the handling of words, there are the words of sense. Then, there are words that generalize and say "without this that thing can't be essence." So you have words like truth and reality. The "real" is bad enough, but at least it's a voice, a kid saying, "For real?" But then the philosopher adds the "i-t-y" and you start playing all kinds of word games and that's non-sense. You can get lost, really lost. But the Hindu knew that all these things existed. They do exist and sometimes you want to record it. So much for epistemology. When I'm sick of it, thoroughly sick of it, I handle it this way. It was *enough* that I wrote five hundred pages of *Bottom*.

Q. What do you mean, you got rid of epistemology in *Bottom*? The work seems to me to be all epistemology.

A. "The questions are their own answers." You want to say "yes," say "yes"; you want to say "no," say "no." It's a useless argument. Well Wittgenstein, . . . he was the kind that wondered why anybody should bother to read him. As at the beginning of "I's (pronounced *eyes*) . . ." the *haiku*—everybody's writing *haiku*. You remember Elsie, Borden's cow? That's what I meant, and I greeted her up on the sign there: "Hi, Kuh." "Those / gold'n bees / are I's." Obviously some apparition or vision. She's up there anyway and the golden bees . . . I don't know, she makes honey. The bees are also "eyes." You were wondering which "eyes" see. On the other hand, suppose, without my glasses, I look out at the tower— "those / gold'n bees / are I's, / eyes, / skyscrapers": all I see is Christmas crystallography. It's wonderful, but absolutely astigmatic.

All right, the epistemological question? I see this? Yes. The eyes see it? But there's also an object out there. All right, whichever way you want.

Q. Where does the idea of love fit in? It seems to be the chief theme of *Bottom*.

A. Well, it's like my horses. If you're good enough to run or feel like running, you run. If you want to live, you love; if you don't want to live, you hate, that's all. It's as simple as that. It's like being and non-being again—just different words for states of existence.

Q. The horses in *"A"*-7 don't have any manes.

A. Oh, those particular horses are sawhorses. They don't have any manes. Oh, I see what you're after. I don't think that way, though. When I say they don't have any manes, that's all I mean. It's like the old song, "Yes, We Have No Bananas."

Q. But you say these sawhorses are also words—so they're not just sawhorses.

A. Then if I say that, they are words. I use words for them; how can I get them across except in words? I say "sawhorse"; otherwise they'd better speak for themselves. That's a case of objectification. There are these sawhorses. All right, somebody can look at them and not bother with them. They interested me. But I wanted to get them into movement because I'm interested in the sound of words. So I got them into movement. Of course, in *"A"*-7 I have also talked about words, what to do with words.

A is written at various times in my life when the life compels it. That also means that my eye is compelling something or my ear is compelling something, the intellect is always working with words. Being a certain creature with my own bloodstream, etc., I will probably, unless I discover something new to interest me or something worthwhile to write about, probably repeat many things. All art is made, I think, out of recurrence. The point is to have recurrence so that it isn't mere repetition, like Poe's "Bells, bells, bells, bells." The idea is to have these recurrences so that they will always turn up as new, "just" different. Something has happened to the movement or you see the thing "differently." Now this business of words occurs in the first movement, *"A"*-1, and though I'd like to forget it, I must say this: I think that too much of our literature is about the craft of literature. Two great faults I'd like to avoid, but unfortunately I'm among men—I live in my times. . . . The other fault is pretension to learning. How can they all know so many things? By the time I'm eighty I hope to be very simple, if I haven't shut up.

Q. Yet there is a great deal of erudition in *Bottom*, isn't there?

A. I never looked at it as erudition. These were the things I read, and I've probably read very little compared to most people. I don't consider myself a scholar. These are the things I've read, the things I've loved. You've asked about love before. I suppose love means if you do something, that's love; otherwise you don't do anything. There can be, I suppose, a purely passive kind of love. I'm certainly not proud of the erudition. On the other hand, notice that much of the citation of Shakespeare is edited, not because of presumption, but because I wanted to show off the good things.

Q. [Student:] I've been reading the French poet, Ponge, who's extremely interested in words and objects, too. And Sartre, in a little essay on Ponge called "Les Mots et les choses," mentions that he feels Ponge participated in a kind of crisis of language between 1918 and 1930, and that he was trying to make a word an object like the objects he saw. I was wondering whether you felt that you also participated in a crisis of language, a kind of devaluation of words.

A. Well, things happen, you know, in one's time. I've read some of Ponge and recently Cid Corman printed a good deal of him, at any rate a notebook. He's trying to write a poem in the old-fashioned style about pines, so that it will turn out to be like something by Valéry or Hérédia—the Parnassians or the post-Parnassians, something like that. And no, he felt these *things*; they were, of course, botanical things. (Incidently, I wish that

instead of studying philosophy I had studied some botany.)
One of the nice statements Ponge makes is that the poet who
falsifies the object is an assassin; instead of calling the object
what it is, this kind of poet develops grand metaphors and all
the "baroque" curlicues. Well, I suppose you get to a time
where worlds apart two people might be doing similar things.
The work itself, of course, is different. Ponge is consistenly
concerned with botanical objects, just to describe pine needles,
for instance. On the other hand, will they—the pine needles—
help him? The one line about pine needles in the *Cantos*—the
feeling of the redness of the pine needle in the sun—does what
Ponge didn't succeed in doing in that notebook at all, though
I admire what he is after. It's certainly more worthwhile than
attempting another imitation of Baudelaire. I mean either you
show that you're alive in this world, in making something, or
you're not [102/730: "the pine needles glow as red wire"].

Q.   Would you mind commenting on *"A"*? Do you conceive of the
     poem as having an overall structure?

A.   I don't know about the structure of *"A."* I don't care how you
     consider it, whether as a suite of musical movements, or as
     something by a man who said I want to write *this* as I thought
     I saw the "curve" of it in twenty-four movements, and lived
     long enough to do so. I don't know, how would you consider
     Mahler's *Song of the Earth* or something like that? No, I didn't
     think of Mahler. I simply want the reader to find the poem not
     dull. As I said on another occasion, not anxious to say it then:
     "Written in one's time or place and referring to other times
     and places, as one grows, whatever ways one grows, takes in,
     and hopes to survive them, say like Bach's music." Maybe
     you get that out of it; maybe it will make its music. I feel a
     curve or something like that. But in working it out . . . it's
     the detail that should interest you all the time.
         I feel that life makes the curve. That's why Williams kept
     adding to *Paterson*; he found he had more and more to say and
     that it was all part of the poem. (You know, the poet is in-
     satiable. I could go on talking forever.) Otherwise, you get
     down to the old argument, there is no such thing as a long
     poem; there are some good lines, and so forth. Maybe, I don't
     know. A long poem is merely more of a good thing, shall I
     put it that way? So the nice thing is, for instance, that Pound's
     Cantos are still coming out. I hope he isn't crazy devoting so
     much time to the idea that they charged six-percent interest
     in Pisa, and how wonderful it was. No—rather "Imperial power

is / and to us what is it? / The fourth; the dimension of stillness." That's the great Pound. Or in a very late canto, "When
one's friends hate each other / how can there be peace in the
world?" And with that I leave you.

L. S. DEMBO

*LOUIS ZUKOFSKY: OBJECTIVIST POETICS AND THE QUEST FOR FORM**

Admired by Charles Olson, Robert Duncan, Robert Creeley, and a generation of avant-garde writers who esteem Ezra Pound and William Carlos Williams, Louis Zukofsky remains an enigmatic and generally misunderstood figure. Even the members of the so-called Objectivist group that gathered around him in the thirties often found his work impenetrable, and today the situation has been compounded by the appearance of his five-hundred page "metaphysics of cognition," *Bottom: On Shakespeare*, and his still unfinished masterpiece, *"A,"* a quasi-autobiographical poem written over a lifetime.[1] Just as the theories he presented as guest editor of the Objectivist issue of *Poetry* in 1931 were met with silence or confusion, so he has rarely been discussed outside the little magazines. But Zukofsky is more than a coterie poet or a man who owes his place in literary history chiefly to his association with Ezra Pound. To the contrary, he is, for all his eccentricity, both a germinal part of the whole nominalist trend of twentieth-century poetry and a craftsman of extreme subtlety.

I have limited myself in this study to a consideration of Zukofsky's "objectivist" theories of poetry and what I understand to be the conceptual basis of his early poems. As one might expect, Zukofsky is impatient with labels; he accepts the term "objectivist," but (William Carlos Williams notwithstanding) he denies that there is or ever was any thing called "Objectivism." Still, his poetic values do spring from a coherent philosophic

*Reprinted with permission of Professor Dembo and the editors from *American Literature*, Vol. 44, No. 1 (March, 1972).
1. For an account of the Objectivists see "The 'Objectivist' Poet, Four Interviews" (George Oppen, Carl Rakosi, Charles Reznikoff, and Louis Zukofsky), along with my introduction in *Contemporary Literature*, X (Spring 1969), 155-219. [The Zukofsky part reproduced herein pp. 265-281.]

context; they embrace not only technical devices but a particular mode of perception and expression. Finally, many of the poems, implicitly, record the efforts to achieve ideal "objectivist" perception and to discover the form that will turn sensations and impressions into poetry.

I

Although Zukofsky's statement in the special number of *Poetry* reveals a particular kind of sensibility more than it outlines a program, it is an important document in the history of modern poetics.[2] Partly polemical, it attacked, as Harriet Monroe subsequently lamented, the "proud procession of poets whom in our blindness and ignorance, we had fondly dedicated to immortality." For Zukofsky, contemporary poetry, except for certain new writers (Pound, Eliot, Cummings, Stevens, Williams, and Charles Reznikoff, among others), had "neither consciousness of the 'objectively perfect' nor an interest in clear and vital particulars," two of the chief virtues of "objectivist" technique. Calling these virtues "objectification" and "sincerity," Zukofsky elaborated an abstruse but clearly nominalistic theory in which he defined "sincerity" in part as "thinking with the things as they exist," an expression that underlies his whole view. As Zukofsky later explained it,

> I come into a room and I see a table. Obviously, I can't make it eat grass. I have delimited this thing, in a sense. I call it a table and I want to keep the word for its denotative sense— [keep it] as solid as possible. The only way it will define itself further will be in a context. In a way it's like grammar; only grammar is more abstract. In traditional grammar, you start with a *subject*. "I'm going to talk about *that*," says Aristotle. What are you going to say about *it*?" "Well, what can I say about it?" says Aristotle: "It is, it exists, or it acts; or sometimes you hit it on the head and it seeks an action . . . ."[3]

René Taupin's "Three Poems by André Salmon," translated by Zukofsky for the special number, gives a clue to the meaning of this statement. Taupin contends that with *Les Féeries* Salmon

---

2. *Poetry*, XXXVII (Feb., 1931), 268-284. Actually, Zukofsky's commentary is divided into two adjacent parts, "Program: 'Objectivists' 1931" and a longer piece entitled "Sincerity and Objectification, with Special Reference to the Work of Charles Reznikoff." Zukofsky was made guest editor by Harriet Monroe at the insistence of Ezra Pound, who overwhelmed Zukofsky with advice on what and what not to include in the issue. The correspondence is held by the Beinecke Library at Yale. Zukofsky's essays, revised from the originals, were collected in *Prepositions* (London, 1967).
3. "Interview," p. 203 [herein, pp. 266-267].

began to write "Nominalistic poetry,"

> poetry which was neither dreamy nor sentimental, but a matter
> of neat and simple notation. . . .
>
> Would the image no longer do? The *real* would: the poet
> was now obliged to find it in all its intensity, in its anxiety to be
> handled . . . . Nominalistic poetry is a synthesis of real detail,
> similar to the art of the primitives. . . .
>
> The first requisite was to avoid the betrayal of words and
> emotions, so that the real would strike the poet directly . . . . The
> most direct contact is obligatory, more striking than any meta-
> phor tainted with impure interpretation.[4]

For Zukofsky, "direct contact"—thinking with the things as
they exist—begins in a physiological response; the "thinking" or
intellectual aspect, as in Pound and Williams, comes out of the
physiological and is free of sentiment and other distortions of the
generalizing mind. The thought of which Zukofsky speaks never
really seems to transcend its aesthetic origins; one of its highest
forms is music. This is not to say that all the senses are not important to the poet; in fact, sight is primary among them. Yet in poetry, sight still translates itself into sound: "because of the eye's
movement, something is imparted to or through the physical
movement of your body and you express yourself as a voice . . . .
the eye is a function of the ear and the ear of the eye."[5]

Whatever the case, "the word is a physiological thing," intimately related to the poet's direct response to things as they exist.
It can be misused, but ideally its "articulation, as against that of
other words, will make the object."[6] Zukofsky cites a line by
Chapman in which words and the cadence into which they are arranged recreate verbally or express the original perception or sensation: "the unspeakable good liquor there." "Obviously, the man
who wrote that knew what it was to gargle something down his
throat."

"The worth of nominalistic poetry," wrote Taupin, "depends
not only on the value of the subject, but on the energies and active
manifestations of the subject." For Zukofsky it is the "energies
and active manifestations" of words that characterize the poetry

---

4. *Poetry*, pp. 290-291.
5. "Interview," p. 205.
6. The idea of the poem as object was outlined by William Carlos Williams in his *Autobiography*: "The poem being an object (like a symphony or cubist painting) it must be
the purpose of the poet to make of his words a new form: to invent, that is, an object
consonant with his day. This was what we wished to imply by Objectivism, an antidote
in a sense, to the bare image haphazardly presented in loose verse." (New Directions,
1951, p. 265). Although one of the major proponents of a poetics of Objectivism, Williams was not, according to the others, a member of the group per se.

of "sincerity." Simply put, sincerity is "the care for the detail." One might call it the first phase of nominalist perception rendered into a poem:

> In sincerity shapes appear concomitants of word combinations, precursors of . . . completed sound or structure, melody or form. Writing occurs which is the detail, not mirage, of seeing, of thinking with the things as they exist, and of directing them along a line of melody. Shapes suggest themselves, and the mind senses and receives awareness.[7]

That is, in sincerity form is limited to word combinations; such combinations might point to or suggest an overall melodic line, but they do no more than provide hints. Reznikoff's one-line poem, "Aphrodite Urania," is a model of sincerity: "The ceaseless weaving of the uneven water." According to Zukofsky, each word possesses "remarkable energy as an image of water as action." Again, each word recreates the physiological experience of observing the ocean, sound, sight, and meaning being integral. Of another poem Zukofsky says, "There is to be noted in Reznikoff's lines the isolation of each noun so that in itself it is an image, the grouping of nouns so that they partake of the quality of things being together without violence to their individual intact natures."[8]

"Objectification" occurs in a poem when a complete structure is actually realized and not merely suggested; the sense of "rested totality" results—"the apprehension satisfied completely as to the appearance of the art form as an object": "That is: distinct from print which records action and existence and incites the mind to further suggestion, there exists . . . writing (audibility in two dimensional print) which is an object or affects the mind as such."[9] Reznikoff's "Hellenist" is an example:

> As I, barbarian, at last, although slowly, could read Greek,
> At "blue-eyed Athena"
> I greeted her picture that had long been on the wall:
> The head slightly bent forward under the heavy helmet,
> As if to listen; the beautiful lips slightly scornful.[10]

Here is Zukofsky's analysis:

> . . . the purposeful crudity of the first line as against the quantitative . . . hexameter measures of the others, the use of words of two syllables . . . with suitable variations of words of four and three . . . the majority of words accented on the first syllable, all

---

7. *Poetry*, p. 273.
8. Ibid., p. 278.
9. Ibid., p. 274.
10. Ibid., p. 275.

> resolve into a structure (which incidentally translates the Hel-
> lenic) to which the mind does not wish to add; nor does it, any
> more than when it contemplates a definite object by itself.[11]

The "rested totality" that Zukofsky sees in this poem is, characteristically enough, a prosodic one. That he should think of the
mind as wishing or not wishing to add to such a structure all the
more confirms the aesthetic nature of nominalist "thought" as he
conceives it. The theme of the poem seems to be of no consequence to Zukofsky, even though it is precisely the haikuesque
turn of thought that most strikes the reader. Simply, the poet, a
"barbarian" who has painfully mastered Greek, is trying to read to
the picture of the goddess; he now sees her in a new perspective,
her head bent forward *as if to listen*, and, because of his awkwardness, her "lips slightly scornful." The title "Hellenist," which Zukofsky says is unnecessary because the poem is complete, is, of
course, ironic and adds to the charm of the conceit. If the poem
"incidentally translates the Hellenic," as Zukofsky argues, it
should perhaps do so haltingly.

But Zukofsky did have a polemical point in regard to Reznikoff; namely, that the verbal qualities of his shorter poems were
more than "mere pretty bits" and involved the "process of active
literary omission." If, as Reznikoff confessed, he could not wholly
follow the discussion of sincerity and objectification, he at least
shared with Zukofsky a belief in concision and he at least was
attracted by the idea of a poetry that relied on rhythm, not metaphor, for its chief effects.

Ostensibly, Zukofsky took the term "objectivist" from "an
objective," for which he provided the following elliptical definitions: *"(Optics)—The lens bringing the rays from an object to a
focus. (Military use)—That which is aimed at. (Use extended to
poetry)—Desire for what is objectively perfect, inextricably the
direction of historic and contemporary particulars."*[12] In regard
to the definition applicable to poetry, what is important is that
the poet is concerned with particulars (sincerity) and their direction (objectification). In " 'Recencies' in Poetry," the preface to
The "Objectivists" Anthology, brought out in 1932, Zukofsky
added to the definition, "A desire to place everything—everything
aptly, perfectly, belonging within, one with, a context." "Context" seems to be the nominalist's means for arriving at the universal. For Pound, Zukofsky, and later, Charles Olson, poetry was
essentially ahistorical: all (good) poetry was contemporary. Poems

---

11. Ibid., pp. 275-276.
12. Ibid., p. 268.

were "only acts upon particulars," but "linguistic usage has somewhat preserved these acts which were poems in other times and have transferred structures now." If true poetry was a "process of words acting on particulars," such words had a context "capable of extension from its time into the present." Even if the initial context could not be apprehended, the classic poem reached "an equilibrium of meaning determined by new meanings of word against word contemporarily read." Ultimately, "the direction of historic and contemporary particulars" led to a " 'musical' shape."

Appropriately, Zukofsky turned to Pound's "principles of poetic invention" for clarification of his own poetics. As Reznikoff said, Pound, with his insistence on direct treatment, concision, and metrical innovation, greatly influenced the entire group. "Exclusion" (eliminating "clutter") became one of Zukofsky's, as Pound's, chief antidotes to conventional versifying. But more, Pound's division of poetry into melopoeia, phanopoeia, and logopoeia was particularly relevant to Zukofsky's ideas on the aesthetic-musical nature of poetic form: melopoeia is poetry that "moves by its music, whether it be music in words or an aptitude for, or suggestion of, accompanying music." Phanopoeia is "imagism"; and logopoeia is "poetry that is akin to nothing but language which is a dance of the intelligence among words and ideas and modifications of ideas and characters." In short, these terms stand for "movements" affecting the ear, the eye, and the brain. But rather than viewing them as independent or separate, Zukofsky sees them as fused into a single "emotion which in its movement, in its verbal existence, sensuously and intelligently manifests poetry." The "poet's image is not dissociable from the movement or the cadenced shape of the poem."

This movement seems to be the vital force of the poem (perhaps leading to "equilibrium") and it is apparent in each of the components. It directs (as well as arises from) the diction, images, and meanings. Zukofsky has always been concerned with the "musical shape" of the individual word ("the sound and pitch . . . are never apart from its meaning") and indeed he is almost equally interested in the aesthetic effect of individual letters: "most western poets of consequence seem constantly to communicate the letters of their alphabets as graphic representations of thoughts—no doubt the thought of the word influences the letters but the letters are there and seem to exude thought."[13] This is as close as the western writer can come to achieving what

---

13. Louis Zukofsky, ed., *An "Objectivists" Anthology* (New York, 1932), p. 20.

the Chinese writer does by means of the ideograph, which is "felt" by the reader. (I don't believe that Pound, with his ideogrammic method, ever went quite so far as to extend aesthetic effect to single letters.)[14]

The poetic translation of "thinking with the things as they exist," then, was "exactness of utterance," this exactness involving "measurement" by words (*"Poetry / For My Son When He Can Read"*). Consistently the realist, at least in his efforts, Zukofsky believed that there was a standard for writing poetry just as there was one for making tables, and this standard made moot all epistemological problems. The "physical intricacies of fact" were the references for the intricacies of words ("which are the semblances of the things") and the "choice for science and poetry when symbols or words stop measuring is to stop speaking." The major aim of the poet was "not to show himself but that order that of itself can speak to all men." Again, the order that most sought to speak to all men was found in music; poetry was therefore "nothing else but the completed action of writing words to be set to music."

The trouble was that the transmutation of things and feelings into verbal music did not always provide a shape that could speak to all men. Indeed one wonders whether Zukofsky really intended to do so, despite his strong belief in the measurable qualities of poetry and the necessity for objective standards. As much the solipsist as the realist, he has always been something of a recluse and it is typical that, while he is quite willing to talk about his work, his interpretations often turn out to be as esoteric as the poems themselves. His long poem *"A"* deals with personal subjects elliptically, but Zukofsky firmly refuses to talk about his life in any way that will provide an insight into himself or his poetry. "By the time I'm eighty I hope to be very simple," he said, "if I haven't shut up."

II

But Zukofsky's remark has, I think, a deeper significance, for if simplicity can be equated with clear musical articulation, and hence harmony and form, it is a goal that the poet is ever struggling to attain. This struggle for "objectification" seems to be a central theme in Zukofsky's otherwise themeless poetry:

---

14. But Isadore Isou, with his *Lettrisme*, did after the Second World War, and the German Dadaist, Raoul Hausmann, preceded him by a generation.

> If his notes could not extricate themselves from this complicated
> mass, they would be to his tactility like meeting at a point with-
> out further coincidence or intersection. If they did extricate
> themselves, they would, moving towards a definite shape, become
> capable of being apprehended, themselves their own existence in
> the plain of surrounding existence, tactility of material become
> tangible.[15]

This latter, I take it, indirectly describes an ideal poem, which,
like an ideal of sculpture, is rarely attained. Thus in a poem dedicated to the sculptor, Osip Zadkine, Zukofsky wrote:

> In the art of stone it is hard to set one's own
>   seal upon the idea of stone,
> And in a world from which most
>   ideas have gone
> To take the wreck of its idea
> And make it stone. . . .
> But of stone to be seen in the sun,
> Is harder.
> There are almost no friends
> But a few birds to tell what you have done. (p. 99)

In a sense the aim of Zukofsky's art is the "stone to be seen in the
sun," the "definite shape" that is its "own existence in the plain
of surrounding existence, tactility of material become tangible."
The problem is that the material resists becoming tangible, and so
tactile or apprehensible.

Consider, for example, this typical description:

> A last cigarette
> a companion
>
> dark, spring's
> green smells
>
> and the work
> is in mind
>
> a love's
> unclouding it
>
> the spontaneous
> idea
>
> is not yet
> called up (p. 92)

The poet is stimulated, but all remains potential. In a sense, he has
achieved "sincerity" (the eye for detail) but he has not found the

---

15. Untitled prose piece in *All: The Collected Short Poems, 1923-1958* (New York,
1965), p. 70. All page references in the text are to this edition. Quotations are by permission of W.W. Norton & Co., Inc.

"direction for the . . . particulars." The "love" that is unclouding the work in his mind (or his mind itself) is simply his urge to create—an expression of his vitality—as Zukofsky's definition suggests: "If you're good enough to run or feel like running, you run. If you want to live, you love; if you don't want to live, you hate, that's all."

The poem continues elusively:

> a green light
> of the subway
> entrance
>
> to let spring ask
> is the world
>
> at the World's Fair
> any more
> than an action sings.

The syntax here is confusing, but the implication is clear: the poet seems to be asking whether the world (reality) is any more the World's Fair (science and technology) than it is poetry. ("Is the World / at the world's fair" means, I think, not just "Is everybody attending the fair?" but literally "Is the World's Fair the whole world?") For, according to the poet, his method and the scientist's are alike:

> Science, too, posted
> after all smells
>
> carefully fostering
> cadres
>
> not grudging
> time
>
> patiently
> "bothering."

For the scientist, the result was represented by the World's Fair; the poet hopes his "method" will end in an "action" that "sings." But the fact is that it is only a hope, that he is still "fostering/ cadres" (in the sense of frameworks), still waiting for the intuition that will give shape (objectification) to his sensations on a spring day.

Zukofsky's attempt to understand a dream presents a similar problem. "A coffin launched like a ship's hull / Sped as from a curtain afire / Draped to the keystone of an arch" provides the stimulus (p. 94). The coffin sinks and wakens

> under the stream and in me
> A set of furtive bells, muted
> And jangling by rote "What does this say? . . ."

In this case the meaning of the vision is essential to the poetic realization of the experience, and the speaker tries to apprehend what it was in his own mind that caused such a dream. His conclusion is as hopeful but as uncertain as it was in the poem previously discussed:

> "Eyes, looking out,
> Without the good of intellect,
> Rouse as you are used to:
> It is the bad fallen away,
> And the sorrow in the good.
> You saw now for your book, *Anew*."

This response is part of what the bells cited above jangled by rote; in other words, it is still part of the dream and seems to be only scarcely less enigmatic than its context, for the poet is in fact looking out without the good of intellect, and the poem remains a demonstration of its theme.

A statue in a Washington cemetery provides another encounter with the inapprehensible. The poem that presents this experience is entitled, significantly enough, "1892-1941," an indication of the total knowledge that can be derived about the figure represented. "Characterless lips, straight nose, sight, form no clue/ (are none too great sculpture) to portrait or you" (p. 100). The statue is bad (formless) art and the spectator has only the unpleasant sensation that some person is dead and buried.

In most instances musical form did not necessarily involve "meaning" in the discursive sense. A poem in which Zukofsky felt that he had succeeded, "Glad they were there" (p. 102), contains no predication and, on the face of it, is no less baffling than normal. Here is the entire piece:

> Glad they were there
> Falling away
> Flying not to
> Lose sight of it
> Not going far
> In angles out
> Of ovals of
> Dances filled up
> The field the green
> With light above
> With the one hand
> In the other.

The note to this poem quotes passages from Dante (the dance of the blessed in the Paradiso), Marx (the dialectical movement of the process of exchange), Lorentz (the motion of particles in a magnetic field), and Cavalcanti (an image fragment involving light and the color green). The poem borrows phrases from all these sources and is apparently intended to be an example of what it presents. As with Dante's souls, Marx's exchange and use values, and Lorentz's electrons, the source or inspiration of the motion is hidden and all that is visible is the effect. "Although we never lose sight of it," Lorentz wrote, "we need by no means go far in attempting to form an image of it and, in fact, we cannot say much about it. . . . only the resultant effects . . . are perceptible to our senses" (p. 114). The poem, then, is supposed to provide the purely aesthetic effect of rotation, and the reader can penetrate no deeper than the movement of words and images. Indeed the poem graphically resembles a whirling figure.

Patterns that are the results of mysterious or awesome forces are discoverable in nature (perceived by the "clear, physical eye"), but they are also created by the "wordsman." The title poem of *Anew*, for example, plays off in counterpoint two views or "experiences" of summer; the form of the poem provides an aesthetic order for the sensations described. The speaker begins with the sensations of a man looking up at trees on a hot day:

> Anew, sun, to fire summer
> leaves move toward the air
> from the stems of the branches
>
>   fire summer   fire summer (p. 87)

He imagines how people at sea, who have been cheated of late spring and early summer, would view the same scene from offshore; for them, "the green leaves that fill up the day":

> blow up on the trees of the cliff
>
> on the top
> the mill with the clock-tower
> fires summer
>   over a midsummer shore.

Nothing is being said here; Zukofsky is merely expressing "the intense vision of a fact" from two points of view that reinforce rather than counteract one another and form a "cadre" for the experience.

Like "Glad they were there," "Anew" probably was regarded by Zukofsky as a successful attempt to achieve an aesthetic or conceptionless form. The poet's musical notes detached

themselves from the mass and moved toward as definite a shape as
they could achieve, I think, when the materials were taken from
nature, as they were in most of the shorter poems. (The first section of poems in particular offers abundant examples of Zukofsky's attempt to capture verbally light, sound, and motion in his
surroundings.) The problem of achieving such form, however, was
recurrent:

> Has the sum
> Twenty-five
> Reduced the years
> Of the live songs
> To one-quarter
> Of a century
> Become cold mortar
> Of a pyramid? (p. 88)

The speaker here seems to be concerned that his poems, written
over twenty-five years, are, like the mortar of pyramids, no more
than the cement for a cold memorial. Regarded rationally, the
number twenty-five is simply a matter of mortal chronology. But
there is another way of regarding it:

> Forget the number
> Think of an entablature of snow
> Engraved there 2 a bird-prow
> Taking 5 in tow. . . .

Seeing the number and the years it marks as a hieroglyph—apparently one in which Ra, the falcon-headed sun god, reveals himself—is to gain an insight into the hidden form that animates a life
and a lifetime of poetry:

> Then Ra look down
> The figure shining thru the measure
> Each song the midday
> A sum of each year's leisure.

As the next poem confirms, however, the form is musical, not
rational:

> For you I have emptied the meaning
> Leaving the song
> Or would a god—a god of midday
> Have been brought in by the neck
> For foes to peck at

"Meaning" in the conventional sense belongs to the secular world
and Ra was never intended to be held up and "pecked at" by
meaning-hunters and other empirically-minded foes of mystery.
Such men can only hold the poet in contempt:

> *God[,] the man is so overweening*
> *He would prolong*
> *A folly of thought see 2 as a bird*
> *And what not that we rid day of*
> *So that we may think in our time*

That is, the empiricist rids day of myth (Ra) so that he can "think in his time" and in these lines he attacks the poet for not following his example. But the poet can see a vitalizing form to which the sceptics are blind; moreover, he is capable of the intense aesthetic vision that is appropriate to love:

> Two birds tip on the guy wire
> The green rained on
> Is coppered by sunset, a treeling's
> So black (together we hush a response) between
> Its trunk and silk mesh of kirtle showed evening.

Perhaps the implication here is that love is the "form" of life, just as music is the form of poetry. The final poem in the series reads in its entirety:

> What are these songs
> straining at sense—
> you the consequence?

This statement itself strains at sense, but its context does give it the meaning that Zukofsky explicitly denied to it.

The most detailed and elaborate account of the psychology of the objectivist poet in his quest for form appears in the companion pieces " 'Mantis' " and " 'Mantis,' an Interpretation," the latter being not only an explanation of the former but, again, a re-enactment of the processes it describes. The original is a sestina that plays upon the poet's responses to a mantis encountered in the subway. Thus the first stanza reads:

> Mantis! praying mantis! since your wings' leaves
> And your terrified eyes, pins, bright, black and poor
> Beg—"Look, take it up" (thoughts' torsion)! "save it!"
> I who can't bear to look, cannot touch,—You—
> You can—but no one sees you steadying lost
> In the cars' drafts on the lit subway stone. (p. 73)

As we shall see in a moment, the sestina represents the formalization of the diverse thoughts inspired by the mantis. It is important to emphasize here that Zukofsky is not interested in the mantis as a symbol or even as an object; rather he is concerned with the total "happening" of the encounter—that is to say, with "thoughts' torsion" of which the mantis is only a stimulus. The mere fact, for instance, that the mantis flew at his chest and showed its ungainliness is of no inherent interest:

But *all* that was happening,
The mantis itself only an incident, *compelling any writing*
The transitions were perforce omitted.

Thoughts'—two or three or five or
Six thoughts' reflection (pulse's witness) of what was happening
All immediate, not moved by any transition. (p. 75)

This is precisely the same kind of process that was intimated in a poem in which the speaker awaited the calling up of the spontaneous idea that would give shape to his sensations on a spring day (p. 92). And just as in this poem the poet was "fostering cadres," so here he asks,

Feeling this, what should be the form
Which the ungainliness already suggested
Should take?

                —Description—lightly—ungainliness
                With a grace unrelated to its surroundings. (p. 75)

But this is merely the initial problem. More difficult is capturing

la battaglia delli diversi pensieri . . .
the battle of diverse thoughts—
The actual twisting
Of many and diverse thoughts
What form should *that* take?

A possible solution lies in

The sestina, then, the repeated end words
Of the lines' winding around themselves,
Since continuous in the Head, whatever has been read,
                whatever is heard,
                        whatever is seen
Perhaps goes back cropping up again with
Inevitable recurrence again in the blood
Where the spaces of verse are not visual
But a movement,
With the vision in the lines merely a movement. (p. 76)

The sestina records a movement in the blood and in the mind, just as the mantis, a "small incident of one's physical vision," affects "nerves, glandular facilities, electrical cranial charges." It represents the "recollection" of the multiple intellectual, as well as sensual, possibilities of one's encountering a mantis on a subway: "entomology," "biology," underground rhythm, "economics of the poor" (the lost insect suggests to Zukofsky the "oppression of the poor"), myths and folk legends about the mantis, "airships," and so forth. This whole conception seems to have something in common with I.A. Richard's impulse theory of mental operations and their goal of "equilibrium."

Actually, Zukofsky sees himself here as having an affinity with Dante in *La Vita Nuova*, although Dante's context is a far different one. The subtitle of the interpretation is *"Nomina sunt consequentia rerum, names are sequent to the things named,"* an axiom Dante cites in Chapter Thirteen when making the point that since the name of love is sweet, the effects of love must be so. Zukofsky goes on to allude to the opening lines of the *Vita*: "Incipit Vita Nova / le parole . . . / almeno la loro sentenzia / the words . . . at least their substance." The original reads:

> In that part of the book of my memory before the which is little that can be read, there is a rubric, saying, "Here beginneth the New Life." Under such rubric I find written many things; and among them the words which I purpose to copy into this little book; if not all of them, *at least their substance.* (my italics)[16]

This concern with recollection and the means of recording it is expressed by Zukofsky toward the end of the interpretation: "The Head remembering these words exactly in the way it / remembers/ la calcina pietra / the calcined stone." The calcined stone recalls the whole quest for the "definite shape" discussed above.

What is most significant, perhaps, is that the *Vita* has a literary as well as a psychological dimension. Dante is at pains not only to recount his feelings per se, in regard to Beatrice, but to present, complete with explication, the sonnets that these feelings occasioned and in which, conversely, they were formulated. What would appeal to Zukofsky here is the problem of the "transcription" of words from the "book of memory" to the literal book— from psychological reality (thoughts' torsion) to the poem in which the mental processes are accurately objectified and hence formally realized.

Despite the complexities of the sestina, the main "movement" in the original is clear: the poet is at once repelled by and sympathetic to the mantis, which threatens to alight on his chest and, at the same time, seems doomed to be trampled. Furthermore, the speaker fluctuates between perception of the actual mantis and the associations, chiefly with the poor, that it calls up, "the poor's helplessness / The poor's separateness, / Bringing self-disgust." Insofar as the sestina is based upon repetition through rearrangement of words, the dialectic is maintained up to the last stanza, where the poet finally breaks the circle of his feelings by calling upon the mantis to fly and the poor to arise. The coda reads:

---

16. *La Vita Nuova*, tr. D.G. Rossetti, in *The Portable Dante* (New York, 1947), p. 547.

> Fly, mantis, on the poor, arise like leaves
> The armies of the poor, strength: stone on stone
> And build the new world in your eyes, Save it! (p. 74)

Zukofsky was fully aware that he was risking a social message here and the interpretation argues, with nominalist logic, that the "invoked collective"

> Does not subdue the senses' awareness,
> The longing for touch to an idea, or
> To a use function of the material:
> The original emotion remaining,
>   like the collective,
> Unprompted, real, as propaganda. (p. 79)

Commenting favorably on a translation of Ovid by Golding, in which a wild boar is described, as compared with a similar description by Shakespeare in *Venus and Adonis*, Zukofsky wrote: "The Golding written 28 years before the Shakespeare SEES MORE than the Shakespeare. The Ovid-Golding wild-boar registers the social and economic scene *besides* his merely physical presence."[17] And he added that one "should distinguish . . . between a poet who writes perfectly about one detail, and another who writes perfectly about the same detail and a host of other detail covering a phase of civilization." In short, there is room in a nominalist poetic for social implication, just so long as it inheres naturally in perception and "thought." Pound, of course, was proof of that.

As interpreted by Zukofsky, "Mantis" is an example of what Williams meant when he said that the poem is "an object that in itself formally presents its case and its meaning by the very form it assumes." A more expressionistic example of a poem that works in this fashion is "Poem Beginning 'The,' " a semi-farcical piece that, like *The Waste Land*, presents a chaotic sensibility in quest of order. With its welter of literary, personal, and general allusions, its individually numbered lines, and its non-logical, "musical" movements, the poem is an imitation of Eliot—or Pound (in whose *Exile* it first appeared). Or perhaps it is intended as parody (Zukofsky even provides an untranslated epigraph in Arabic script and an index to the allusions). As in *The Waste Land*, the disjointedness of the form reflects the disjointedness and disorientation of the poet seeking values in a morally destitute society. The wind that blows aimlessly through Eliot's world reappears in Zukofsky's:

---

17. *A Test of Poetry* (New York, 1964), p. 54.

14   But everywhere only the South Wind, the
              sirocco, the broken Earth-face.
15   The broken Earth-face, the age demands an
              image of its life and contacts. . . . (p. 12)

In this self-acknowledged reference to Pound's *Mauberley*, and in
turn to works by Lawrence, Joyce, George Moore, Eliot, and Cummings, Zukofsky is apparently lamenting the inevitable destruction
of the poetic sensibility ("why are our finest always dead?") and
envisioning himself as another starved prophet exploring the
wasteland.

   Just as Tiresias is unable to unify his perceptions, the speaker
in "The" cannot find a pattern in the flux of his thought:

69   How the brain forms its visions think-
              ing incessantly of the things. . . .

71   the things themselves a shadow world
              scarce shifting the incessant
              thought. . . .

Given to puns and prosaic, no less than lyrical, statements ("On
the stream Vicissitude / Our milk flows lewd") the poet sees himself as a prowling, complaining cat in a "cat-world," or more
powerfully, as a mortal, failed Christ ("Do you walk slowly the
halls of the heavens" or "Feel only the lull, heave, phosphor /
change, death. . . ."). A quotation from Yehoash, the pen name of
Samuel Bloomgarden, the Russian-American Yiddish writer, epi-
tomizes the poet's failure and hope for restoration:

110   And his heart is dry
111   Like the teeth of a dead camel
112   But his eyes no longer blink
113   Not even as a blind dog's.

114   With the blue night shadows on the sand
115   May his kingdom return to him,
116   The Bedouin leap again in his *asilah*,
117   The expanse of heaven hang upon his shoulder. . . .

But this lyrical vision is immediately followed by the return to an
absurd reality.

   In the two final movements the problem of identity is viewed
in autobiographical terms. The disorientation of the poet in
modern society is reflected in Zukofsky's own sense of "self-exile"
both from Russian-Jewish and American cultures. Partially
parodying Herrick, he attempts to find the lost poetry in his
mother's past:

187   How long ago is it since you gathered
           mushrooms,
188   Gathered mushrooms while you mayed.

In a possible allusion to revolutionary Russia, he asserts that it "is your Russia that is free mother." Whatever the case, the writings of Yehoash again provide the lyrical analogy of the poet's quest:

205   Winged wild geese, where lies the passage,
206   In far away lands lies the passage.
207   Winged wild geese, who knows the pathway?

This section reaches a climax in a vision of horses, whom Zukofsky views as aesthetically ideal creatures apparently identified with the poet himself:

226   Lord, why not give these bright brutes—
           your good land—
227   Turf for their feet always, years for their mien.

238   If horses could but sing Bach, mother,—
239   Remember how I wished it once . . . .

The truth, however, is that horses can't sing Bach nor can Zukofsky "sing" like Yehoash, who, we might assume, was closer to the "epic" of the Russian-Jewish experience. "Assimilation is not hard," Zukofsky explains, "And once the Faith's askew / I might as well look Shagetz [gentile] just as much / as Jew." On the other hand, he can really identify himself no more with middle-class American civilization than he can with Jewish. His appeal to his mother is, in effect, an appeal to a muse, and the words of a Jewish lullaby become "the words of the prophet . . ./ Likely to save me from Tophet."

Actually, as do many other modern poems that express poetic despair, "The" concludes optimistically. If the poet cannot make "great songs" based on religious faith, he can make "kleinen lieder" that are "joy, against nothingness." Yehoash again speaks for Zukofsky:

318   By the wrack we shall sing our Sun-song

323   Sun, you great Sun, our Comrade,
324   From eternity to eternity we remain true to you,
325   A myriad years we have been,
326   Myriad upon myriad shall be.

This declaration is akin to that uttered by Pound periodically throughout the *Cantos*, Crane, *The Bridge*, Williams, *Paterson*, and Olson, *Maximus*. What faith might have meant to Yehoash and to Zukofsky are, needless to say, quite different. For the latter, it could have been simply the belief in art and song for their own sakes.

I have scarcely meant to imply by this analysis that "Poem beginning "The" " is a wholly coherent work, and, in fact, the explication leaves out a great deal. As in Pound and Olson, a studied obscurity is part of a larger metaphysic in which the poem is not simply an interpretation of experience but an expression of the poet's very attempt to arrive at an interpretation. And inasmuch as their efforts are unsuccessful, it is doubtful that what is obscure to the reader is much clearer to the poet.

The quest for form carried with it, as I have suggested, an attempt to perceive in a particular way; that is, with the "clear physical eye." And just as the poet frequently failed to achieve form, so it was frequently difficult for him to perceive in the ideally "objectivist" manner. The elliptical poem called "Immature Pebbles" deals with this problem. Zukofsky begins with a quotation from Veblen that he himself found obscure: *"An imponderable is an article of make-believe which has become axiomatic by force of settled habit. It can accordingly cease to be an Imponderable by a course of unsettling habit."* The central problem in the poem is the poet's observation of a spring scene (young people bathing in a lake) to whose perennial recurrence he has become habituated. This "observer's irrelevancy / of April" does not bode well for the rest of the season:

> Should then this repeated objectless
> of inconsequence, following and May
> bring the expected to the accustomed
> in this place,
> the surprise will, it can be seen, not exceed
> legs of young men and women
> bathing in a lake—
> summer's inaction colored hot. . . . (p. 46)

Zukofsky commented that "obviously, this man . . . is looking at things the 'wrong' way and he wants to get away from the scene," and the speaker himself concludes that "such matters of photography" are handled "more pertinently from a train window."

But to return to the relation between perception and form, Zukofsky felt that because the poet could here see only photographically, the poem itself was no more than a photograph. Apparently basing his remarks on the fact that newspaper photographs are composed of dots, he asked:

> . . . is it as good as Seurat's painting? It may have rendered as much as Seurat in words. Obviously, Seurat was happier with his points of paint than I was with my words. . . . These kids are

> pebbles; they're a part of nature, they're "nice," but I'd rather
> see them through a train window. I didn't want to make a photo-
> graph and yet I did. . . . I prefer singing to this type of thing, but
> there it is.[18]

Because the habits of vision could not be broken, all that could be
achieved was a kind of literary *pointillisme*.

The opposite seems to be the case in Zukofsky's poem about
his washstand (p. 59). Here, there

> Comes a flow which
> if I have called a song
>   is a song
> entirely in my head
>
>   a song out of imagining
> modillions descried above
>   my head   a frieze
> of stone completing what no longer
>
>   is my wash-stand

This poem presents the same kind of interplay between subject
and object that was found in " 'Mantis' "; the difference is that
while the latter remains within the range of logical, associative
thought, the former is clearly an exercise in imaginative observation, as is its companion piece, " 'Further than'—" (p. 72), in
which, drying from the shower, the poet reads a complete geo-
graphy and geometry into the bathroom floor.

The most extreme form of breaking the "settled habits" of
vision appears, however, in poems that are of obviously nominalistic inspiration. Here is a bizarre little piece in which the poet and a
flower look with the same kind of eyes at a hatless, baldheaded
man on a warm day in Autumn:

> Ears beringed with fuzz
> owned a man's sculpturing head
> autumn's regard
>   for weather like spring
> holed shoes meeting the pavement (p. 58)

This may well be the poet's description of himself; in any case,
the features that he singles out strike the flower as well:

> If, when,
>   introduce these to
> a fuzzed flower   Petal will
> declare as of carving   "bluish soles'
> walk, head, ears' hair: greeting"

---

18. "Interview," p. 213.

Like the poet, the flower perceives in terms of particularities, not rational wholes. Actually, the flower and the man seem to inhabit the same world and to exist as equals. If the subject is in fact the speaker himself, the identification of man and nature is all the more profound.

My aim in this discussion has been to do no more than shed some light on Zukofsky's objectivist vision and I have concentrated only on a small number of his earlier poems. But no single article can really do justice to Zukofsky's achievement. The later lyrics, *Bottom: On Shakespeare, "A"* (presently extended to twenty-one books), phonetic experiments with Catullus, and the fiction—each presents its own problems of exegesis and requires separate, intensive study. These works carry Zukofsky's objectivist inspiration to fruition and, I believe, give him the scope and depth of a major poet. Zukofsky may never reach the ultimate simplicity he desires but perhaps no genius does.

CID CORMAN

IN THE EVENT OF WORDS

Introduction

The move into sounded words was pointed early along. The versions of Catullus picked up the charge increasingly as they developed. The play of—not only on but in and through—words was implicit—if not explicit—from *THE* on. In *LITTLE* he spells it out for us:

> rabelais H. *rab*, master, *le(t)z*, jester; *rab lavi* (Egy. *lawai*) m. lion;
> or diminutive possessive, *rebele's*?

As Zukofsky says further on in that text—as he begins his soundings into English of Welsh poetry: "(Z) moved to compassion by the wide back span of the old man's uplifted head longed to master more than a little Welsh—thinking: if only he could render its sounds in English that made sense . . . ."

Nearer the end of the book—which is often clearly a transcription of literal event—and makes an excellent introduction to the temper of the Zukofsky family—he introduces us—in advance—to the notion of an *anthology*—a culling of plants familiar in and around the house:

> [Z] wrote in the shadow of the privet, his eggshell (he called it) protected . . . from neuralgia . . . . She clipped a blossoming spray of privet hanging over the neighbor's wire fence, but kept it arching for shade and for them . . . . Their large leaves had become a weed as he untangled a small brier from them to train it on the rock back wall . . . . Then, overseer, he walked toward the hydrangea. "Hope springs coternal" . . . blending his Latin and Greek—*eternal* and *cothurnal* . . . .

So we know what we are up against.

LZ's sense—from as far back as *THE*—that the reader should work. There he provided—partly Eliot in cheek—lots of leads. But in *"A"*-7 and 9 and 22 and 23 as well as *RUDENS*—in the later

Catullus poems—in parts of *LITTLE* and "Thanks to the Dictionary"—the thrust towards getting us to SOUND the words and discover sense—to bring us into play—to participate—goes beyond the
efforts of Mallarmé and Joyce—of Eliot and Pound—of Olson.

You can say: but it seems pedantic as well as obscure. And
you can miss it completely and wilfully as do the classical scholars
et al who put down the Catullus versions as nonsense. It wont do.
If you want the poetry of it you have to sound it—you have to
make each word of it yield. Nothing less will do. Too much? If a
good thing can be too much. One thing is certain—if you do the
work prescribed—you will come out of it educated—poetically
educated.

Perhaps—as usual—the most that can be said of the work
L.Z. has pre-empted us by/with in saying (in *"A"*-23 —which was
completed as *80 FLOWERS* was beginning in earnest):

(after noting Celia's making a home-place out of seemingly
nothing he notes)

> her logic's unanswerable refurnishing from
>
> nothing: unstopping motion whose smallest
> note further divided would serve
> nothing—destined actual infinitely initial,
> how dire his honor who'll
> peddle nothing: rendered his requiem
> alive (white gold-autumn-leafed mat cut
> down to 1-foot circle and
> tasseled) would praise when 80
> flowers the new lives' descant
> thought's rarer air, act, story
>
> words earth—the saving history
> not to deny the gifts
> of time where those who
> never met together may hear
> this other time sound *one.*

(This—no doubt—relates to the final move from the City to
Port Jefferson and reminds already of our:

> Heart us invisibly thyme time . . .)

For *les mots sous les mots* we have an extraordinary preface in 23
—whose clear spelling-out can be seen in:

> . . . *ait, aight, eyet,*
> *eyot, eyght* sing *the same*
> . . river . . among green aits . . *eye-land*
> islands and meadows. A laugh . .
> and not butt my head.

And this precise presentiment as well (how often L.Z. lounges bright-eyed sharp-eared at the threshold of death):

> . . . Let
> Bee-sting hold back, the flowers
> arrive she nurtures them—waggery,
> gravity (patience upon approbation) can
> creep for the flower-of-a-leaf—
> man and earth suffer together:
> two centuries touching cold-ridge inventoried
> abreast of '10 years—80 flowers' . . .

Nothing enjoins us more at the end of *"A"* but his joy of Celia's sensing returns—in the face of his devoted devotions:

> the gift—
> she hears
> the work
> in its recurrence

Sawhorses, racehorses, the horses of heroes and of the gods —workhorses—usses.

☩☩☩☩☩☩☩☩☩

> These flowers are like the pleasures of the world.
> (*Cymbeline*, IV, ii, 296)

Louis left us his *80 FLOWERS* with a clear injunction to sound words and syllables—if we care to see what he means. The legacy of this garden is transcendantly clear: (*hortus*)—

> Heart us invisibly thyme time . . .

These words flower and the ripening seed "unwithering gaping" requires our making. There is perhaps no other poet who evokes more the poet in us to complete his work.

As a beginner—and to be brief in the face of a text demanding time—thyme time—coming into good odor—best to give you a little opening—to give you a sense of what is going on—without implying any exhaustiveness.

The book involves 80 flowers (broadly-speaking): it actually mentions more. And each page contains 8 verses of 5 words—though many of the words are compound. He has—in fact—worked the scope of his limits to the breathbone. Plus the introductory poem—similarly constructed—which I have quoted from above. The quincunctial structure Zukofsky had already heavily invested in *"A"*-21 thru *"A"*-23. And these flowers do connect back:

increate
garden . . .
reading earth's scripture . . .

And with each plant involved we cannot help seeing that he
saw and saw through his words as well—finding them breathing
(living) them.

I take one example out of the many—but it can stand as a
partial paradigm of what is going on.

PRIVET

League gust strum ovally folium
looped leaf nodes winter icejewel
platinum stoneseed true ebony berries
gray-jointed persistent thru green hedge
ash-or-olive order white panicles heavy
with daffodil doxy red blood pale
reign paired leaves without tooth
on edge primmed private *privet*

All these poems (the style Apollinaire?) do without punctuation. But the ear finds its way to sense—if attentive. Typical of
Zukofsky—when he is in full flight—it is virtually impossible to
jump his gun. One word leads to the next—but you would never
know what word until you do. Those who refuse to "buy" his
handling of Catullus are not going to be any happier here. The
temptation to imitate and parody is too patent. And evasive. In
short—unless you stay open to the event—let it occur to you—
patiently learning as you sound each word combining—it is un-
yielding.

Privet is the hedge—as it happens—most common to my childhood in Boston. The opening verse will seem impervious to most.
But merely saying the words aloud at once reveals a Latin sounding just below the surface. I turn to the dictionary and find:
Ligustrum ovalifolium (California privet). He has wrung a deeper
music of sense from the bareness of that. The Latin word itself
referred to the hedge. And it must be related to the Latin word
"ligo" for binding. The word "League" is not inappropriate. The
"strum" ("um") sound persists into the "primmed private *privet*"
at the close.

If you try to resolve the poem syntactically you will get
lost. Each word moves within the local thrust. The word "strum"
has a strong verbal—gently imperative—force that plays into our
reading. We feel the hedge shaking in the winter scene—a hardy
shrub (one reason for its popularity). He shares with us the plant's
appearance in apt detail—appraising it even as he does: "winter

icejewel." Because of his making us read each line with deep sounding—we are likely enough to discover more than perhaps he intended: perhaps the word "terrestrial"?

The close examination of the berries—even to the pits ("stoneseed")—into the branches and summer blossoms (where "ash-or-olive" suggests "dead-or-alive").

He uses the Miltonic splitting of adjectives in "white panicles heavy" but in a way that Milton would hardly have thought possible. And then we are cast into syncopation of Autolycus' song in the midst of Act IV of *The Winter's Tale*:

> When daffodils begin to peer,
>   With heigh! the doxy over the dale,
> Why, then comes in the sweet of the year;
>   For the red blood reigns in the winter's pale.
> The white sheet bleaching on the hedge,
>   With heigh! the sweet birds, O, how they sing!
> Doth set my pugging tooth on edge;
>   For a quart of ale is a dish for a king . . .

It ties in with his description of the toothless oval paired leaves of the hedge and does so with extraordinary finesse—altering the song to his own use exactly. And bringing the rhythm exquisitely to bear.

And he brings us to coda with a sense of the word's etymology—which has been thought of as coming from the word "prim" (verb)—which is close to the idea of "trim." He doesn't want us to overlook the seeming literal connection with "private"—since that is a function of the hedge—in fact. It also prevents us from eavesdropping on the aunts tumbling in the hay.

The play of the poetry is unmistakable. There is a feeling of delight and splendor—in the inextricably verbal nuance and wit: "Eden gardens labor":

> . . . consonances
> and dissonances only of degree, never—
> Unfinished hairlike water of notes
> vital free as Itself—impossible's
> sort-of think-cramp work x: moonwort:
> music, thought, drama, story, poem
> parks' sunburst—animals, grace notes—
> z-sited path are but us.

Which takes us also beyond *"A"*-24 into the posthumous.

The Texts*

Poetry if anything has a sense for everything. Meaning: without
poetry life would have little present. To write poems is not enough
if they do not keep the life that has gone. To write poems may
never seem enough when they speak of a life that has gone. The
poet may visibly stop writing, but secretly measures himself
against each word of poetry ever written. Furthermore, if he is of
constant depth, he thinks of others who have lived, live, and will
live to say the things he cannot say for the time being. People who
do this are always working. They are not ashamed to appear idle.
The effort of poetry is recognizable, as against a great deal of
timely writing, despite the dress and respites of poets. Poetry has
not one face one day to lose face on another. A person would
show little thought to say poetry is opposed to—since it is added
to like—science . . . .

This translation of Confucius may not be all that one looking at a
face one respects might want it to be, but the love one respects it
for is clear: "Education begins with poetry, is strengthened
through proper conduct, and consummated through music."

"Education begins with"—looked at either as process or structure,
poetry apprehending, intense, disinterested, informs skills and the
intellect. "Is strengthened"—grows with integrity, an ability to
select and relate what is worth knowing and to defend it for
men's welfare. "Consummated through music"—the aim of an order that might perhaps be communicated to all men.

. . . poets measure by means of words, whose effect as offshoot of
nature may (or should) be that their strength of suggestion can
never be accounted for completely.   ̄

. . . Poems are but phases of utterance. The action that precedes
and moves towards utterance moves toward poetry . . . .

---

*Cid Corman has collected here what appear to him to be Zukofsky's most central and
formative, critical statements. They are given here to speak for themselves and form
what he calls "a Zukofsky critique." The source of each quote is given in brackets following it, and the quotes are separated from each other by four asterisks as a device.

With respect to such action the specialized concern of the poet will be, first, its proper conduct—a concern to avoid clutter no matter how many details outside and in the head are ordered. This does not presume that the style will be the man, but rather that the order of his syllables will define his awareness of order. For his second and major aim is not to show himself but that order that of itself can speak to all men . . . .

Always concerned with saying as much as possible and speaking to the full, never lost in the overfall, he steers from discourses on his art to a simple inventory of the poetry in one line or so many lines, yet never presumes that identifying a poem by length is more than a tag he uses while he sorts value . . . .

. . . The poet wonders why so many today have raised up the word "myth", finding the lack of so-called "myths" in our time a crisis the poet must overcome or die from, as it were, having become too radioactive, when instead a case can be made out for the poet giving some of his life to the use of the words *the* and *a*: both of which are weighted with as much epos and historical destiny as one man can perhaps resolve . . . .

Poetry never exaggerates or destroys the thing it is. It may border on the perilous or record the sentimental among other events and remain poetry . . . . [*POETRY*:1946]

* * * *

. . . Writing occurs which is the detail, not mirage, of seeing, of thinking with the things as they exist, and of directing them along a line of melody . . . .

. . . each word in itself is an arrangement . . . .

. . . Properly no verse should be called a poem it it does not convey the totality of perfect rest . . . .

The economy of presentation in writing is a reassertion of faith that the combined letters—the words—are absolute symbols for objects, states, acts, interrelations, thoughts about them. If not, why use words—new or old?

. . . the sound and pitch emphasis of a word are never apart from its meaning . . . .

. . . Poems are only acts upon particulars . . . .

The good poems of today are not far from the good poems of yesterday. [*AN OBJECTIVE*: 1930, 1931]

* * * *

. . . good poetry? It is preçise information on existence out of which it grows, and information of its own existence, that is, the movement (and tone) of words. Rhythm, pulse, keeping time with existence, is the distinction of its technique. This integrates any human emotion, any discourse, into an order of words that exists as another created thing in the world, to affect it and be judged by it. Condensed speech is most of the method of poetry . . . . The rest is ease, pause, grace. If read properly, good poetry does not argue its attitudes or beliefs; it exists independently of the reader's preferences for one kind of "subject" or another. Its conviction is in its mastery or technique. The length of a poem has nothing to do with its merits as composition in which each sound of a word is weighed, though obviously it is possible to have more of a good thing—a wider range of things felt, known, and conveyed.

It is quite safe to say that the *means* and *objects* of poetry (cf. Aristotle's *Poetics*) have been constant, that is, recognizably human, since ca. 3000 B.C.

I. The Means of Poetry: *Words*—consisting of *syllables*, in turn made up of *phones* that are denoted by *letters* that were once graphic symbols or pictures. Words grow out of affects of

  A. Sight, touch, taste, smell
  B. Hearing
  C. Thought with respect to other words, the interplay of concepts.

II. The Objects of Poetry: *Poems*—rhythmic compositions of words whose components are

  A. Image
  B. Sound
  C. Interplay of Concepts (judgments of other words either abstract or sensible, or both at once).

Some poems make use of —i.e. resolve—all three components. Most poems use only A and B. Poems that use B and C are less frequent, though C is a poetic device (invention) at least as old as Homer's puns on the name of Odysseus: "the man of all odds", "how odd I see you Od-ysseus." (cf. also the earlier, homophonic devices of syllabaries.)

. . . From the preceding analysis of the components of poems it is clear that their forms are achieved as a dynamics of speech and sound, that is, as a resolution of their interacting rhythms—with no loss of value to any word at the expense of the movement . . . .

. . . No verse is "free" . . . if its rhythms inevitably carry the words in contexts that do not falsify the function of words as speech probing the possibilities and attractions of existence. This being the practice of poetry, prosody as such is of secondary interest to the poet. He looks, so to speak, into his ear as he does at the same time into his heart and intellect. His ear is sincere, if his words convey his awareness of the range of differences and subtleties of duration. He does not measure with handbook, and is not a pendulum. He may find it right to count syllables, or their relative lengths and stresses, or to be sensitive to all these metrical factors. As a matter of fact, the good poets do all these things. But they do not impose their count on what is said or made—as may be judged from the impact of their poems . . . .

. . . The least unit of a poem must support the stanza; it should never be inflicted on the least unit . . .

The best way to find out about poetry is to read the poems. That way the reader becomes something of a poet himself: not because he "contributes" to the poetry, but because he finds himself subject to its energy. [*A STATEMENT FOR POETRY*: 1950]

* * * *

. . . the real underlying ground in my imagination of the character of Washington—or Shakespeare. There is something there, underneath the dynamo of intelligence—of life itself that is crude, rebellious—the lack of which, or the denial of which . . . makes an ass. [Letter to W.C.W.: Oct. 22/35]

* * * *

. . . Detachment and the poet's receptivity for torment were part of him from the beginning . . . .

He could express feeling that carried accents of restraint . . . .

. . . gave the impression of precise phraseology and order of thought—two prerequisites not the least important for a poet; and of hidden paradox not in the least to be dispensed with by a wit.

Leaving art to make the best of death . . . .

. . . In the end, all Thought was identical; travelling through constant contradictions it returned upon itself in silence . . . .

. . . unusual emotion ordered by more than usual mind . . . .
[*HENRY ADAMS*: 1924]

* * * *

The test of poetry is the range of pleasure it affords as sight, sound, and intellection. This is its purpose as art . . . . I believe that desirable teaching assumes intelligence that is free to be attracted from any consideration of every day living to always another phase of existence. Poetry, as other object matter, is after all for interested people.

Translators or adaptors have to find an equivalent in English . . . . The emotional drive must be retained . . . . A simple order of speech is an asset in poetry.

Prose chopped up into "verses" of alternately rhyming lines of an equal number of syllables is not poetry. A good poet never uses a word unless it adds to the meaning of the thing said. A good poet writing in English usually writes good English, unless the nature of his subject matter compels otherwise.

Different attitudes towards things and events are at the base of different poetic content . . . .

Poetry convinces not by argument but by the *form* it creates to carry its content.

Great poets are implicitly good critics of poetry . . . .

A poet's matter should be criticized for what he intended to present, rather than for what he did not intend to present . . . . One should distinguish, however, between a poet who writes perfectly about one detail, and another who writes perfectly about the same detail and a host of other detail covering a phase of civilization.

A valuable poetic tradition does not gather mold; it has a continuous life based on work of permanent interest (quality). This tradition involves a knowledge of more than English poetry . . . .

There are all kinds of measure (metre) in verse. No measure can be bad if it is a true accompaniment of the literal and suggestive sense of the words.

The spelling should help sound the words. Sounded, they make sense . . . .

Shakespeare, writing a play, concerns himself again and again with the actor sounding his verses before an audience.

The sound of the words is sometimes 95% of poetic presentation . . . . If, in any line of poetry, one word can be replaced by another and "it makes no difference," that line is bad . . . .

Good verse is determined by the "core of the matter"—which is, after all, the poet's awareness of the differences, changes and possibilities of existence. If poetry does not always translate literally from one language to another, from one time to another, certain lasting emotions find an equivalent or paraphrase in all times. The equivalent or paraphrase, if it be done well, is poetry in its own right, not merely translation.

. . . the accurate transmission of feeling through words . . . what the art of poetry consists of . . . .

Simplicity of utterance and song go together . . . . Effective rhyme furthers the poet's statement and is never a stop-gap in the movement of the lines or their meaning.

Folk art occurs with inevitable order as part of the growing history of a people. Its technique is the result of their lives, their enterprises . . . . the *essential* technique of folk art—its simplicity, its wholeness of emotional presentation—*can* serve as a guide to any detail of technique growing out of the living processes of any age.

It is the hardest task for even great POETS to limit the number of words used to maximum advantage . . . .

. . . The emotion is not less for following an organic exactness of speech, rather than a series of poetic allusions or profuseness of sentiment.

. . . a poem is an emotional object defined not by the beliefs it deals with, but by its *technique* and the *poetic conviction or mastery* with which these beliefs are expressed.

There probably is no such absolute dictum as the "non-poetic" word; any word may be poetic if used in the right order, with the right cadence, with a definite aim in view: whether it be music (i.e. lyricism) of statement; suggestion of an accompanying tune;

image; relation of concepts or ideas; or a context which is all of these things at once . . . .

Condensation is more than half of composition. The rest is proper breathing space, ease, grace.

Writing presents the finished matter, *it does not comment*. Satiric verse, at its best, does not exist in a vacuum of abstractions . . . . A poet's dramatic sense is often a short cut to effective implication *as well as* to effective presentation.

Poetry is information: the effectiveness of the cadence of a line is usually in direct proportion to the definiteness of the words used in that line. Cadence plus definite language equal the full meaning.

. . . Elegance and correct versification meant for declamation are not enough to compel permanent interest, as poetry. As poetry, only objectified emotion endures . . . .

Good poetry is the barest—most essentially complete—form of presenting a subject; good poetry does not linger to embroider words around a subject . . . . Good poetry is definite information on the subject dealt with, on the movement of the lines of verse, and on the emotion of verbal construction . . . .

The cadence when its emotional integrity is tenuous, becomes too facile. The words are too often carried along in a *lull* of sound (of no intrinsic value) till they lose their connotative meanings. Or, the lines become banal.

The cadence, its emotional integrity, tends to be so carefully true, worked out, measured, that the attention is forced to stop and define almost every word. The connotations of the words are never passed over, but they are often so rich in suggestion . . . that the result is an ambiguity of meanings giving the effect of vagueness . . . .

The emotional quality of good poetry is founded on exact observation which is often a combination of humor *plus* sense.

. . . The poet's actual writing down of his poem may be pretty much, or very much, an unconscious (as opposed to a logical) process. But when the words of a poem, intended to denote certain "happenings" or "things", are jogged about so that only a noble vagueness is denoted, the poet has failed in his task of *presentation*.

Poetry does not arise and exist in a vacuum. It is one of the arts—
sometimes individual, sometimes collective in origin—and reflects
economic and social status of peoples; their language habits arising
out of everyday matter of fact; the constructions which the intelligence and the emotions make over and apart from the everyday
after it has been understood and generally experienced . . . .

The less poetry is concerned with the everyday existence and the
rhythmic talents of a people, the less *readable* that poetry is likely
to be. But the forms of particular communication—which are
necessary enough for a varied life—may never, in any society, be
absorbed as automatically as air. [*A TEST OF POETRY*:1948]

* * * *

Symbol of our Relatively Most Permanent Self, Origin and Destiny—Wherever the reference is to the word Mother, *The Bible*.
["Poem beginning "The" "]

* * * *

        in that this happening
                is not unkind
        it put to
                shame every kindness

. . . He was in his own time, his fears too much aroused and pro-
longed, teased by repeated disappointments in the attainment of
his object. If his notes could not extricate themselves from his
complicated mass, they would be to his tactility like meeting at a
point without further coincidence or intersection. If they did extricate themselves, they would, moving towards a definite shape,
become capable of being apprehended, themselves their own
existence in the plain of surrounding existence, tactility of materials become tangible . . . .

        The figure shining thru the measure
        Each song the midday
        A sum of each year's leisure.

        For you I have emptied the meaning
        Leaving the song . . .

        I am like another, and another, who has
                finished learning
        And has just begun to learn . . .

patiently
"bothering."

If number, measure and weighing
Be taken away from any art,
That which remains will not be much: —
At least nothing like an
Appreciation of dawn
After the sixth day of work in one week: —
Or of snow melting from trees
If it falls with a sound of leaves.

What sorrow do you fear?
Ask, will you, is it here
Distrust is cast off, all
Cowardice dies. Eyes, looking out,
Without the good of intellect,
Rouse as you are used to:
It is the bad fallen away,
And the sorrow in the good.
You saw now for your book, *Anew*."

"To enhance justice on earth
        and to make the world one household . . ."

The lines of this new song are nothing
But a tune making the nothing full
Stonelike become more hard than silent
The tune's image holding in the line.

In the art of stone it is hard to set
        one's own seal upon the idea of stone . . .

In any case, if it happens,
        I will not regret it one day
        That I am plain to the simplest.

All creation into being
Is poetry or making.
But that
Made with music
Is named poetry
The same holds
Of love, only desire
Of good
Is the fire and light
Power of love . . .

That year's
poem
will be
better

if tears
show him
to the
letter.

Care
Is
Clear.

So the song be for good
and that time a new's written
the water flow on,
as there now, it be a completion
to wharves below, a street
away.   A way —

. . . what is after begins what was about.

If undersigned
Has wonder signed
It is not *prior to*,
Neither/nor, nor *and/or*.

Delight, Amadeus, to light

The music of a little night.

All who matter have come
without effacing *ever* . . .

. . . so pride loving itself looks
to more fortunate glory, with a power
apart from the trembling sense
only glory restores.

To perfect
        makes
practice . . .

That song
      is the kiss
it keeps
      is it

The
      unsaid worry
for what
      should last . . .

Trust: to lip words
briefs what great (?) discourse well.

freedom also happens
tho a tradition precounts

but someone before him
is counting for him
unless it happens

that the instant has him
completely absorbed in that someone:
a voice not a meter

but sometime a meter's a voice.

art is not covetous
whose root is long [*ALL*: 1923-1964]

* * * *

Love, or—if one wishes to explain—the desire to project the mind's peace, is one growth . . . .

The words show their task: a pursuit of elements and proportions necessary for invention that, like love as discerned object, is empowered to act on the intellect . . . .

The basis for written characters, for words, must be the physiological fact of love, arising from sight, accruing to it and the other senses, and entering the intellect (which, not Time's fool, does not make the eye untrue), for the art of the poet must be to inform and delight with Love's strength (and with Love's failings only because they are necessary).

The tendency . . . is for the sound to persist as pun or tenuous intellectual echo, unless these words are spoken over and over again or, what amounts to the same process, unless the actual print preserves them for the eye to fathom but not to see . . . .

Constantly seeking and ordering relative quantities and qualities of sight, sound and intellection, the action of the words moves also with a craftsman's love: a love totally unrequited only when the craftsman stops writing . . . .

The form of all uttered drama must arise from the measured order of words moving to a visual end . . . .

. . . how can the action of learning be over-precise! Its scope appraises a refinement of eyes into mind, *affined* (in the sense . . . of being *bound by obligation*) to judgment as a phase of taste, when the sense of the tongue is changed into a draught and a morsel of thought.

. . . lovely and loving implications of words . . . .

. . . Shakespeare's characters, if they may be imagined gratifying one another as mutual incentives by speaking, must speak also to Shakespeare—who is at once dead in them and has still to live in them.

Insight moves sight to the site, or the site moves sight to insight. Each makes *natural* sense: i.e., a purposeful thought; a thought felt as purposeful. But the term *site* must always be there with the other two—sight and insight—or they will not be there.

. . . precisely the value of reading Shakespeare—or for that matter anyone who is worth reading— . . . is, the feeling that his writing as a whole world *is*, compelling any logic or philosophy of history not to confuse an expression of *how it is* with *that world is*. The thought that *it is* has, of course, no value, is rather of a region where thought is free and music is for nothing—or as eyes see and go out. The value of the thought *how it is* is that it is against confusing expression.

The roots and stems of grammar are foresights and hindsights so entangled that traditions and chronologies mean little if not an acceptance, a love of certain, living beings for words as seen things.

. . . the sensible subject of Cabbalah was the visible creation, no matter how the Letters group, emanate, go secret.

. . . a clockwork prosody cannot allow Shakespeare a speaking voice or cadences that keep pace with ranging and rhyming eyes; or hear *where* ordered necessity of that voice may not escape rhyme tho rhetoric conceives verse as "blank"; or presume to translate the misplaced concreteness of rhyme in Homer into nonclassical, modern tongues. When ancient hexameters, the editing of Greek scholiasts may not, by modern prosodic tests of where a line ends, rhyme on the nose, no rhyme can be *seen* tho print shows it within a line or within lines not far apart. It has been said that rhyme should be heard and not seen; but that it must not, of course, be heard when a late mind thinks of the quantity of rhymeless "classic" feet.

That art is "good" which does not presume or run out on the world but becomes part of visible, audible, or thinkable nature:

an art reached with scaled matter, when it is, as in Shakespeare with words, in Bach with sounds, in Euclid with concepts, or in Ravenna mosaic with small colored stones.

Art is to see.

If, unlike the disciplined scholar, I must still look up the numbers of the lines ((in Shakespeare)) to give them to you, it is because the aptness of that sort of memory, as of all memory, does not usually approach the poetry anew as does turning the pages to part of a crowded column of print where the eyes may see again what is there and read—happy.

. . . the great poet, like the great violinist, marries his instrument, syllable or fiddle, so his recklessness sees him thru—never deterred by the barometric pressures of virtuosity and doctrinal accomplishments of trite interval and tone. Tho he no doubt has all of the virtuoso's technique for radiating polish its calculated evidence as mere accessory to life must largely appear—to him, *if you wish*, he says, *to his foolishness*—loveless and unreasonable. His necessary love, a recklessness having no earlier comparable end is about all there is for him in art or performance. And when it is thru with him his art must always suggest more recklessness to enact in existence than the order of a cultured memory can reclaim from it as a guide for others' practice. Cultivated thought mostly furthers his virtuosity, feeding on him for the sociableness of obviously calculating and self-decimating witnesses to art among audiences that the human family has become.

Oratio, speech, language, utterance, tongue moved for a time to sound; barring confusion as the push of *this* animalcule—as against *that*—curving a lobe of itself around food particle or dust; or a humane red showing thru a translucent film of cells of one life, or the sallow green of another—follicles hairing views—spectra. Or they see as eyelashes flicker; or come out one by one, air without hairs, eyes—round, unfringed.

. . . A translator *should* maybe essay transliteration: phlox, *flame* (Gk.), be tried by the *sound* of *flux* rather than *fire* . . . .

Without demonstration, the *Poetics* ((Aristotle)) granted that everyone knew melody. The *Metaphysics* praised sight. Both discoursed as parts of Aristotle's greater grammar—his whole work. When he thought of it metaphysics nourished grammar. In *it* his work has being, as Homer's has without it, at least like a face, a voice to sing, an eye to see, letting others find grammar there.

The poet perfects the mother tongue with eyes and ears until grammarian and metaphysician see the structures of paradigm in him. His fate then—or choice—is a poetry of grammar, or to forget grammar or hack it. Running together, the human animal's late taste and smell run the risk of refining the witless specialties of bees and dogs . . . .

No abstract note equals the material sound . . . . In music, no produced note is ever equal to itself or equal to equals. Apart from gauge, tension, weight of a string—all tolerances—the fingering hearing mates the sense known as perfect pitch.

The words of Shakespeare's song keep the feeling of old dance, as against ear busy hearing more than one voice in the counterpoint of his stage iambics. But in both sung and acted lines, as the Book Bahir says, "the vowels abide in consonants like souls in bodies." Or—as happens so often with the sounds of his words the transformation is expected . . . .

If a man spend all time furthering himself where will he be? The reed of the grass discloses the wind; the musical reed, moisture of breath and touch. The voice or the tune is never seen. Riffling flows away on the shape of the riffle. Vico fabled: man sung before he spoke. A man longs, how can he get back what he once sang into speech . . . . It is literally not sense*less* . . . to speak of the surest sense . . . . The apparent intransigence of thought in such distinctions devolves from words . . . that twine as some stems one around another, and the intervals at which they twine are of interest only mutually—considered "perfect" or "short of the perfect" as the case may be or as the consideration comes up. That is the interest of the arts . . . the feeling that even the most intellective of them are *tangible* . . . . Under the aspect of eternity, where all things exist equally with the same force as when they began to exist, nothing of the mutual need of course be *said*; thought is only conflation of extension, and extension of thought, *until* the bass-string of humility is suddenly aware of the presumption of having said something about the holiness of the treble . . . . The impression Shakespeare's text leaves a reader who is inclined to feel that one book judges and is judged by all other books is a comment on music thru history. (It) also conveys the impression that whatever Shakespeare's dramatis personae have to say about good music their analysis has, as self-proof, less harmony to offer than a song: for a song when heard by inexplainable proof of its own has that sense of the *substantial* known rather like the seeing of the eye than the idiom of the brain. Affected by both impressions the reader whose craft is not music thinks of the violinist keeping the sound together by his orderly fingering at which he looks while playing—his eyes exercised to effortless fleetness; but he limits his looking as he listens not to outrun tangibly the critically fleeting visible order, so that no wrong twisting of fingers can effect a frightened look that the sound may not come clear . . . . So that the reader whose own craft can never solidly stake some object like a "thing" of music finds whatever notions of its history that he has sidling the comments of Shakespeare's characters on it.

. . . if an artist's power of action is not destroyed by conceiving himself after a nature not his own his only fear is the unnecessary . . . . And if the musician's ear does not love its song as the lover's eyes their sight, he will not know it as "a type of human nature to which we may look."

. . . as the master of music sleeps to be restored under rarest sounds of the round above him, the wisest or most loving beholder cannot say whether his importance is joy or sorrow.

. . . the modern poet fretted by his sense of some unmistakable clear end of expression . . . compelled . . . to be aware of other *languages* where the world is both one and varied . . . .

. . . if that intellective portion of mind that is music can make poetry and prose interchangeable, because there is a note always to come back to . . .—sung to the scale the "subjects" of speech are so few and words only ring changes one on another, the differences perceived by their fictions are so slight music makes them few. Up, down, outwards—for even inversions and exact repetitions move on—are the melodic statement and hence the words' sense: or after syllables have been heard before in contiguity, they may also be augmented or diminished, or brought to crowd answer on subject in a great fugue . . . .

"A"—pronounced how? With a care for the letters and out of them their sound. [*BOTTOM: ON SHAKESPEARE*: 1963]

* * * *

. . . poems come as you live them.

. . . life is longwinded, art is winded . . . .

I too have been charged with obscurity, tho it's a case of listeners wanting to know too much about me, more than the words say.

Concrete poetry—a hundred years ago it was marble . . . .

. . . disliked spreading thru space, preferred things small and compact, a small table for desk, a narrow shelf of books over it: so that when he was not writing it was a blank table, never a display of creativity . . . . [*LITTLE*: 1950-1969]

* * * *

. . . especially . . . writing prose . . . . The difficulty is to judge without seeming to be there, with a finality in the words that will make them casual and part of the story itself, except perhaps to another age . . . .

[T]he story must exist in each word or I cannot go on. The halt seems likely to be permanent in the worst of the grind—when the words of an insoluble sentence written down, written over, crossed out, add up to indecisions making situations and characters empty. I feel I have not the sense in which, along with the story, I must live—and seem merely to glance at a watch . . . .

And a writer's attempts not to fathom his time amount but to sounding his mind in it . . . . I wanted our time to be the story, but like the thought of a place passed by once and recalled altogether . . . a solid—defying touch . . . . [*IT WAS*: 1941]

* * * *

. . . The more the words of others impressed him with their factual content the more he felt he must wait for his own facts before being tempted into words . . . .

. . . too much of a hit or miss affair, like aimless words, to pass for action . . . .

The sunlight through a closed window fell on his hand and made him think of the limitless range even the smallest choice could contain.

. . . The dance of the words, and the dance they followed called *estampeda*, was among the earliest that gave his people a tongue....

To sing well, without attracting attention, and to show them
another local tree . . . . [*FERDINAND*: 1940-1942]

* * * *

. . . everything worth remembering insists on now. [*ARISE,
ARISE*: 1936-1940]

* * * *

. . . I can't get excited about any *poetics* finding special terminol-
ogies to cover what is the general case, or should be: *it moves* and
someone is moved . . . . [Letter to Cid Corman: July 11/60]

* * * *

. . . "A" 's references—as you say, the context must "explain"
'em or reveal them. They are usually *constructs*, telescoping of
several actual references . . . . And anyone who goes off on exact
"identification" I needn't tell you is not reading or hearing . . . .
[Letter to CC: Aug. 13/60]

* * * *

. . . what interests me most on top of it as I am—too damn close
for a guy who can't avoid "ideas" tho these interest him least—
is not the ideas but the way the recurrences & reflections (your
shadows) come welling up tho I don't *consciously* try anything
like plotting 'em, of all the other movements of "A" . . . as for
what else in the way of *content* ten years have accumulated the
sooner I get that out of the way & buried in the music of the
whole thing the better . . . . [Letter to CC: Aug. 25/60]

* * * *

. . . I've been reading Monkey (Wu Chang-En)—to see what in my
ignorance I may have "repeated". One third thru, pleasant enough,
but certainly not more than Tom Nashe's Jack Wilton. As for
"influence" on L.Z. I am my own Chinee . . . . Just as I'm my own
Gagaku (as I say in iii)—I mean don't take my dance to be a literal
report of the dances I "saw" performed—if I haven't said this
before. As a matter of fact I take off from two dances *I* saw & mix
'em up—all this in case you meet an authority who'll complain

about the letter and look down on a poor spirit who wants to dance at all . . . . [Letter to CC: Sept. 30/60]

* * * *

Desire longing for perfection

Not boiling to put pen to paper
Perhaps a few things to remember —

Clear music

The music is in the flower . . .
Each leaf a buttress flung for the other.

. . . The music steeps in the center

This is my face
This is my form.
Faces and forms, I would write you down
In a style of leaves growing.

The song out of the voices.

Song's kinship,
The roots we strike.

One horse
Walked off,
The trees showing sunlight
Sunlight trees,
Words ranging forms.

My one voice. My other: is
An objective—rays of the object brought
    to a focus,
An objective—nature as creator—desire
    for what is objectively perfect
Inextricably the direction of historic
    and contemporary particulars.

Sounded contacts

Spoke: words, words, we are words, horses,
    manes, words.

bringing together facts
which appearances separate:
all that is created in a fact
is the language that numbers it,
The facts clear,

breath lives
with the image each lights.

We are things, say, like a quantum of action
Defined product of energy and time, now
In these words which rhyme now how song's
    exaction
Forces abstraction to turn from equated
Values to labor we have approximated.

. . . Flourish
By love's sweet lights and sing *in them*
    I flourish.

. . . song sounding
The grace that comes from knowing
Things . . .

So goes: first, *shape*
The creation —
A mist from the earth,
The whole face of the ground;
Then *rhythm* —
And breathed breath of life;
Then *style* —
That from the eye its function takes —
"Taste" we say—a living soul.

. . . the kinship of what is in what is not.

Sense sure, else not motion,
Madness to ecstasy never so thralled
But showed some quantity of choice . . .

If each time a man writing a word
Thought it most completely distils him
Or did not write it . . .

Measure, tacit is.

Durable fire.

Voice: first, body —
Speak, of all loves!

An integral
Lower limit speech
Upper limit music

. . . understands me best
Because he does not understand.

Speech moved to sing

. . . the noblest embraces the whole art
Involving by no means
The smallest traction of reason.

The horse sees he is repeating
All known cultures
And suspects repeating
Others unknown to him,
Maybe he had better not
Think of himself
Hunting so to speak
Sowing so to speak
Composing always.

Together men form one sky.

One sky is rich in each of us,
Undivided.

Art pursues no one, is rather pursued,
But everyone wants to fly before he has
                    wings.

The horse plods and learns
Neither sleep nor Sabbath can rest him
If he is called upon to write a book
And it is put by for a life
Nothing fails it
Cared for in his mind,
He need not rush at the book.
It is never late
What must be form.

To plod is not hobble.
Each time has Love's way with music.

He who knows nothing
Loves nothing
Who does nothing
Understands nothing.
Who understands
Loves and sees,
Believes what he knows,
The horse has large eyes
Man's virtue his feeling.
His heart treasures his tongue . . .

What stirs is
                    his tracing a particular line,
Tracing of lines

Meeting by chance or design.
With him *ornament*,
    acquires
A precision of appeal . . .

. . . all actions
Which passions determine
Are determined better
By a reason like love.

If it sang then
It still sings.

Can love rouse a thing of the past
And not see it as present?

The song does not think
To say therefore I am,
Has no wit so forked.

. . . Each writer writes
one long work whose beat he cannot
entirely be aware of. Recurrences
follow him, crib and drink from a
well that's his cadence—after
he's gone . . .

The way
Things are,
Quiet
Is happier
Than most words.

. . . art that has cannot have more or less

My poetics has old ochre in it
On walls of a civilized cave,
Eyes trapped in time, hears foam over horses,
All of a style, surge
Over six thousand years
Not one of their mouths worrying a bit.

— Tell me

— Tell *you*

Live to a great age
Each led—let each
Yield a little time

To the persuasive song
Of which each part
Must end . . .

The infant laughing to its parent
Theory starts with that which is
Nature and art with what is to be —

Things that stay, and a taking off . . .

Love's leisure is
The prime end of all action

You wish me well

. . . the harmony of chances.

How mean of me ridden by words
Always to think at first of being disturbed
          by the dissonance
When the years make their order.

Listening behind me for my wit . . .
The pricked horse's (inner?) ear.

. . . with his dichotomy
Dick and a cot and o me
Isorhythm—I—so rhythm . . .

. . . hay, bee, sea.

. . . an exchange between an intellective
          portion
Of head and that part it calls music
Meaning something some time to come back
          to a second time . . .

Only the image of a voice:
Love you

measure only

bounds excess

. . . I
don't like
work I

like what
is *in*
the work"

Innocence *in-*
nocere not
to do

hurt to . . .

. . . Why

not 'speech
framed to
be heard

for its
own sake
even over

its interest
of' (de-)
'meaning'

. . . Reading's profitable
pleasure—not much —
attracts judgment to

task I'll not
remember rather'll fire
my mind than

furnish it—song
does not work
my judgment, dazzles

my clear look
(luck?)—if not
the weight of

what I write
perhaps its intricacy —
o you'll regret

I pothered but
you'll have bothered'
Catullus played Bach

((please note the playback here: CC))

. . . poetry's of
the grief, politics
of the grievances . . .

I've counted words,

selected all my
life.

. . . my "Cats"

chaste—eyeing passionate
Italian lips two
thousand years near

to sharp them
and flat them
not in prurience —

of their voice . . .

I cannot now
get around
thinking I am dead
where with you
now I have no place
as I say
it now
and you sense
it always said.

Goal's naturally breathless, look back,
        an, a the —
praise or as you wish the reticence of
all my omissions, not "smarter" than
          Catullus, thank

you . . .

. . . chances of
ordered changes changes of ordered
     chances, song that
literally came into and out of one's ears

Sensible people fable the truth.

. . . what is eternal
is living . . .

. . . the law, water, shaped
to the container it's in.
Strength's perfection asks no prayer,
redeems every fault, dreams no
hell. Devotion cannot add or
subtract . . .

Temple altar light unextinguished *yes*,
sleep waylaid, mused more hours,
in a fire of coals —
bread: their past 5000 years
not duped by studied words
an idea meant a name
calls soul in me if

erased by drunken elephants or
ignored exile, born for fellowship,
no share, only all welcome
related by good nature, inviolable
adversity, ardor, actions animate rest . . .

. . . A
child learns on blank paper,
an old man writes palimpsest,
a good heart dejected brings
others peace, asks no returns,
assumes milestones guide all and
belong to each so no
one people can claim to
excel . . .

. . . . "not mine" comes from
the sage calling fig *fig* . . .

. . . bread, not arrogance.

. . . read, not into, it:
desire until all be bright.

. . . all
things began in Order to
end in Ordainer . . .

what hurries? why hurry? wit's
but the fog, the literal
senses move in light's song
modesty cannot force, blind call
its own, nor self-effaced fled

to woods perpend without pride
Stone into lotus.

. . . research won't guarantee;
tongues commonly inaccurate talk viable
one to one, ear to
eye loving song greater than

anything . . .

renew—whirligig punning tempest . . .

. . . a song worth
50 cows . . .

Your nest among the stars. .
peace..flame..fields..BRANCH..

a thought not your thought
..wholeness..tracing see into grain..

Tesserae Graces . . .

. . . as to what rarest
temper reads our matter, post
fate her time-veined glory, kin
air too late . . .
                    our book's *my own*:
delight seen one time: so:
married *once*: mirrored fire admired
animal probities father risk. Keys
punt: arbors tutor us: air
is, air is, short or
long sounds air's measure . . .

young name grew old, older
names another: hermit yoke shuns
trafficked humility. Mudguard beggars mud,
a hermit cloud creates itself —
none knows me, why rankle:
..*man's life's.. to say "One."*

. . . 'blazed, man, trove-airs
occlude sots, grant chant's precise
that's its praise—none "equal", touch'

. . . You spoke
for me of *my* cell,
I'll not work its silence
and peace again—now anybody's
sloth to stretch in, psalter
and breviary: ashes, I a
breviary better lug stone . . .

. . .'Null all true,
see chanting, trust descant scaling.'

. . . 'not for them
but with them, prest lips
voice the bent dray-horse, pack
illumined sweat-light, hair grows long
fern-mane rises, ears-ringing words start.'

An art of honor, laud —
'pleasures do' wit's joys accord:
so on hand-vowed integrities, unaltered
syllables, the fended wrist, fires'
light rest: bourne eyed'll guide
gar them hear draw ear
brute dear up-on a rouncy
aske nomore..go.

series distributes harmonies, attraction
                         Governs
destinies. Histories dye the streets:
intimate whispers magnanimity flourishes:
                         doubts'
passionate Judgment, passion the task.

Most art, object-the-mentor, donn'd one —
smiles ray *immaterial Nimbus*. [*"A"*: 1928-1974]

JONATHAN GREENE

ZUKOFSKY'S FERDINAND *

I

Jung in the Prologue to his autobiography states, "We are a psychic process which we do not control, or only partly direct." Zukofsky's Ferdinand doesn't even have the pretense of partly directing his life and it is only at the end of the narrative that in a dream a deeper self takes over and, as is often the case in emergencies (even dreamt ones), knows what to do in such a manner that instinct suddenly is wisdom and tells the other parts of self what it had long partially or fully repressed.

At one point Zukofsky has Ferdinand thinking with direct focus on the question: "He suspected that then also he would be dying of inanition, finding no steady pleasure in any bit of the earth as his own and professing to be glutted thinking whether others could." Part of that inanition can be traced to the ways Ferdinand was protected: having been raised by aunt and uncle, hardly knowing his parents, his life was directed by others, especially an older brother, an object of Ferdinand's resentment (he is the practical materialist). His father and brother scheme a career for him and Ferdinand follows their plans after he overhears that his own secret unacted-upon plan has had a boulder plummet onto its path.

That secret pipe dream is the touchstone of a life in which he could have called a "bit of the earth" his own by knowing it *if only* he could go back to Italy and marry his childhood companion, Nina. There he could learn from her father, their former gardener, his knowledge of vineyard and the natural world's secrets. That daydream is shattered when Ferdinand overhears that Nina has married; he relapses into the passive self-absorption that has ascendancy in him.

Thus, after being brought up by the Mediterranean and attending school in Paris, Ferdinand enters the French embassy in America, the future plotted out for him. Zukofsky's description

---

*Reprinted with permission of author from *MAPS*, No. 5, 1973.

as follows is clearer in its emotional history than we could ever suspect Ferdinand of stating:

> His lot, the result of habit, stopped him from running away from the childless love of aunt and uncle or to a desire out of the past for possibilities like Nina and the gardener. Practical in risking little, he saw in himself and detested the straight-laced wariness of his brother who without real feeling would never give up the duty of taking care of him. In the same way he took care of his own constraints, emphasizing his emptiness and affecting to be quiet.

Without the self-awareness and self-humour of Musil's "hero" in *The Man Without Qualities*, both Ulrich and Ferdinand share similar reclusive natures through which they perceive the world as too absurd to be intimate with or accept.

Yet, perhaps in spite of himself, Ferdinand does find that he has three close friends, all exiles: a White Russian, an Englishman, and a New York Jew, "the rabbin." Behind the character of the Englishman one might posit Basil Bunting, both in his ability to quote Firdusi and in his readiness to enlist in the Second World War. And in the bookish "rabbin" we might sense a veiled projection of Zukofsky himself, bookish and self-defensive about that in a world of materialism and (then) war.

After years of the delights of a quiet and secretive life, earning what one imagines a quite decent wage, Ferdinand over and over again sees as an image of his existence the "creeping Charlie" or Wandering Jew (the *Commelina Virginica*) for like this weed "he was getting to feel more like an American, ruggedly free, affecting to send out roots, never long rooted." Then, suddenly after thinking of himself as one with little sense of attachment to a personal past, Ferdinand is visited by his aunt and uncle escaping from a France defaulted to the Germans.

This visit opens out into an interlude in Ferdinand's routine existence in the midst of which this short novel ends. Ferdinand is taking a tour of the state with his aunt and uncle when the armour of his personality breaks down and the matter of his life passes before him in deep dream/vision. In the Arizona desert, Ferdinand glimpses an Indian maiden and soon after meets a gardener both of whom merge with Nina and her father having both literal "real" connections (the maiden's name is said to be Nina, the gardener is distantly related to Nina's father) and identity with them in the primal world of Vision.

This dream/vision, which enters the narrative abruptly as if "reality," lets in all the primordial elements of Ferdinand's inner life. The dream images come with a feeling of great speed, but in the seeming jumble there is a discernable coherence. Ferdinand wakes with a unitive acceptance of his brother, inherits his past in that way:

> He might please his aunt and uncle and speak again to his brother from whom he had become estranged. In that case, he could never get himself to tell this story or as much of it as the *rabbin*, who had lived in his time, could guess.

Which, if the "rabbin" is Zukofsky, is a good tongue-in-cheek way of finishing the narrative.

II

The automobile is the major image/symbol of *Ferdinand*. The story opens with his waiting to beg a ride in Monsieur le Millionaire's car, but in this he is thwarted. The very next day a toy car arrives, a gift from his father, and he is almost drowned riding it into the sea. The gardener thinks to himself "of the boy possibly wasting a life on a kind of toy such as had nearly drowned him that day" and at the end of the narrative Ferdinand fantasizes having died while actually only denting a fender. So at the beginning, we have a prefiguration of the end and the division of personality that can list Genoa, vineyard, pastoral existence on one side of a ledger (the unacted-upon) and cities, worldliness, sophistication, his brother, etc. on the other.

The whole story can almost be told through the car events and analogies:

> he enjoys rides in the country with a fellow student, who then lets him drive it alone

> his mother dies in a car

> he is then shipped off to America with a new car in the hold—this car's wheel is on the "wrong" side, a distinction abandoned as he "Americanizes"

> his latent fear of accidents, of car breakdowns

> "The development of successive car models forced him, when he looked back on them, to dwell on parts of himself he had superseded like the machines."

> the knock in the motor as a disturbance in himself, a fault of character, that would need fixing

> being at times solicitous of himself and car, at times abandoning that concern

being stalled "Like the dying said to see images of their earliest
life—or all their past through a child's eyes—the three were stalled
as if they had a moment in the present."

to the end where the car identification is complete: "His heart
pounded, causing him to recall that the piston rod of his car had
leaped through its hood and breaking the plate glass had killed
him."

The car, as American symbol of rootlessness and materialism is
central. Ferdinand rides the plateaus and highways, ignoring the
smaller roads that are pitted with possible dangers. The psychological correspondences are obvious, if not heavyhanded. If one is to
keep to a surface existence, then one must keep one's possessions
in perfect repair. Things become obsessive since they are the
underpinnings of a lifestyle: if the car falls apart it threatens the
fragile course of events, the balance of personality. If one's means
of escape from where one is falters, then one would have to deal
with elements of oneself that float to the surface when one is not
moving restlessly away from them, the emptiness, etc. In the end
he dreams of leaving the car to search on foot for the gardener and
the Indian girl, the rejected part of the past which, once acknowledged, can heal.

III

Ferdinand was first collected in *It Was* published by Origin
Press in 1961. It is the most interesting and least dated story in the
book (the slangy humour makes *A Keystone Comedy* the most
dated). The collection's title piece acts as prologue to the book
and pronounces its aesthetic:

> This story was a story of our time. And a writer's attempts not to
> fathom his time amount but to sounding his mind in it. I did not
> want to break up my form by pointing to well-known place
> names and dates in the forty years that I had lived—events famil-
> iar to most of us, to some more than myself. I wanted our time to
> be the story, but like the thought of a place passed by once and
> recalled altogether: seen again as through a stereoscope blending
> views a little way apart into a solid—defying touch. I was saying
> something that had had a sequence, like the knowledge of taking
> a breath, and hiding it, because one breathes without pointing to
> it before and after.

Thus, *Ferdinand* has a firm place in a historical setting that is the
backdrop to the story. Though its language is formal and somewhat old-fashioned (with his mother's death "he reached his majority"), the most awkward moments are to be found rather in

Zukofsky's penchant for literary quotes and allusions. Perhaps these can be excused since Ferdinand's background is cultured and early on we are given a poem he wrote as evidence of his once having had literary pretensions. But still the inclusion of the text of a whole sea shanty and the time when aunt & uncle sing with him first a Medieval song, then parts of *Don Giovanni,* then *The Miller of the Dee,* seem obtrusive to the narrative, if not unlikely in realistic terms. The later allusions to Villon and Antigone seem equally precious and forced.

If that allusiveness might be a failing of a poet writing prose, then as a counter-weight we have prose sequences of a fineness many a writer could be jealous of. We might wish to think of the stereoscope in this impressionistic meeting of Ferdinand with his mother:

> As he stepped across the threshold he wanted to turn back, but somehow forced himself to stay, feeling his weight bearing on his heels. He relied on the rare occasions his mother had been mentioned in his life instead of on formal introduction. Civil conduct, he imagined, would protect him. His eyes were focused shyly on the mirror, and as she approached him, he saw her in the length of the glass move further away. Then unexpectedly blurred but magnified, the irises appeared to come close to him.

Or, likewise at the reunion with aunt and uncle which also augurs change, we have a succession of images that correspond exactly to the psychological state described:

> He could hardly believe, now that he would do all that he once confided to himself he could never do, there was so little to worry him. His loneliness seemed to move in the distance, offering no explanation as to why he had once brought it on himself, seemed reflected like the numbness of bitter cold when several senses at once begin to feel warm.

Such prose descriptions as well as a sentence as rich as: "It was a pity that people did not risk enough to speak out in behalf of one another's happiness and their own." make *Ferdinand* worthy of one's attention.

THE TRANSLATOR

L.Z., 1976 (Photo by Hugh Kenner)

BURTON HATLEN

ZUKOFSKY AS TRANSLATOR

To Zukofsky, Creeley says, poetry represents a way of seeing "words as in the world in much the same way that men are."[1] Words and men alike are "in the world," to Zukofsky, as material objects. All of Zukofsky's philosophic masters (Aristotle, Spinoza, Marx, Wittgenstein) insisted that the only reality is the world that offers itself to our senses, the material world. In Zukofsky himself we also find an insistence upon living in *this* world, a resolute refusal to seek a transcendent realm "beyond" the immediate particulars of experience. Zukofsky's sense that men and women are "in the world" primarily as material beings has ample precedent not only in the philosophies of Aristotle *et al.*, but also in the poetry of Ezra Pound and William Carlos Williams. But in seeing words too as material objects, Zukofsky opens up a radically new way of thinking about language. To such relatively (compared to Zukofsky) traditional modernists as Pound and Williams, words are of interest because they have meaning, because they point beyond themselves toward a "reality" that the words "name"—always more or less imperfectly, since the particular word can never totally body forth this "reality." From this perspective, writing becomes a quest for "*le mot juste*," the word that most closely approximates the "reality" (whether mental or physical) that the writer wants to express. For Zukofsky's principal poetic mentors, Pound and Williams, the reality which words attempt to seize for us is composed essentially of images: the sensory particulars of experience. "No ideas but in things" Williams proclaimed; and for Pound a "truth" that cannot be apprehended by the senses is no truth. But despite their devotion to the concrete particulars of experience, Pound and Williams were still inclined to see words as

---

1. Robert Creeley, "A Note," in *A Quick Graph* (San Francisco: Four Seasons, 1970), p. 133.

symbols which point toward these particulars. It remained for Zukofsky to take the materialist way of thought one step further and to see words themselves as particulars in their own right, not essentially different from Williams's white chickens, or Pound's petals on a bough. Unlike the verse of his great predecessors, Zukofsky's poetry is relatively barren of images. Instead he gives us *words*. He writes "skinny poems" so we will be forced to look at one word at a time. The effect is to break us out of habitual syntactic patterns, so that we can see the word as a thing, an object in space. But the material world is temporal as well as spatial, and Zukofsky's words therefore also move in time, in a sometimes grave, sometimes gay, always orderly melody. ("The melody!" Zukofsky cries in *"A"*-6; "the rest is accessory."[2]) Primarily, then, Zukofsky's words are objects-in-motion which exist within a space-time continuum. As such, they are perhaps best envisioned as pulses of energy. (One of Zukofsky's most obscure publications is an anonymous translation of a forgotten biography of Einstein. I don't want to exaggerate Zukofsky's scientific attainments, but I think he learned as much from Einstein as he did from Marx or Pound or Wittgenstein.[3]) Each of these energy pulses, furthermore, also has a history. All words, even "the words *the* or *an*," are, says Zukofsky, "weighted with . . . epos and historical destiny."[4] The word moves, then, not only within the "time" of the poem but also within historical time; at any moment it gathers up in itself its entire history. But note that even yet we have not come to a realm of "meaning," as something that exists beyond and above the words. And if we are tempted to think that we have detected a "meaning" of this sort in a Zukofsky poem, we are, I think, almost certainly mistaken. (For example, the horses that canter through *"A"* do not, as Kenner notes, symbolize anything at all.[5]) Rather, the consistent aim of Zukofsky's poetry is to deny the possibility of moving beyond words, into the realm of ideas. For his is a poetry that insists upon the words themselves, as material artifacts, and as notes in an unending melody.[6]

The poetic principles that I have here spelled out rigorously govern Zukofsky's poetic practice, in his translations no less than

2. Louis Zukofsky, *"A"* (Berkeley: University of California Press, 1978), p. 26.
3. At least one commentator on Zukofsky agrees: cf. Stephen Roy Mandell, *The Finer Mathematician: An Introduction to the Work of Louis Zukofsky* (Temple University dissertation, 1975), esp. pp. 73-118.
4. Quoted by Creeley, p. 135.
5. Hugh Kenner, "Of Notes and Horses," *Poetry*, 111 (Nov., 1967), 118.
6. The most useful discussion of Zukofsky's non-referential approach to language is Thomas Anthony Duddy, *Perception and Process* (S.U.N.Y. at Buffalo dissertation, 1972), pp. 11-19.

in his own poetry. We have in this century become fairly accustomed to poetry that subverts our normal expectations about
words and the way they "mean." But translations which treat the
"original," not as a pattern of meanings, but rather as a sequence
of irreducibly material syllables, or as a sequence of musical notes,
are likely to startle the most favorably disposed reader. Zukofsky's
two major translations are a complete translation of Catullus's
poetry, prepared in collaboration with his wife Celia, and the
translation of Plautus's *Rudens* that constitutes movement 21 of
"A."[7] These two translations have in common a refusal, unique
among any translations that I know, to pander to our fear of
language, our hunger to escape from words into "meanings."
Most translations treat the meaning of the original as separable
from its words. This meaning, the translator assumes, is hovering
somewhere above the words, like a Platonic ghost. All the translator need do, therefore, is de-code this meaning from the words
of the original and then re-encode the meaning in a new language. Implicit in all of this is the assumption that words are mere
husks, to be stripped away so that we can get at the "meaning"
concealed within. Of course, every poet knows that this way of
thinking about language is false. But translators who are also poets
usually, after a *pro forma* apology, go ahead and translate "meanings" anyway. Zukofsky refuses this easy way out. Instead his first
goal as a translator is to establish the physical reality of his own
English words, thereby also forcing us to come to terms with the
physical reality of Catullus's or Plautus's Latin words. His second
aim is to carry over into English some of the energy patterns that
control the movements of the words in the original text. And his

---

7. The Catullus translations are collected in the magnificent Cape Goliard edition:
Catullus, trans. Celia and Louis Zukofsky (London: Cape Goliard and New York: Gross-
man, 1969). This edition is not paginated, so I shall refer to poems by number only.
In a personal communication, Celia has described the precise form of her collaboration
with Louis in this project, and it might be well to put her comments on record: "I did
the spade work. I wrote out the Latin line and over it, indicated the quantity of every
vowel and every syllable, that is long or short; then indicated the accented syllable. Below the Latin line I wrote the literal meaning or meanings of every word indicating
gender, number, case and the order or sentence structure. I used Lewis & Short *Latin
Dictionary* (Oxford Un. Press) and Allen & Greenough *Latin Grammar* (Ginn & Co.).
Louis then used my material to write poetry—*good poetry.* I could never do that! I
never questioned any of his lines, just copied his handwritten manuscript to facilitate the
typing" [C.Z., Sept. 12, 1978]. Given the systematic collaboration of Louis and Celia on
this project, I shall generally describe the Catullus translation as the work of the Zukofskys (plural). But since Celia herself here says that it was Louis who transformed her
prose version into poetry, it also seems to me legitimate to treat the translations as part
of Louis Zukofsky's poetic *oeuvre.* I shall therefore from time to time describe the
poetic voice that here addresses us as the voice of Zukofsky (singular). The *Rudens*
translation was first published in *"A" 13-21* (Garden City: Paris Review Editions,
1969). *"A"*-21 is now most conveniently available in the University of California Press
edition of *"A."*

third aim is to place all the words here at issue—the Latin words of the original and the English words of the translation—within an historical continuum. The methods which Zukofsky employs to arrive at these goals differ somewhat in the two translations here under discussion. Yet both translations, as I shall try to show, achieve the three goals that I have here spelled out. Both translations are also characterized by a virtually fanatical rigor of method. And both translations (the Plautus perhaps less than the Catullus) are likely to strike the unwary reader as decidedly bizarre, perhaps even perversely idiosyncratic. I cannot here presume to offer a complete guidebook for the perplexed reader of Zukofsky's translations. But I do believe that, if we are patient, we will discover that everything in these translations makes sense. I have, in feeble imitation of Zukofsky, chosen this last word (" 'sense,' from L. *sensus*, the faculty of perceiving") with some care. To "make sense" is to make a pattern that the senses can apprehend with delight. Zukofsky's translations, like his own poems, offer to our senses rich, complex, and (I hope here to demonstrate) delightful patterns. Both the Catullus and the Plautus translations "make sense," in all possible meanings of that phrase; and in the remainder of this essay I shall try to show the various kinds of sense that these two translations make. At the same time I also want to show that the critics who have denounced Zukofsky the translator as a fool or a charlatan are wrong; and to this end I shall pause from time to time to quarrel with one or another of Zukofsky's detractors.

I

The method of translation which the Zukofskys have employed in the Catullus translations is explained in the preface to the Cape Goliard edition:

> This translation of Catullus follows the sound, rhythm, and syntax of his Latin—tries, as is said, to breathe the "literal" meaning with him.

The quotation marks around "literal" are crucial, for in effect the Zukofskys are here redefining this word. In ordinary usage, the literal translation is the translation that most closely approximates the plain prose meaning of the original. But the Zukofskys remind us that the "*littera*," the letter, is an aural and visual shape, not a "meaning." In practice, the Zukofskys force our attention back toward the "literal" by treating each of Catullus's words as a sequence of syllables. The Zukofskys have translated every surviving scrap of Catullus's verse. Each translated poem has exactly the same number of lines as the original; each line of the translation contains exactly the same number of syllables as the equivalent line in the original; and as far as possible the length and the sound of the English syllables echo Catullus's Latin syllables. Thus the translation constitutes a syllable by syllable metamorphosis of Catullus's Latin into English: a strange sort of English, admittedly, and often a very obscure sort of English. But the principle seems clear: the Zukofskys are determined to remain faithful to Catullus's syllables, as tactile, sensory objects. If they can get some of Catullus's meaning into English, that's fine; and the meaning never slips away entirely—even in the most obscure passages it hovers behind the words, like a half-heard melody. But the audible melody, the music of the syllables, is always first. The response of academic critics, in particular academic Latinists, to this enterprise has been generally a sclerotic rage, matched only by the initial response to Pound's *Homage to Sextus Propertius.* "If Pound were a Professor of Latin," Professor Hale tactfully suggested when the *Homage* was first published, "there would be nothing left for him but suicide."[8] Taking his cue from Hale, Alan Brownjohn, the *New Statesman* reviewer, compared the Zukofskys to ignorant school children: "It all reads like unseen stabs at unseen translation when one hasn't done the homework of the night before: knotted, clumsy, turgid and ultimately silly." And he wondered if perhaps they were insane: except for a few brief passages, the translations were, he reported, marked only by "complete lunacy" and "unbelievable crankiness."[9] Robert Conquest, writing in *Encounter*, went a step further, and suggested that the Zukofskys were barbarians celebrating the destruction of civilization itself: "The Hun," he concluded, "is at play—worse still, *at work*—among the ruins."[10] A year or so after Conquest's assault on the Zukofskys, an American academic, Burton Raffel, joined the chorus:

> To whom is this translation of Catullus . . . of any use? The Latinist can read Catullus in Latin; he does not need, nor presumably is he interested to read, that "a ventum horribilium atque pestilentem" can be aped (but not translated, no) as "o vent them horrible, I'm not quite, pestilent mm." The non-Latinist wants to know, as well as he can, what Catullus said and how he said it. Can he get anything—*anything*?—from this?[11]

8. "Pegasus Impounded," *Poetry*, 14 (1919), 55. Quoted in J.P. Sullivan, *Ezra Pound and Sextus Propertius* (Austin: University of Texas Press, 1964), p. 6.
9. Alan Brownjohn, "Caesar 'ad Some," *New Statesman*, 78 (Aug. 1, 1969), 151.
10. Robert Conquest, "The Abomination of Moab," *Encounter*, 34 (May, 1970), 56.
11. Burton Raffel, "No Tidbit Love You Outdoors Far as a Bier," *Arion*, 8 (1969), 441.

The Catullus translations have found some defenders, but even they often seem uneasy. Kenner, writing in 1968, lauded the Zukofskys for their determination to treat the Latin "not only as a source of 'meanings' but as a graph of breathings and intonation." Yet, he went on, "the achieved English is irremediably strange"; and only "the sheer scale of the enterprise, which . . . offers . . . Catullus whole, subdued after unimaginable trouble," can turn the "strangeness . . . into virtue" (Kenner, p. 113). Guy Davenport, celebrating a poetic idiom that he finds both Joycean and Shakespearean, nevertheless confessed that "on every page we find ourselves looking for the place where Zukofsky has charmed his monstrous method into allowing the poet to get through a glorious passage on his lute unpestered."[12] And Cid Corman, while insisting upon the poetic virtues of the Zukofsky adaptions, seems willing to agree that perhaps they aren't really translations: "There is no point in comparing these versions with any other versions of Catullus. . . . The only accuracy must occur within the work itself as poetry."[13]

To refute the charges of critics like Brownjohn, Conquest, and Raffel, we need only look (but we must look long and hard) at what the Zukofskys do with a specific poem:

XXXII

Amabo, mea dulcis Ipsithilla,
meae deliciae, mei lepores,
iube ad te veniam meridiatum.
et si iusseris, illud adiuvato,
nequis liminis obseret tabellam,
neu titi lubeat foras abire.
sed domi maneas paresque nobis
novem continuas fututiones.
verum, siquid ages, statim iubeto:
nam pransus iaceo, et satur supinus
pertundo tunicamque palliumque.

32

I'm a bow, my dual kiss, Ipsithilla,
my daily key, eye, my eye's little leap-horse,
you bid me to "when," I'm your meridian.
That: so you see as sure as that adjuvant,
no case, limb, menace obscure your tableland,
no tidbit love you outdoors far as a bier.
Stay home, my man he asks we pair us—no bis—

---

12. Guy Davenport, "Zukofsky's English Catullus," *MAPS*, 5 (1973), 72.
13. Cid Corman, "Poetry as Translation," in *At Their Word* (Santa Barbara: Black Sparrow, 1978), p. 19.

nine continuous gasps, no refutations.
Very, so he could, yes start if you bid to:
he's primed now a joke-stuffed satyr, so pin us!
pert under the tunic, pulling up the quilt.

The translation, it is clear immediately, makes no sense apart from
the original: without the Latin *"amabo" en face*, the import of
"I'm a bow" will be lost upon us. But when the original and the
translation are read in conjunction, as they are printed in the Cape
Goliard edition, a powerful energy begins to leap back and forth
between the two texts. The translation forces us to look back at
the original, and to see it in a new way. The Latin *"amabo"* becomes three words in English: "I'm a bow." The effect is to frac-
ture the Latin word into a sequence of syllables, each of which becomes a pure sound value: "a," "ma," "bo." Only *after* we apprehend *"amabo"* syllable by syllable are we allowed to see it as a
word, a unit of meaning. (If, at the back of our heads, we hear a
juvenile voice chanting *amabo, —bis, —bit,* that's all right too.)
The Latin syllables take on density; each has its own color, weight,
and shape. And the English syllables take on equal density, as the
vigorously colloquial, assertively American idiom of the translation is, if only through conjunction with Catullus's Latin, trans-
muted into poetry. The translation thus reproduces, with exact
precision, the syllabic music of the original. But the Zukofskys
have also reproduced the currents of energy that flow among
Catullus's syllables and galvanize them into life. Consider the
opening phrase, for example. Catullus isn't talking about bows,
of course. But neither is he talking about "love" in some vague,
"spiritual" sense. Rather he is talking about sexual desire, and before the poem ends he tells us that his desire has assumed the concrete form of an erect penis. Anyone who has ever seen an erect
penis knows that it is a "bow" in at least three senses: it curves
like a bow, it is aimed at an object of desire, and it is ready to
shoot. As Catullus's Latin is metamorphosed into English, a metaphor is released. But the Zukofskys clearly do not simply "make
up" this metaphor. Rather the metaphor was latent in Catullus's
Latin all along, waiting to be freed. Or take the middle section of
the translation. The sixth line so offended Raffel that he quoted
it, derisively, in the title of his essay on the Zukofsky translation,
with the implication that the line is pure nonsense. But I would
argue that this section of the translation does make sense, and I
would paraphrase the fifth and sixth lines as follows: "Make sure
that no clothes, hands, or threats prevent me from enjoying your
cunt; and don't go out lest some little shrimp ('tidbit' refers both
to the supposed rival and his genital) fuck you to death ('far as a

bier')." My English here is more idiomatic and more colloquial than the English of the Zukofsky translation; but I do not think that I have added many, if any, additional "meanings." Not all these meanings are "literally" present in the original. My diction-ary, for example, translates *"liminis"* as "barriers," whereas the Zukofskys give us, not the abstract noun itself, but three possible varieties of barriers. Yet here, as in the metamorphosis of *"ama-bo"* into "I'm a bow," all these new meanings are latent in the or-iginal. The translation unfolds, amplifies, explicates Catullus's Latin poem; but it is never false to the original, and unlike my paraphrase it is faithful to the sound as well as to the sense of the original.

That the Zukofskys have succeeded in reproducing both the *melopoeia* (the term is Pound's, and it means "a musical property which directs the bearing or trend of the meaning") and the *logo-poeia* (to Pound, the "dance of intellect among words"[14]) of the original is also clear in my second example, the most acid of all the Lesbia poems:

LVIII

Caeli, Lesbia nostra, Lesbia illa,
illa Lesbia, quam Catullus unam
plus quam se atque suos amavit omnes,
nunc in quadriviis et angiportis
glubit magnanimi Remi nepotes.

58

Caelius, Lesbia new star, Lesbia a light,
all light, Lesbia, whom Catullus (o name
loss) whom his eyes caught so as avid of none,
none else—slunk in the driveways, the dingy parts
glut magnanimous Remus, his knee-high pots.

Caelius is, of course, a man's name; but the word also means "heaven," and so the metamorphoses of *"nostra"* into "new star" and of *"illa"* into "a light" not only echo the sound of the original but also pick up meanings which are present in the Latin, but which no other translation that I have seen reproduces. The re-iteration of Lesbia's name and Catullus's reference to himself in the third person underscore the dual nature of names: they both belong to us (*"suos"*) and *are* us (*"se"*). To lose one's name is to lose all, and the line break between "name" and "loss" in the translation suggests a total severing of all ties—with the past and its illusions, and with a selfhood that was founded upon these

---

14. Ezra Pound, *Literary Essays* (New York: New Directions, 1968), p. 25.

illusions. For a moment, in the last part of the third line, the memory of these old illusions hovers before us. But the abrupt "unc" sound ("*nunc*," "slunk") marks a shift to a new and terrible vision of Lesbia, of woman, of human existence. The transformation of "*quadriviis*" ("crossroads" in my dictionary) into "driveways" is obviously wholly appropriate. "Dingy parts" refers both to the alleys (*angiportis*) in which Lesbia carries on her trade, and to her own soiled genitals. The later meaning is not explicit in Catullus; but it is clearly relevant. Through the fourth line, then, the Zukofsky translation is both lucid and faithful to Catullus. The last line, however, calls for more detailed comment. The first word of Catullus's last line is, I would propose, a true touchstone—though not quite in Arnold's sense of this term. My dictionary says that "*glubo,—ere*" means "to peel," as in peeling the bark from a twig; and it coyly suggests that Catullus uses the word in a "transferred" sense. Is Lesbia peeling back the foreskins of the nephews of Remus? Is she, as my local Latinist suggests, "milking them down"? Perhaps. But Catullus's metaphor also suggests oral sex (cf. our words "glug," "glub," and "gulp," all of which imitate the sound of swallowing); and "*glubit*" also uncannily echoes the sound of a male genital moving within a well lubricated female genital. "*Glubit*" is the perfect union of sound and sense; and Catullus puts this word at the place where it will have the maximum shock effect, immediately after the line break. The feelings that surround this word seem clear enough. Sex here seems dirty in all possible senses: we (and Catullus) feel disgust as we watch Lesbia ply her trade, and we also want to wallow in the mud with her. But Catullus's dazzling success in condensing all these possibilities into a single word poses an enormous problem for the translator. For several years after I first read this poem, I speculated about possible translations of "*glubit*." I once thought that "fucks" would be as close as one could come to a satisfactory equivalent: the word is ostentatiously vulgar, it has (or had) a shock value, and it is (like "*glubit*") faintly onomatopoetic. But the Zukofskys, letting sound rather than meaning guide them, have clearly found the right word. "Glut" has the vulgar, gutteral sound of the original. It also has many of the meanings of "*glubit*." And the Zukofskys allow the other meanings of "*glubit*" to emerge later, in the last words of the line. The "knee-high pots" here mentioned long seemed to me very mysterious. Everything else in the translation became, after a little effort, reasonably clear. But what were the pots doing in the poem? Finally a colleague, Professor Paul Bauschatz, suggested a solution. The pots are toilets. (Is there any other kind of pot that is "knee-

high"?)[15] And Lesbia, it seems, has become a public toilet, available to any male Roman who needs to discharge something from
his penis. Again, Catullus's poem says nothing about pots, knee-
high or otherwise. But the image of Lesbia as a public toilet unerringly re-produces the feeling of the original. As such, it is the perfect conclusion to a perfect translation.

But why Catullus? What lead the Zukofskys to embark upon
the enormous project of metamorphosing each of Catullus's syllables into English? One reason is that the New York poet Louis
Zukofsky is a direct descendent and heir of the Roman poet
Catullus. The historical continuity that links the two is clearly
visible in the language of these translations. The English of New
York has many progenitors, but the Latin of Augustan Rome is
certainly one of the most important. Our own speech is clotted
with Latin syllables, and in these translations we stare, astonished,
as English devolves back into Latin. But if Zukofsky is in one
sense Catullus's heir, in another sense he is his brother, for a principal motive of these translations seems to be Zukofsky's sense
that he and Catullus were caught within similar historical situations. Both were inhabitants of imperial cities. Both, therefore,
heard about them a cacophony of tongues and idioms emanating
from a wildly heterogeneous citizenry. In the Zukofsky translation, the jostling of Latinate polysyllables and street slang suggests this cacophony. If there was little linguistic commonality in
these imperial cities, there was little cultural or religious commonality either. Both Catullus's Rome and Zukofsky's New York were
fragmented, secular cities. Both poets could see about them com-
patriots who had responded to fragmentation and secularization
by embarking on frantic religious quests, but neither took this
easy way out. Instead both took upon themselves the more demanding task of discovering a way of affirming the possibility of
love in a world that seemed to negate that possibility. A common
conviction that love alone can redeem this world is, in fact, the
most important similarity between the two poets. The Zukofsky
versions of Catullus's longer poems reveal this shared concern most
fully. Catullus's short poems are primarily satiric pictures of contemporary Rome; his longer poems instead invoke a ritual or my-
thological world of love and order—they establish, in fact, a stand-
point from which he can summon degenerate Rome to the bar of
judgment. The longest of these poems is number 64, an epyllion
in honor of the marriage of Peleus and Thetis. The marriage of the

---

15. An alternative explanation has been offered by Gilbert Sorrentino in "Louis Zukofsky," *Paideuma*, 7 (Winter, 1978), 401. I still prefer my reading of the line.

hero and the goddess becomes an emblem of cosmic unity, as all opposites (water and land, female and male, divine and human) here come together. In this respect Catullus's poem is the model of such magnificent Renaissance celebrations of marriage as Spenser's "Epithalamion." Like Spenser's poem, Catullus's number 64 is written in a high ceremonial mode. In this poem we are offered, not a continuous narrative, but emblematic processions. And all these processions center on the marriage bed, where the union of opposites will take place:

> Ipsius at sedes, quacumque opulenta recessit
> regia, fulgenti splendent auto atque argento.
> candet ebur soliis, collucent pocula mensae,
> tota domus gaudet regali splendida gaza.
> pulvinar vero divae geniale locatur
> sedibus in mediis, Indo quod dente politum
> tincta tegit roseo conchyli purpura fuco.

> I see his Seat, say this, honeycomb opulent aisle recesses
> ranging on, fulgent and splendent aureate and argent hall.
> Candid ivory solely ease, goblets light pour cooly men sigh
> to the home whose good wit regales a splendid eye gazing.
> Look now where Her Own Divine nuptial bed will glow on their
> State abodes in midway ease, Indic white elephantine tooth
> tinct with coveted rose of conchylium purple spread—full glow:

Passages such as this make clear what Catullus and Zukofsky had in common. The translation reproduces the lavish sensuality of the original, a sensuality flavored by a touch of urban (and urbane) irony. But the glow that emanates from the marriage bed is no illusion. For both poets, this bed is sacred. In this bed the one true mystery, the coming together of man and woman, is consummated; and in this bed occurs also the one true miracle we know, the creation of new life.

If Catullus and Zukofsky share a conviction that all human life revolves around the marriage bed, however, their views of love differ in one important respect. To Catullus, the love and wholeness represented by the marriage bed is now gone forever from the world, whereas to Zukofsky love is an immediate and daily presence. Here again Catullus's Peleus and Thetis poem is a useful test case. This poem includes two long interludes, the first of which describes the coverlet on the marriage bed. On this coverlet are embroidered scenes from the life of Theseus: his triumph over the Minotaur, his repudiation of Ariadne, and the mistake over the sails that results in the death of Theseus's father, Aegeus. A second major interlude tells how various heroes and gods come, in solemn procession, to the wedding. The last to arrive are the

Fates, who prophesy a joyous marriage, but who also predict the
death of Thetis's son, Achilles, in the Trojan War. Both the Theseus segment and the procession of the gods segment thus move
from triumph to tragic loss, from joy to grief. And the poem as
a whole follows a similar pattern. Catullus, although he would like
to believe in the gods, cannot summon up any real belief. Thus it
is not only Aegeus and Achilles but the gods themselves who are
here dying; in the end the poem becomes a lament over the departure of the gods from this earth. The departure of the gods has
left the earth barren, as Catullus suggests in the concluding lines of
this great poem:

> sed postquam tellus scelerest imbuta nefando,
> iustitiamque omnes cupida de mente fugarunt,
> perfudere manus fraterno sanguine fratres,
> destitit extinctos natus lugere parentes,
> optavit genitor primaevi funera nati,
> liber ut innuptae poteretur flore novercae,
> ignaro mater substernens se impia nato
> impia non veritast divos scelerare parentes:
> omnia fanda nefanda malo permixta furore
> iustificam nobis mentem avertere deorum.
> quare nec tales dignantur visere coetus,
> nec se contingi patiuntur lumine claro.

> Said past come tell us sclerous crime imbued earth, men founder,
> justice has gone and always cupidity and mind figure ground,
> perfidy on their hands brothers now strangle their brothers,
> destitute extinct those sons who looked after their parents,
> mourned them, but today's father primps at junior's funeral
> libertine impatience bother to deflower his new mother,
> innocent martyr son steered to impious incest,
> impious no fear or taste divines scald wrath of her parent gods:
> all law once founded unfounded malice a mixture of furor
> justifying no blest mind may await gods' ray where or home.
> Where there are no tales dignifying Their Ways They cut us,
> nor seek contingent patient touch to illumine clear air.

Justice is gone; love is gone. We are left with the bestial struggle of
each against all. Such is Catullus's vision of life in Rome. For Zukofsky, in contrast, the gods (and justice and love) were alive and
well, and living in Brooklyn. In the poetry of Catullus, the possibility of a direct apprehension of love was a memory and a hope;
to Zukofsky, Venus daily offered herself to his senses, in the person of Celia. Lesbia is the archetype of love betrayed, denied, lost;
Celia is the archetype of love found and refound each day. In the
total corpus of Zukofsky's work, then, the Catullus translations
represent not only an act of affirmation but also an act of purga-
tion. In this translation, Zukofsky confronts the possibility of love

denied. But as the lucidity and purity of the final sections of *"A"* demonstrate, Zukofsky wrestled with the demon and won. It therefore seems to me useful to think of the Catullus translations as the "shadow" (in the Jungian sense) of Zukofsky's generally sunlit poetic *oeuvre*. Without the shadow, Zukofsky's triumphant celebration of love would seem too easily won. But for the song of triumph itself we must turn to *"A,"* especially the final movements; and it is to one of these "crystal cabinets" (the phrase is Rexroth's), *"A"*-21, that I shall now turn.

II

Zukofsky's translation of Plautus's *Rudens* seems to have escaped the attention of the Latin professors, perhaps because it is buried in *"A."* But Zukofsky's admirers have also, perhaps for the same reason, had little to say about this translation. If the *Rudens* translation has aroused less controversy (but also, apparently, less interest) than the Catullus translations, no doubt one major reason is that here Zukofsky's labors issue in something that looks more or less like "normal" English. But if the *Rudens* translation is less obviously idiosyncratic than the Catullus translations, the two works nevertheless share a common determination to give us, not disembodied meanings, but *words*, as particles of matter in motion. Plautus's Latin text is not included in *"A"*; and it is not essential to our understanding of the translation, for Zukofsky does not here attempt to echo the sound or syllable structure of the original. Yet he does preserve a rigorous fidelity to the line pattern of the original, by giving us precisely one line of English for each line of Latin. The translation also maintains an absolutely regular pattern of five words to each line, even though Plautus's lines vary in length. In fact, Zukofsky has here created a new kind of poetic line. Earlier poets counted accents or syllables; Zukofsky has decided to count words. The regularity of Zukofsky's line, and the exact correspondence between his lines and Plautus's, tends to establish the line as an irreducible unit both of sound and of meaning. As syllables (the word as broken down into parts) function in the Catullus translations, so the line (the word as part of a larger rhythmic—but not syntactic—whole) functions here. In both translations we are invited to look at words from a non- (in one case a sub- and in the other a trans-) verbal perspective, while at the same time our impulse to see the word as nothing more than a pawn in the game of "meaning," a variable in a syntactic "string," is thwarted. The effect is to allow us to see the word as a three-dimensional object in space. In the *Rudens* translation, since there is no effort to match the English to the Latin, the words at issue are Zukofsky's, not Plautus's. In this respect, Davenport is correct in describing the *Rudens* translation as "so many English words set to [the music of] Plautus's Latin."[16] The translation is also Zukofsky's in another sense: it is an integral part of *"A,"* and it helps carry the themes (I am using this word in a musical rather than in a philosophic sense) of Zukofsky's epic an important step toward resolution. Zukofsky also marks this work as his own by including a running off-stage commentary which owes nothing to the Latin text. Yet even after we recognize that the *Rudens* translation is no less Zukofsky's poem than the *Homage to Sextus Propertius* is Pound's poem, an awareness of the precise relationship between the translation and the original seems to me useful both to an understanding of Zukofsky and to an understanding of Plautus. Indeed, if we look at Zukofsky's and Plautus's texts together, it becomes clear that a powerful (and decidedly sexual) energy flows between the two, that Plautus's text stands to Zukofsky's as father to child (with the poet himself as "mother"), and that Zukofsky's poem itself is in the fullest sense an act of love.

To see precisely how Zukofsky's five-word line here functions, it will be useful to juxtapose a passage of Plautus's Latin, a conventional translation of the passage, and Zukofsky's version of the same passage. The passage I have selected is the opening soliloquy of Palaestra (Zukofsky trans-literates her name as "Polly"). At the beginning of the play the boat in which Palaestra has been traveling runs aground. As she wades ashore, she speaks as follows:

> nunc quam spem aut opem aut consili quid capessam?
> ita hic sola solis locis compotita sum.
> hic saxa sunt, hic mare sonat,
> neque quisquam homo mihi obviam venit.
> hoc quod induta sum, summae opes oppido.
> nec cibo nec loco tecta quo sim scio:
> quae mihist spes, qua me vivere velim?
> nec loci gnara sum, nec vidi aut hic fui.
> saltem aliquem velim qui mihi ex his locis
> aut viam aut semitam monstret, ita nunc
> hac an illac eam, incerta sum consili;
> nec prope usquam hic quidem cultum agrum conspicor.
> algor, error, pavor, me omnia tenent.
> haec parentes mei haud scitis miseri,
> me nunc miseram esse ita uti sum.

---

16. Guy Davenport, "Zukofsky's *"A"*-24," *Parnassus*, 2 (Spring-Summer, 1974), 327.

libera ego prognata fui maxume, nequiquam fui.
nunc qui minus servio, quam si serva forem nata?
neque quicquam umquam illis profuit qui me sibi eduxerunt.[17]

Zukofsky's version of this passage reads as follows:

No one consoles me, I'm
alone one with this place,
here rock here sea groans
no man comes my way:
these rags endow my dowry,
no sop or sleep welcomes,
hope's mist, must I live?
I will never know here.
Show me the way out
someone, show me a narrow
path—here or there riddles,
nothing here grows I see.
Cold, loss, fear tear me
and my parents don't know
my misery, torn from them
born free presumably to quicken
sorrow, judged like the poor,
little profit life brought them (*"A,"* p. 446)

For purposes of comparison, here is E.F. Watling's competent but banal English version of the same passage:

Now there's no hope, no help, no one to turn to. . . .
    All alone . . . in this lonely desolate place. . . .
Rocks, and the sea . . . no one will ever find me.
I've nothing, but these clothes; no food, no shelter,
No hope . . . oh, what have I got to live for?
Where shall I go? I've never seen this place,
Never set foot on it before. There's no one
To show me where to find a road or path.
I don't know where to go . . . this way, or that way? . . .
    I see no sign of cultivation here. . . .
I don't know where I am . . . I'm cold . . . I'm frightened.
Oh father and mother, if you only knew
Where your poor daughter is, and what she suffers.
If this is I, your daughter born in freedom,
I might as well have been a slave; such sorrow,
Nothing but sorrow, have I brought you. . . .[18]

The Latin line has an amplitude that is largely absent from Zukofsky's English. Watling's English line looks closer to Plautus's. Yet in Watling's version Palaestra sounds coy, giggly, a little silly: Pauline fleeing from one of her perils, perhaps. *We*, of course,

17. Text from the Loeb Classics edition of Plautus, ed. Paul Nixon (London: William Heinemann, 1932), IV, 306.
18. Plautus, *The Rope and Other Plays*, ed. and trans. E.F. Watling (Baltimore: Penguin, 1971), pp. 97-98.

know that Palaestra is in no danger. The play is a comedy, so we are confident that things will turn out all right. Furthermore, Arcturus has already told us, in the prologue, that everyone on the wrecked boat has come safely to shore. But if we know that all is well, Palaestra does not. She must seem genuinely terrified and grief-stricken in this scene, or the whole play will begin to seem like a parody. And she must seem truly "lost," if the moment when her parents find her is to retain its poignancy. In Zukofsky's version, far more than in Watling's, Palaestra seems truly frightened and truly lost. The compressed five-word line gives to Polly's speech a terse dignity. Her very refusal of rhetoric becomes a measure of the intensity of her pain: a parallel case might be the river merchant's wife, in Pound's great translation of Li Po's poem. Zukofsky achieves this effect primarily through a meticulous control of each word. When necessary, Zukofsky's line edges close to the Latin: thus Plautus's "hic saxa sunt, hic mare sonat" becomes "here rock here sea groans," and "algor, error, pavor me omnia tenent" becomes "Cold, loss, fear tear me." The Latinate patterns of these lines imperceptibly undercut the normal patterns of English syntax. The effect is to isolate the individual word: "cold," "loss," "fear"—the words drop into our minds one by one, and the ripples spread. In many of Zukofsky's lines there are also touches of assonance or of alliteration: cf. "fear tear" in one of the lines already quoted, and numerous other examples—"alone one," "endow my dowry," "sop or sleep," "mist, must," "show me a narrow," "little profit life." A distinct Anglo-Saxon echo seems to hover over these lines: an important model, both here and in other sections of Zukofsky's translation, is Pound's "Seafarer." Finally, there is a careful, virtually Miltonic counterpoint of syntax and line. As we read through even so brief a passage as this, the five-word line begins to control our rhythmic expectations. Indeed, the line break becomes so powerful a structural tool that it serves at times as a substitute for punctuation: "here rock here sea groans/ no man comes my way." Unconsciously we begin to anticipate a syntactic shift at the end of each line. And Zukofsky controls our responses by satisfying this anticipation at times ("these rags endow my dowry,/ no sop or sleep welcomes,/ hope's mist, must I live?") and frustrating it at other times, as the syntax drives on across the line break ("Show me the way out/ someone, show me a narrow/ path. . . ."). The poetic voice we are here hearing is, I submit, the voice of a master. Cid Corman has said that Zukofsky had the finest ear of any poet of our time, and a careful examination of the quoted passage lends credence to Corman's thesis.[19] The words, the measure—these are Zukofsky's. But at the same time Plautus is here as well served as we (or he) could ask.

But a play, as Aristotle noticed a long time ago, is not a collection of words or even a collection of lines. Rather it is a sequence of *actions*; and a play as a whole is a single extended action. Zukofsky, who studied Aristotle with care, understood the centrality of action in drama. The proof is *Arise, Arise*, one of the most genuinely dramatic plays ever written by a poet. It is no accident that the title of this play is a verb. And *Arise, Arise* does not merely talk about "arising." The title is not only a verb but specifically an imperative, and by the end of the play we find ourselves (along with at least some of the characters) obeying this command. Given Zukofsky's awareness of the role of action in drama, it seems important to ask what sort of action is at issue in *Rudens*, and why this action interested Zukofsky. The modern reader, coming to *Rudens* for the first time, is likely to feel that he has read this play a dozen times before. And in a sense he has, for the plot of *Rudens* is one of the great archetypal plots of comedy: the story of the Lost Child Found. There is little suspense here, for the Prologue tells us everything that will happen in the play:

> fisheRman's sea   net dragged Up a leathery wicker
> rattling the baby's charms for his master's Daughter
> a leno had kidnapped for his slave brothEl.
> unknown to her father she was his little ward
> after her shipwreck: later they fouNd out—
> she married her Sweetheart   a young man (*"A,"* p. 438)

But if this plot generates little suspense, it does evoke a sense of wonder. The plot of the Lost Child Found receives its fullest treatment in the luminous miracle plays with which Shakespeare closed out his dramatic career: *Pericles, Cymbeline, The Winter's Tale,* and *The Tempest*. In all of these plays the apparent loss of a child (Marina, Guiderius and Arviragus, Perdita, Ferdinand) leaves a great wound, not only in the hearts of the characters, but in nature itself; and the recovery of the lost child miraculously attests the presence of grace (I am not using this word in a specifically theological sense—rather I would have the reader associate this word with ideas like "rightness," "harmony," "wholeness," "light") in the world. Zukofsky was, of course, a devoted student of Shakespeare, especially of the late plays. It is therefore not surprising that Shakespeare's voice often intervenes—sometimes

---

19. Cid Corman, "Love—In These Words," *MAPS*, 5 (1973), 30.

explicitly, for there are quotations from Shakespeare scattered through the text—in the dialogue between Zukofsky and Plautus. Zukofsky's reading of *Rudens* is, I am suggesting, consciously "Shakespearean."[20] Zukofsky's *Rudens*, like Shakespeare's romances, begins with a shattering of the world, and it moves toward a vision of a world made whole again through love. In all of Shakespeare's late plays a storm-caused shipwreck triggers the action. The storm augers the "breaking of nature's germans," and in at least two plays (*Pericles* and *The Tempest*) it separates parent from child. But the storm is also cleansing; out of it may come, as we see in *The Tempest*, a world made whole again. *Rudens* too begins in storm and shipwreck, but we know from the beginning that this storm will blow the lost child back to her parents. The destructive force in this play is Leno, the pimp, who has bought Palaestra/Polly, the Lost Child, from a slave dealer and is carrying her off to a life of prostitution. Leno here represents the demonic urge to reduce love to lust, and to turn all human life into a commercial transaction. But the counterforce is love itself, which manifests itself not only in the creative wind, Arcturus, which blows the boat ashore, but also in the fortuitous series of accidents that constitutes the plot of the play. These chance occurrences bring Palaestra/Polly to the home of her parents, and at the same time bring the tokens of her identity (these are in a rope chest which is conveniently fished from the sea at the appropriate moment) to the right place at the right moment. It is significant that the action of the play takes place around the temple of Venus, for Venus is here the force that moves the sun, and the wind, and the hearts of men, drawing all together in a final harmony. This harmony unites master and servant, and it even unites pimp and proper citizen, for Leno is at the end invited to dinner. (As Erich Segal notes, the pimp in Plautine comedy is usually an object of total scorn, and a reconciliation which includes the pimp is unusual.[21]) But, more important, it unites man and wife, father and daughter, within the family. Familial love is, in fact, the *rudens* (the rope) of the title; for it is love that twines us together and makes us one.

---

20. ""*A*"-21 is," says Guy Davenport in his terse summary of *A* 13-21, "a translation of Plautus' *Rudens*. Why? Well, because it is the source of "Pericles," the most beautiful of Shakespeare's plays in Zukofsky's assessment . . . ," ("Louis Zukofsky," *Agenda*, 8 [Autumn-Winter, 1970], 135). I have not yet found an editor of Shakespeare who believes that *Rudens* is the "source" of *Pericles*. But Davenport's suggestion that the Shakespearean overtones of *Rudens* stimulated Zukofsky's interest in the play seems to me correct.
21. Erich Segal, *Roman Laughter* (Cambridge: Harvard University Press, 1968), p. 165.

If *Catullus* confronts the specter of love denied, therefore, *Rudens* is a vision of a world made new by love. *"A"* as a whole is a quest for such a world: a quest that ends in the grand harmonies of *"A"*-24, as the music of Handel draws together the various voices of Zukofsky (P the Poet, D the Dramatist, T the Thinker, and S the Storyteller) into an integral whole. The *Rudens* translation is an important moment in this quest. *"A"* begins with a sense of loss: a harmony has been broken, a friend (the mysterious Ricky) has been lost, perhaps at sea. Beginning in *"A"*-12 Zukofsky begins to recover the past; and in *"A"*-21 he burrows his way back through Shakespeare's England, and through Plautus's Rome, to arrive finally at the long lost Greek play which was, presumably, Plautus's source. There is no first term to this process, and no last term. Zukofsky's *Rudens* is no less (but no more) original that Plautus's. Both are part of the on-going process that is Life, and Art as well. Thus the past becomes, not the "cause" of the present, the "original" that we imitate, but rather simply a moment that precedes ours. So too the future also becomes a movement into possibility, where the lost friend can be recovered in a new form: the form of the daughter that Zukofsky never had. To go back is to go forward. By going back to *Rudens*, Zukofsky moves forward on his own perilous quest. That such is, for Zukofsky, the import of this enterprise becomes clear in the "voices off" passages which Zukofsky interpolates into the text. A few of these passages are spoken by characters in the play; but most are spoken by Zukofsky himself, and they provide a sometimes obscure but often richly suggestive commentary on the play. The most remarkable of these interludes, in my judgment, is the long meditative lyric incorporated into Act IV. As the offstage voice speaks these lines, the chest containing the tokens that will establish Palaestra's/Polly's identity is being pulled on-stage, and therefore the action of the play is rapidly moving toward a climax. But action itself, the mystery of our endless questing forward within time, is the theme of this meditation. We are all, Zukofsky suggests, carried forward by something which both is and is not under the control of the human will, and the writing of a sentence is as good an example as any of how this happens:

> so life writes
> out the desirability
> felt, perceived not
> one's own: gift
> of an if
> that trembles a
> disorder, conceives order:

> safe wording what
> is it to
> say *I meant*: ("*A*," p. 477)

But the mystery of time gathers up not only words, but leaves and
our lives:

> friends hard to
> hold, leaves' sway
> on fall's branch
> all colors remembered
> delight the ground
> tho't blows. Like:
> the river Epirus
> puts out the
> torch, lights it:
> and the drafts
> hurt: all fishermen
> transfigured: cuttlefish casts
> a long gut
> out of her
> throat: a certain
> age hermit crab
> occupies empty shell,
> studying a wind—
> discerning spared injuries:
> for *their* discourse
> seems to be
> music: ("*A*," p. 477)

Even the cuttlefish and the crab, it seems, live in time, casting
themselves forward into the future, carrying on their backs the
shell of the past. We're all in the river, or on it:

> And be still
> moving a fly
> upon the water
> you yourself being
> also always moving
> down stream—caterpillars
> moving not unlike
> waves of the
> sea . . . . ("*A*," pp. 478-479)

The mood here is reconciliation: it is the mood of Plautus, and of
Shakespeare at the end. And Zukofsky too, like Shakespeare's
Pericles, came at last to hold his lost daughter in his arms, and
to hear the music of the spheres:

> Most heavenly music!
> It nips me unto listening, and thick slumber
> Hangs upon mine eyes: let me rest.

GUY DAVENPORT

*ZUKOFSKY'S ENGLISH CATULLUS**

1. English is well advanced into its inevitable process of becoming pidgin. Inevitable, because when a speaker of English is unaware of the components of words he must speak by formula, rote, and custom, deaf to historical nuance and blind to the structure of a word.

2. English has four vocabularies: Old English, French, Latin, Greek. *Fire, flame, conflagration, holocaust. Sickness, malady, infirmity, epidemic.* There is, as in every language, a fifth source of coinage and borrowings *(boss, kangaroo, kleenex).*

3. English is Zukofsky's second language, after Yiddish.

4. The expansion of French poetic diction, already begun in Hugo, characterizes the end of the century, and distinguishes the style of Apollinaire, the subject of Zukofsky's first critical study.

5. The two great writers of English whose styles could accommodate the full range of the four English vocabularies are Shakespeare and Joyce.

6. Zukofsky's English, like Pound's, is basically eighteenth century, neo-classical. Zukofsky uses with ease such a word as *commonage*, which is in Johnson's *Dictionary* but no longer in spoken English. To this elegance of diction he adds the musical resonance of Renaissance English and the vulgate of his time, the thin earnest American English of the professional classes.

7. Zukofsky's profession was teaching. Elucidation of words was his daily exercise. Habit becomes second nature. Williams' ability to move from medical terminology to the vulgate can be seen in his honest plainness. Zukofsky's skill in talking about Shakespeare in the classroom shows in his precision of phrasing. Language,

*Reprinted with permission of the author from *MAPS*, No. 5, 1973.

like a hand, is shaped by use.

8. Diction, a free choice of words, is never free. It is always a game with rules. Gertrude Stein and Wittgenstein became intensely aware of this at the same time, and found the rules of diction inside a language. Language left to itself is a tautological social gesture.

9. The poet makes his own rules. Metre, diction, assonance, consonance, tone, rhythm, symbolism, correspondences.

10. As Zukofsky progressed into his canon, he seemed to fall in love with rules all but impossible to keep, such as finding the phrases for a *translation* in the Everyman edition of Marx's *Capital*, or creating images that look like *"A"*'s. Or of making a translation sound like the original.

11. Joyce is the immediate model here. Throughout the text of *Ulysses* the adventures of Odysseus are always on display, in every word, like the twelve notes of Schoenberg's scale, over and over and over. Other systems of allusion are simultaneously worked into the same words. "Genius is the ability to pay attention to two things at once." (Kafka)

12. To translate all of Catullus so that the English sounds like the Latin Zukofsky had to pay attention to three things at once: sound, rhythm, and syntax. The choice of each word therefore involved three decisions. This is of course impossible, but with a language containing four (and in a pinch five) vocabularies one can at least get close.

13. The first implication of Zukofsky's game is that diction as every other poet has known it must go by the by. He needs the entire dictionary to supply him with words.

14. *O quick floss silk of the Juventii, form*. This sounds Joycean. That "floss silk" is singing along with *flosculus*, diminutive of *flos*, flower. Here the method Zukofsky has committed himself to rendered a daring phrase which another translator might never have searched for, much less found.

15. Zukofsky's method keeps producing phrases from the diction of Nashe, Greene, Jonson, Udall: "cony cully," "salt hacks, tavern boys," "cocksure cockeye," "tour-pickled, low-puling long nosed," "looting, lupine whore," "do you faggot as my old salt dollies."

16. Catullus' obscenity has never been done better than in this translation:

> Bared dentures rinsed with a wash of spanish urine
>
> . . . raped by radishes and mullets.
>
> no sacred armpits lair hops as that he-goat's

17. Shakespeare-Zukofsky:

> and insolently toss a minute at my will magnified
> and soon dispensed with in a marring sea and in insane wind.
>
> . . . it is the crest of passion quieted
> gives way to this small solace against sorrow,
> could I but lose myself with you as she does . . .
>
> down there, where it is granted not one comes back.
> On you be the curse of the blind and dead shade
> Orcus, hell that destroys all beautiful things.
>
> . . . or as if to trumpet Jupiter
> lit instantly astern to fill the favored sheets

18. On every page we find ourselves looking for the place where Zukofsky has charmed his monstrous method into allowing the poet to get through a glorious passage on his lute unpestered:

> no, let her not look back at me as she used to,
> at her love whose fault was to die as at some
> meadow's rim, the blossom under the passing
>   cut of the share's thrust.

A young poet could get the world's attention with writing like that.

19. Zukofsky's stubborn intrepidity has already given the critics colic, and will blind readers to this translation for years:

> pro tale, o rig it all, me I cogged kiddie

Such opacities shift our eyes to the Latin: *pro telo rigida mea cecidi.* We note that he got the Latin sound, but where is the sense? The words are all there in the dictionary.

20. That there is no freedom except in discipline is a Judaeo-Christian idea. Twentieth-century artists working in a received form quickly exhausted it: Hemingway and the novel, for example. Perhaps we must distinguish between form and formal arrangement. Form commands intelligibility; formal arrangement is the passionate love of design, and is strongest in peasant art and under

intellectual control.

21.   In all of Zukofsky's writing the beginning is passion—excite-
ment of eye or ear, love for people, places, objects, a driven soli-
citude for a virtue or a quality. Expression is then carried out in
severest discipline, a discipline that can (as in the Catullus) constantly hamper clarity. But that is the game.

22.   William Carlos Williams intuited the rules shaping his poetry
as he went along; so did Pound, to a lesser extent.

23.   Zukofsky would chain fire, if he could, and have the wind
move in regiments of cubed air.

24.   Most translators fail their originals. Zukofsky transposes his
original into a different set of gestures: Picasso repainting Velas-
quez. *Ubi cymbalum sonat vox, ubi tympana reboant* becomes
"o be cymbal, loom sounded voice, o be tympana rebounded."
That loom, complex of meaning, is Zukofsky's. It is as if he *found*
it in Catullus.

25.   Abraham Cowley translating *Carmen XLV*:

> My dearest *Acme*, if I be
> Once alive and love not thee
> With a passion far above
> All that ere was called Love,
> In a *Lybian* desert may
> I become some Lions prey,
> Let him, *Acme*, let him tear
> My Brest, when *Acme* is not there.

Zukofsky doing the same:

> Acme, Septimius sighs so amorous,
> tenoned, sighing agree, "my" and quiet "Acme
> knee too pretty to mar, what qualm, I pore oh
> on my sum I see due, and if years part us
> a wan tomb cool my pluck, may it perish
> solus in Libya or India, tossed a
> case of—went and met with a blue-eyed lion."

26.   Blue-eyed lion! Said creature being from the mind of Bottom. There is more of the playful, smiling, silly lover in Zukofsky's version than Cowley could get there in a budget of continuous Sundays. It is a fair guess that Shakespeare would have
had Septimius produce that blue-eyed lion for Acme's tickled ear.

27.   A poet zones off his diction from the rest of a language's
vocabulary. Even dictionaries are so zoned. My grandmother used

to say, "I hear the fire reels charming out of the guardhouse." If you are a Russian using Webster's Third International, you will not find *fire reel*, nor an adequate definition of *guardhouse*, and you will have to infer that *charm* as "a blended or confused noise" is appropriate English for the bells and trumpets of fire reels. This is like Shakespeare's "When turtles tread," which students take to be terrapins walking rather than doves mating. Zukofsky, Shakespearean of Shakespeareans in our time, prefers the chord of words, or tone cluster, to the prepositional phrase ("furtive a vocal low quaint time"). Whatever is native to English, however archaic or elliptical, he can use—"cold how mean," "quick come day prone now precipitous valley volute hues."

28.   The reader bewildered by Zukofsky's text (*all* readers, without exception) can first of all go through and underline the passages which are indisputably magnificent poetry:

> Time poured there white, my prime vested me, I trod out the purest . . .

> Advent and yet to be, come portent and hope . . .

> . . . nor do we see the knapsack on our back's the ghost.

29.   Then the lines where Catullus has come alive, as alive as if he were breathing garlic in your face, through the Zukofskian laying on of hands:

> Void, vile, now be interred, and goodbye to you
> ill look into hell where your dead feet let you,
> incommodious cycle, pests of poets.

> pert under the tunic, pulling up the quilt

> . . . laud her, hang cavil.

30.   Yet I suspect that the best of these poems are the lines that seem to be ugly, angular, and strange. Familiarity alone will get us near them. Catullus is not all that approachable a poet. Much of him is shadowy and psychologically dark. Zukofsky can transmit Catullus' lewdness, but not his salacity.

31.   Contemporary New York is probably as close an historical rhyme to Catullus' Rome as we are likely to find, unless you would like to think of mediaeval Kyoto or Berlin in the 1920s.

32.   The only other modern Catullus is Carl Orff's. The *chuckle* there, and rattling dicebox, are Zukofskian. Otherwise they are distinct in spirit.

33.   The real achievement in translating classical poetry is not linguistic but guessing the right tone—the hang of the spirit. It is
probably always wrong to bring the past into the present. The true
poet finds the present in the past. Pound's Propertius is about
London, an imperial capital containing poets and bores, lively girls
and refrigerators patent.

34.   Had the Kerensky Republic not fallen to the Bolsheviki,
Zukofsky would have been a poet in the circle of Khlebnikov or
Mandelstam. He would still have written *"A,"* but probably not
the *Catullus*. He needed New York, *Roma nova*, for that.

35.   Zukofsky's English is like, and is the opposite of, Doughty's.
They both wrote by choosing each word by theory and by the
rules of a game. Homer's words came to him like ants to spilt
honey. Both Zukofsky and Doughty had to resuscitate dormant
and obsolete words and make them function beside living English.
Each wrote idiomatic English, and each had another language in
mind phrase by phrase. Technique, for each, was all.

DAVID M. GORDON

THREE NOTES ON ZUKOFSKY'S CATULLUS
I "CATULLUS viii": 1939-1960[1]

Miserable Catullus, stop being foolish
And admit it's over,
The sun shone on you those days
When your girl had you
When you gave it to her
           like nobody else ever will.
Everywhere together then, always at it
And you liked it and she can't say
                 she didn't
Yes, those days glowed.
Now she doesn't want it: why
          should you, washed out
Want to. Don't trail her,
Don't eat yourself up alive,
Show some spunk, stand up
              and take it.
So long, girl. Catullus
          can take it.
He won't bother you, he won't
          be bothered:
But you'll be, nights.
What do you want to live for?
Whom will you see?
Who'll say you're pretty?
Who'll give it to you now?
Whose name will you have?
Kiss what guy? bit[e] whose
             lips?
Come on Catullus, you can
          take it.

Miser Catulle, desinas ineptire,
et quod vides perisse perditum ducas.

---

1. *Anew* (Prairie City, Illinois: The Press of James A. Decker, 1946), p. 32.

fulsere quondam candidi tibi soles,
cum ventitabas quo puella ducebat
amata nobis quantum amabitur nulla.
ibi illa multa tum iocosa fiebant,
quae tu volebas nec puella nolebat.
fulsere vere candidi tibi soles.
nunc iam illa non vult: tu quoque, impotens, noli,
nec quae fugit sectare, nec miser vive,
sed obstinata mente perfer, obdura.
vale, puella. iam Catullus obdurat,
nec te requiret nec rogabit invitam:
at tu dolebis, cum rogaberis nulla
scelesta, nocte. quae tibi manet vita?
quis nunc te abibit? cui videberis bella?
quem nunc amabis? cuius esse diceris?
quem basiabis? cui labella mordebis?
at tu, Catulle, destinatus obdura.

A careful paraphrase which reflects on the concision of Bunting, Pound, Reznikoff, Cummings and Williams; keeping a certain directness and driving straight to the point, it skips over subtleties that do not immediately rise into crucial prominence. A wiry muscularity, lean, deft, "And admit it's over" for "et quod vides perisse perditum ducas" [prose, "and concede as lost what you see is lost"]. LZ is concerned about the meaning; e.g., "The sun shone on you those days," but notice how the idiom of *In Our Time* and *Tropic of Cancer*[2] modifies the original [*it*, "sexual intercourse," *OED*]. We are struck by the unaffected realism of a first hand experience, the flowing simultaneity of metonymically detailed time, place, and oomph in a world closed to all else, and after which a prose Catullus is flat, "Wherever the girl led you, when you went around with her, she was loved as no one shall ever be loved, then when there were so many joyous times, which you liked and the girl didn't dislike."

But the 1939 poem maintains a vernacular point of view. And the tough guy tone continues, "Now she doesn't want it." In the parlance, *impotens* becomes *washed out*. "Don't eat yourself up alive" explains "nec miser vive," as he keeps an eye on *vive* for *alive*. The stubbornness of "obstinata mente" is highlighted in "show some spunk," and he repeats "and take it" from "obdura." There is an acerbity in "He won't bother you, he won't/ be bothered:/ But you'll be, nights," which seems to go beyond the original. The ending continues in the voice of the South Side and Brooklyn, knowing from the gut, when it comes to love, "quem

---

2. Pound was interested in this novel for a time around 1935 [see *Letters*, pp. 272, 301].

nunc amabis," "who'll give it to you now?" Is the bell-mouthed horn and voice of "Satchmo" overheard in that music's background?

Then at the age of 56, after twenty-one years of serious research and music, LZ demonstrates how good an ear he has in this version that he produced in partnership with Celia,[3]

> Miss her, Catullus? don't be so inept to rail
> at what you see perish when perished is the case.
> Full, sure once, candid the sunny days glowed, solace,
> when you went about it as your girl would have it,
> you loved her as no one else shall ever be loved.
> Billowed in tumultuous joys and affianced,
> why you would but will it and your girl would have it.
> Full, sure, very candid the sun's rays glowed solace.
> Now she won't love you: you, too, don't be weak, tense, null,
> squirming after she runs off to miss her for life.
> *Said* as if you meant it: *obstinate, obdurate.*
> Vale! puling girl. I'm Catullus, *obdurate,*
> I don't require it and don't beg uninvited:
> won't you be doleful when no one, no one! begs you,
> scalded, every night. Why do you want to live now?
> Now who will be with you? Who'll seee (sic) that you're lovely?
> Whom will you love now and who will say that you're his?
> Whom will you kiss? Whose morsel of lips will you bite?
> But you, Catullus, your destiny's *obdurate.*

Beyond all of his other effects in this translation, LZ's line pulses with the feel of the Latin rhythm of the original: we seem to actually sense the choliambic verse,

$$\breve{\vphantom{l}} \colon \diagup \ \cup \diagup \breve{\vphantom{l}} \ \diagup \ \cup \diagup \cup \mathord{\smash{\llap{\diagup}}} \ \diagup \ \cup$$
Miss her, Catullus? don't be so inept to rail[4]

His line keeps the same number of syllables. Yet it is not precisely the choliambic, but rather his creative rendering of it that dovetails quantity and stress in order to enliven the English line.[5]

Now a much wider range of word-power asserts itself, but this is no passive imitation of a prose meaning. Out of the interstices of the carefully calibrated rhythm and meaning, "don't be so inept," a new addition crops up, "to rail." But is it extra? How

---

3. *Catullus (Gai Valeri Catulli Veronensis Liber)*, translated by Celia and Louis Zukofsky (London: Cape Goliard Press, 1969), VIII.
4. From Allen and Greenough's *New Latin Grammar* (1888; rev. New York: Ginn and Company, 1931) which Celia and Louis used for details, p. 415.
5. Apparently he would get the Latin rhythm down as a basis for a theme, or thematic rhythm, and then play an original figure on that basis, remembering EP's "I think progress lies rather in an attempt to approximate classical quantitative metres (NOT to copy them) than in a carelessness regarding such things" (*Literary Essays*, 13). Celia adds, "Yes, Louis was always concerned with using the Latin quantity to *enhance* the flow of the English line of verse" (in a letter to the author March 21, 1979; my italics).

does one make *inept* into a verb, as it is in Latin, "to play the fool"? The slightly archaic "inept to rail" prepares the ear for "against fortune," but instead we get a literally correct, "at what you see perish when perished," with the Brooklynese echo of du- cas, "is the case," as the perfectly appropriate joinery. Or, in the fully translated third line, ". . . once, candid the sunny days glowed . . ." there is the addition, "Full sure . . . solace." But *solace* (etym., *solor*) seems to derive from *soles* (the comfort of sunshine), and *full* and *sure* are suggested by *soles* and solace.

The sexually pregnant *it* of the 30's reappears from the earlier poem, "When you went about it as your girl would have it." But this time the finer shading, "went about it," from "ven- titabas"[6] is less heroic and final, and more self-assured than "when you gave it to her/ like nobody else ever will" [Lesbia, not the poet, is the subject of the verb amabitur], compared with, "You loved her as no one else shall ever be loved." Here the tone is of the still-in-love lover: "Now she won't love you: you, too, don't be weak, tense, null." The Latin, *impotens*, is given neurasthenic implications, a precision far beyond the impressionistic, "washed out." "Squirming after she runs off to miss her for life," aligns *sectare* ["eagerly pursuing"] with the writhing anguish of love as a more mundane sensation of the groin than the figurative, "Don't trail her,/ Don't eat yourself up alive."

In "I don't require it and don't beg uninvited," there is a more yielding attitude than in "He won't bother you, he won't/ be bothered." And, "Won't you be doleful when no one, no one! begs you" accurately indicates more sympathy with the girl's plight than the cold finality, "But you'll be, nights." "Morsel of lips" is etymologically related to "labella mordebis," even ef- fecting the same diminutive play: *labellum* ["little lips"]. And note how he catches the sweep of elision in "ibi illa" for "bil- lowed."

Thus we find that the earlier version is elegiac, tight-lipped, edgy, acrimonious, and tough, whereas the later version is polished, urbane, sophisticated, humane, and assured. Beyond these dif- ferences are of course the major technical approaches to the trans- lation. Do the later techniques of translating improve on the earlier? I think the answer is yes, because although the earlier ver- sion is a beautiful independent poem, still as *translation*, and all the qualities endeavored after in translation, the later version

---

6. Pronounce *ventitabas* with a Yiddish-German *W*,

ven ti ta bas
ven ta bou tit

has more to do with the original.

For Catullus' poem was not written in the actual bitterness of his final revulsion against Lesbia, but rather during what seemed to be a minor and temporary tiff, and the poem, while complaining of her coldness, does look forward to reconciliation, "and don't beg uninvited." We need only look at the real bitterness of his last poems to Lesbia to see that LZ has caught the correct mood and tone, "who'll see that you're lovely?" in this more genial and sunny later version.[7]

II Technique

That the Latin is absolutely essential to the text is a staunch tenet that LZ developed from studying Pound's translations. LZ was a very careful student of Pound's as Pound himself recognized; for example, when LZ sent *A Test of Poetry*[8] to him in 1954, Pound said, "Looks like he is following *ABC*."[9] LZ has brought up to date the translating techniques of the Renaissance and especially those of Chapman, e.g., LZ has projected new life into the elaborated conceit. Chapman changes a line of Homer [prose, "I am not yet practiced in clever speech, *Od*. iii, 320], into the involuted,[10]

> My youth by no means that ripe forme affords
> That can digest my mind's instinct in words
> Wise and beseeming th'ears of one so sage.

And similarly, notice how Zukofsky changes a line of Catullus, "Quae simul ac rostro ventosum proscidit aequor" [prose, "She at the same time ploughed the windy sea with her prow," LXIV], into "Wild sea mull ache rose throe wind tossing prow scudded ichor." Here "throe-wind tossing prow-scudded ichor" gives in imaginative but accurate paraphrase the meaning of the Latin [*ichor*, "humeur aqueuse"[11]]. And what is "Wild sea mull ache rose"? [*Mull*, "coastal headland"]. It is a beautiful concretized conceit of the emotional depiction of a stormy sea-scape upon a headland, that moves from the precise music of the line. And with this conceit he sets the tone for the entire poem.

---

7. Cf. *Catullus*, ed. Elmer Truesdell Merrill (1893; rpt. Cambridge: Harvard U.P., 1951), p. 17.
8. (New York: The Objectivist Press, 1948).
9. In conversation with the author in early September, 1954.
10. *Chapman's Homer*, ed. Allardyce Nicoll (London: Routledge & Kegan Paul, 1957), iii, p. 44.
11. Emile Boisacq, *Dictionnaire Etymologique de la Langue Grecque*, from the 2nd edition (Heidelberg: Carl Winter's, 1923).

Or LZ turns the line, "sed non videmus manticae quod in tergost" (XXII) into "nor do we see the knapsack on our back's the ghost." Here, after strictly rendering the meaning he lifts the whole poem by the conceit of the seeing, unseeable *ghost*. Or from, "qualis sit solet aes imaginosum" [prose: "(she never asks) the bronze mirror what she is like," XLI], LZ extends the amazing conceit, "What lies sit solid ice imagine o some"; or in "sidereal moult" (VII) from "sidera multa," the shedding off of stars as a chicken moults feathers.

And just as Chapman moralizes Homer, e.g., coining of Odysseus not wanting to bathe in the presence of Nausicaa's young women, "He taught these youths modestie by his aged judgement,"[12] LZ also had a curious moral feeling about Catullus; he remarked to me that he didn't want his translation to "titillate the passions."[13] But with his equally strong commitment to the integrity, music, meaning, even the breathing pattern of Catullus, what about the obscenity? The result is a careful transposing, sublimating, and uplifting into wit of all that is "titillating" by means of the most ingenious figures of speech; e.g., in the case of seeking something stronger than insults to use against a woman who has stolen his poems, "sed no est tamen hoc satis putandum" [prose, "But we must not think this is sufficient" XLII], LZ quips, "Say, there isn't a name chokes this pudendum." His outrageous Rabelaisian buffoonery is unfig-leaved wit which leaps on absolutely any innocent looking Latin word and commits logopoeic rape.[14]

III *Progression d'effet*

And in regard to the whole work of LZ's *Catullus*, there is a steady progression of effect in the translations that moves from the simple to the complex in style, in technique, in intellectual growth, and in verbal, musical and metrical brilliance. A gradual development in the techniques of the translation takes sensitive account of the emotional maturation in Catullus' poems themselves.[15] For example, in looking comparatively (in the manner of *ABC* and *Test*) at a few lines (a prose version is added in parenthesis),

---

12. Chapman, vi, p. 113.
13. On June 15, 1975 in Orono, Maine, at the Memorial celebration for Ezra Pound, organized by Carroll F. Terrell.
14. Cf. Burton Hatlen, "Catullus Metamorphosed," *Paideuma*, 7-3, p. 539.
15. Celia concurs with this position, "Correct, the carmina have the same increase in complexity." From a letter of March 2, 1979.

1

Whom do I give my neat little volume
slicked dry and made fashionable with pumice?

Cui dono lepidum novum libellum
arido modo pumice expolitum?

12

How spiced is your wit? Just fidgety—stupid?
qualmish, sordid and entirely wanting in taste.

hoc salsum esse putas? fugit te, inepte:
quamvis sordida res et invenustast.

("You consider this a good joke? It escapes you, dummy;
entirely an ill-bred thing and in the worst taste.")

14

how, why have I gone wrong, quipped what so luggish

nam quid feci ego quidve sum locutus,

("What have I done, or what have I said.")

22

Suffenus he's one Capricorn milked cuss, fusser,
rear sass of hate or ton of bore the hack mutates.

Suffenus unus caprimulgus aut fossor
rursus videtur: tantum abhorret ac mutat.

("Suffenus is only a goatherd or ditch-digger
to see him again, so outlandish and changed.")

28

Piso's own comates, his, corps an inane as
opt sad sarks—kin no less—'at's expedited!

Pisonis comites, cohors inanis
aptis sarcinulis et expeditis,

("You followers of Piso, a needy train
with ready baggage that is earily carried")

35

Poet I'm too near your and my sod daily—
well I'm, Caecilius, as this papyrus asks—

Poetae tenero, meo sodali
velim Caecilio, papyre, dicas

("Papyrus leaf, I want you to tell the tender
poet, my friend Caecillius")

37

Egnatius, opaque whim of bone and faked beard, and
Egnati, opaca quem bonum facit barba
("of Egnatius of whom a bushy beard made a gentlemen")

39

Egnatius, candid as his horse-bit white dentures,
grins right on, cocksure cockeye. Say a rare venting
sobselling counsel's oratory squeeze folk tears,
he'll grin right on.

Egnatius, quod candidos habet dente,
renidet usquequaque. si ad rei ventumst
subsellium, cum orator excitat fletum,
renidet ille.

("Egnatius, because he has white teeth
he smiles on every occasion. If he come
to the prisoner's bench, when counsel is making all cry,
he just smiles.")

44

ferret the freak
whose tongue wagged me to eat his glum liver logic

ferat frigus,
qui tunc vocat me, cum malum librum legi.

("let cold come to him
who invited me just when I'd read a stupid book.")

51

linked tongue set torpid, tenuous support a-
flame a day mown down, sound tone sopped up in its
tinkling, in ears hearing, twin eyes tug under
    luminous—a night.

lingua sed torpet, tenuis subartus
flamma demanat, sonitu suopte
tintinant aures, gemina teguntur
    lumina nocte.

("but the tongue becomes torpid, a slight
flame flows in my limbs, with their own sound
the ears tingle, and my eyes become covered
with darkness.)

54a

Irascibly iterating my iambics—
unmerited, unique eh—imperator.

Irascere iterum meis iambis
immerentibus, unice imperator.

("You will again be irascible at my innocent
iambs, you, our one and only general.")

63

Spurred altering wake toss Attis his craft racing till marled in the

Super alta vectus Attis celeri rate maria

("Carried in his fast ship over deep seas, Attis")

78

Gallus ha' but brothers: bro one's lady slip's make so young she's
all there i' this lap that feels—heir (whose) all that broth'r two has

Gallus habet fratres, quorumst lepidissima coniunx
    alterius, lepidus filius alterius.

("Gallus has two brothers; one has a very nice wife,
    the other a handsome son.")

85

O th' hate I move love. Quarry it fact I am, for that's so re queries

Odi et amo. quare id faciam, fortasse requiris.

("I hate and love. Perhaps you want to know why I do this.")

95

Purvey me my intimate's core, dear monument's all that there is,
    let th' populace (tumid or gaudy) eat Antimacho.

parva mei mihi sint cordi monumenta sodalis,
    at populus tumido gaudeat Antimacho.

("Let the small remembrances of a friend be important
to me, and let the populace enjoy the boastful Anticachus.")

112

Mool 'tis homos' Naso, 'n' queer take 'im mool tis ho most *he*
    descended: Naso, mool'tis—is it pathic, cuss.

Multus homo es, Naso, neque tecum multus homost qui
    descendit: Naso, multus es et pathicus.

("You are many men's Naso, but not many men
go to town with you Naso: you are many men's pathic.")

114

how coop he o many guineas, fishes, prod tract, arable, fur, ask we.

aucupia omne genus, piscis, prata, arva ferasque.

("All kinds of bird-catching, fish, pasture, corn-land and game")

Fragmenta 3.

—O—O O day my own liquor airing libido's.

—O—O O de meo ligurrire libidost.

("I would like to taste for my own reasons.")

[*NOTES*:] We see that he starts out in 1, with a "pure" translation. In 12, there is a more direct use of the Latin word which
keys the English play against it, "fidgety . . . qualmish." And in
14, a 17th century idiom, "luggish" ["miserly"] is used. In 22,
the word choice is much freer and there is a mixing of idioms,
"rear sass of hate," a person secretly spreading hatred. In 28, an
increased breaking up of, and placing of phrases that fit and rhyme
with the Latin but make inventions of the sense. Here we shall
find LZ's answer to Joyce's portmanteau word from *Finnegan's
Wake*. LZ builds in 35, his whole phrase upon the shifted meaning
of "sodali-sod daily" (antanaclasis). In 37, there is a more striking
and yet controlled use of Latin sound to invent an English coun-
terpart for the literal sense. But 39 offers a combination of a
straight translation along with a raucous echo of the Latin in
modern English slang to produce a law-court idiom. The invention
in 44 mixes modern with Elizabethan slang. In 51, there is a further development of the English short phrase given as a quasi-
etymological definition of the Latin word, "sound tone sopped up
in its/ tinkling." And LZ develops his use of the two-or-more-
word phrase as his molecular unit, in place of the word by itself.
In 63, the phrase is larger, more flexile, taking in a much larger
range of words and rhythms; he produces a floating and suspended
sense of movement which moves. Here is an interesting example of
the evolving of LZ's "asyndetic parataxis" (as William Ringler
used to call it), phrases placed together without any joining particles. Also interesting use of paratactic phrases in 64. In 78, the
sexual pun shows a continued development, ladyship-"lady slip's,"
in order to present the just overheard and breathily retailed bit of
gossip, interrupted to explain and include complications of a
tricky liaison. But 85 reveals epigrammatic tightness, density
("quarry" ["to dig stone"]); power-punch without losing creative
freedom. In 95, we meet an especially successful bringing together
of a number of these techniques, the finely balanced and cadenced
emotion, and yet with no subsiding of his logopoeic inventiveness.
In 112, the play on "mool" ["grave"], "homos" ["humus"], and
"ho" ["heel"], transmogrifies the Latin and seems to comment on

the "Hades" of *Ulysses*. Fragmenta 3, a further unfolding of cantabile vowel-leading. Thus *Catullus* manifests a technical *tour de force* that recalls the "progression of styles" Joyce used in his own particular way in *Ulysses*, and Pound, in his, in the "ordering of the resources of English poetry," in his Confucian *Odes*.[16]

---

16. Hugh Kenner has made this amazing observation in both cases. See his *Dublin's Joyce* (London, 1956; rpt. Boston: Beacon, 1962), pp. 242 ff. And his *Gnomon* (New York: Obolensky Inc., 1958), pp. 97 ff. And see his remarks on style in *Joyce's Voices* (U. of Cal. Press, 1978), pp. 73, 77, 79, 84.

THE TESTAMENT

L.Z.'s desk, Port Jefferson, N.Y., Aug., 25, 1978
(Photo by Fred Siegel)

CELIA ZUKOFSKY

*YEAR BY YEAR BIBLIOGRAPHY OF LOUIS ZUKOFSKY**

1922

(poetry)   Vast, tremulous (used in 'A'-18).

1923

(poetry)   tam cari capitis.

1924

(poetry)   Not much more than being; Tall and singularly dark you pass among the breakers - ; Millenium of sun; Cars once steel and green, now old.

(prose)   Henry Adams: A Criticism in Autobiography (original version).

1925

(poetry)   Close your eyes; Aubade, 1925; Ferry; And looking to where shone Orion; O sleep, the sky goes down behind the poplars; Memory of V.I. Ulianov; Passing tall; Run on, you still dead to the sound of a name.

1926

(poetry)   Poem beginning 'The'; Like the oceans, or the leaves of fine Southern; Only water; We are crossing the bridge now; How many / Times round; Stubbing the cloud-fields — the searchlight, high; During the Passaic Strike of 1926.

1927

(poetry)   A dying away as of trees; Song Theme.

1928

(poetry)   Blue light is the night harbor-slip; Ask of the sun; Buoy — no, how; Cactus rose-mauve and gray, twin overturned; And to paradise which is a port; Cocktails; 'A'-1, 2, 3, 4 (original versions); 'A'-7 (begun).

*From *A Bibliography of Louis Zukofsky* by Celia Zukofsky, Black Sparrow Press, Los Angeles, 1969. Supplemented by additions of works from 1967-1978.

1928

(prose)　　Henry Adams: A Criticism in Autobiography (additions); Beginning Again with William Carlos Williams (postscript to Henry Adams).

1929

(poetry)　　Two Dedications.

(prose)　　Henry Adams: A Criticism in Autobiography (*Hound & Horn* version); Ezra Pound: His Cantos (original version).

1930

(poetry)　　'A'-5, 6 (*An "Objectivists" Anthology* version); 'A'-7 (completed *An "Objectivists" Anthology* version.

(prose)　　Sincerity and Objectification I-V; American Poetry 1920-1930; Review of R. Taupin's *L'Influence du Symbolisme sur la Poésie Américaine de 1910 à 1920* (used in *Prepositions*).

1931

(poetry)　　Prop. LXI; Train-Signal; Madison, Wis.; Happier, happier, now; her soil's birth; Immature Pebbles; *An "Objectivists" Anthology* (collated).

(prose)　　Program: "Objectivists" 1931; Recencies in Poetry (both used in *Prepositions*).

1932

(poetry)　　To my wash-stand; in that this happening; It's a gay li-ife; No One Inn; Imitation; Who endure days like this; The sand; For the cigarette finished; The mirror oval sabres; Do not leave me; Crickets / thickets; Ears beringed with fuzz; In Arizona; Snows' night's winds; Whatever makes this happening; Arizona.

(prose)　　Thanks to the Dictionary (appears in *It was*); The Writing of Guillaume Apollinaire (original English version of *Le Style Apollinaire*).

1933

(poetry)　　Song 3/4 time; A Junction; Home For Aged Bomb Throwers; Checkers, checkmate and checkerboard; This Fall, 1933; N.Y.

1934

(poetry) Mantis; Specifically, a writer of music; The Immediate Aim; Alba (original version of Alba, 1952).

1935

(poetry) Further than; A madrigal for 3 voices; 'A'-8 (begun).

(prose) *A Test of Poetry* (begun); Review of Lewis Carroll's *Russian Journal* (used in *Prepositions*).

1936

(poetry) *Arise, Arise* — A Play in Two Acts (original version).

(prose) *A Test of Poetry* (cont.); Modern Times (used in *Prepositions*).

1937

(poetry) Che di lor suona su nella tua vita; The green plant grows; One lutenist played look; Motet; 'A'-8 (revised and completed).

(prose) *A Test of Poetry* (cont.).

1938

(poetry) Glad they were there; So sounds grass; For you I have emptied the meaning; Anew, sun, to fire summer; Ah spring; When the crickets; Has the sum; What are these songs; 'A'-9, first half (begun).

(prose) *A Test of Poetry* (cont.); "aids" and restatement for 'A'-9 (begun).

1939

(poetry) Drive, fast kisses; Catullus 8; A last cigarette; Gulls over a rotting hull; My nephew; The rains, the rains; The men in the kitchens; The lines of this new song are nothing.

(prose) *A Test of Poetry* (cont.); "aids" and restatement for *First Half of 'A'-9* (completed); Henry Adams (revised); Ezra Pound: His Cantos (revised); Preface to Sincerity and Objectification (used in prefatory note in *Prepositions*). N.B. Sincerity and Objectification, once intended as the title of a book, was (with omissions) later absorbed in *Prepositions*.

1940

(poetry) The bird that cries like a baby; The world autumn; Light 2 and 15; Light 11 (original version); 'A'-9, first half (completed); 'A'-10; Arise, Arise (revised).

(prose) *A Test of Poetry* (completed); Ferdinand (begun).

1941

(poetry) No it was no dream of coming death; Strange; 1892-1941; And so till we have died; In the midst of things; Guillaume de Machault; Belly Locks Shnooks Oakie; Light 6, 8, 9, 10, 13, 14; Light 11 (revised).

(prose) Ferdinand (cont.); It was; A Keystone Comedy (later collected in *It was*).

1942

(poetry) One oak fool box; Celia's birthday poem; Or a Valentine; Can a mote of sunlight; One friend; In the midst of things (revised); A marriage song; 'A' 1-6 (revised).

(prose) Ferdinand (completed); Dometer Guczul (used in *Prepositions*).

1943

(poetry) You three; After Charles Sedley; To my baby Paul; Light 3, 5, 7, 12.

(prose) Basic (used in *Prepositions*).

1944

(poetry) It's hard to see but think of a sea; for Zadkine; The Letter of Poor Birds; I walk in the old street; Even if love convey; Sequence 1; Light 1.

1945

(poetry) A Song For The Year's End 1, 2; Light 4; Sequence 2, 3, 4 (original versions).

1946

(poetry) A Song For The Year's End 3; Sequence 5.

(prose) Poetry / For My Son When He Can Read (used in *Prepositions*).

1947

(poetry) Sequence 2, 3, 4 (revised); Michtam 1; que j'ay dit devant.

(prose) *Bottom: on Shakespeare* (begun).

1948

(poetry) So That Even A Lover; Light 1-15 (order of poems arranged); Michtam 2, 3; 'A'-9, second half (begun).

(prose) An Old Note on William Carlos Williams (used in *Prepositions*); The Case of Ezra Pound (used in *Prepositions* as Work / Sundown); *Bottom: on Shakespeare* (cont.).

1949

(poetry) Chloride of Lime and Charcoal; Non Ti Fidar; Xenophanes; Some time has gone.

(prose) *Bottom: on Shakespeare* (cont.).

1950

(poetry) Reading and Talking; As To How Much; Air; Perch Less; And Without; George Washington; 'A'-9, second half (completed); 'A'-11; 'A'-12 (begun).

(prose) Review of V. Koch's *William Carlos Williams* (see 1948 item on W.C. Williams); Little Baron Snorck, chapters 1-8 (later entitled *Little*); A Statement for Poetry (used in *Prepositions*); *Bottom: on Shakespeare* (cont.).

1951

(poetry) To My Valentines; Pamphylian; 'A'-12 (completed).

(prose) Review of G. Santayana's *Dominations and Powers* (used in *Prepositions*); *Bottom: on Shakespeare* (cont.).

1952

(poetry) Spook's Sabbath; Alba (1952); On Valentine's Day To Friends; Old.

(prose) *Bottom: on Shakespeare* (cont.).

1953

(poetry) The Judge and The Bird; All of December Toward New Year's; Songs of Degrees 1, 2; Songs of Degrees 3 (original version); For Selma Gubin's Umbrellas; All Wise; H.T.

(prose) *Bottom: on Shakespeare* (cont.).

1954

(poetry) Songs of Degrees 4, 5.

1954

(prose)   *Bottom: on Shakespeare* (cont.).

1955

(poetry)   Songs of Degrees 3 (revised); Songs of Degrees 6, 7; The Guests; Claims; The Laws Can Say; An Incident; Shang Cup.

(prose)   *Bottom: on Shakespeare* (cont.).

1956

(poetry)   The Record; This is after all vacation; *Barely | and | Widely | love.*

(prose)   *Bottom: on Shakespeare* (cont.).

1957

(poetry)   Stratford-on-Avon; The heights; The green leaf; A Valentine; Send regards; 4 Other Countries (begun).

(prose)   *Bottom: on Shakespeare* (cont.).

1958

(poetry)   4 Other Countries (completed); This year; Ashtray; Another Ashtray; Head lines; Catullus 1, 2, 2a, 3, 4, 5.

(prose)   A Citation (used in *Prepositions*); Foreword (used in prefatory note to *Prepositions*); *Bottom: on Shakespeare* (cont.).

1959

(poetry)   Homage; Her face the book; Hill; 1959 Valentine; Wire; Jaunt; Peri Poietikes; I's; To Friends, For Good Health.

(prose)   Little Baron Snorck (outline, chapters 9-35); *Bottom: on Shakespeare* (cont.).

1960

(poetry)   I's (Azure); (Ryokan's scroll); 'A'-13 partita; Catullus 6-9.

(prose)   *Bottom: on Shakespeare* (completed).

1961

(poetry)   Daruma; Catullus 10-17, 21-50.

(prose)   Bottom, A Weaver (used in *Prepositions*); Translators' Preface to Catullus.

1962

(poetry)   The Old Poet; Atque in Perpetuum; The / desire / of / towing; Pretty; The Ways; Catullus 51-63, 65.

(prose)   Prefatory Note to *Prepositions* (revised); Found Objects (1962-1926) (used in *Prepositions*).

1963

(poetry)   Finally a valentine; Catullus 66-69; 'A'-16, 17, 20; After reading, a song.

(prose)   Beginning Again with William Carlos Williams (final version as used in *Prepositions*).

1964

(poetry)   Catullus 70-80; The translation; 'A'-14, 15; 'A'-18 (begun); 'A' Libretto.

(prose)   The 'Form' of 'A'-9; (revision of *First Half of 'A'-9*, 1940).

1965

(poetry)   Catullus 81-116; Catullus fragmenta; Catullus 64 (begun); 'A'-18 (cont.); 'A'-19 (begun).

(prose)   Pronounced Golgonooz̀a? (used in *Prepositions*), Henry Adams (final version as used in *Prepositions*); Prefatory Note to *Prepositions* (final version).

1966

(poetry)   Catullus 64 (completed); 'A'-18, 19 (both completed); 'A'-21 (begun).

1967

(poetry)   'A' / Cantata; 'A'-21 (completed).

(prose)   Foreword / 'A' (to Paris Review Edition of 'A' 1-12; *Little* (chapters 1-8, revised); *Little*, chapter 9; *Little*, chapter 10 (begun).

1968

(poetry)   Preface to *L.Z. Masque* ('A'-24).

(prose)   *Little*, chapter 10 (completed); *Little*, chapters 11-27.

1969

(poetry)   Prefact to *L.Z. Masque* ('A'-24) (revised).

(prose)   *Autobiography* ms. arranged; *Little*, chapters 28-35; "To Daryl Hine for Nov. 1969 *Poetry* for Henry Rago."

1970

(poetry)   AN ERA / ANY TIME / OF YEAR ('A'-22); *Initial*
                ('A'-22).

(prose)   Introduction to L.Z. reading from *Little* for "Spoken
                Word Program" of Radio Station WNYC-FM, N.Y.C.,
                Sept. 15, 1970; Corrections of the unauthorized pub-
                lication of *The Gas Age*; Foreword to *'A' 1-12*,
                Doubleday/Paris Review Edition (revised).

1971

(prose)   Notes for Wallace Stevens Memorial Lecture delivered
                at Univ. of Conn., Storrs, 4/29/71; Taped lecture
                transcribed and revisions made for printed text.

1972

(poetry)   'A'-22.

1973

(poetry)   'A'-22 (completed), 'A'-23 (begun).

1974

(poetry)   'A'-23 (completed); *80 flowers* (begun).

1975

(poetry)   *80 flowers* 1-23.

1976

(poetry)   *80 flowers* 24-50; Index of Names and Objects to
                'A' 1-24; Index to Prepositions.

1977

(poetry)   *80 flowers* 51-77.

1978

(poetry)   *80 flowers* 78-80; *Gamut: 90 trees* (begun).

(poetry)   *"A,"* University of California Press. The complete
                poem.

(poetry)   *80 flowers*, special limited edition of 80 copies.

MARCELLA BOOTH

THE ZUKOFSKY PAPERS: THE CADENCE OF A LIFE

> Each writer
> writes one long work. . . .
> . . . Recurrences
> follow him, crib and drink from a
> well that's his cadence.[1]

Since 1961 the Humanities Research Center at The University of Texas at Austin has been acquiring the papers of Louis Zukofsky. In 1969 when I catalogued this collection there were manuscripts for the following items: 17 books of poems including 2 unpublished volumes, *The First Seasons* and *The First Book*; 2 collections of translations and adaptations; 238 published poems; 14 unpublished ones; 6 books of criticism; 32 essays and reviews; 3 novels; 2 short stories; 2 dramas. In all, more than 12,000 pages of manuscripts for all Zukofsky's published and unpublished works from 1920 through 1968.[2] In addition there were numerous miscellaneous manuscripts: bibliographical lists, his work in the 1930's for the Index of American Design, Zukofsky's proposed works, his readings, and others, such as notes on poetics and the English translation of Ives Tinayre's French parables. Also included in the collection were 468 items of correspondence to Cid Corman, Edward Dahlberg, Ian Hamilton Finlay, James Joyce, Ezra Pound, William Carlos Williams and others. The largest, most informative file in the correspondence contained letters to Lorine

---

1. Zukofsky, *"A"* (Berkeley, University of California Press, 1978), p. 214.
2. Marcella Booth, *A Catalogue of the Louis Zukofsky Manuscript Collection* (Austin, Humanities Research Center, The University of Texas, 1975) gives a complete description of each of these manuscripts. The Catalogue, hereafter cited as *LZ Catalogue*, traces the development of Zukofsky's works by following them in the manuscripts from earliest versions through revisions and final printings. The miscellaneous manuscripts and the Zukofsky letters listed below are also described in *LZ Catalogue.*

Niedecker written over a period of 30 years.[3]

Celia Zukofsky continues to send her husband's papers to Texas: manuscripts for *"A"-22*, *"A"-24*; *A Bibliography of L.Z.* (Black Sparrow Press); *Little*; performance materials (*Autobiography* performance by Metropolitan Opera Studio, March 31, 1971; *Arise, Arise* performance at Cinemateque Theatre, New York City, Aug. 6-27, 1965); and miscellaneous items: readings, tapes, letters, notes, and photographs.[4] When Celia adds the residual manuscripts now in her care to the collection, the record will be complete; but there is already enough material, 60 years of life and letters stuffed into cardboard boxes, to keep critics of poetry busy well into the next century.

The extensive collection is a valuable source for scholars not simply because of its size (all of Zukofsky's major works are represented by a series of manuscripts), but also because the papers are carefully crafted and heavily annotated. The poet's habit of listing sources, his numerous drafts, his tendency to revise in various shades of ink and pencil, dating each revision, all enable the critic to read in graphic form the progress of a life's work.

Sometimes a single manuscript reveals years of that work. Two examples are the earliest notes and outline for *"A" 1-24* and the plan for "An Alphabet of Subjects" in *Bottom: on Shakespeare*. The back and front of each of the manuscripts and all margins are completely filled with Zukofsky's very small handwriting; words are crowded into every available space. Different colored ink and pencilled notations indicate that Zukofsky came back to each manuscript time after time, jotting down ideas as his thought developed. The poet describes such manuscripts as these in *"A"-12*: "Much of it in pencil—blurred—other / notes written over it./ I can't read back thru the years."[5]

But the critic who examines the collection will find that Zukofsky has so crafted his papers that one can indeed read back through the years. There are over 50 years of *"A"* to be read: sixty separate manuscripts—the earliest notes and those that followed, the many drafts and revisions, plus the numerous manuscripts for the separate and collected printings of the various movements.[6]

---

3. The number of LZ letters to Lorine Niedecker can not be determined because she has censored the letters by cutting them into fragments. When there is no date, the letter is identified by fragment and folder numbers.
4. Listed in a letter to me from Celia Zukofsky, 6 June 1979.
5. *"A,"* p. 251.
6. This count does not include the manuscripts added to the collection after it was catalogued.

There are 20 years of *Bottom*: thirty separate manuscripts which include preparatory notes, early holograph notes in spiral notebooks, various typescripts with their revisions, and the final master copy. There are also galleys, page proofs, and layouts of the book. Forty years of additional criticism can be read in the manuscripts for *Prepositions*. These manuscripts coupled with the analysis of writers and literature that are in the 44 years of Zukofsky letters make up a literary history of the modern movement in poetry.

Individual poems are also well represented in the collection. Zukofsky spent only 2 years on the title poem I'S (PRONOUNCED *EYES*),[7] but the 82 manuscripts for the single poem indicate that he labored longer over determining the sequence of its eleven stanzas than he did over the arrangement of all the poems he included in the book *I's (Pronounced Eyes)*. He first wrote these stanzas as separate poems, then experimented with various sequences, and finally decided on the published version.

As the critic reads back through the years, he will begin to see certain patterns in the work. For example, Zukofsky follows the same process of combining separate poems into one poem in the manuscripts for the volume *Some Time*. The stanzas or sections of the poems SEQUENCE 1944-6, LIGHT, QUE J'AY DIT DEVANT, and MICHTAM were first written as individual poems before they were published under their subsequent titles. He explains the process of making a new form from several existing ones as follows: "A later poem sparked a new form in which I saw the reason for the miscellany that had preceded, and which I might have otherwise discarded."[8]

The manuscripts indicate that Zukofsky is not content until the one form which is organic to the work shows itself to his awareness. Certain that the form "is in germ in the first words," and that it is "indeed compelled by all the words of the poem," he will deliberate for years, quite patiently letting the work progress until the form comes of itself.[9]

The poem LIGHT, made up of fifteen stanzas first written as separate poems, shows his refusal to hurry the process. LIGHT 2, 11 (original version), and 15 were written in 1940; LIGHT 6, 8, 9, 10, 11 (revised), 13, and 14 in 1941; LIGHT 3, 5, 7, 12 in 1943; LIGHT 1 in 1944; LIGHT 4 in 1948. Celia Zukofsky

---

7. Zukofsky's practice of capitalizing poem titles is followed throughout the text.
8. Quoted in a letter to me from Celia Zukofsky, 13 February 1969.
9. *Prepositions: The Collected Critical Essays of Louis Zukofsky* (New York, 1968), p. 17.

indicates in a letter to me dated 13 February 1969, that it was LIGHT 1 in 1944 that prompted Zukofsky's vision of the final poem. Autograph notes on the manuscripts indicate, however, that the order of the poems was not determined until 1948. If Zukofsky's practice in other manuscripts (those for *"A,"* for example) is any indication, he was quite capable of holding the form in his head from 1944 when LIGHT 1 was written to 1948 when LIGHT 4 was written and the final order was recorded.

The same patience that centers on a concern for form can be traced in the prose. For example, three earlier essays are revised and combined under one title, "William Carlos Williams," for publication in *Prepositions.* "William Carlos Williams. A Citation," written in 1958 is Part I of the new essay; "An Old Note on William Carlos Williams," written in 1948 is Part II; and "Beginning Again with William Carlos Williams," written in 1923, is Part III.[10] By combining and condensing the separate works, and by reversing their chronology, Zukofsky works backward to the original insight. The new form gives time new direction, and thus brings into Zukofsky's prose what had become in *"A,"* Pound's *Cantos,* and Williams' *Paterson* an ordering principle for personal epic: the treatment of time as that "instant which is a complex large enough to include past and present and even indicate further direction.[11]

The manuscripts of *"A"* give the most sustained account of the struggle for form. Zukofsky began the poem in 1926 right after he had finished THE. Then, with two years work (a single manuscript attesting to the intensity of the effort),[12] he had the design that he would hold in his mind for 50 years as he committed the parts of that design to paper. The early *"A"* 1-4 was finished by 1928. *"A"* 1-7 was completed the summer of 1930, revised in 1940, the revisions mostly in the form of cuts. The fact that Zukofsky worked the poem in blocks, *"A"* 1-4, then *"A"* 1-7, suggests that the single movements were always in a sense both prompted and controlled by the larger design. The manuscripts reveal his struggle for the form of each movement, but that struggle was always governed by an awareness of what the longer form *"A" 1-24* demanded.

The dates of the manuscripts are important because they

10. The descriptions above of the manuscripts for the Williams essay, the sequence poems in *Some Time,* and the poem I'S (PRONOUNCED *EYES*) were first published in Marcella Spann, "The Zukofsky Papers," *The Library Chronicle of The University of Texas at Austin* (November, 1970), pp. 54-55.
11. Zukofsky, "A Draft of XXX Cantos by Ezra Pound," *Front* 4 (June 1931), p. 365.
12. The earliest notes and outline for "A." See *LZ Catalogue,* p. 38.

allow the scholar to reconstruct the creative process. He can observe Zukofsky's focus on detail, he can trace his construction of a single movement, and he can follow the poet working backward and forward as Zukofsky fits the movements into a larger design.

The manuscripts for "A"-8 and "A"-9 show the poet's attention fixed on sound. Zukofsky begins by marking the r and n sounds in his drafts of "A"-8, studies the way they fall into pattern naturally from his own voice, and then writes the ending of "A"-8 by mathematical formula: the r and n sounds are arithmetically precise, there are more diagrams and equations for "A"-9; Zukofsky then constructs the five strophes of "A"-9 by formula; that is, the ratio of the two sounds (r, n) are functions of coordinates (x, y) moving on a circular path.[13]

After observing this kind of attention to detail, the researcher can trace the progress of a single movement. The dates reveal that there were seven years after "A"-7 before "A"-8 was written. Of course time was needed for the necessary research of the subject matter (a list of sources on the manuscripts often indicate the nature of the research), but a major effort was obviously the working out of the form. In a letter to Lorine Niedecker dated 28 January 1937, Zukofsky explains the musical form of "A"-8 which gives "the effect of a 'mirror' figue"; that is, the poem divides into two parts (two fugues), "each of a pair (of fugues) being the exact inversion of the other, as if it were seen in a mirror." He goes on to give an account of the composition:

> But I'd be crazy & chust superhuman if I sat down to figger out an exact order of the materials going up to make up each fugue, because fugues in words don't really exist, because all the words go in one order—give one melodic line & can only suggest others between the lines going on at the same time, while in music you can & do have 2 or 3 or 4 melodies (voices) going on at the same time. So as I said—I've let the intensity with which I've felt the material determine its order & the *effect* or *suggestion* is something like a mirror fugue in this section.

Zukofsky then explains the contribution of detail to form:

> I hope this will make the whole easier to read and show the real meaning of the detail (as part of the music, the general occupation). Otherwise of course I mean the detail—the facts said in 'em —to be very clear, very simple, even obvious, & let the emotion of the whole carry 'em. . . . Not that each fact follows out of the previous—obviously from my musical order that wdn't be the case, but there is always some suggestion of one fact that

13. For more detail, see *LZ Catalogue*, pp. 53-54.

> prompted the next to come into the order, i.e., the "transition"
> from *so the green mold grew* to the green, yellow of Peter's gar-
> den. And that's sumpin like good orchestration—displaying all
> your timbres, sound capacity of various instruments but gradu-
> ating your passing from one instrument to another or bringing
> out a dissonance—& I do that both by suggestion of individual
> sounds & groups of 'em and single images & (star) clusters of
> 'em.[14]

Such explanation adds a good deal of meaning to Zukofsky's
"Impossible to communicate anything but particulars."[15]

Zukofsky's concentration on technique and form placed him
in the main stream of what Pound termed the new poetry. And
Zukofsky, like Pound, pushed the known techniques and the new
discoveries (they might term them rediscoveries) to their limits in
the most demanding form in the movement, the long epic poem.
An aside that I witnessed in Washington D.C. in 1958 might *hint*
at the nature of the accomplishment; at least, it registers one
man's awareness that such accomplishment is significant. When
Ezra Pound was released from Saint Elizabeths Hospital after
twelve and a half years, he was asked by a reporter about Frost's
efforts on his behalf. Pound replied: "He ain't been in much of a
hurry." The press pounced on this criticism of Frost, but I remember a more telling criticism given on the same occasion. The reporter, aware that it was Pound who managed to get Frost's first
book published in England, tried to get an evaluation of Frost's
more recent work. Not receiving the quotable answer he was
hoping for, the reporter pressed the point with the suggestion that
Frost's continued success, which overshadowed Pound's, perhaps
indicated that Frost was the better poet. Pound's only reply was
"He didn't write a long poem."

Zukofsky did write a long poem, and in *"A,"* as in Pound's
Cantos, the classic matter of the epic is assimilated into new
poetic creation in a prodigious major work that required the effort of a lifetime.

The new poetry held firmly to the cannon that "all new subject matter is ineluctably simultaneous with 'what has gone before.' "[16] Its practitioner, therefore, would have to be a critic as
well as a poet. The critic/poet would determine the nature of what
had gone before; the poet/critic would present the past as present
experience. Zukofsky saw early the necessity of dual awareness:

14. This excerpt and the one above from LZ letter to Niedecker were first printed in
Library Chronicle, pp. 52-53.
15. *Prepositions*, p. 24.
16. *Prepositions*, p. 71.

"a critic began as a poet, and that as a poet he had implicitly to be a critic."[17]

In *Prepositions*, Zukofsky's collected criticism, he gives us his definitions for "pure poetry." The prose definitions have the same source as his poetry, "a poetically charged mentality."[18] It is this kind of mind, with its two-fold vision, that makes the papers at Texas such a valuable collection. The critic's eye is always governing the poet's hand; and the poet's eye, the critic's hand. The craft in the manuscripts and the lengthy explanation of that craft in Zukofsky's letters give us an unpublished treatise on poetry. Zukofsky's published work gives us the poet's form, and this is the form he wants read; but critic that he is, he carefully preserved the papers that give another form—the form that led to the poetry. Zukofsky would approve the reading of that form as well. As he said in another context, "The omissions are part of the poem."[19] There are quite a few omissions to be read in the manuscripts of a poet who believed that "Condensation is more than half of composition."[20]

Ezra Pound, known for his ability to spot talent early, was one of the first to recognize Zukofsky as both poet and critic. In 1928, he published Zukofsky's poems in *Exile 3* and *Exile 4*. A few years later, he was made aware of Zukofsky's skill as a critic. The younger poet's article in *The Criterion* on the early *Cantos* showed he had understood what Pound was about long before other critics had done so. Pound, who thought one ought to read poetry for oneself, complained that his critic had told too much. Zukofsky gives this account to Lorine Niedecker:

> I think I did the E.P Criterion . . . to surprise a friend. He wuz so stunned someone shd. have fathomed him—when I saw him in 1933 he still thought—& said sadly—"you told the public too much."[21]

Pound had obviously taken the young man's measure when he gave the beginning poet the advice about writing that Zukofsky would remember all his life: "Look into thine own ear and read." Louis could be trusted to look until he had caught the cadence of a life: "If my poems are worth anything, they are my biography."[22] He could also be trusted to recognize *poems* as an

---

17. *Prepositions*, p. 22.
18. *Prepositions*, p. 22.
19. See *LZ Catalogue*, p. 190.
20. Zukofsky, *A Test of Poetry* (New York, Jargon/Corinth, 1964), p. 81.
21. Fragment #199; no date given.
22. In a letter to Jessie McGuffie, 24 February 1962. See *Library Chronicle*, pp. 58-59, and *LZ Catalogue*, Letter Section, pp. 233-248 for an indication of the biographical information to be found in the Zukofsky Collection.

inclusive term. The word *craft* holds in it the meaning of a company of practitioners, the guild. Zukofsky has said of literature that it "is in a way another's account / Which if I can carry / May add up to my own."[23]

The serious writer will always concern himself with determining where he stands in the literary tradition that has passed into his care, and Zukofsky's manuscripts and letters show him searching that tradition for his place in it. His mind ranged freely from Homer to Shakespeare to Catullus to Pound. He would compare Lorine Niedecker's verse with Emily Dickinson's. He would place such disparate writers as Henry Adams and William Carlos Williams side by side and see connection. He would go from Whittier to the Beats, and then back to Whitman. And he would always see his work in relation. His papers show him to be the kind of writer Henry James extols, one of those people "on whom nothing is lost."[24] In fact Louis Zukofsky's published works and the manuscripts behind them might very well be viewed in much the same light as James' novels and his prefaces that elaborate those novels. One man's work gave us the art of fiction; the other gives us the art of poetry.

---

23. *"A,"* p. 238.
24. Henry James, "The Art of Fiction" in *The Writer's Craft* edited by John Hersey (New York, Alfred A. Knopf, 1974), p. 20.

CARROLL F. TERRELL

A BIBLIOGRAPHY OF WORKS ABOUT
LOUIS ZUKOFSKY WITH EXTENDED COMMENTARY

The bibliography given here lists all of the significant writings about Louis Zukofsky and his work which have appeared since WW II. The title was contrived to suggest its function in this book, which makes it different from an ordinary checklist. The annotations are extended (1) if the subject matter has not been treated elsewhere in the book at sufficient length or (2) if the article is both valuable and difficult to obtain. For instance, the best collection of exegetical materials available is *MAPS*, No. 5, 1973, edited by John Taggart. Since *MAPS* is out of print and extremely rare, I have given more lengthy summaries of the pieces from it, particularly if they have dealt with subjects not treated elsewhere.

The basic work for the bibliography was done by Winifred Hayek, a Master's degree candidate in English at the University of Maine at Orono. Miss Hayek did all the time-consuming search for the materials and produced an alphabetical listing of everything written about Zukofsky since WW II. She read most of the articles and wrote brief annotations for many of them; for the dissertations listed, she summarized what was given in *Dissertation Abstracts*. When her work has been adequate for the book's design, I have used the prose she gave me followed by her initials in brackets: [WH].

The bibliography has been organized and numbered, *seriatim*, according to the date that the critical pieces appeared, beginning with the knowledgeable piece by Lorine Niedecker in 1956 and ending with the contents of the memorial number of *Paideuma* (Vol. 7, No. 3), Winter, 1978. If a date is ambiguous (that is designated roughly as Spring, Fall, etc.), the order has been first topicality or failing that alphabetical. Each of the items treated has been numbered for easier reference. The work has been preceded by an index alphabetized by author and followed by the number of the item.

‡‡‡‡‡‡

‡‡‡‡‡‡

1. Niedecker, Lorine. "The Poetry of Louis Zukofsky." *Quarterly Review of Literature*, 8 (April, 1956), pp. 198-210.

   Lorine Niedecker, a major poet of the Zukofsky school herself, is inclined to let the poetry speak for itself. She quotes extensively until a general overview of some key characteristics of *"A" 1-12, 55 Poems*, and *Anew* evolves. Niedecker feels *"A"* moves out of the time framework of most poems: "As the world continues, the poem is whirled into liveforever." She quotes short passages from different movements of *"A"* and then focuses more closely on the themes of *"A"*-8, the canzone form of *"A"*-9, the historical subjects of *"A"*-10, and the tone of *"A"*-11. The cyclical form of most of *55 Poems* is stressed, as is the personal tone of the works in *Anew*.

2. Rexroth, Kenneth. "From the Past, Two Familiar Voices." *New York Times Book Review*, July 28, 1957, p. 5.

   In this review of *Some Time*, Rexroth finds Zukofsky to be one of the most important, mainstream poets of the 20th century. "Actually, Zukofsky's style is part of a worldwide movement of anti-Symbolism." Most of the poems here, except the one or two "best described as knotty, gnarled epic-elegies of the mind struggling with reality," are "exercises in absolute clarification, crystal cabinets full of air and angels."

3. Beum, Robert. "Epic and Lyric." *Poetry*, 91, No. 4 (Jan., 1958), pp. 266-68.

   Includes a review of Zukofsky's *Some Time* in which Beum is struck by "the superiority, with very few exceptions, of the later to the earlier lyrics." He finds that the poems have "become clearer and above all more musical" and that "Williams and Pound alone . . . have a surer ear."

4. Williams, William Carlos, intro. *"A" 1-12*. Kyoto, Japan: Origin Press, 1958.

   An informed and perceptive end-note to this first collection of the first twelve movements of *"A"* by one who followed Zukofsky's work more closely and intimately as a friend than anyone else. He explains how for years Zukofsky's poetry seemed difficult because he tried to read him as an Imagist: "Intent on the portrayal of a visual image in a poem my perception has been thrown frequently out of gear. I was looking for the wrong things. The poems whatever else they are are grammatical units intent on making a meaning *unrelated* to a mere pictorial image."

5. Levertov, Denise. "A Necessary Poetry." *Poetry*, 97, No. 2 (Nov., 1960), pp. 102-09.

> In this review of *"A" 1-12*, Levertov cites the several points WCW makes in his end-note to the collection and quotes from the work to show that Williams is correct: "In reading Zukofsky, then, we must try to avoid taking the visual image on its face value, or demanding of it a sensuous richness he is rarely concerned to give it; we must try to awaken our own intelligence to follow the intricacy of his thoughts . . . ." Levertov admires much about the book but has some reservations: "Of his craft in total construction I am less sure . . . . I don't see in it the architechtural strength of, say, *Paterson*." She also finds some sections of the poem too dense—in fact "impenetrable." But "these objections or doubts are relatively minor."

6. Stafford, William. From "Touching Sacred Objects." *Poetry*, 102, No. 2 (May, 1963), pp. 117-18.

> Includes a review of *16 Once Published*. Stafford finds the book "elegant" in design. "The poems live by a constant intention—a readiness to be rapt about small experiences and their finest, remotest effects."

7. Rich, Adrienne. "Beyond the Heirlooms of Tradition." *Poetry*, 105, No. 2 (Nov., 1964), pp. 128-29.

> A review of *Found Objects*, which the author finds contains poems that are "delicate" but "often labored." The poet "brings to the battle some inherited stratagems of Pound (heavy use of allusion and quotation) and Williams (a short breath-phrased line, too often here a one-word line)." Much of the review concerns *Mantis*, which Rich finds is "an interesting study of one deliberately consciously avant-garde poet's pain and concern with the possible limitations of *two* traditions": the European and the American.

8. Clark, Thomas. "Zukofsky's *All*." *Poetry*, 107, No. 1 (Oct., 1965), pp. 55-59.

> In this review of *All: The Collected Shorter Poems, 1923-1958*, published by W.W. Norton, Clark finds the *melody* of the pieces the most striking thing to mention. "In the more extended pieces the counterpoint of ear and mind by 'imitation' (as Zukofsky explains the term as title of one poem— 'the repetition of a phrase or subject in another voice-part or in a different key') enacts the odd weaving effect to be found also in parts of *'A.'*" Clark isolates "Mantis" and "4 Other Countries" for special comment. "If . . . Zukofsky's poems are musical

in the sense Mallarmé's poems are . . . by the solidity of their contact
. . . they also return again not to history but to human space: the *now*
of the senses gives intelligent presence."

9. Creeley, Robert. ". . . Paradise/our/speech . . . ." *Poetry*, 107,
No. 1 (Oct., 1965), pp. 52-55.

A review of W.W. Norton's collection, *All,* in which Creeley quotes to
illustrate some of the most significant nuances of Zukofsky's music.
He says of the poet: "It is his belief that a poet writes one poem all
his life, a continuing *song,* so that no division of its own existence can
be thought of as being more or less than its sum. This is to say, it *all*
is." Remarking on the diversity contained in the volume, Creeley concludes: "I can think of no man more useful to learn from than Zukofsky, in that he will not 'say' anything but that which the particulars
of such a possibility require, and follows the fact of that occasion
with unequalled sensitivity."

10. Davie, Donald. "After Sedley, After Pound." *Nation,* 201
(Nov. 1, 1965), pp. 311-13.

An appreciative review of *All: The Collected Shorter Poems, 1923-
1958* published by W.W. Norton. Davie praises Zukofsky's respect for
language and grammar, his concentration and compactness, and a
style "to which the norms of prose syntax are essential (hence the
very sedulous punctuation); though it breaks the norms even as it
respects them." Davie sees Zukofsky clearly in the Pound tradition
but "within hailing distance of a quite distinct tradition which for a
long time was more influential among us—the wit writing of Allen
Tate, say, or William Empson." He deplores the fact that the "new
criticism," which ought to have hailed Zukofsky, ignored him so that
"among his peers it was Pound and Williams who appreciated and
helped."

11. Malanga, Gerard. "Some Thoughts on *Bottom* and *After I's.*"
Poetry, 107, No. 1 (Oct., 1965), pp. 60-64.

Malanga is specific: "The most impressive thing about the structure
of Louis Zukofsky's *Bottom: On Shakespeare* is its substantiality. It
is of this world as much as is Pound's study of George Antheil. There
is often beauty to it, but it is never ineffable." He quotes an often
cited passage on the theme *"love: reason::* eyes: mind," the passage
which begins: "Love needs no tongue of reason if love and the eyes
are 1—an identity. The good reasons of the mind's right judgment are
but superfluities for saying: *Love sees*—if it needs saying at all in a
text which is always hovering towards *The rest is silence.*" He finds
the passage "often cited as giving the heart of Mr. Zukofsky's views
of writing and the world in general, is, . . . typical in its conception
of what constitutes structure, or *its* structure." As for *After I's,*
Malanga finds these short poems "are definite enough in limb and
movement, [but] they remain curiously abstract and, for all their
tremendous agonies and perturbations, cold to the sympathies and
imagination of the reader." The review closes with a note on Celia

Zukofsky's score for *Pericles*. He says: "The result is a music that is rhythmically alive, accurate, and colorful."

12. Creeley, Robert. "Louis Zukofsky." *Agenda*, 4, Nos. 3-4 (Summer, 1966), pp. 44-45.

Creeley begins his review of this first volume of *All* by citing some critical precepts of Zukofsky, stated in other places such as *A Test of Poetry* (1948) and *"A"*-12. From *A Test . . .* , he quotes: "The test of poetry is the range of pleasure it affords as sight, sound, and intellection. This is its purpose as art . . . ." From *"A"*-12 we look at the magnificent opening lines which express the deep need a poet has to be a poet. We see how *shape, rhythm,* and *style* express the most human attributes of the human. And we see how the lines starting with *"Out of deep need . . ."* explain much and justify more:

> *Out of deep need . . .*
>
> So goes: first, *shape*
> The creation—
> A mist from the earth,
> The whole face of the ground;
> Then *rhythm* —
> And breathed breath of life;
> Then *style* —
> That from the eye its function takes—
> "Taste" we say—a living soul.

This state of things had a long beginning and a longer evolution:

> First, glyph; then syllabary,
> Then letters. Ratio after
> Eyes, tale in sound. First, dance. Then
> Voice. First, body—to be seen and to pulse
> Happening together . . . . [*"A"*-12]

Creeley notes the "lovely note of *time*" in some of the songs, but is most interested in the technique of "Mantis" as well as *"Mantis," an Interpretation*. To him, the important consideration is that "Zukofsky feels form as an intimate presence, whether or not that form be the use or issue of other feelings in other times, or the immediate apprehension of a *way* felt in the moment of its occurrence." Here, he is concerned with Zukofsky's reasons for using the sestina for "Mantis" even though the form is intricate for the 20th century.

As a distinguished poet himself, Creeley says "I am embarrassed to deal with all that in this poem excites and informs me."—that, because his notes have to be brief. And as a poet, Creeley knows better than most the great value of Zukofsky's work to any other disciplined poet: "It is a peculiar virtue of Zukofsky's work that it offers an extraordinary handbook for the writing of poems. His particular sensitivity to the qualities of poetry as 'sight, sound, and intellection' marks the significance of his relation to Ezra Pound, who dedicated *Guide to Kulchur* 'To Louis Zukofsky and Basil Bunting strugglers in the desert.' "

Creeley closes his all-too-brief review with a note written by Zukofsky:

> . . . How much what is sounded by words has to do with what is
> seen by them, and how much what is at once sounded and seen by

them crosscuts an interplay among themselves—will naturally sustain the scientific definition of poetry we are looking for. To endure it would be compelled to integrate these functions: time, and what is seen in time (as held by a song), and an action whose words are actors, or, if you will, mimes composing steps as of a dance that at proper instants calls in the vocal cords to transform it into plain speech . . . .

13. Bernlef, J. "Louis Zukofsky: Het ritme van ogen." *De Gids*, 130, No. 3 (1967), pp. 179-81.

Frits Vosmon (University of Maine Physics Department) provided me with a ten paragraph summary of the ten-paragraph Dutch article by J. Bernlef whose real name, he says, is H.J. Marsman. In a note accompanying his precis he says, "I have the impression that [he] . . . likes the poem, although he remains very objective." Vosman further says that most of his summary is literally translated lines from the article. Bernlef makes several points: There are several poems in 20th century Anglo-American literature which range from long (Eliot's *The Waste Land*) to very long (Pound's *The Cantos* and W.C. Williams' *Paterson*). A long poem gives many opportunities and when produced over a number of years reflects the writer's growth and change, but because of this the long poem may fail in unity of vision and thus disappoint. Zukofsky's *"A" 1-12* is the first half of a long poem which, if finished, will have 24 movements. Although Zukofsky has published 18 books since his early work as an "objectivist," it is *"A"* that makes him an interesting poet today.

Bernlef notes several other circumstances: (1) Zukofsky is accepted by all as a disciple of Ezra Pound; (2) Compared with *The Cantos*, *"A"* is second-rate: "It has too much in it and not enough form even though Zukofsky orders a lot less than Pound"; (3) Zukofsky's language is close to the language of William Carlos Williams "without being shamelessly obvious"; (4) Once in a while it is eccentric and makes Bernlef think of "a calf with three heads." But after all reservations he sees *"A"* as a valuable effort to create form out of an essentially formless daily life: *"A"* is "a little world full of holes and references to this big world."

14. Carruth, Hayden. "Louis Zukofsky." *Poetry*, 110, No. 6 (Sept., 1967), pp. 420-22.

A review of the second volume of *All: The Collected Short Poems, 1956-1964*, published by Norton. As a poet of great sensitivity himself, Carruth finds these volumes may present a danger. After a poet has written for years in relative obscurity, when he is discovered he may find "the pendulum of his reception has swung from uninformed neglect to uninformed adulation." Thus Carruth finds work which is pedestrian along with what he calls "peaks": "Zukofsky's virtue appears best in relation to his elders, especially Pound and Williams. Where Pound called for a new heave forward, and Williams for a new beginning, Zukofsky seems to say, yes, 'heaves' and 'beginnings' are fine, but there is also such a thing as a 'peak.'" In an analogy from music, he lists Bach, Vivaldi, and Corelli before coming to Mozart whose work is even more splendid. "At its best Zukofsky's poetry has an intricate, ascending lucidity that is truly Mozartian . . . ."

15. Creeley, Robert, ed. and intro. *"A" 1-12*. New York: Double-day and Co., Paris Review Editions, 1967.

As Zukofsky favored in Shakespeare and Whitman the "clear physical eye" as against "the erring brain" so Creeley favors in Zukofsky the same quality of clearly seeing things as they exist. Key words often re-peated in *"A" 1-12* are "all" used in the sense of "one" (implying the unity of life) and "leaf" at times echoing *Leaves of Grass*. Says Creeley: "the experience of one's life as one is given to have it, and as relationships of its nature are found, unfold, then, as *leaves*, finding home in time far past or in the instant now." Creeley quotes from *"A"*-2 written in 1928: "The music is in the flower,/ Leaf around leaf ranged around the center;/ Profuse but clear outer leaf breaking on space,/ There is space to step to the central heart:/ The music is in the flower./ . . . the leaves never topple from each other,/ Each leaf a buttress flung for the other." Twenty-two years later, Creeley notes that Zukofsky wrote in *"A"*-11: "His voice in me, the river's turn that finds the/ Grace in you, four notes first too full for talk, leaf/ Lighting stem, stems bound to the branch that binds the/ Tree, and them as from the same root we talk, leaf/ Over leaf of his thought . . . ." Creeley finds the idea of "His voice in me" to be significant: "that men do so move, one to one—here grandfather, to father, to son—but that also, as Zukofsky thinks possible, it may be that Shakespeare had read Catullus, and that men who may so read the same text may so *in time* relate." The implications are tremendous: Pound's idea of "Sagetrieb" or "handing on the tradition" and having the vital tradi-tion live and be re-lived to the latest generation. *"A"* opens with an Easter Sunday performance of Bach's "St. Matthew's Passion" at Carnegie Hall. After the concert, Zukofsky took a walk with Bach's form, notes and leaves growing in him. Creeley quotes Zuk: "I walked on Easter Sunday,/ This is my face/ This is my form./ Faces and forms, I would write you down/ In a style of leaves growing." And Zuk quotes Pound: "Hast 'ou fashioned so airy a mood/ To draw up leaf from the root?" Lines which, says Creeley, "give measure for such occasion."

Creeley goes on to give other examples of the poetry and themes and then devotes the remainder of this introduction to a synopsis of Zukofsky's life and work from the 20's into 1967.

16. Kenner, Hugh. "Of Notes and Horses." *Poetry*, 111, No. 2 (Nov., 1967), pp. 112-21.

A review of *"A" 1-12* published by Jonathan Cape and of *"A" 1-12* published by Paris Review Editions, Doubleday. Kenner outlines the publishing history of *"A"* and estimates the difficulties the rarity of the text has caused. A reader "who wasn't so blessed as to be in touch with Cid Corman," who did *"A" 1-12* in Japan in 1958, had to do without. Of *"A"* as a whole Kenner writes: "Like *Leaves of Grass*, like *The Cantos*, it's a poem-in-progress to encompass the poet's life; but unlike Whitman and Pound, who knew at the start what kind of texture they wanted and little else, Zukofsky began about 1927 with a formal plan, a plan of the form, which means in practice (1) an in-tuition of the poem without any words in it, a silent structural eloquence; and (2) a sequential table of difficulties to be overcome." Kenner illustrates Zukofsky's way with words and sounds by quotes from his *Catullus* and *"A."* He offers some theories about the poem as a whole: "It is a curious possibility that the whole poem may be an exegesis of the indefinite article, and so of cases standing for kinds, and so of a tension between the kind of reality kinds have and our stubborn pragmatic intuition that our need for a filing system has merely divised them." If, indeed, "the" may stand for a particular item of Being, then "A" may well be taken as the general term for Being: thus do we have the ontological question, which harassed Zukofsky more than any other, posed. Kenner may well be right. Epistemology meant to Zukofsky not only the knowledge of knowledge but most of all knowledge of Being. And he did say he wrote *Bottom: on Shakespeare* "to do away with all philosophy."

17. Donoghue, Denis. "That Old Eloquence." *New York Review of Books*, 10, No. 8 (April 25, 1968), pp. 16-18.

In a review of *"A" 1-12*, along with two other books, Donoghue sees the major thrust of *"A"* to be an expression of form and music. Citing from *"A"*-2 the lines: "this is my face/ This is my form,/ Faces and forms, I would write you down/ In a style of leaves growing," he says, "Organic form, then, but the form starts from the object, apprehended with love." Donoghue then places *"A"* among other long works being done at the same time, among them Pound's *Cantos*, Eliot's *The Waste Land*, and Cumming's *Him*, and adds: "If we ask where Pound is to be felt in the *Cantos*, the answer is: 'in his own lines which are all his other people.' He is to be found, that is, in the musical measure, the song while it sings of other people and other things." Donoghue is a discriminating reader: "This verse in a style of leaves growing, the extant world and all minor worlds certified by the propriety of the voice. So the words are found: about the finding, there is nothing to be said, except that it is a consolation to know that it can still be done."

18. Dembo, L.S. "The 'Objectivist' Poet: Four Interviews." *Contemporary Literature*, 10 (Spring, 1969), pp. 155-219. (Interview with Louis Zukofsky, pp. 203-19.)

Much of this interview of May 16, 1968 covers questions suggested by "Sincerity and Objectification." Throughout the interview Zukofsky largely controls the flow of conversation, jumping to new observations by association from the original question or by his own train of thought. Zukofsky protests that he would like to avoid discussions of philosophy, criticism, theory of knowledge, and the explanation of poems. He does, however, amplify his use of the terms "sincerity," "objectification," and "spontaneous idea." Zukofsky quotes from and comments on "The Old Poet Moves to a New Apartment 14 Times," uses "Not much more than being" and "Immature Pebbles" in dialogue about objectivist versus abstract writing, and speaks of making the sestina new in "Mantis." Other significant topics include the physiological importance of words and the overall "curve" of *"A."* [W.H. The Zukofsky part of the text is reprinted herein, pp. 265-281.]

19. Raffel, Burton. "No Tidbit Love You Outdoors Far as a Bier: Zukofsky's *Catullus.*" *Arion*, 8 (1969), pp. 434-45.

> Raffel's thesis is solidly stated: "Different translation theories, different translation practices, can achieve different levels of communication, but without communication I think that no translation occurs" (p. 436). Raffel feels that theories of translation are only important insofar as they help the translator, that they are meaningless in themselves. Zukofsky's translation of *Catullus* fails, except in isolated sections where he releases himself from his theories, because his attempt to suggest the sound of Latin results in poetry which is not Latin but which also fails as English communication. Along with clearly communicating the meaning, a successful translation of poetry also displays poetic merit. In this light, Zukofsky had the potential to have been more successful than other translators translating this work. [W.H.]

20. Spann, Marcella. "An Analytical and Descriptive Catalogue of the Manuscripts and Letters in the Louis Zukofsky Collection at the University of Texas at Austin." *DAI*, 30:5459A. Univ. of Texas, Austin, 1969.

> This dissertation includes not only a complete catalogue but also a history of each work, showing stages of development and publishing information where applicable and giving textural variations. The catalogue is organized by genre.

21. Stock, Noel. "Balancing the Books." *Poetry Australia*, 30 (Oct., 1969), pp. 46-52.

> According to *Abstracts of English Studies*, 14, No. 3 (Nov., 1970), pp. 196-97: "Two hundred years of science have incapacitated poets for a total vision. None since Baudelaire has been able to look at his world and perceive a unity and arrive at a meaning. Pound's *Cantos* exhibit modern man's 'collapse into a sea of matter and fact.' Williams aimed at and achieved merely a vision of facts. Zukofsky and the Objectivists arrived only at a precision of fact and image."

22. Davenport, Guy. "Louis Zukofsky." *Agenda*, Vol. 8, Nos. 3 & 4 (Autumn-Winter, 1970).

> A critical article on the occasion of the publication of *"A" 13-21* by Jonathan Cape and *Catullus* by Cape Goliard noted by *Agenda* to be now available in England for 42 and 38 shillings respectively. Davenport gives a 4,000 word statement about Zukofsky's work as a whole and shows how this new sequence of movements from *"A"* fits into the work as perceptible up to that time. He takes notice, in passing, of *Bottom: On Shakespeare, All, Prepositions, It Was*, etc. He remarks on the lack of enthusiasm with which the long poem, as a form, has been received in America. He notes the quite impossible feat Zukofsky set himself in the *Catullus*. He gives examples of how the English is made to sound like the Latin and adds: "There is no point in our saying 'You can't do that' to the poet, for we might note that his liberty to do it has already bound him to a set of rules which he alone is willing

to observe with delight . . . ."

He lingers to examine some of Zukofsky's amazing verbal resources from the time of such early works as *Le Style Apollinaire*, a study of the French poet who, taking the next revolutionary step after Rimbaud, Laforgue, and Corbière, "threw the diction of French poetry wide open, cancelling the rules by which poetry was restricted to these words only and never those." He lines up anecdotes of a similar situation in English poetry noting "Dr. Johnson's outrage at seeing the word *rat* in a poem," etc. Most valuable to new readers of Zukofsky are his brief notes on parts of *"A"*:

> What Zukofsky is about in his poetry is always reasonably obvious, often so obvious that we reject what we can see and look for matters which we suppose to be wonderfully hidden. *"A"*-13, for instance, is a father talking to his son, playing at being Polonius. The parts are arranged as variations on a theme, dancing successively to five tunes. The beauty of these sixty pages is the jig of words, the rise, probe, jab, and flash of intellect. Transposed into a prose statement, these partitas would render up a fat volume of essays, the subject of which would range from heaven to earth and back again. *"A"*-14 is a soliloquy beginning and ending with an image of the sun; in between in a meditation—the mind at peace and reflecting on itself, arranging its elements, supplying its own light and warmth. *"A"*-15 reaches back to the earlier portions of *"A"* in which Lenin and Gibbon are allowed to debate the condition of man; here arising from the anguish of the Kennedy assassination, Gibbon's Roman sanity would seem to have the better of the argument, but we must remember that we are reading an unfinished poem. *"A"*-16 has but four words, one of which is compound: "An/ inequality/ wind flower." The windflower, or anemone, is in Hebrew the Na'amon flower, in honor of Adonis, its English name being a supposed etymology from the Greek *wind*. The imagist knot here is a kind of emblem between elegies, alluding to the brevity of individual lives and to the continuity of life. Life seeds life; the wind moves over the flower scattering its seed. *"A"*-17 is both an elegy for William Carlos Williams and a celebration of the friendship of the two poets. *"A"*-18 is a peroration (or as much of one as we are likely to see in Zukofsky), speaking with an emotion unlike anything else in *"A."* It is basically a soliloquy, but very much meant to be overheard; it is about "the times," the Vietnamese war, the public mine, the tenor of modern thought. For sheer intellectual passion there is little in modern literature to equal it. *"A"*-19 is a long lyric. Like the lyrics outside *"A,"* it is a brilliant piece of metaphysical wit, whimsical, satirical, and essentially light. *"A"*-20 is about Paul Zukofsky, the poet's son, composer and concert violinist. *"A"*-21 is a translation of Plautus' *Rudens*. Why? Well, because it is the source of "Pericles," the most beautiful of Shakespeare's plays in Zukofsky's assessment; because it is the good-natured mind of Plautus, a *balanced*, sane, stoic, Epicurean mind honoring love's *reason*—and opposite end of the Roman spectrum of mind from Catullus.

Davenport compares his man with Joyce: "The poet speaks for himself and his family; he is the counter-vision of the inarticulate Bloom and the nightmare of industrial city man in *Finnegan's Wake*." He makes a pertinent judgment.

23. Spann, Marcella. "The Zukofsky Papers." *Library Chronicle of the University of Texas*, 2 (1970), pp. 49-59.

An eleven page description of the contents of the Zukofsky archive at the Humanities Research Center at The University of Texas at Austin. Or in other words, a summary statement of Marcella Spann's catalog of "the more than twelve thousand pages, in addition to letters, now in the collection," which is growing rapidly. The catalog was published by the University of Texas in 1975. See Marcella Booth's account pp. 393-400 herein.

24. Cox, Kenneth. "The Poetry of Louis Zukofsky: *"A."" Agenda*, 9-4 through 10-1 (Autumn-Winter, 1971-1972), pp. 80-89.

> Cox was the first, so far as I know, to say: "Zukofsky's poetry is the most important yet written in English by anyone born in the twentieth century." Also, in this review, he emphasizes the significance of the architecture of *"A"*: "the quality of Zukofsky's poetry is everywhere equal . . . ." Its power is in its "macrostructure." Examining the question whether he was "a poet's poet," Cox says, "All poets are poets' poets . . . ." But, he goes on: "Zukofsky's poetry has however a side ordinary experience can respond to as a scope which shifts the perspective other poetry is seen in. Like all other poetry, it differs from all other poetry and makes some of the other look an aspect of itself." Cox's enthusiasm of Zukofsky as a craftsman knows no bounds: "beside him even Pound can look meretricious." Cox goes on to comment on the parts of *"A"* (thru 21) available to him as well as to describe briefly *Bottom: On Shakespeare* and *Prepositions*. Finally he places Zukofsky in the tradition with conviction: "On the evidence so far available *"A"* is the poem of today which best stands comparison with the *Cantos*. It is less adventurous but more reflective and at the centre more certain . . . . In the *Cantos* man dares, exercising the arts of speech to protect and protest: they tend towards record, memorial, definition. In *"A"* man leads a domestic existence blessed by luck and love and governed by abstractions known through science and the mass media: it tends toward satisfaction, praise, song."

25. Dembo, L.S. "Louis Zukofsky: Objectivist Poetics and the Quest for Form." *American Literature*, 44, No. 1 (March, 1972), pp. 74-96. [Reprinted herein pp. 283-303]

26. Duddy, Thomas A. "Perception and Process: Studies in the Poetry of Robert Creeley, Robert Duncan, Denise Levertov, Charles Olson, and Louis Zukofsky." *DAI*, 33:305A-06A. S.U.N.Y., Buffalo, 1972.

> Discussions of the individual poets are presented as basically separate essays. The section on Zukofsky focuses on *"A."* Duddy explains what he believes these "Black Mountain Poets" most essentially share: "Creeley's formulation that 'form is never more than an extension of content' is perhaps the clearest theoretical expression of the principle which binds each of these poets to another." [W.H.]

27. Suter, Anthony. "Basil Bunting et deux poètes américains: Louis Zukofsky et William Carlos Williams." *Caliban*, 9 (1972), pp. 151-57.

According to *Abstracts of English Studies*, 17, No. 5 (Jan., 1974), p. 315, "Bunting imitated stylistic devices of Williams, in *The Oratava Road*, and of Zukofsky, in his *Odes, I, 33*." [W.H.]

28. Cox, Kenneth. " *"A"*-24." *Agenda*, 11, Nos. 2-3 (Spring-Summer, 1973), pp. 89-91.

Cox gives us a 3-page discription of this most remarkable piece of work, a poem which, everytime I look at it, suggests not "A Round of fiddles playing Bach," but the Chorale of Beethoven's 9th. Cox suggests in brief compass a number of internal correspondences *"A"*-24 has with the 23 movements which come before it. He notes that the poem is a masque—"Celia's L.Z. masque"—in two acts (nine scenes) which is scored for five parts as the preface says: "Music, thought, drama, story, poem." Celia wrote: "Handel's Harpsichord pieces are one voice. The other four voices are arrangements of Louis Zukofsky's writings as follows:

Thought (T) — *Prepositions*

Drama (D) — *Arise, arise*

Story (S) — *It was*

Poem (P) — *"A"*

The masque is centrally motivated by the drama. Each character *speaks* in monologue . . . . Performance time approximately seventy minutes." The text of *"A"*-24, organized with 3 musical staffs per page, is 243 pages.

The four dramatic lines running concurrently under the music reflect and derive from the poet's whole creative life. Says Cox: "*It was* is the title given to the collection of Zukofsky's narrative writings . . . . *Arise, arise* is a play in two acts written in 1936 . . . . By it the masque is 'centrally motivated'; occupying the middle of the five voices, it provides a driving linear centre. There is however a deformation. Each character of the drama appears in one scene of the masque and in that scene speaks all his lines in sequence and in monologue. The drama has thus been sliced lengthwise into acting parts distributed among its nine characters." Cox elaborates an apt insight: "Without trying to reconstitute its single multipersonal form . . . one can see the drama is of death and generation, revolution and resurrection. The source of its title [*Arise, arise*] is Donne's sonnet beginning *From the round earth's imagined corners blow* . . . ." Cox has a number of conclusions: "More than through any other movement of *"A"* there comes through *"A"*-24 the power of woman." Or: " *"A"*-24 is a work of massive simplicity." His final conclusion is also pointed: "Yet it would be pointless to look everywhere for internal correspondences. In *"A"*-24 Zukofsky's work has been recalled and rearranged by a devoted ear, as in course of time it will be differently recalled and differently rearranged in the minds of distant readers and alien cultures. In this sense it is already a resurrection, a life abandoned and renewed, a model for incorporation of the work into the common tradition. And it teaches that perfection of the life and of the work are not incompatible, that a lifework can be completed within marriage without wound or subjection."

29. Charters, Samuel. "Essay Beginning 'All.'" *Modern Poetry Studies*, 3, No. 6 (1973), pp. 241-50.

> Charters' essay is in the form of an interior monologue about the experience of and challenge of reading Zukofsky's short poems. Charters is enticed by "The possibility that the whole man is in it" (p. 241) but sees this possibility as one source of difficulty: "All of Zukofsky is left in, and that is the dimension that has no edge to pick up and look under, no divisions where lines can be picked apart" (p. 242). Dangers to the reader come from how much Zukofsky has included, from the fact he has no predetermined stance but has found a form for each situation. The reader must go slowly and find the "consistency of the inconsistencies" (p. 245). Charters closes by thinking about several influences on Zukofsky, influences which were first absorbed by Zukofsky's mind and which therefore never inspired imitative poetry. "Zukofsky is only like himself . . ." (p. 250). [W.H.]

30. Duddy, Thomas A. "The Measure of Louis Zukofsky." *Modern Poetry Studies*, 3, No. 6 (1973), pp. 250-56.

> Duddy believes that "What is unique about the work is . . . that it is a poetry *reaching out* toward a system of measure which, in this sublunary world, is best exemplified by music, and best of all by Bach" (p. 251). For Zukofsky, "Music here is epistomology" (p. 251), says Duddy. The mathematical-musical concern with sound and structure, such as found in *"A,"* in the translation *Catullus*, and in the *Autobiography*, are unique with Zukofsky and separate the format of *"A"* from the more sprawling *Paterson* and *Cantos*. Duddy stresses the organic relationship between meaning and sound in Zukofsky's work. [W.H.]

31. Cox, Kenneth. "Zukofsky And Mallarmé: Notes on *"A"*-19." *MAPS*, No. 5 (1973), pp. 1-11.

> Kenneth Cox examined Zukofsky's technique in *"A"*-19 and came up with one of the best illustrations of the poet-at-work to be found. He gave us his findings in a 6-part study which John Taggart used as his lead piece in *MAPS* , No. 5, a special issue devoted to Zukofsky. One can neither summarize nor improve what Cox says in Part I:
>
>> " *"A"*-19" is composed of a prelude of eight quatrains and a piece of 72 strophes each of 13 lines except the last, which has 12. Occasional irregularities apart, there are two words a line in both prelude and piece except that the last line of each strophe has three. The prelude gives occasion for the poem. It sets the scene, establishes mood and introduces motifs: most of its words recur in the piece. The setting is preliminary to a violin concert; it is snowing. The piece itself opens with extreme obscurity and some discord from which threads of sense or melody emerge fitfully. Syntax is tenuous, interest is primarily in single words ground out, like chords with passing notes, for the sake of their constituent meanings and total tonal values: it might be described as vertical writing. The writing clears and there follows a humoresque based on the rules for the competition in which the players are taking part. It is written in a springy tempo and with an imbecile lucidity and precision but with faults of idiom and spelling due to a substrate of Italian: the competition was held in Genoa. The last and longer

part, after announcement of the result, consists of free-moving and far-ranging variations often much condensed. It is fast loose sceptical merry and reflective. The prizewinners perform, there is a party, themes touched lightly rush, crisscross, drift, fall in flurries, in a tourbillion of snowflakes. The close is calm; it returns to the mood and setting of the prelude, the snow has settled.

Cox goes on to develop the thesis [with a nod toward Joyce] that "the poem is perceptible under one of its aspects as itself the piece the violinist plays." The two-word lines are down-strokes or up-strokes of the bow. Irregularities in the line are thus accounted for as giving special violin effects such as grace-notes, changes in pitch and duration, or even trills. He gives "their impalpable/ conscionable double" as a trill and notices "the suffix -le recurring frequently as tremolo." Thus: "The semantic gaps between successive words are recognizable as intervals large or small, the phonetic continuity or discontinuity of the words as legato or staccato." Cox gives other examples to show how music relates to form and even how "form is also the subject of the poem." He does some glossing on the way, such as the following comments on the lines opening the first strophe ("No ill-luck/ if bonding/ tohu bohu"):

> *No ill-luck* averts omen (13 lines to the strophe) and predicts safety in the process of creating form out of the crude and chancy. *Bonding* is the physicist's word for the event typified by *An other*. *Tohu bohu* are Hebrew words for the original state of things without form and void (Genesis I,2), used in French to signify disorder. The very first word *No* may also be read not as negation but as abbreviation of *Number*.

If one knows how much significance Zuk attached to Pythagoras, especially the relationships between his theory of numbers and music, one finds Cox's further analysis quite likely indeed:

> Two being given as principle of formation, the structure of the poem is intelligible as number as well as perceptible as music for violin. Based on a foot of two words it is made up of a prelude consisting of 2^3 quatrains each of 2^3 words and a piece of 2^3 x 3^2 strophes each of 3^3 words. The final strophe, bad luck having been made good and the poem completed, has not 13 but 2^2 x 3 lines (2^3 x 3 words), but this is not evident till the last word is reached. And the number of strophes (72) mirrors the number of words per strophe (27).
>
> The numerical structure also symbolizes the development of the single person, one becoming two by marriage and three by begetting a child. The poem is both a private valentine to the poet's wife and a public performance by their son, the violinist. Familial and social coefficients raise the accident of individuality to powers of two and three: two is both the sum of one and one and an entity made up of one and another. It can be the sex of a human being, the spin of a particle, the lefthandedness or righthandedness of an optical isomer, a binary digit of information.

In section IV, Cox gives the 13 lines of the first strophe in full, the 12th and 13th line being: "Misfortune Place/ it futile range" and then makes the connections with Mallarmé:

> As far as [the word] *misfortune* this draws on a poem of Mallarmé's, *Le guignon* (run of bad luck). It is an early work, one of the first in which Mallarmé applied to needs of his own the sonorous rhetoric he had inherited from Baudelaire and perhaps from Victor Hugo.

After giving examples he summarizes the way in which the poet uses his source:

> Nearly all the words of the opening strophes are from Mallarmé. The passage is not simple translation or imitation or condensation or evocation or refabrication but sometimes one, sometimes another: there are obscure lines where Mallarmé comes through scarcely changed, clear lines where he is hard to recognize. It may be compared with a palimpsest where the later writing covers the earlier here heavily, here lightly; or with a version which reproduces the words now by sound, now by sense, by calque or transformation; or with a medium who both transmits and resists the spirit who possesses her; or with a ventriloquial act.

Cox gives the major elements in his conclusions in parts V and VI:

> This technique of writing resembles in one respect an executant's performance of a piece of music composed by someone else. In another respect it is not a special technique at all but a concentrated example of the only operation at the disposal of a writer: the use of pre-existent words. There are various stages of pre-existence and several varieties of use. Later in the poem Zukofsky quotes from Mallarmé and adapts him, he *voices thru* Demetrius of Phaleron and transcribes passages from Sextus Empiricus, and the words of Shakespeare he knows so deeply surface here and there.
>
> The whole of poetry may be regarded as pedigree, as a succession of affiliations which skips the apparent diversity of idioms. A special interest attaches to personal acknowledgements, to those of the verbal imagination at points of juncture and transfer: they constitute the family tree of the art.

But just as Cox's words only scratch the surface of *"A"*-19, so these words here only faintly suggest the whole content of his analysis.

32. Kenner, Hugh. "Too Full for Talk: *"A"*-11." *MAPS*, No. 5 (1973), pp. 12-21. [Reproduced herein pp. 195-202]

The shortest of the 24 movements of *"A"* is *"A"*-16, which contains only 4 words strikingly arranged on one page. Two movements, *"A"*-11 and *"A"*-20 are contained in only two pages but since *"A"*-20 has shorter lines than does *"A"*-11, it is the third briefest movement of the poem. Thus Kenner has a point when he opens his piece by saying: "Your impression may well be that if *"A"*-11 would go by more slowly you could follow it. . . ." One has a lot better chance of following it if he heeds the information Kenner gives in this brief analysis.

33. Heller, Michael. "Some Reflections And Extensions: Zukofsky's Poetics." *MAPS*, No. 5 (1973), pp. 22-25.

Heller's reflections concern the "timely, timeless" aspects of Zukofsky's art: "Timely and timeless, in that one could always return to such statements as those in *Prepositions*, in the poems of *"A"* and *All*, and recover the sense of being a poet, recover the sense or nonsense of a modality of craft." He remarks on the qualities of "rigor within a generosity and openness" and says that the poet is aware, also, "how the human and worldly touch, how meaning is not to be evaded." With examples from *Prepositions*, he says, "What we call 'tradition' is simply meanings offered and meanings surpassed by meanings offered." This wheel, we note, is one which can go around and around without offering the reader a place to get off. So Heller notes: "And these meanings are more or less inclusive than those which they surpass, are temporal [note "times and timeless" above] — not prejoratively—because they embrace both the sense and nonsense of their time and are altered by both 'progress' and forgetfulness." For these and other considerations, Heller sees that perhaps "Zukofsky's poetics are to the poetry of our time . . . a profoundly conservative effort"; and that its value to the poet "lies precisely in its conservatory nature, a nature which is yet open to the possibility of any linguistic usage as long as that usage grounds us in the world, as long as it appears to be necessitous and not dilution or decor."

34. Cid Corman. "Love—In These Words." *MAPS*, No. 5 (1973), pp. 26-54.

Zukofsky's "Barely and Widely" was first published in 1958 as a 78-page facisimile of the poet's handwriting. It was an edition limited to 300 numbered and signed copies. Corman's article is a lengthy review and reaction to the poem; his technique is to hold numerous passages up to view so that the reader can see how "the poet makes the language sing sense." He is at pains to show that "Zukofsky has the finest ear, certainly, of any poet in our time . . . ." and that his "music is always also involved with the melody of meaning; that is, to move with his mind, in its leaps and turns, in its dips below the surface and it opens into mellifluousness or unexpected stops" which "creates a world of poetry that is of such freshness as to make one wonder where poetry had been 'all this time.'"

35. Melnick, David. "The 'Ought' Of Seeing: Zukofsky's *Bottom*." *MAPS*, No. 5 (1973), pp. 55-56.

This account has a brief foreword and two parts: (1) *Bottom: On Shakespeare* as theory and (2) *Bottom: On Shakespeare* on Shakespeare. The foreword is a reaction to Zukofsky's Wisconsin interview with L.S. Dembo [pp. 265-281 herein] in which Zuk pretends to have done away with epistemology, a wry irony on a sequence of ironies. Melnick declares that his accent, following the poet's, falls on Aristotle, Spinoza, and Wittgenstein. In the theory section he finds that *Bottom* "returns often and with approval to Aristotle's quarrel with Plato over the nature of the mind's objects—a quarrel that went far toward formulating the maxim, 'no ideas but in things.'" Aristotle vascillates between ideas and things: "an old story of culture." When we get away from the concrete, "we feel Nostalgia." This is the crux: "Zukofsky believes that the connections he discovers in this regard . . . as between Aristotle and Shakespeare, Spinoza, and Wittgenstein, reveal fundamental aspects of their character, and, by inference, of all human nature." But the real crux is Plato's "Love that moved men to recall and rejoin pure Being." For Zukofsky, "Love is the mind's desire and the eyes' achievement." Having established these premises (and many more), Melnick, applies them to *Bottom: On Shakespeare* and finds Shakespeare often wanting but more often discerning whether with "eyes" or "I's": His images are his people. "Whether fierce, false, melting, or precious, the eyes in these images make judgments, express feelings, reveal attitudes, biases, characteristics . . . . They are available to Shakespeare as a ready means—to acknowledge, ignore, entreasure, threaten, welcome, submit. They are proofs, not cures, of passion." And passion is motion, the opposite of the stillness of Love in pure Being. If Melnick's account tends to be circular, so is Zukofsky's in the 400 pages of *Bottom*. In ten pages, Melnick gives the key poles and points of this densely contrived book better than any other account I've seen.

36. Davenport, Guy. "Zukofsky's English Catullus." *MAPS*, No. 5 (1973), pp. 70-75. [Reproduced herein pp. 365-370]

37. Mottram, Eric. "1924-1951: Politics And Form In Zukofsky." *MAPS*, No. 5 (1973), pp. 76-103.

Eric Mottram's 27-page piece is divided into two parts roughly equal in length: the first has to do with the ideas of people who helped form the ideas of Zukofsky as they relate to his form, and the second shows how his form accommodates his ideas and politics. Since he follows Zukofsky's prose pieces gathered in *Prepositions*, he finds Henry Adams, Ezra Pound, Shakespeare, Spinoza, Wittgenstein, Apollinaire, Santayana, Lenin, and Einstein, as well as Rene Char and Charlie Chaplin among the significant thinkers behind Zukofsky's thought. *The Education of Henry Adams* is as significant as any other book in the education of Louis Zukofsky. But the thought of Lenin, as perceived through many "eyes" and "I's," especially Pound's in the early 20's, had more to do with his politics. Mottram quotes Zukofsky who quotes Pound in 1928: "Lenin invented . . . a new medium, something between speech and action, which is worth . . . study." But the formative ideas of Lenin in the 20's were one thing which both Zukofsky and Pound clearly distinguished from the conclusions of other people in the 30's.

Mottram quotes William Carlos Williams who said Zukofsky had admitted that "love of literary fame" was his ruling passion and that he then developed beliefs "which although not strong in *"A"* are present in *Bottom*: his sense of a life-force in great men (Washington and Shakespeare are his examples)." Then he goes on to say:

> While he is not a thoroughgoing thirties vitalist (in Eric Bentley's sense), he recognizes "something there, underneath the dynamo of intelligence—of life itself that is crude, rebellious—the lack of which, or the denial of which . . . makes an ass." [*Prepositions*, 1967, pp. 41-42]. The work of this man would reveal him: "It is in complexities that appear finally as one person that the good of a life shows itself—ringing all together to return the world to simplicity again . . . like a good picture: a sharp differentiation of good from evil"—"a sound to add still more to the intelligent, the colorful, the whole grasp of feeling and knowledge in the world . . . ."

Mottram, at several points, isolates concepts of coherencies that enter Zukofsky's works from one or another major figure in the poet's circle of friends as they inform the work of Zukofsky: William Carlos Williams' idea of politics as a science of humanity applying also to art; and the Poundian idea that art means standards as well as

recurrences. But the recurrences made by man must inform the coherence in thought, the universe in action, as well as art. So in *"A"*:

> The coherence, as in *"A"* is exemplified in Einstein: "Everything
> should be as simple as it can be, but not simpler" as "a scientist's
> defense of art and knowledge—of lightness, completeness, and ac-
> curacy." Twenty years earlier Zukofsky defines the coherence
> through Adam's *Mont St. Michel and Chartres*: "What was intended
> to be impersonal has the element of the personal diffused through
> design. The struggle of the American mind for the ciborium not
> its own casts the spell of tragedy through the calm of structures"
> [Ibid., 46].

Mottram is astute in distinguishing Zukofsky and his recurrent co-
herences from the quests of those he knew best in books or in person,
in particular Williams whom he knew by both:

> But Williams [as perceived by Zuk] was not nostalgic for the cup
> of any European Eucharist to save America; the Grail is not
> hunted in America; Eliot shifted his Harvard Jacobinism to Europe
> precisely in order to take part in the ancient chase for the in-
> fallibly holy and authoritarian. Zukofsky sees that *In the Ameri-
> can Grain* and *A Voyage to Pagany* resist tragedy: "there can be
> no lingering for what is final, for what resolves into unity. Fact—
> impels from incident to incident, because the Beginning comes
> only with the finish of what is Past."

But when we come to explicit political steps Zukofsky goes to Santayana's *Dominations and Powers*. Mottram says, "Santayana on the
arbitrariness of detailed contingent life and 'contrary moralities' is
central for *"A"* and Zukofsky's other major works." He cites part of
a passage Zukofsky cites from Santayana:

> Victory or prosperity for one's own people or one's own civili-
> zation will no longer seem an ultimate or unqualified good . . .
> only manifesting, in one arbitrary form, the universal impulse in
> matter towards all sorts of harmonies and perfections. Then all
> the other harmonies and perfections, not attainable here, perhaps
> not attained anywhere, will come crowding to the gates of our
> little temple. And the spirit will be tempted to escape from that
> particular sanctuary, to abdicate its identity with the society that
> bred it, and to wander alone and friendless . . . .

Zukofsky's essay, "The Effacement of Philosophy," conveys a
number of other value judgments which are based on "Santayana's
debt to Spinoza," and, says Zuk, "Spinoza may be said to be the last
great Western philosopher. He based his *Ethics* on a single definition
that was integrated in the manner of Bach's *Art of Fugue*. Materialist
philosophers of history may do well to think about Bach's remark:
"The order which rules music is the same order that controls the
placing of the stars and the feathers in a bird's wing." Zuk ends his
brief note with a quote from Spinoza who said: "The superstitious,
who know better how to reprobate vice than to teach virtue, have
no other intuition than to make the rest as miserable as themselves"
[*Prepositions*, 50]. Mottram mentions some of these things as well as
Santayana's sense of harmony all of which are relevant to *"A"* as a
whole and *"A"*-12 in particular. Also:

> Santayana's harmony is so expanded as to need "a new ear to hear
> it." Zukofsky counters with Spinoza: "Many errors consist in this
> alone, that we do not apply names rightly to things." Men seem to

err "because we think they have the same members in their minds
as on the paper." The politics of *"A"* is the pain and joy in being
aware of the need to bring universal perfection into relation with
family and society, in a time when state and international politics
prove disastrous to human life.

Mottram's concluding paragraph for the first part of his essay is a
balanced judgment of the enormous complexities and perplexities of
the 30's, 40's, and 50's, or, for a poet, of all ages when it comes to
political and moral affirmations and poetic action:

> But the political poem which activates the possibility of a fu-
> ture action for change and is not totalitarian is rare. It is more usu-
> ally a matter, however, of "this is hell, nor are we out of it"—and
> Marlowe himself was once caught by the Star Chamber. The poli-
> tical poems of the 1930's often reported Hell and claimed its per-
> manence (stoicism) or its imminent overthrow (revolution). But
> Hell is the knowledge that there is always someone above to cas-
> trate, rape or exhaust you, with the violence of inverted Eros sup-
> porting him. Beauty—that harmony and perfection so yearned for
> throughout Zukofsky—is neither Eros nor Hell. It, too, is a term
> which takes its meaning from history and from the nature of the
> proportions between labour and leisure. Poetry has not usually
> been written from within the working class because leisure for the
> proletariat has consisted of recovery from exhaustion, and a re-
> covery manipulated, since the advent of the mass media, by rulers
> and owners. The integrity of a slave is worthless. Skinner's law—
> that the rat is always right—was a discovery sponsored and paid for
> by Washington and its business lobbies. Stevens and Frost are
> loved by the frightened middle-class reader, and his critical men-
> tors, for their sense of immutability, rigidified in conventions of
> non-participatory and ruling-class criteria of beauty (and San-
> tayana was also Stevens' advisor for perfection and harmony.)
> Thirties writers found it difficult to grasp the principle of a style
> as a "germinative phenomenon," or the necessity for "writing de-
> gree zero." Craft risks in the service of an analysis of tradition;
> workmanship in the service of non-fascist persuasion; poetry as
> part of revolutionary mutual aid—it is easy to list the needs out
> like this. Zukofsky is a poet who lived through the first climactic
> decades of catastrophe which we inherit. *Prepositions* and *"A"*
> and *Bottom* are his entirely honorable survivalist strategies—not
> only examples of method and technique but of handling the
> proper materials of major poetry.

In Part II of his essay Mottram gets more down to cases. The
politics of the earlier movements of *"A"* may well stand for the rest
of it. Such lines as "desire longing for perfection" from *"A"*-1 may be
a paradigmatic theme for the poet and artist in politics as well as in
art. Such desire for perfection may be an urge of "both the totalitarian *L*eft and totalitarian *R*ight." Says Mottram:

> A liberal humanist has to define his position with great care if it
> is to partake of neither extremism: provided, that is, he has that
> need. The typical juxtaposition of *"A"*-1 is: Pennsylvania miners
> "again on the lockout," irony about relief for those who can af-
> ford it, while resisting "a mass movement," and Bach's music, like
> natural cells, "before the eyes, perfecting" (in *"A"*-2: "The music
> is in the flower"). These *Bottom* materials are in turn placed with
> the muddled cruelty of capitalist relations between production,
> employment and consumption; the primary example is the fascism

of worker chain gangs in the Argentine. *"A"*-2 (1928) goes further into Easter as celebration of salvation and perfection out of sacrifice. Art and society should be like the music of nature (but there is no mention of the ecological sacrifice in nature). In *"A"*-3 (1928) the poet is prompted to see himself as Arimathea to a young suicide's Christ, but it is not clear what the salvation connection is. In *"A"*-4 (1928) the father-son structure of continuous human history and religion is part of "the courses we tide from," but there is no hint that inheritance programmes may be at the root of social corruption. By 1930, these themes have intensified in American life. *"A"*-6 expresses fear of "a mutual, common level,/ Everyone the same," that Bach's fugue may become "a music heap," that music may become like Beethoven's—"melody forced by writing." Zukofsky requires a kind of naturalist classicism—Bach is natural and society should be another such instance; but there is little to suggest the degrading aristocratic conditions within which Bach toiled. All we get is "He who creates/ Is a mode of these inertial systems." (Bartok understood the relationship of leaf-structure to his music, *and* maintained a social conscience.) Zukofsky's eye is rather on perfection—and this persistence is most celebratedly given in lines quoted in section 3 of "An Objective" (1930-1):

> An objective—rays of the object brought to focus
> An objective—nature as creator—desire
>   for what is objectively perfect
> Inextricably the direction of history and contemporary
>   particulars.

Mottram goes on to cite examples from *"A"* to detail Zukofsky's attitude to the various political movements of the 20's and 30's. The concern is clear as is the record of dramatic events, but the poet's own commitment is less so: "Did Zukofsky after all, like Pound and D.H. Lawrence, hang on to belief in vitalistic leadership? (If not Lenin, who exactly?)" Since *"A"*-8 has the strongest political implications, much space is devoted to it and to the various Marxist elements which support it. But, he says: "The finest section of *"A"*-8 shows Zukofsky a major describer of the liberal issues—complete, late on, with loving quotations from both Brooks and Henry Adams, but still not isolating their sense of political and technological power." But his technique, in Mottram's eyes, weakens parts of the poem:

> Zukofsky then lowers the interest of his poem by plodding through notorious fake justifications of "business" and its obscene profits. But he puts his finger precisely on the way in which Americans' belief in their way of life thrives on a reliance on how "our ancestors/ Lived in times of revolution" rather than an analysis of capitalist exploitive incompetence. At this point, Zukofsky is at his most understanding. He isolates Henry Adams' despair in 1901, owing to his lack of ability to jettison the whole pattern of capitalist violence—"this is what satiates my instinct for life," and, in common with Brooks, his 19th century belief in blind force actions, a form of romantic organicism dear to the despairing reactionary. Russia is therefore early given as the reserve of "civilization" although at the time it looked like residual "energies" turned to "inertia." But Zukofsky understands the limits of such application of physics to human society—they are the limits of coherence again: "the facts can never be complete,/ And their relations must be always infinite." The bridge passage concerns Zukofsky's father arriving with other Russian Jews in New York, emigrants in Pennsylvania, and the relations between "grass roots" within and outside America which provide part of the enabling impulse to strike in 1935 for survival.

Mottram takes care to accent the poet's care in isolating motivations always as a reflection of deep need and aspiration. It is a real desire for "coherence and perfection" that makes thoughtful revolutionaries "set themselves above the law." It is from the parallels that can be drawn between the American worker and the labor-exhausted lives of workers in Italy, Germany, and Hungary that Zukofsky addresses America: "You are not the most favored nation,/ the seaman are striking, will the longshoremen come out for the shape-up?" Mottram sees what Zukofsky sees is really at stake in these agonized political confrontations as well as why Zuk did not, as many of his closest friends did, go for Russian leadership in the 30's:

> What is at stake in the American inheritance of Locke on liberal paternalism, with its aristocratic authoritarian actuality; although *Bottom* is more or less blind to Shakespeare's manic authoritarianism, *Coriolanus* seems to be a basis for criticism here:
>
>> Workers and farmers are no Roman mob.
>> They are not maintained by the State.
>> They maintain the State by their work.
>
> Zukofsky did not plump for Russian leadership in the Thirties; *"A"*-8 shows him mistrusting fetishism of the International, inevitable Left Revolution, and "the sexual theories" of political action—"literature which/ Flourishes in the dirty soil of society" and "middle class morality." Nor is the answer the abstraction of "Indian" detachment. Reading *"A"* one is continually reminded that Marxism never bit into American assumptions of social inequality with any widespread strength, but Zukofsky does not get through to the consequences, any more than Ginsberg will do many years later in "Wichita Vortex Sutra," the true successor to *"A"*-8. Both poems reflect the obsessive American need to re-establish confidence in American *mores* rather than change them radically from the base up.

The inflamed political passions of the 30's, which saw the formation of the Abraham Lincoln Brigade to defeat the Falangists in Spain, are recorded at the end of *"A"*-8 as if an emotion recollected in doubt:

> *"A"*-8 concludes with the Spanish Civil War action against fascism, a much clearer political action, in the poem, than any American revolt; a summary of method; and an effort at return to possible rebirth. But the Civil War was not in fact as clear-cut as this, and the method is arbitrary:
>
>> bringing together facts
>> which appearances separate:
>> all that is created in a fact
>> is the language that numbers it,
>> The facts clear,
>> breath lives,
>> with the image of lights.
>
> The fact is that clarity may bring about a swifter decision to criminal action, and one is bound to add that Jefferson cannot stand simply for *sinceritas* and *claritas.*

Mottram deals briefly with other themes and modes as they occur in the poems from *"A"*-9 through *"A"*-11, but reserves most of his remaining space for *"A"*-12. Between the writing of *"A"*-8 and *"A"*-12 a number of things happened: Louis and Celia were married; World War II started and finished; their son Paul was born and shadowed his future as a child-prodigy on the violin; the Bollingin award was given to Pound; and Senator McCarthy began raising all Hell in Washington. Thus, "Concord" becomes a strong hope and "Love" a stronger dynamic in his vision of the world to come. But the family from now on remains the most central and most celebrated force:

> Ten years after the second twentieth century collapse of inherited dominance-submission patterns, the poet continues in late Shakespearian modes with a fine work addressed to Celia and Paul as family and as musician-composers, placed in the centre of traditional order represented by China and Greece. Love is exemplified by the honour of music made by his family for him—a form of paradise which organizes the play between natural (the leaf structure again) and man-made (music), itself the core of the previous sections of *"A."* So that *"A"*-12 can begin again with Bach— "out of deep need" in 1950-1—the measure of perfection, and proceed to become the first major fulfillment of Zukofsky's career, a work to put with the best of *Paterson*, the *Cantos* and *Maximus*. The first thirty-eight pages have a beauty of organization and sustained lyrical variation—mainly in short Shakespearian cadences —which remain a pleasure at each reading. Explicit poetics is juxtaposed with material for poetry—theory exposed with the *prima materia*. Shape, rhythm and style— " 'Taste' we say—a living soul" —are initially isolated and then re-form into:
>
> > Ratio after
> > Eyes, tale in sound. First, dance. Then
> > Voice. First, body—to be seen and to pulse
> > Happening together.
>
> Creation of music and poetry imitates, in the classical sense, the Creation, and without blasphemy. Marriage is celebrated through the celebration of *A Midsummer Night's Dream*: "The parts of a fugue should behave like reasonable men in an orderly discussion." Yet, here once again Zukofsky is unconcerned with the palpably hierarchical nature of Shakespeare's order. "Concord" is his theme, traditionally presented through the nature/creation dialectic he used in the 1920s and 1930s parts of *"A"*:
>
> > The order that rules music, the same
> >   controls the placing of the stars and the feathers
> >   in a bird's wing.
> > In the middle of harmony
> > Most heavenly music
> > For the universe is true enough.
>
> Concord is the hope for the post-Thirties, post World War II poet. It is mutual exchange in creative love—"Everybody take. Here/ And owe nothing," acting "without the mask." Concord is freedom: "Only free (often wordless)/ Men are grateful to one another." The poet's isolation—"I speak to myself most often"—is tolerable only in the paradise of family concern (Zukofsky's feeling is remote from the challenges of Engels' *The Origin of the Family*) and the pleasure of art: "Measure, tacit is." Bottom's naive need to perform his art redeems his clumsiness and so he survives the fairies, the wood and the Court.

As he closes his essay Mottram notes that for Zukofsky, "Perfection in *"A"*-12 is the nuclear family": wife, father, and son. The human condition has remained the same, but the accent and significance of events and of what is to be most valued has altered. Drastic events took place but, "Out of the 1920-1950 catastrophe Zukofsky retrieves an order of what men can do at their finest—craftsmanship and art." Mottram says "Amen" to this by a last paragraph which puts all his findings into one sentence, built with craftsmanship and the nicest of art.

> To read *"A"1-12* in 1972 is to enter a rare privilege: the continuous action of a man working out his necessity for confidence in a time which militates against it, and making a poem as a raft for survival, even if the chart of currents and treachery may appear to undermine of itself the urge to perfection and coherence.

38. Greene, Jonathan. "Zukofsky's *Ferdinand.*" *MAPS*, No. 5 (1973), pp. 131-136.

> This is a descriptive review of *Ferdinand/Including It Was*, a 96-page prose work first published by Origin Press in 1961, and republished by Jonathan Cape in London in 1968. The 6-page review has 3 parts: the first deals with the genesis of Ferdinand as a character dominated by family and siblings, and dying of a kind of spiritual inanition. Ferdinand seeks identity and escape through fantasy: "that secret pipe dream is a touchstone of a life." Greene compares Ferdinand with Musil's *The Man Without Qualities*, in which Ulrich is so much a package of the qualities of his time that he can hardly be identified himself. Greene finds Ferdinand to be "Without the self-awareness and self-humour of Musil's hero." But Ferdinand does have "three close friends all exiles: a White Russian, an Englishman, and a New York Jew." He finds Basil Bunting behind the Englishman, and Zukofsky himself the Jew. In the 2nd part, the automobile is seen as the major symbol of a mechanistic civilization, and in the 3rd part he concludes that, in spite of a far-fetched and forced elusiveness, *Ferdinand* is "worthy of one's attention."

39. Quartermain, Peter. "Louis Zukofsky—re: Location." *Open Letter*, 6 (1973), pp. 54-64.

> That "Zukofsky's rhetoric . . . is a rhetoric of activity" is a main point to this discerning article which develops the theme that "Zukofsky's poems, like those of W. C. Williams, are machines, machines made out of words." Quartermain cites a brief poem entitled "FOR" which has three lines: "Four tubas/ or/ two-by-four's." and analyses the "palindromic echoes" in it at some length as an exemplum of the poet's technique in most of his work. It is a small machine. "The poem as machine is a valuable metaphor, for in an industrial and urban world the machine has an inescapable effect upon the quality and organization of our perceptions and responses to them." What we see as a germ in "FOR" we find at large in *"A"* presented in the cadences of·music, and "the music is a music of meanings as well as of sounds." But as Zukofsky says: "Poems are only acts upon particulars, outside of them . . . only through such activity do they become particulars themselves—i.e. poems."

40. Davenport, Guy. "Zukofsky's *"A"-24.*" *Parnassus: Poetry in Review*, Vol. 2, No. 2 (Spring-Summer, 1974), pp. 15-23.

> Davenport opens his 8-page statement with brief background information on the writing and publishing history of *"A"*—a sad and traditional history of long poems in America: "(the first thirty of Pound's

Cantos were set by French, the eighty-fifth through ninety-fifth by Italian compositors; the first half of Olson's *Maximus* was printed in Germany, the second half in England; Walt Whitman himself set *Leaves of Grass*; Melville paid for the printing of *Clarel* . . .)." His conclusion: "It cannot be demonstrated that the American public has ever clamored to read a long poem by an American poet." So with *"A"*: The first parts, *1-12*, were collected and printed in Japan, and a photocopy of this edition, financed by *The Paris Review*, has been long out of print. *"A" 13-21* came out of England in 1969. In 1974, 22 and 23 were still being worked on while *"A"-24* was being reviewed. These data are significant: the long critical silence about Zukofsky is in large part caused by the unavailability and lack of promotion of his work.

Davenport gives us 5 pages of illustrations from the poem as a whole: Zuk's associations of mind in *"A"*-7; his *buffo glissando* and pantomimic brio in *"A"*-13; his way of counterpointing themes in the manner of Charles Ives; and more.

The Ives' technique, with its clowning, needs emphasis for it bears on *The Cantos* as well as *"A."* Both poems range from tragedy and high seriousness to raucous buffoonery and include *all* aspects of life which can be evoked by verbal exploitation. Says Davenport: "Ives' 'Concord Sonata' begins its 3rd movement with what sounds like variations on the initial theme of Beethoven's Fifth Symphony; we discover later that the joke is Louisa May Alcott trying to play Wagner's piano redaction of the noble symphony, making a mangle of it and faking difficult passages with phrases from the Calvinist hymns with which her fingers are most comfortable; but a musicologist can tell us that the phrase isn't Beethoven at all, but a Scots folk melody that sounds like Beethoven, just as in the grand theme of the Second Symphony we are convinced we are hearing the National Anthem ('Columbia Gem of the Ocean' at that time) whereas we are hearing yet another Scots tune, 'My Bonnie Lies Over the Ocean.' This is all very Zukofskian." It is indeed. Davenport concludes: "There is enough narrative and anecdotal matter in *"A"* to make a shelf of novels." There is indeed. All the words used in *"A"*-24 are taken from the poet's previous works so that we can expect this climactic movement to express the major themes of a lifetime's thought and sensibility. The masque begins with a harpsichord arpeggio while a voice begins to read from an essay called "A Statement of Poetry." Against this background, the voice says: "And it is possible in imagination to divorce speech of all graphic elements, to let it become a movement of sounds." Davenport says: "While we hear this voice speaking about the movement and tone of words, a second voice, lower, speaks disjunct lines, as if at random from the script, from the play *Arise, Arise* . . . . Simultaneously a third voice recites from the story 'It Was.' The loudest voice, coming in at the second bar of the music, speaks the lyric 'Blest/ Infinite things' from *"A"* -14." If Davenport seems difficult to follow, there are good reasons for it. So, until we are quite familiar with it, is *"A"*-24, which goes on like this for an hour and ten minutes: "four voices," says Davenport, "speaking simultaneously to a constant glory of Handel." Still, says he, this form is quite justified: "Nothing let us note is being obscured by all these voices talking at once. We have no more right to complain that we can understand nothing (as indeed we can't) than to complain of Ives' *Putnam's Camp, Redding, Connecticut* that we can't make out what two military bands are playing (separate tunes simultaneously on top of some lovely ragtime and a bit of *Tristan*). The elements exist elsewhere, and can be consulted. This is Celia's *Masque of LZ; she* knows the parts off by heart, and if it pleases her to hear them this way, then that is the symbol, the figure as she makes it out in the carpet. She typed all these words in a house with a violinist constantly practicing." Davenport closes his statement with remarks on Zukofsky's reputation for obscurity—but more than that on Zukofsky's lack of reputation, which Davenport attributes to a number of causes. Lack of availability of the works for one, and his technique of making all his works interdependent, back and forth in time, for another. To know any of it is to know all of it and *vice versa*: "Familiarity is the condition whereby all of Zukofsky's work renders its goodness up . . . . Once we know that every phrase is an ultimate condensation of what the same concepts would be in a windier poet, we can then gear our wits to Zukofsky's finer machinery."

41. Carruth, Hayden. "The Only Way To Get There From Here." *Journal of Modern Literature*, 4, No. 1 (Sept., 1974), pp. 88-90.

> Carruth, a poet of consequence himself, gives us here a brief exhortation "to read the poems" which is "the best way to find out about" the work of a poet. "Look, he has his faults, granted. Verbosity here, attenuation there—I presume the chief danger of musical talent is etherealization. But of all times, old and new, he has one virtue in greatest degree, that *all* his words inhere, all, within one another's meaning conforming centrally to the unsayable."

42. Yannella, Philip R. "On Louis Zukofsky." *Journal of Modern Literature*, 4, No. 1 (Sept., 1974), pp. 74-87.

> Zukofsky's poetry is distinguished by its "grace and harmony," its musicality and fugal structure, its "intellectual range [to which] . . . we are . . . unaccustomed in our time," its dedication to love, particularly familial love, which gives us poems "which function on the levels of pure simplicity and pure grace." Yarnella's discerning article opens by bewailing the neglect Zukofsky has experienced, especially at the hands of English professors—even professors of contemporary poetry—who should know better. But then he accounts for the condition by the lack of availability of the poet's work. Still, young poets such as Duncan and Creeley hunted his poetry up and followed him as the next-generation master in the Pound-Eliot-Williams tradition. Yarnella explores the ways in which Bach informs not only the music and meaning but also the total structure of *"A,"* which he says is, indeed, the "poem of a life." But he finds good results even in the bad: "Zukofsky's endurance of the general lack of attention paid his art seems only to have strengthened his resolve as an artist."

43. Lang, Warren P. "Zukofsky's Conception of Poetry and a Reading of His Poem of a Life—*"A."*" *DAI*, 35:2279A-80A.

Indiana, 1974.

> Zukofsky's poetic principles, particularly "objectification" and "sincerity," are explained and then applied to *"A"* as an explanatory tool. Chief areas of focus include musical structures and thematic leitmotifs. Lang adds a conclusion which studies the reasons for *"A"*'s potential appeal to the reader.

44. Taggart, John Paul. "Intending a Solid Object: A Study of Objectivist Poetics." *DAI*, 36:332A. Syracuse, 1974.

> This dissertation focuses on the three key phrases associated with Zukofsky's work: "the poem as solid object," "sincerity," and "objectification." In discussing sincerity, the role of love and the importance of sight are emphasized and sections of *"A"*-12 and "Mantis" are used as examples and tests of "the proposed composition sequence of the sincere poet." Under "objectification," Taggart relates cubist theory in art to objectivist poetics and explores the influence of Pound on Zukofsky's poetics. He shows how objectification produces unity and musicality. Conclusions concern the nature of "solid" as applied to a poem: giving the poem properties of three-dimensional art and also "carrying some obligation for its reader to re-examine his universe." [W.H.]

45. Booth, Marcella. *A Catalogue of the Louis Zukofsky Manuscript Collection.* Austin: Humanities Research Center, Univ. of Texas, 1975. [See item 20 above.]

46. Kenner, Hugh. "Bottom on Zukofsky." *Modern Language Notes*, 90 (1975), pp. 921-22.

> Kenner quotes Zukofsky's summation of the major premises of *Bottom* . . .: "All of Shakespeare's writing embodies a definition, a continuing variant of it over so many years. It is a definition of love that the learning of the later (specifically English) Renaissance had forgotten: The definition of Love as the tragic hero. He is Amor, identified with the passion of the lover falling short of perfection . . . at those times when his imagination insufficient to itself is an aberration of the eyes; but when reason and love are an identity of sight its clear and distinct knowledge can approach the sufficient realization of the intellect." Kenner thinks that the longer one reflects on Zukofsky's continual use of love as a major motivating force in his work (as well as in all life), the more one becomes convinced that the content of the word has been extended way beyond its ordinary (or even any other specialized) use: perhaps somewhat in the way Pound extends intelligence to include whatever force it is that makes the cherry produce a cherry tree. He thinks that Zuk finds similar depths of perception in Shakespeare: "The more detailed precisions or obscurities of this definition of love in early Renaissance writing are beside the point. Its origins and changes are many and complex: Greek mysteries, Ovid, . . . Oriental and Arabian sources, Provençal extensions and intensities. Continental and English philosophy of the 13th century, configurations of Cavalcanti, Dante and other Italians." Kenner concludes that the results of these perceptions are "thousands

of parallelisms and meditations" of which he gives examples. He closes his article by returning to another premise of Zukofsky: "It is simpler to consider the forty-four items of the [Shakespeare] canon as one work, sometimes good, sometimes great always regardless of time in which it was composed, and so, despite defects of quality, durable as one thing from 'itself never turning.'" Says Kenner to this: "Zukofsky on Shakespeare, which we may also read as Bottom on Zukofsky."

47. Mandell, Stephen Roy. "The Finer Mathematician: An Introduction to the Works of Louis Zukofsky." *DAI*, 36:3715A. Temple, 1975.

> Mandell shows the musical qualities of Zukofsky's poetry, particularly the contrapuntal, fugue-like quality which allows complex discussions of relationships. The form helps create the unity of the poem. Past, present, and many facets of experience including Zukofsky's own family life are brought together in *"A,"* which "transforms a life into a poem."

48. Slate, Joseph Evans. "Williams at Austin." *William Carlos Williams Newsletter*, 2, No. 2 (1976), pp. 14-15.

> Included is the facsimile of a letter from Williams to Zukofsky. Slate briefly summarizes the content of the Williams manuscript holdings of the Harry Ransom Center of the University of Texas at Austin and particularly stresses the holdings related to Louis Zukofsky—reviews of Zukofsky's books and close to five hundred letters directed to Zukofsky "the advisor and friend so strangely missing from Williams' *Autobiography*" (p. 14). The letter reproduced as a representative example is breezy and personal, discussing, among other topics, Williams' appreciation of Zukofsky's critical comments and opinions. [W.H.]

49. Roubaud, Jacques, trans. and intro. "Poèmes." *Europe*, 55, Nos. 578-79 (June-July, 1977), pp. 78-91.

> Poems chosen from *All: Collected Short Poems* (Norton, 1965) are presented in what Roubaud calls a first attempt to translate Zukofsky into French. Roubaud's brief introduction (in French) calls Zukofsky, along with Pound, the most important American poet of our time, gives a brief publishing history of *"A,"* and explains his belief that Zukofsky's style is essentially opposite to Pound's because of the influence of Dante and Arnaut Daniel's sestina and Cavalcanti's canzone upon Zukofsky. [W.H.]

50. Corman, Cid. "At: Bottom." *Word for Word, Essays on the Art of Language*. Vol. 1. Santa Barbara: Black Sparrow, 1977, pp. 128-69.

> Corman begins this long essay-review of *Bottom: on Shakespeare* with a brief disquisition on the nature of art. He then attempts, by directions and indirections, to find Zukofsky's finding of Shakespeare out. Corman's thesis is forthright: "Not since Coleridge has any poet attempted to such an extent to bring to weight the complete work of

Shakespeare as Zukofsky has here. It answers, far more cogently than any argument, also for the relation that obtains between the English language as it is handled now anywhere and as it has been anywhere." Zukofsky quotes Ben Jonson about Shakespeare's unblotted lines. Corman quotes Zukofsky on Jonson: "Jonson's lines convey the contest any poet has with his art: working towards a perception that is his mind's peace, he knows, unfortunately, that his writing with fleshly pencils will be loosely considered the issue of himself."

Thus Corman as poet looks at Zukofsky as poet who has looked at Ben Jonson as poet looking at Shakespeare, first of all, as poet. Therein is the difference and the significance of Zukofsky's work. Looking at the tradition of Shakespearean criticism, Zukofsky the poet finds that the plays and poetry have been used or seen to illustrate stages in Shakespeare's life or the development of his art: the state of his mind or the shape of his poetic line. Such approaches are to Zukofsky out of focus: they ask the wrong questions and put the emphasis in the wrong place. His major intent in *Bottom . . .* is to "mildly and firmly" set the "scholar critics" on a better course:

> Guessing at the chronology of the forty-four items of the canon, the critics have been insistent on seeing his ideas grow, his feelings mature, his heart go through more exploits than a heart can, except as may be vaguely intimated from the beat and duration of any of the lines or works. It is simpler to consider the forty-four items of the canon as one work, sometimes poor, sometimes good, sometimes great, always regardless of time in which it was composed, and so, despite defects of quality, durable as one thing from "itself never turning." So growth is organic to decay and vice versa.

To this remarkable statement Zukofsky appends even more remarkable ones such as:

> Love, or . . . the desire to project the mind's peace is one growth.

> Love's not Time's fool.

> Love looks not with the eyes but with the mind.

> The form of all uttered drama must arise from the measured order of words moving to a visual end. "Arise arise . . . ."

Corman, unerringly, zeros in on the most striking of Zukofsky's revealing commentary. For one who has a number of times taught such plays as *The Tempest* and *Hamlet*, it is a heady experience to encounter such stunning statements as these:

> The best in the writing called *The Tempest* resembles, after all, the corporeality of Ariel's songs, not what finally happens to Ariel when his freedom becomes as insubstantial as Love's asking, tragic, fractious "mind."

Or:

> He sees, as few seem to have seen, that *Hamlet* is the tragedy of love's innocence brought to terrible wisdom and the dignity that hollows out justice from it: "The *tragic* theme," as he says, "of love's division from reason because it cannot see and 'will not know what all but he do know.'"

To elucidate Zukofsky on Shakespeare, Corman calls upon such writers as Joyce (*Stephen Hero),* Zimmer (*Philosophies of India*), Gerard Manley Hopkins (*Journal*), Baldwin (*Nobody Knows My Name*), Basho (*Oku-no-hoso-michi*), Rilke (*Letters*), as well as Martin Buber and Hasidic lore, *passim.* To elucidate Shakespeare, Zukofsky calls upon Homer, Aristotle, Aquinas, Spinoza, Henry Adams, Henry James, and Wittgenstein to name the most significant few. Says Corman:

> In the longer concluding segment of Part Two Zukofsky extends the purview of his book in time, from Aristotle to Wittgenstein, retaining the instances of Spinoza as pivot, finding in all their work Shakespeare's projections focussed *as* thought, and creating a nexus of man's capacity eloquently attested to. Whether the ability and the care to make so magnificent an "integration" of "minds" and "eyes" and "love" occurs in art elsewhere today so extensively remains a task to see. In any event, this (*Bottom*) is an opportunity that has called only in our time and only an intelligence equally aware of the rest of the world's achievements could amend fully what is given here. (And it is a sign of Zukofsky's clairvoyant love that it sees *that* possibility and intimates as much.)
>
> Zukofsky also sees that Shakespeare knows
>
>> No tongue! all eyes! Be silent
>
> which discovers answer in Paulina's words to Leontes:
>
>> Behold, and say 'tis well.
>> I like your silence, it the more shows off
>> Your wonder: but yet speak. . . .
>
> But now the proportion:
>
>> *love : reason :: eyes :mind*
>
> Perpends. And the author explains: "Love needs no tongue of reason if love and eyes are 1—an identity. The good reasons of the mind's right judgment are but superfluities for saying: *Love sees—* if it needs saying at all in a text which is always hovering towards *The rest is silence."*

51. Howard, Ben. From "Comment, Four Voices." *Poetry,* 130 (August, 1977), pp. 290-92.

In a review of *"A"*-22 and -23 along with three other books, Ben Howard finds that "Louis Zukofsky's new long poems make a very different first impression." But that impression is on the whole good. As one would expect, no reader could expect to make much out of this final volume which completed *"A"* until he could get his contextual bearings for the twenty-four movements as a whole. As Howard says: "the reader who wishes to get his bearings can refer to the earlier poems in the sequence and can also consult the author's frequent comments on his work. Evident in both is a preoccupation with what Zukofsky terms 'an intense vision of a fact,' or 'the physical intricacies of fact,' and with representing those intricacies in the texture of his verse." Howard also says: "A dense verbal texture is a hallmark of Zukofsky's mode of thought, a radical nominalism whose enemies are abstraction and symbol." To this we can say with the youth of some yesterday, "Right on, Brother!"

52. Ahearn, Barry. "Origins of *"A"*: Zukofsky's Material for Collage." *ELH*, 45, No. 1 (Spring, 1978), pp. 152-76.

For Ahearn, the collage described in *"A"*-12 presents a symbol of the entire organizational pattern of most of Zukofsky's poems, particularly *"A."* Ahearn shows how the contrast of rather mundane, everyday subjects and a sophisticated treatment of the relationships between these subjects (as in a collage) appeared in poems as early as "Poem Beginning "The,"" and provides a key to the complexities of the poems. *"A"* 1-7 is examined. Biographical events and avant-garde trends in the arts are both presented as influencing Zukofsky to adopt the collage style. Connections made between the biography and the poetry are occasionally tenuous, but the article is readable and perhaps suggestive of further areas of study. [W.H.]

53. Corman, Cid. "Poetry as Translation (Zukofsky)." *Word for Word, Essays on the Art of Language*. Vol. 2. Santa Barbara: Black Sparrow, 1978, pp. 16-30.

A defense of the Zukofskys' version of Catullus, a book which, says Corman, "has been formidably attacked in some of the respectable English periodicals (*Encounter* most notably) and where it has been found acceptable has been quickly glossed over." Corman's opinion is quite different. He says: "I feel no need to mince words in this matter." And mince them, he doesn't. He gives a chapter and verse account of Zukofsky's expertness as a translator of poetry, and demonstrates the time (years) and labor (arduous) he put into it.

54. Kenner, Hugh. "Louis Zukofsky: All the Words." *The New York Times Book Review*, June 18, 1978. Reprinted in *Paideuma*, Vol. 7, No. 3 (Winter, 1978), pp. 386-89.

On the occasion of Zukofsky's death, Kenner gives us some of his memories of the man as well as some of the characteristic signatures of his work. He remembers his stance of heavy eyebrows; his playfulness among friends; his hypochondria which even he came to know as hypochondria; his unlimbering of septuagenarian legs to give a little dance; and his life with his other half, Celia, who, by dint of Ellis Island inventiveness, became Celia Thaew. Kenner points to Zuk's lifelong love of words: little words, big words, strange words, all words. To Zuk, words were objects in the world like stones or trees. He records evidence of his wit, his love of family, and life, and poetry, and the many friends who cherished his work. He closes by presenting evidence from Zukofsky's own verse that his greatness will prevail and finally be recognized by all discriminating readers of the future.

55. Zukofsky, Celia and Others. "Dove Sta Memora." *Paideuma*, Vol. 7, No. 3 (Winter, 1978), pp. 371-406.

This issue of *Paideuma, A Journal Devoted to Ezra Pound Scholarship*, was devoted to the works and memory of Zukofsky, a friend of Pound from their first meeting in 1927 to Pound's death in 1972. Thus Celia Z. entitled her note in the memorial section "1927-1972." Fifteen others contributed to this special section: Basil Bunting contributed a note entitled "Pound and 'Zuk'"; George Oppen gave us

"My Debt to Him." Ian Hamilton Finlay expressed the sense of most of the others in his brief "In Memory": "The operation of intelligence, as seen in the poetry of Louis Zukofsky, is one of the things which for me redeems the idea of 'man.' I say this on the simplest possible level, recording a simple sense of gratitude that this poetry, this evidence of intelligence actually exists." By "intelligence," Finlay, the Scottish concrete poet, specified that he meant something "other and better than thought." Gael Turnbull, Ronald Johnson, Thomas A. Clark, and Michael André Bernstein wrote memorial poems. Robert Creeley contributed a quite human and touching account of his first meetings (as a literally penniless storm-drenched poet) with the Zukofskys. Hugh Kenner, Harvey Shapiro, Hayden Carruth, and Guy Davenport reported their encounters with the man and his work as did Robert Kelley. Gilbert Sorrentino and Ron Silliman suggested how much Zukofsky had become a model for them and many another younger poet.

56. Hatlen, Burton. "Catullus Metamorphosed." *Paideuma*, Vol. 7, No. 3 (Winter, 1978), pp. 539-45.

This article summarizes the critical debate aroused by Zukofsky's translation of Catullus; locates these translations in relationship to the Poundian heritage; and offers close readings of two Catullus/Zukofsky poems, with the purpose of showing how the translation "unfolds, amplifies, explicates" the Latin original, while remaining faithful to "the sound as well as to the sense of the original." Some portions of this article are incorporated into "Zukofsky as Translator," printed in this volume.

57. Ignatow, David. "Louis Zukofsky—Two Views." *Paideuma*, Vol. 7, No. 3 (Winter, 1978), pp. 549-551.

As an important poet in his own right, David Ignatow expresses some ambiguous feelings about Zukofsky, mainly concerned with L.Z.'s refusal to believe that Pound was really antisemetic.

58. Kenner, Hugh. "Loove in Brooklyn." *Paideuma*, Vol. 7, No. 3 (Winter, 1978), pp. 413-20.

A poem by Zukofsky, entitled "A foin lass bodders," published for the first time in the memorial issue of *Paideuma* is followed by this remarkable analysis by Kenner. The poem itself, a canzone of 5 sonnets and a 5 line coda, is the most striking, elaborate, internal and external rhyming structure one could imagine: a tour de force one is not likely to see elsewhere. Kenner's analysis is an equal tour de force. Zukofsky follows in English all the intricate rules followed by Guido Cavalcanti in his "Donna mi prega" as mapped out by Pound: "Each strophe is articulated by 14 terminal and 12 inner rhyme sounds, which means that 52 out of every 154 syllables are bound into pattern." Says Kenner: "Pound saw little for English to do with the pattern save acknowledge it . . . [and] made no effort to follow Guido's rules. Zukofsky did, to the letter: every rhyme in its place." This kind of thing is not easy even in Italian, but English? One would suppose,

"No way!" But that's only the beginning: the whole poem is done in a Brooklyn accent. The opening lines of the poem are

A foin lass bodders me I gotta tell her
Of a fact surely, so unrurly, often'
'r 't comes 'tcan't soften its proud neck's called love mm. . .
Even me brudders dead drunk in dare cellar
Feel it dough poorly 'n yrs. trurly rough 'n
His way ain't so tough 'n he can't speak from above mm. . .

Kenner's opening comment is

Donna — "A foin lass" — *mi prega* — "bodders me:" what proportion of the great Canzone is literary convention? And what happens if its substance be moved in the direction of *volgari eloquentia*, vernacular speech? Speech of a time and place: Brooklyn: the 1930's. Guido's *stil nuovo* was allegedly grounded on Florentine vernacular of the 1290's, a diction of which we possess no tape recordings. Zukofsky's version of c. 1938 is a comic *tour de force* and a four-way commentary: on Guido's Canzone, on Pound's 1928 and 1934 versions, on the possibility of American local speech and underpinning philosophic song. Literary historians are glib in their talk of speech. To make speech course through verse means imagining, impersonating a speaker.

After this, the analysis becomes more and more breathtaking— so breathtaking it cannot be summarized and the results only hinted at.

59. Quartermain, Peter. "Recurrencies: No. 12 of Louis Zukofsky's *Anew.*" *Paideuma*, Vol. 7, No. 3 (Winter, 1978), pp. 523-38.

This article is a detailed exegesis of one of Zukofsky's most difficult poems. While reading it one is reminded of a precept Zukofsky quotes from Einstein: "A thing should be as simple as it can be, but no simpler." The poem was written toward the end of WWII while Zuk was writing instruction manuals for radios, bombsights, etc., as an employee of the Hazeltine Electronics Corporation. It opens: "it's hard to see but think of a sea/ Condensed into a speck." Soon after this, we know that we will be concerned in some very abstuse matters of contemporary light-heat-wave-energy physics and analogies of "seas" with fields of force.

60. Seidman, Hugh. "L.Z. at Polly Tech." *Paideuma*, Vol. 7, No. 3 (Winter, 1978), pp. 553-58.

Candid camera glimpses of Zuk as a teacher in and out of the classroom. [Reproduced herein, pp. 97-102]

61. Schimmel, Harold. "Zuk. Yehoash David Rex." *Paideuma*, Vol. 7, No. 3 (Winter, 1978), pp. 557-69.

A four-part study of the ways in which Zukofsky makes use of the work of the Yiddish poet Yehoash (pen name of S. Bloomgarten) in his own, especially "Poem beginning "The." " [Reproduced herein, pp. 235-245]

62. Ahearn, Barry. "The Adams Connection." *Paideuma*, Vol. 7, No. 3 (Winter, 1978), pp. 479-93.

> Barry Ahearn consulted many unpublished letters and other documents in the Zukofsky Collection at Austin, Texas. The results show that *The Education of Henry Adams* had more extensive effects in more different ways upon Zukofsky than one would gather from his essay on Adams. Even the title, *"A,"* quite likely comes from a germ in Adams. [Reproduced herein, pp. 113-127]

63. Byrd, Don. "The Shape of Zukofsky's Canon." *Paideuma*, Vol. 7, No. 3 (Winter, 1978), pp. 455-77.

> As his title suggests, Byrd steps back and looks at Zukofsky's work as a whole. He finds it possible to make assertions which show how the parts ramify but still cohere. [Reproduced herein, pp. 163-185]

64. Corman, Cid. "The Transfigured Prose." *Paideuma*, Vol. 7, No. 3 (Winter, 1978), pp. 447-53.

> Corman quotes a long passage from Charles Reznikoff's prose dramatization of an encounter with a dog. He then shows how Zukofsky transmutes—"transfigures"—the essence of the prose into a poetry segment of *"A"*-12.

65. Dawson, Fielding. "A Memoir of Louis Zukofsky." *Paideuma*, Vol. 7, No. 3 (Winter, 1978), pp. 571-79.

> The story of a relationship with the warmth and wit Zukofsky will be much remembered by. [Reproduced herein, pp. 103-111]

66. Duncan, Robert. "Reading Zukofsky." *Paideuma*, Vol. 7, No. 3 (Winter, 1978), pp. 421-27.

> A major 20th century poet gives an account of how Zukofsky, among such others as Pound, Joyce, Williams, and Olson, created an excitement in the 30's which became formative upon his own work. Reflecting now upon the urgencies of that decade and the dismay of some of the political affirmations made by poets then, Duncan says, "Whatever a poem meant in its truth of particulars it was not a political directive. The truth of a poem was the truth of what was felt in the course of the poem, not the truth of a proposition in whatever political or religious persuasion outside the poem. The particulars of the poem were in process."
>
> Thus does Duncan arrive, as a poet must, at Eliot's earlier conclusion: Poetic affirmation does not require philosophical assent—or maybe the other way around. If I remember correctly his example was that one does not have to believe Milton's curious theology in order to affirm the poetic quality of *Paradise Lost*.
>
> Duncan's conclusions are important and need to be repeated again—and again—and yet again: "What mattered was that this poet Zukofsky had indeed read his Pound and his Williams and in the course of his reading derived a new art, an art that has anticipated problems of the poems that I have found essential in my own work as it has developed [N.B. important because most poets writing

today must concur]. In the work of poets from Creeley to Michael Palmer I see the implications of Zukofsky carried further than I know in my own work. Not to praise or appraise, but to bear testimony to the enduring resource: his work in *All*, in *"A,"* in *Bottom: On Shakespeare*, and *Catullus* stands as primaries of all of us at work in the closing decades of the Twentieth Century."

67. Gordon, David. "Zuk and Ez at St. Liz." *Paideuma*, Vol. 7, No. 3 (Winter, 1978), pp. 581-84.

A discriminating, candid-camera, account of Zukofsky with Celia and Paul visiting his old friend Pound at St. E's in August 1954. Gordon here has a fine eye and ear as he records seeing the trio waiting for the bus, arriving at the hospital, and making a mere visit into a great memory: "Three sauntered. Stopped for trialogue. Then resumed a savoir-bus-waiting-faire." Just to think of Zukofsky is to fall into word patterns and puns he might smile at: "All three, unified, neat and thin; a young boy coming up to his mother's shoulder, an attractive young woman, slightly shorter than the older, thinner man, who was gaunt, but not frail." Gordon gives us an extraordinary image in action of the poet in and out of the world around him, this time communing with an elm tree over him: Celia carried Paul's violin [he was going to play the Janequin bird song, Canto 75 for Pound] while "the boy as the man seemed to become more rapt in the world of live wood overhead":

> It was an intently quiet and mysterious moment having to do with the elm tree. He moved inconspicuously along the sidewalk without direct outward manifestation of any action. There was only a registration in the extremely sensitive lines of his face of some supra-awareness; that was unmistakable. And in the alternate light and shade of the afternoon he seemed to give the illusion of rising on his toes, becoming a bit taller, almost moving upward. He was fervently scrutinizing the boughs and leaves and seemed to be imperceptively drifting toward them, almost as if he would have been pulling himself up there with his arms, had his hands not been clasped behind his back. Although his feet were in contact with the pavement he no longer appeared to be really depending on them. . . . The whole thing was in the attitude, not only of his most expressive eyes, but of his entire body; it was not exactly elastic, but there was a lightness, he seemed about to be gathered into the ascending sweep of the tree. His features did not go slack, but kept a kind of deep imperturbability as of one in the uttermost leap of concentration—the faculties brought all to one determinative act of perceiving. . . .

Otherwise the piece describes the arrival and departure of the family at St. E's as given in "Conversation with Celia" [see 69 below].

68. Taggart, John. "Zukofsky's 'Mantis.'" *Paideuma*, Vol. 7, No. 3 (Winter, 1978), pp. 507-22.

A telling and graphic hypothesis and exegesis of one of Zuk's "denser" works. [Reproduced herein, pp. 247-262]

69. Terrell, Carroll F. "Conversations with Celia." *Paideuma*, Vol. 7, No. 3 (Winter, 1978), pp. 585-600.

This article is based on a question and answer session with Celia

Zukofsky taped in early September, 1978. The two incidents published here concern the family's visit to Pound in 1954 and the events leading up to Celia and Zuk's marriage in 1939. Complete transcripts of all the sessions will be housed at the University of Texas at Austin, at the Beinecke Library at Yale, as well as at the Pound Archive at Orono.

70. Tomlinson, Charles. "Objectivists: Zukofsky and Oppen, a memoir." *Paideuma*, Vol. 7, No. 3 (Winter, 1978), pp. 429-45.

[Reproduced herein, pp. 79-95]

INDEX OF PEOPLE, BOOKS, AND THINGS

The items indexed include the names of people, the titles of books or musical compositions, and most other capitalized words or concepts, except for the names of cities and publishing companies in bibliographical notes. The works of Zukofsky are indexed under his name with *"A"* first followed by the titles of sections of *"A"* (such as *"A" 1-12* and *"A"-24* which appeared as separate books) and then followed by the sequence of movements: *"A"*-1, *"A"*-2, etc. Zukofsky's other works follow in alphabetical order.

Perforce, a standard editorial procedure to deal with the titles of Zukofsky's works had to be adopted. Decisions were arbitrary, because the poet himself used different forms at different times, but his latest practice has been used most often. Thus, the titles of books containing sections of *"A"* have all been italicized: e.g. *"A" 1-12* and *"A"-24*. However, the *"A"* in references to individual movements is in italics but the number of the movement is not: *"A"*-1. Since "Poem beginning "The"" never appeared separately, and the first double quote around "The"is part of the title, a second double quote has been used as the best of unhappy alternatives. Otherwise, the form used by Celia Zukofsky in the Bibliography has been taken as final: thus, *Arise, arise* is referred to as *Arise, Arise*. But verbatim quotes from sources have sometimes been allowed to stand as written even though the form varies from the standard adopted for this book. The editor is indebted to Roland Nord for assistance in the indexing process.

‡ ‡ ‡ ‡ ‡ ‡

A

Acoetes, 192
Adams, Brooks, 114, 116, 117, 118, 119, 120, 123, 123n, 124, 125, 126, 209, 423
Adams Jr., Charles Francis, 120, 120n, 121, 122, 123

Adams, Henry, 19, 113, 114, 114n, 115, 116, 117, 117n, 118, 119, 120, 120n, 122, 123, 124, 125, 126, 127, 155, 167, 205, 205n, 206, 207, 209, 210, 211, 212, 213, 217, 220, 221, 222, 223,

203n, 393
Daniel, Arnaut, 206, 208, 255, 261,
    430
Dante, 15, 34, 164, 191, 201, 205,
    206, 207, 217, 232, 248, 255,
    259, 261, 275, 292, 297, 429,
    430
Dante's Lyric Poetry, 259n
Das Kapital, see "Capital"
Davenport, Guy, 8, 16, 17, 20, 28,
    109n, 184, 211, 212, 235, 239,
    350, 350n, 358, 362n, 365, 412,
    413, 420, 426, 427, 428, 434
David rex, 245
Davie, Donald, 407
Dawson, Fielding, 8, 19, 103, 110,
    436
Dawson, Susan, 103
Degnan, June Oppen, 91
*Degradation of the Democratic Dog-
    ma*, 116, 123-127
Dembo, L.S., 8, 24, 25, 26, 265n,
    283, 283n, 411, 414, 419
Descartes, 217, 219
Descriptive Catalogue, A, 206
Desert Music, The, 238
Detail and Parody, 133
Dial, The, 16
Dickinson, Emily, 400
Dictionary, 365
Dionysius, 192
Dionysos, 164
Discrete Series, 82
Divina Commedia, 164
Dominations and Powers, 421
Don Giovanni, 341
Donna mi prega, 22, 214, 219
Donne, John, 41, 42, 231, 415
Donoghue, Denis, 411
Doughty, 370
Douglas [Major], 59
Dream/Thunder Road, The, 105
Dryden, John, 203, 203n
Duchess of Malfi, 68
Duddy, Thomas Anthony, 346n,
    414, 416
Duncan, Robert, 72, 73, 75, 79,
    109, 138, 206, 206n, 213, 257,
    283, 428, 436
Dynasts, 71

E

Echanges, 48
Edison, Thomas, 217
Education of Henry Adams, The,
    113, 114, 118, 124-127, 420, 436
Einstein, Albert, 99, 346, 420, 421,
    435
Electrons and Waves, 214, 219, 221,
    223
Eliot, T.S., 16, 20, 22, 32, 33, 33n,
    71, 87, 164, 164n, 170, 171,
    172, 181, 207n, 237, 284, 298,
    299, 305, 306, 409, 411, 421,
    428, 436
Emerson, Ralph Waldo, 270
Empson, 191, 407
Encounter, 349, 433
Engels, Friedrich, 42, 169, 182,
    209, 221, 425
Ephraim, Morris, 28
Epicurus, 413
Epstein, 32
Erskine, John, 48
Escudero, 69
Eshleman, Clayton, 101
Euclid, 322
Exile, 16, 231, 235, 298, 399
Eyore, 108

F

Ferlinghetti, 72
Feuer, Lewis S., 169n
Fiedler, Leslie, 248, 248n, 261,
    261n
55 Poems, 23, 133, 144, 172, 237,
    405
Fink, Mike, 118
Finlay, Ian Hamilton, 79, 92, 393,
    434
Finnegan's Wake, 88, 380, 413
Fisk, James, 120
Flaubert, G., 79
Ford, Worthington Chauncey, 124n
Foster, K., 259n
Foucault, Michel, 206, 206n
Frost, Robert, 87, 398, 422